LYRICAL-ANALYSIS

LYRICAL-ANALYSIS

The Unconscious Through *Jane Eyre*

Angelyn Spignesi

Chiron Publications • Wilmette, Illinois

Quotations from *The Newly Born Woman* by Hélène Cixous and Catherine Clément are reprinted by permission of the University of Minnesota Press, © 1986. Quotations from *Desire in Language* by Julia Kristeva are reprinted by permission of Columbia University Press, © 1980. The lines from *The Aeneid* by Virgil, trans. Robert Fitzgerald, are reprinted by permission of Random House, Inc., © 1983.

Library of Congress Catalog Card Number: 89-25217

Printed in the United States of America.
Book design by Siobhan Drummond Granner and Nancy R. Snyder.

Library of Congress Cataloging-in-Publication Data:
Spignesi, Angelyn
    Lyrical-analysis : the unconscious through Jane Eyre / Angelyn Spignesi.
        p. cm.
    Includes bibliographical references.
    ISBN 0-933029-54-3 : $16.95
    1. Brontë, Charlotte, 1816-1855. Jane Eyre. 2. Psycho analysis and literature. 3. Subconsciousness in literature. I. Title.
PR4167.J5S65 1990
823'.8—dc20   89-25217
                                                    CIP

ISBN 0-933029-54-3

For my father, Giro

Contents

Introduction 1

    Language 9

    Metaphysics and the Authority of Legitimization 16

    Transference/Countertransference 26

Chapter 1:   Windowseat 33

Chapter 2:   Mirrored Phantom 45

Chapter 3:   Apothecary 63

Chapter 4:   Black Pillar 85

Chapter 5:   Lowood 113

Chapter 6:   Helen Burns 129

Chapter 7:   Natural Curl 143

Chapter 8:   The Seed-Cake 169

Chapter 9:   Crib White Curtain Covering 187

Chapter 10: Pillowed Voice of Advertisement 207

Chapter 11: Thornfield 227

Chapter 12: Gytrash 249

Chapter 13: Men in Green 273

Chapter 14: Restory 291

Afterword I 313

Afterword II 333

Acknowledgments

Writing a work such as this, which is a detailed analysis of the unconscious (exploring its meanings, its language), involves a long solitary stay in the unconscious. The seeds of this project began in 1981, and, since fall 1982, I have been working on this book which required years of living in and traversing through regions of the unconscious. In many ways, I was guarded and guided "spiritually" during these years. I'm fairly certain that Brontë herself was a constant guardian, and for that I'm extremely grateful: it could not have been done without a sort of felt dialogue between us.

Such a work requires much silence and hermetic sealing and is not something in which others really can participate: this one required these seven private years of distillation, coagulation, refinement of word and rhythm, etc. The first people to read the manuscript were the publishers to whom I sent it when it was completed. Yet there were those who witnessed: my family somehow understood that day after day, year after year, I had to write in isolation a text which may or may not be inaccessible and/or misunderstood; also a few close friends were supportive during this work which really could not be shared as well as my loneliness which very often was — and for that I'm deeply appreciative. Also over the years I was given support through reading drafts of singular chapters to the Connecticut Association for Jungian Psychology, a seminar on French feminism at Yale University, the Pittsburgh Jung Society, the National Women's Studies Association at the University of Illinois, and the Wainwright Institute of Depth Psychology.

Once the book was finished, there came unexpected and very helpful assistance in the publishing process. Edward S. Casey reviewed the Introduction sections, Afterword I, and Chapters 1 and 2, suggested that I not alter them, and gave me detailed information concerning publishing houses which was a crucial motivating force in my getting underway the publishing procedure. Patricia E. Sabosik took professional risks in endorsing, in the publishing world, such a work that could not be easily "categorizable," and also offered me much support and guidance throughout the publishing procedure, for which I am very grateful. Nathan Schwartz-Salant, a publisher to whom I sent the manuscript, though a stranger to me and my work, immediately appreciated the findings on the unconscious in the work as well as the place of language in it, and he offered me complete editing rights which was a decisive factor in the choice of a publication route. Both he and Murray Stein have been open and sensitive to the nuances involved in my writing such a book, and helped to make its publication much easier than it could have been otherwise. For her love of the music of language and her overall precision, a bow of gratitude to Siobhan Granner, Managing Editor at Chiron Publications, as well as her assistant Ellen Keith who made most of the editing suggestions. Ms. Granner oversaw the entire publishing project with extreme skillfulness and calm. Imagine what it would be like to type a few pages of this text, and here is the good-hearted fortitude, clear mindedness, and technical ability of Debbie Sestito who typed the entire manuscript.

Introduction

In Brontë-esque fashion, this work begins with its negative, with what it is not. It is not an attempt to construct classifications of the novel in order to displace previous ones; it is not an exploration of the epistemological structures of rhetorical tropes or the development of a system of relations between figure and sign, sign and referent. One can locate here a certain analysis of rhetorical tropes and issues pertinent to "representation," yet its primary attempt is to study the unconscious of a woman in its own terms without appropriating that unconscious to conscious structures, that is, models of conscious thought.

Whose terms? What unconscious? What is a female unconscious? To that arises the now commonplace question: is she one or does she have one?[1] She has been so occupied being the unconscious of Western culture that she has only begun to step out of her position as the "unruffled surface" reflection of man's "Other" and venture into her own.[2]

During the years the Brontës lived, it was particularly necessary that a woman physically extricate herself from men and society to explore her

---

[1] This question — "Is woman the unconscious or does she have one?" — is Luce Irigaray's addressed to Jacques Lacan, which is discussed by her in *This Sex Which Is Not One*, trans. Catherine Porter (Ithaca, N.Y.: Cornell University Press, 1985), p. 60-61, 123ff. His response, in *Encore: Le séminaire XX, 1972-3* (Paris: Seuil, 1975), which in part is translated as "God and the *Jouissance* of the Woman" and "A Love Letter," trans. Jacqueline Rose, in *Feminine Sexuality: Jacques Lacan and the école freudienne*, eds. Juliet Mitchell and Jacqueline Rose, (New York: Norton, 1982), is further discussed by Alice Jardine in *Gynesis: Configurations of Woman and Modernity* (Ithaca, N.Y.: Cornell University Press, 1985), p. 168.

[2] See Lacan's discussion of imago and the "pure mirror of an unruffled surface" in "Aggressivity in Psychoanalysis," in *Écrits: A Selection*, trans. Alan Sheridan (New York: Norton, 1977), p. 15. Also his view of woman as Other in the sexual relation and with regard to what can be said of the unconscious, in "A Love Letter": "By her being in the sexual relation radically Other, in relation to what can be said of the unconscious, the woman is that which relates to this Other" (p. 151). Jane Gallop discusses this "unruffled surface" and the distinction of likeness and mirror in *Reading Lacan* (Ithaca, N.Y.: Cornell University Press, 1985), p. 62.

unconscious, the "unthought"[3] of the philosophical systems governing thought, and articulate the findings. It is not an arbitrary occurrence that all Brontë sisters wrote their novels sequestered and unmarried, not in broad social relation. Charlotte Brontë came the closest to such intercourse, and her (forced) extrication from that became the initiation of her novels, pen to the blank page entry to know it instead of being his.[4]

In this work, I take a different position than do others interested in the "feminine" unconscious. To the question about an unconscious which would be a woman's, Luce Irigaray suggests that since the feminine may be included in the unconscious (that it pertains to what is operating in the name of the unconscious), we first need to determine what the unconscious has borrowed from the feminine before we can arrive at a question of a feminine unconscious.[5] She also raises the issue that since the unconscious is a property of discursive logic, still belonging to that system as do others misrecognized by it (savages, children, insane, women), it remains as an outside-other which that primary system continues to appropriate thematically as "object" without eradicating completely its (inferior) difference.[6]

It cannot be denied that the study of *any* unconscious has to occur within the context of the conscious system of discourse, but from the beginning of this study, I have refused to translate or return the workings of the unconscious to that system of discursive thought or even its syntax. My sense is that to continue to study the unconscious as it is now defined (in Freudian and Jungian schools) in order to ascertain what it has repressed of the feminine is to use the prior as primary. That is, to begin from an unconscious explored by male theorists, the unconscious of the theoretical man, to find what it contains of the feminine (and it must since the unconscious consists of un-conscious, other-gender material), requires essentially keeping it a study of man: the base would still be the classical philosophical tradition, a classical unconscious.

Instead, I have preferred peering strategically into the unconscious of a woman, which I have found to be quite different from a feminine uncon-

---

[3]See Jardine (*Gynesis*, p. 92ff) on the exploration of the "unthought" which master discourses of the West have had to confront since the 19th century.
[4]The biographies on Charlotte Brontë which I read for this study are the following: Elizabeth Gaskell, *The Life of Charlotte Brontë* (Baltimore: Penguin Books, Inc., 1975); Helen Moglen, *Charlotte Brontë: The Self Conceived* (New York: Norton, 1978); Winifred Gerin, *Charlotte Brontë: The Evolution of Genius* (London: Oxford University Press, 1967); Margot Peters, *Unquiet Soul: A Biography of Charlotte Brontë* (New York: Atheneum, 1986).
[5]Irigaray, *This Sex*, pp. 122-23.
[6]Ibid., p. 124.

scious or the feminine component of the unconscious of a man. Therefore, I prefer to call it a female unconscious, an unconscious of those who are literal women.[7] My sense is that those studying the unconscious and its relation to body have been so threatened by the essentialism critique,[8] and of the body's power to literalize (that is, paralyze) psychological thought, that they have not respected the almost commonplace idea that psyches work through bodies and bodies are a manifestation of psyche, not its destiny but its *speaking*, a discourse of the very unconscious we claim to be studying.

I am not, however, suggesting that man and woman exist outside the symbolic register (linguistic, social, aesthetic, theoretical, economic, and political frames of reference), or that they can be excluded from it. Instead, I am indicating that the literal woman and her body must be used as base for formulations of the unconscious and its symbolic registers.

Therefore, my starting point is not the classical unconscious with an attempt to disconnect what is feminine from its current economy, but the unconscious of a woman, the writing of a woman who so precisely articulated her unconscious that she arrived at aspects of *the* female unconscious

---

[7]Note the difference between this question and the one Jardine raises: "What exactly is the metaphorization process surrounding the term 'woman' in contemporary French theory? While avoiding a certain (primarily American) biologistic psychology, one-to-one correspondence of the sign, as well as the notion of a woman's world as separate cultural space or identity, to what extent can we speak of 'woman' *without* referring to the biological female?" (italics hers), in *Gynesis*, pp. 42–43. Also the difference between it and Irigaray's statement: "They should not put it, then, in the form 'What is woman?' but rather, repeating/interpreting the way in which, within discourse, the feminine finds itself defined as lack, deficiency, or as imitation and negative image of the subject, they should signify that with respect to this logic a *disruptive excess* is possible on the feminine side" (italics hers), *This Sex*, p. 78.
[8]On the animadversion to the biological essentialism of Cixous's *l'écriture féminine* and her response to it, see Sandra Gilbert's introduction to Hélène Cixous and Catherine Clément, *The Newly Born Woman*, trans. Betsy Wing (Minneapolis: University of Minnesota Press, 1986), p. xvff. Ironically, Frank Lentricchia criticizes Gubar and Gilbert's, particularly Gilbert's, feminism as "a new name for essentialist humanism," in "Patriarchy Against Itself—The Young Manhood of Wallace Stevens," *Critical Inquiry* 13 (1987), particularly pp. 773–786. I, too, take issue with some of their work, but the tone of his article is disturbing, next to which the following article of Joan DeJean, "Fictions of Sappho," discussing the Phaethon complex of sons critical of recent feminist theorists, is quite satisfying.

which still informs us over a century and a half later.[9] I begin with the premise that if *Jane Eyre* is the manifestation of *a* female unconscious, which because of its acuity and depth, is informative of *the* female unconscious, a study of *that* female unconscious would require the same royal road as any,

[9]The assumption that a classical piece of literature pertains to a study of the unconscious is derived from the work of Freud and Jung. C. G. Jung discussed how the fantasy occurrences which make up the "transcendent function" (which mediates the transition between conscious and unconscious contents) appear spontaneously in dreams and visions and are also the basis of literature, in fact, the productive activity of the unconscious is responsible for major works of creativity. See C. G. Jung, "Symbols of Transformation," in *The Collected Works of C. G. Jung*, vol. 5 (Princeton, N.J.: Princeton University Press, 1976), pp. 3-7, 34-39. Subsequent references to Jung's writings will be to the volumes of *The Collected Works* hereafter abbreviated *CW*. See also, *CW* 6, p. 63; *CW* 7, pp. 80, 96, 175, 180ff, 207, 299; *CW* 8, pp. 84ff, 204. On his discussion of the figures of the unconscious, the *dramatis personae*, see *CW* 14, p. 529, and *The Visions Seminars, Book One* (Zurich: Spring Publications, 1976), p. 56.

Interestingly, a piece of literature was the content of Freud's and Jung's correspondence literally. Jung brought the "Pompeian phantasy" *Gradiva* by Wilhelm Jensen to Freud's attention, and, during the summer of 1906, months before the two met one another, Freud wrote an interpretation of that work ("Jensen's Gradiva" — his first published analysis of a work of literature). In his preface to that work, which he referred to as "genuinely poetic material" (p. 10), Freud states: "For when an author makes the characters constructed by his imagination dream, he follows the everyday experience that people's thoughts and feelings are continued in sleep and he aims at nothing else than to depict his heroes' states of mind by their dreams" ("Jensen's Gardiva," in *The Standard Edition of the Complete Psychological Works*, IX (London: Hogarth, 1959), p. 8. Subsequent references to Freud's writings will be to the volumes of *The Standard Edition*, published by the Hogarth Press between 1953 and 1981, hereafter abbreviated *S.E.* See also pp. 41-44 in the same volume and pp. 91-92, where he states that the creative writer and the analyst draw from the same source and work on the same object: "[The author] directs his attention to the unconscious in his own mind, he listens to its possible developments and lends them artistic expression instead of suppressing them by conscious criticism. Thus he experiences from himself what we learn from others—the laws which the activities of this unconscious must obey" (p. 92).

In a very different context, Jardine states: "For to question figurability, the symbolic status of the image, the paths and impasses of narrative, and so on—to work at the edges of the unnameable—*is* to deal with literature, with the literary substance itself." *Gynesis*, p. 89.

that is, through the dream, so that each chapter will be "read" as a dream.[10]

For about a century now, the tools for dream interpretation have been attained through the meticulous exploration by men of their own unconscious, most notably by Sigmund Freud and C. G. Jung. Could aspects of their tools be used in such a study without confounding those techniques with their findings? It is not a matter of stepping outside their tradition, but of using their tools in exploring spaces "beyond" it. The methodology of dream interpretation employed in this study was a result of an engagement of both Freudian and Jungian schools. From Freudian interpretation, I use the method of segregating the dream-text into its distinct elements and applying free association.[11] Unlike Freudian interpretation, however, I do not consider the manifest text to conceal latent thoughts; rather, the associations themselves reveal the unconscious meaning already residing within the manifest text. The sense is that the dream (or literary) images are not rebuses, arbitrarily connected to one another,[12] but that each image both in its meaningful association to the next and its meaning within itself elaborates the signification of the dream instead of having a dissimilar referent beyond itself to which it latently points.

The latter issue is derived from Jungian methodology, which also advo-

---

[10]Freud, *S.E.* V, p. 608. "*The interpretation of dreams is the royal road to a knowledge of the unconscious activities of the mind*" (italics his). This, of course, is Freud's great discovery. The integrity and thoroughness with which he scrutinized the dream, and through that the unconscious, has been quite important to me particularly at certain crossover periods. I agree with Clément's position regarding him: "It is good enough that, even if unwittingly, he has given us the instruments for thinking of these changes, of their limits, and of something else that may break open these limits." *Newly Born Woman*, p. 49.

[11]Freud, on "free association": "The adoption of the required attitude of mind towards ideas that seem to emerge 'of their own free will' and the abandonment of the critical function that is normally in operation against them . . ." *S.E.* IV, pp. 102-104, 241-242, 280-281; *S.E.* V, pp. 527-532, 635-641; *S.E.* XXII, pp. 10-13.

[12]On dream as rebus that is, "a picture-puzzle" which is nonsensical in itself: Freud, *S.E.* IV, pp. 277-278; Lacan, "Agency of the Letter in the Unconscious," in *Écrits: A Selection*, p. 159; and for an example of a Lacanian dream interpretation based on this principle that the value of the image as signifier in no way pertains to its signification: David W. Stewart, "Lacan's Linguistic Unconscious and the Language of Desire," *The Psychoanalytic Review* 73 (1986), 17-30.

cates the amplification of images.[13] The form of amplification I have
employed in this study, however, pertains more to the "intertextuality"
discussed by Freudian critics and others;[14] that is, it is taken primarily from
other texts to which Brontë referred or actually quoted within her own.
Therefore, I am proposing an intertextuality construed as amplification:
the positing of an intertextuality which does not preclude metaphysics (to
which I will return).

This engagement of Freudian and Jungian schools, which has informed
the entire work, not only has resulted in the use of techniques advanced by
both Freud and Jung, but also includes the contributions of post-schools:
object relations (Guntrip, Winnicott) and Lacanian schools of post-

---

[13]Patricia Berry, "An Approach to the Dream," in *Echo's Subtle Body: Contributions
to an Archetypal Psychology* (Dallas: Spring Publications, 1982), pp. 53-79. She
discusses how the positioning, repetition, emotion and implication of images
matter not as linguistic elements or even a narrative strategy yet as an approach
to the "epistemology of the imagination with which to meet the dream image on
its own level" (p. 78). See also James Hillman, "An Inquiry into Images," *Spring*
(1977), pp. 62-88; and "Further Notes on Images," *Spring* (1978), pp. 152-182.
Both Hillman and Berry continually caution against linguistic and conceptual
interpretations which distance too far from the expression of the images themselves, though at times this privileges the primacy of image as distinct from
language, see Berry, "An Approach to the Dream," pp. 65-66. In my view, such
a distinction is impossible: all images imply word and have discourse, even the
most numinous and intolerable of them can become (indeed their telos is to
become) meaning and even language. On amplification, which is the elaboration of dream-image through parallels from symbology, mythology, history of
religion, ethnology, etc., see Jung, *CW* 8, pp. 281-297. For Jung's comparison
of psychoanalytic and his constructive dream interpretation, *CW* 8, pp. 75-77.
Paul Kugler discusses Jung's positing image as meaning in *The Alchemy of Discourse: An Archetypal Approach to Language* (Lewisburg: Bucknell University Press,
1982) pp. 50-80, and the relation of that to contemporary psychoanalytic posi-
tions. However, a semantics of image has not been delineated by the post-
Jungians.

[14]For Julia Kristeva's definition of intertextuality as the transposition of sign
systems into another, see Leon S. Roudiez's introduction to her study *Desire in
Language*, ed. Leon S. Roudiez, trans. Thomas Gora, Alice Jardine, and Leon
S. Roudiez (New York: Columbia University Press, 1980), p. 15. Also Julia
Kristeva, *Revolution in Poetic Language*, trans. Margaret Waller (New York:
Columbia University Press, 1984), pp. 59-60. Also, Michael Riffaterre, "The
Intertextual Unconscious," *Critical Inquiry* 13 (1987), pp. 371-385; and his "Tex-
tuality: W. H. Auden's 'Musée des Beaux Arts,' " in *Textual Analysis: Some Readers
Reading*, ed. Mary Ann Caws (New York: The Modern Language Association of
America, 1986), pp. 1-13; and Barbara Johnson's chapter "Les Fleurs du Mal
Armé: Some Reflections on Intertextuality," in her *A World of Difference* (Balti-
more: John Hopkins University Press, 1987), pp. 116-133.

Freudian thought; classical (von Franz) and archetypal (Hillman, Berry) schools of post-Jungian thought.

This study is the continuation of an earlier work which was founded on the assumption that any study of the female unconscious necessitates a scrutiny of the relation of daughter to mother, of mother to the unconscious, as well as a reexamination of the consistent and seemingly inevitable opposition of mother to the unconscious[15] (the silence of her unconscious and the necessity of extricating from her, repressing her or placing her as object in both Freudian and Jungian thought). Therefore, this study continues and elaborates upon my examination of mother–daughter symbiosis begun in the earlier work, and it also explores the implications for the unconscious of woman–woman relations extending from the original maternal bond.

In the earlier work, I found a particular constellation of unconscious "figures" to be analogous to, if not responsible for, the structure of a symptom: anorexia. I use "figure" here in the sense employed by Jungian/archetypal psychology, to describe the "people" of the unconscious, the people who, for example, are a primary way the unconscious appears to us nightly. The figures examined in that study emerged from the unconscious of actual women, the symptom was studied as *dramatis personae* and the symptom was one generally considered "female." I discovered in that work that it is through a symbiosis with her daughter that mother manifests aspects of the unconscious pertaining to thwarted or culturally repressed ambitions or desires (including rage). Within the symbiosis, daughter is available to the effects of mother's unconscious, in fact, is dominated by them (imaged often as male tyrants) and then becomes their embodiment (an attempt at articulation as well as being its foreclosure). Within the anorexic syndrome, daughter was found to be a manifestation of mother's unconscious desire not to locate need and appetite in physical satiation, but to locate a nonbiological desire beyond human need, pertaining to the precise articulation of images of the unconscious not before delineated.

Anorexia, therefore, was explored as the moment a daughter embodies aspects of her mother's unconscious desire without yet having a language to speak that unconscious. The acquisition of such a language was determined to be the resolution of the syndrome. This acquisition was discussed in

---

[15]Angelyn Spignesi, *Starving Women: A Psychology of Anorexia Nervosa* (Dallas: Spring Publications, 1983). In that work, I gradually entered into a language of the female unconscious upon which I am elaborating in this project.

terms of differentiation and delineation of the figures and landscapes of the
female unconscious, indeed dialogue with (and through) them.[16]

Freud acknowledged his failure to recognize the importance of the "preoedipal" bond between daughter and mother, and stated that its discovery
was analogous to the discovery of the Minoan-Mycenean civilization, and
as difficult to grasp.[17] In my earlier study, I drew from a Greek myth, the
primary mother–daughter myth (which most likely was derived from
aspects of Minoan-Mycenean civilization). As I worked this myth to
uncover aspects of the preoedipal bond, the writing in the dominant discourse began to break down, as did the *way* I used traditional sources (not
that I used them). This work continues that penetration into the preoedipal
mother–daughter territory, yet uses a narrative closer to the age of modernity. Though I focus on the encounter of the daughter with the various
"male forces" of mother's unconscious, I have found that the classification of
that territory as either "preoedipal" (which still places the Oedipus myth as
primary) or "animus-ridden" (which is more a reversal of findings on anima
and in Irigaray's terms would be Jung's blind spot in an old dream of
symmetry) does not apply. This study is as much as reexamination of the
concept "animus" as it is of "preoedipal."

The issue of symbiosis returns us to how the female unconscious differs
from other unconscious(es). A statement of Irigaray's which has been very
confirming is her reply to the question on what the content of a woman's
unconscious might be: "I might nevertheless point to one thing that has
been singularly neglected, barely touched on, in the theory of the unconscious: *the relation of woman to the mother and the relation of women among themselves*" (italics hers).[18]

A daughter is to a mother in a different relation *to the unconscious* than is a
son to a mother. How a daughter is related to the mother affects both of
their relation to the unconscious. What is different about a female unconscious is precisely this aspect of symbiosis, which, as I discussed in the

---

[16]On Jung's methodology of the interlocution with "others" of the unconscious,
see *CW* 8, pp. 88f; *CW* 9i, p. 5; *CW* 7, pp. 200-205; also his *Memories, Dreams,
Reflections*, trans. Richard and Clara Winston (New York: Vintage Books,
1965), pp. 170-199. It is interesting to compare this with Lacan's sense of the
unconscious as the discourse of the other, that "the unconscious of the subject is
the discourse of the other" ("Function and Field of Speech and Language," in
Écrits: A Selection, p. 55).
[17]Freud, *S.E.* XXI, p. 226. Luce Irigaray discusses this archaic desire of the
daughter–mother relation and Freud's statement about it in *This Sex*, pp.
138-139.
[18]Irigaray, *This Sex*, p. 124.

earlier work, is at once a channel to the unconscious (for mother and daughter alike) as well as serving as a defense against that (articulated) passage. This study explores not only various *sorts of symbiosis* — antipathetic, sympathetic — but also various levels of each, all from the vantage point of the unconscious and the woman's relation to it.

Why the particular novel *Jane Eyre*? The decision to continue my study of the female unconscious through a study of this specific novel arose from pleasure reading during an eye operation that would affect, temporarily, the use of the right eye.[19] In the first chapter of this novel, I was surprised to discover a particular sort of symbiosis, not dissimilar to that of the anorexic syndrome, and there was the mother's "tyrant" whose domination of Jane sends her to another level of symbiosis pertaining more to death and affairs of the unseen, locked further into mother's rule of the unconscious, where indeed she wants to starve herself in the seldom-visited hidden chamber of mother's order.

Because each chapter of my study consists of a close textual analysis of a chapter of *Jane Eyre*, involving an analysis of each image regarded as meaningful in itself and through its association with surrounding images, a brief synopsis of the *Jane Eyre* chapter precedes each analysis. The intricate study of the female unconscious through a close textual analysis (each chapter of the novel being read as a dream) is pertinent to a discussion of (1) language, (2) metaphysics and the authority of legitimization, (3) transference/countertransference, and (4) the specific contributions of certain French feminists (this latter discussion became the first afterword).

Language

The entry to and interpretation of the unconscious of another woman's text began to break down the discourse in which I was writing about that unconscious: no longer was I analyzing that unconscious in discursive syntax but another sort of syntax began to emerge. What is the double syntax? Irigaray is asked. Her reply: instead of subordinating the unconscious to a conscious, Freud might have "articulated them and made them work as two different syntaxes." The discursive syntax is, in her view, a means of masculine "self-affection," requiring in its standard of sameness

---

[19]Later I learned that it was during her father's eye operation for cataracts, for which she alone accompanied him to Manchester, August 1846, that Brontë began *Jane Eyre*. And, of course, there is Rochester's eye problem at the end of the book, the result of his finally grappling with Bertha, to her death.

that female "self-affection" be impossible ("the feminine is never affected except by and for the masculine").[1]

Discussed in her essays, and through some experimentation in two of them, Irigaray attempts to discover/recover a female syntax. Her belief is that women will not know their desire, what they want, and will remain severed from themselves and one another until they return to the syntax allowing their self-affection.

Throughout many drafts, a language began evolving out of my analysis of the unconscious through *Jane Eyre*, a "female syntax" evolved which in itself was closer (than discursive syntax) to the unconscious being analyzed. This study is written, therefore, in a psychological language, a language of the female unconscious which also analyzes the unconscious: the unconscious simultaneously generating its own language and its own analysis.

Although it is not precisely *l'écriture féminine*,[2] I have been encouraged by readings in French feminist theory to continue in the evolving syntax, which clearly was a breaking down of discursivity. Xavière Gauthier:

> And then, blank pages, gaps, borders, spaces and silence, holes in discourse: these women emphasize the aspect of feminine writing which is the most difficult to verbalize because it becomes compromised, rationalized,

---

[1]Irigaray, *This Sex*, pp. 132–137.

[2]*L'écriture féminine* is a writing privileging the female body, emphasizing diffusion, fluidity, nonaggression, and emphasizing sexual difference in language and text, and is primarily from Hélène Cixous, "The Laugh of the Medusa," trans. Keith Cohen and Paula Cohen, in *New French Feminisms*, eds. Elaine Marks and Isabelle de Courtivron (New York: Schocken, 1981). See also Catherine Clément's essay "Enslaved Enclave," (trans. Marilyn R. Schuster) in that volume, as well as the dialogue between Cixous and Clément in *Newly Born Woman* (also the Introduction, pp. xv–xviii). Also, Elaine Showalter, "Introduction," in *The New Feminist Criticism*, ed. Elaine Showalter (New York: Pantheon, 1985), pp. 9–10, and the following essays in that volume: Showalter, "Feminist Criticism in the Wilderness," (p. 249); Nancy K. Miller, "Emphasis Added: Plots and Plausibilities in Women's Fiction," (p. 341); and Ann Rosalind Jones, "Writing the Body: Toward an Understanding of *l'Écriture féminine*." Showalter speaks of *l'écriture féminine* as a significant theoretical formulation though more a "utopian possibility" instead of literary practice. Miller discusses it as a "hope" but not blueprint for the future.

Makward sees *l'écriture féminine* as the emergence of the writing of Monique Wittig ["To Be or Not to Be . . . A Feminist Speaker," in *The Future of Difference*, eds. Hester Eisenstein and Alice Jardine (New Brunswick, N.J.: Rutgers University Press, 1985)]. For many American feminists, the problem is to relate the practice of feminine writing to a theory of femininity. I have found that the latter (a theory of the female unconscious) could only be attained through the emergence of the former.

masculinized as it explains itself . . . . If the reader feels a bit disoriented in this new space, one which is obscure and silent, it proves perhaps, that it is women's space.[3]

Marguerite Duras states that when women write they translate from darkness and from a silence in which they have lived for centuries.

I think feminine literature is a violent, direct literature and that, to judge it, we must not—and this is the main point I want to make—start all over again, take off from a theoretical platform . . . . I know that when I write there is something inside me that stops functioning, something that becomes silent.[4]

She discusses how in writing she lets something take over that flows from femininity and which is prior to her identity as Duras.

For Hélène Cixous, a most urgent question is the experience of pleasure, feminine sexual pleasure, where it takes place, how it is inscribed at the level of a woman's body, her unconscious, and how to put that in writing, a writing that inscribes femininity which is the inscription of the unconscious female body. "Everything will be changed once woman gives woman to the other woman."[5] (Charlotte Brontë gives Jane to me. I give Bertha to Charlotte.) For Cixous, not fearing the risk of writing as a woman is not to defend against the multiplicity of the unconscious, not to leave its spaces and desires unexplored in themselves—then to attempt to see the other woman not for purposes of a narcissistic strengthening or the verification of a master's power or weakness—it is, rather, to make love better, to invent.[6] Women writing as a woman do not hate, she says; yet I would add that one of the results of writing as a woman is to hate better.

Does the development of a female syntax require only lyrical love inventions? I could not stop there, nor do I think that is "female." I was struck by the "split" between the emotional subtext of anger and cynicism in sections of Irigaray's deconstruction of Freudian and philosophical Western traditions (in *Speculum of the Other Woman*) and that of love in her two lyrical

---

[3]Xavière Gauthier, "Is There Such a Thing As Woman's Writing?" trans. Marilyn A. August, in *New French Feminisms*, p. 164.
[4]Marguerite Duras, "From an Interview," trans. Susan Hesserl-Kapit in *New French Feminisms*, pp. 174–176.
[5]Hélène Cixous, "Sorties," trans. Ann Liddle, in *New French Feminisms*, p. 95; and Cixous, "The Laugh of the Medusa," p. 252.
[6]Ibid., pp. 245–264.

essays.[7] Must anger and dissection remain within the classical philosophical masculine economy and the female syntax be one only of love? I was struck again by the white column running down Julia Kristeva's pages in "Hérethique": on one side the lyrical discourse, on the other a theoretical discourse on mothering.[8]

In another place, Kristeva also speaks of blank spaces and ruptures in language, forces not grasped by the linguistic or ideological system. She states that in a culture where the phallic position requires speaking subjects to be conceived as masters of their speech, the rhythmic and nondiscursive text questions that mastery. Although in the majority of her writings she speaks of the nondiscursive text as feminine in a nonbiological specification, in this essay she discusses the two extremes of (literal) women writing experience, neither of which extremities seems desirable: (1) valorizing of phallic discourse, the privileged discourse of mastery of the (privileged) father–daughter relation; or (2) fleeing from all that is considered phallic, "refuge in the valorization of a silent underwater body, thus abdicating any entry into history."[9]

It is such oppositions that this work aims to traverse. But this work could not have been done before Irigaray's two lyrical essays separate from yet pertinent to her more analytic work, or before Kristeva's white column (I will return to their specific contributions). That my work analytically inves-

---

[7]Luce Irigaray, *Speculum of the Other Woman*, trans. Gillian C. Gill (Ithaca, N.Y.: Cornell University Press, 1985). "And the One Doesn't Stir Without the Other," trans. Helene Vivienne Wenzel, *Signs* 7 (1981), 60–67. "When Our Lips Speak Together," trans. Carolyn Burke, *Signs* 6 (1980), 69–79.

[8]Kristeva first published "L'Hérethique de l'amour," in *Tel Quel* 74 (1977), 30–49; reprinted as "Stabat Mater" in *Histoires d'amour* (Paris: Denoël, 1983), and trans. Leon S. Roudiez in *The Kristeva Reader*, ed. Toril Moi (New York: Columbia University Press, 1986).

[9]Julia Kristeva, "Oscillation between Power and Denial," trans. Marilyn A. August, in *New French Feminisms*, p. 166. She adds that most women novelists reproduce their literal history or constitute an identification through their story (the refuge of narcissism). The "suspended states" of Virginia Woolf, in her view, are not the dissection of language in Joyce. "Estranged from language, women are visionaries, dancers who suffer as they speak." Yet Kristeva does locate a change in the work of one current novelist (Sophie Podolski) indicating both "feminine" language and a sensitivity to language. However, as Jardine notes (*Genesis*, pp. 62–63), women writers are absent from not only Lacan's and Derrida's texts yet even more absent from Kristeva's, Cixous's, and Irigaray's (and other women theorists') texts. ["The women disciples of all of these theorists do sometimes mention contemporary women writers (Michele Montrelay mentions Chantal Chawaf, Marguerite Duras, and Jeanne Hyvrard), but such references are not in any way central to their theses" (pp. 62–63)].

tigates the positional and semantic relations of figures and landscapes of the female unconscious as well as lyrically explores the blank spaces and silences of the text of that unconscious, lyric as analysis, analysis as lyric, in the same sentence and on the same page is the (dare I say logical?) continuation of what women in France have been doing for over a decade. And my work draws toward others of a future where female syntax can be even less dependent on masculine models of discursive thought (for instance, the necessity of this introduction and the afterwords questioned).

The American contribution may be just this requirement that the analytical mode not be segregated from other essays or delegated to another side of the page and exclusively written in discursive language. American psychoanalytic feminists appreciate how several French feminists have turned to "the preoedipal relation between mother and daughter for a narrative of female desire that emerges from the relation to the maternal body," a discourse closer than discursive to the body, *l'écriture féminine*, rejecting Lacan's model of castration, the component responsible for signification in his schema, for its effect of the renunciation of mother by women. They translate and discuss in great detail the possibility of Cixous's and Irigaray's project of a female poetics, language as diffuse and autoerotic, allowing a once-fused mother and daughter "to become women and subjects, in and through language."[10]

Susan Rubin Suleiman worries about the exclusion, however, by French writers of *l'écriture féminine*, of a certain kind of writing pertaining to a "male" discourse of power which could result in a (mere) codification of woman's writing or a fetishization of the female body (privileging of body, voice and lyric over meaning).[11] Ann Rosalind Jones states that resistance to culture always is built on bits and pieces of that culture however they are "disassembled, criticized and transcended."[12] Nancy K. Miller declares that it is pointless to deny the effects of culture on female writing or for women to look for *"uniquely* 'feminine' textual indexes" apart from that culture.[13] Elaine Showalter advises not to exclude from feminist criticism a variety of

---

[10]See the introduction in *The (M)other Tongue: Essays in Feminist Psychoanalytic Interpretation*, eds. Shirley Nelson Garner, Claire Kahane, Madelon Sprengnether (Ithaca, N.Y.: Cornell University Press, 1985), particularly pp. 22–23. Also see *The Future of Difference*, eds. Eisenstein and Jardine; the Introduction and Ann Rosalind Jones's essay in *The New Feminist Criticism*, ed. Elaine Showalter.

[11]Susan Rubin Suleiman, "Writing and Motherhood," in *The (M)Other Tongue*, p. 371.

[12]Jones, "Writing the Body," in *New Feminist Criticism*, p. 374.

[13]Miller, "Emphasis Added," in *New Feminist Criticism*, p. 342.

intellectual tools; whereas a male text is fathered, she says, a woman's is parented and we have to deal with both parents (without women imitating male predecessors or trying to reform them).[14]

Yet, consider Christiane Makward's poignant statement: "If neofeminist thought in France seems to have ground to a halt, it is because it has continued to feed on the discourse of the masters."[15] All this raises the pertinent question: how to use and understand the "male" within female discourse and not rely on the masters (i.e., repeat a masculine discourse on femininity)? This study has attempted that understanding of the place of the "male" in several ways: employing the tools derived from the masculine culture, but then discarding them in the discovery of new ones; a bibliography indicating where masculine theory interacted with or confirmed what it was that was unfolding; inclusion within the study of the effect of male aspects within the female unconscious (Jungians would say considerations of animus; Lacanians the phallic mother). I also maintain a persistent view of female anatomy as its own ground for metaphor,[16] moving it "beyond" its equivalence with a metonymic base of biologistic essentialism (determinism of anatomy) or fetishism.

I would add that the ways "male" has been included in this female syntax of the female unconscious have prevented a certain fusion with mother, not in the sense of Father's Law as wedge (or castrating device) but because mother herself does not want (what does she want?) such a fusion, which obfuscates or denies analysis. This indicates the very possibility, once in the territory of the unconscious, to remain close to _its_ language while still asking questions of meaning.

The language that has evolved out of the interpretation of chapters as dreams, therefore, is no longer one of discursive syntax, but a lyrical-analysis. Whereas analysis emerges from the domain of position, relation

---

[14]Showalter, "Feminist Criticism in the Wilderness," in _New Feminist Criticism_, p. 265.

[15]Makward, "To Be or Not to Be . . . A Feminist Speaker," in _Future of Difference_, p. 102; Showalter also discusses this quote in "Feminist Criticism in the Wilderness," (p. 247) in her discussion of how the feminist obsession with revising, modifying, and attacking male critical theory keeps us dependent upon it. In the same essay, Makward states that neofeminist thought in France is "dangerously close" to repeating traditional formulations of femininity and female creativity. Jardine states (_Gynesis_, p. 43): "To what extent has the attempt in France over the past twenty years to bypass the human subject and dialectics led to the return of traditional notions of the 'feminine'?"

[16]See editors' introduction discussing Derrida's and Irigaray's relation to this issue in _The (M)other Tongue_, particularly p. 24.

and meaning (of the images), lyrical writing comes from extended medita-
tions and associations of body-experience (without reducing that to
biologic-determinism) to the images. The challenge is not to supplement
one mode with another; it is not a matter, for example, of supplementing an
interpretative theory of the dominant discourse with a lyrical rendition
which remains anterior to meaning. It is more a matter of allowing one to
become the other in an oscillating fashion even as that necessitates the
disturbance of the discursive.

Analysis loosens, takes apart "whole" into parts, in order to find the
proportion (portion of parts, their comparative relation); it asks about the
significance of the parts, to themselves, to one another, to the larger text.
Breaking up, analysis lowers, decenters, and language must be changed if
analysis succeeds: one has a choice at that point to write the language as it
breaks down or to translate it to a more familiar language (discursive
syntax). When I did not translate, I found that where the unconscious
pushed logical aspects of conceptualization to their limit, the lyrical style
emerged; the lyric then deepened the analysis further, eventually over-
reaching its limit and becoming again the lyrical, etc. The style is at once
lyrical and analytical: where the lyrical exceeds the analytical, the section is
set off on the page; where the analytical exceeds the lyrical, the introduction
and afterword sections emerged.

"And this involves neither avoiding theory nor embracing it, but playing
it off against itself; placing a violent new thought where the old thought
falters and creating new fictions."[17] I have explored a piece of fiction that I
realized contains a theory of the female unconscious, and in arriving at that
theory through analysis, I ended up with more fiction, other fiction from
behind, beneath the text, subtext, not only within each chapter but in what
became a necessary rewriting of the end of a piece of fiction.

The indistinctness of the lyrical style (its nondiscursive, polyvalent
nature) moves beyond subject–object distinctions, throwing the "Big
Dichotomies" which Alice Jardine discusses so cogently, into question.[18]
This requires an analysis not reliant on previous theories of the unconscious

---

[17]Jardine, *Gynesis*, p. 46.
[18]Ibid., p. 71, her discussion of Meaghan Morris's term "Big Dichotomies." Also
her statement (p. 76): "To think this indistinctness in the twentieth century has
been to think a crisis of indescribable proportions, to throw all of the Big
Dichotomies into question: for if the exterior is interior, then the interior is also
exterior; Man's soul is outside of him-self; history is but the exterior of his own
no longer interior imagination." Though far from her intention, her sense here is
remarkably aligned with Jung's theory of soul.

based on those dichotomies, but one that, like the lyric itself, emerges from the gaps and silences within the text, within the Big Dichotomies which are no longer fundamental.

Jardine discusses "tropological exploration" of rhetorical and thematic spaces, their movement and transformations, which she contrasts with a "topical list of definitions and identities."[19] In this study, such a tropological exploration in itself "produces" an analysis that precludes and even contests topical classification.

Metaphysics and the Authority of Legitimization

Through a lyrical-analysis, therefore, I have written the unconscious of another woman's text. My unconscious interpenetrating hers, the implication of each upon the other. As such, this project bears upon that place where contemporary French theory meets Jungian (archetypal) theory as well as psychoanalytic feminist theory: where one tries to come to terms with the threatened collapse of the dialectic and its representations, as well as the *Cogito* subject, and where one asks about multiplicity/polycentricity of figures and landscapes, circulation in methodology. And, I would add, which pertains to the shift from the primacy of castration as the dominant theme informing the theory of the unconscious.

Critics in France call American feminism pre-Freudian and pre-Saussurian in the ways it espouses natural over psychological life in a refusal of the unconscious, in its insistence on social structures as primary with a self more important than a subject or a multiplicity of reference, and in its view of language as communicative function instead of the effect of a human subject's inscription in culture.[1] What does it mean that I am a female Italian-American depth-psychologist who has written a lyrical-analysis of the female unconscious which moves polycentrically in places where neither subject nor object can be definitively posited? Am I suggesting a new form to be included in American feminism, one based on the primacy of the unconscious? Or am I stating that the study of the uncon-

---

[19]Ibid., p. 47.
[1]On the differences between French feminism and American feminism, see the introduction to *New French Feminists*, pp. xi–xiii; Jardine, *Gynesis*, pp. 42–47, 57–58, 63–64, 146, 233–236; Donna C. Stanton, "Language and Revolution: The Franco-American Dis-Connection," in *The Future of Difference*; Jane Gallop and Carolyn G. Burke, "Psychoanalysis and Feminism in France," in *The Future of Difference*.

scious of a woman is also feminist in the way it disrupts (phallocratic) structures of language and (antinomous) thought?

This study questions the logic of the subject: questions a subject which determines a theory of language, questions a subject acquiring organic unity through cognition, questions a subject which is master of its discourse. The way I have not been master over my discourse is the way "I" let the effects of the unconscious, the language of the unconscious, speak through "me," resulting in a lyrical-analysis.

Who is the subject that is the effect of this? Is it, as it is for Jane Gallop[2] and Catherine Clément and Hélène Cixous,[3] a bisexual subject? Is it, in Irigaray's terms, a subject of self-affection?[4] It is a subject of many "centers," a bisexual subject who knows the conscious and unconscious now through difference not opposition and who finds the shift from one to the other a syntactical, semantic, and a sexual one. Primarily it must be acknowledged that the language emerging from this entry into another woman's unconscious is a language with *no subject* (or object). No subject is the effect of this study, yet a person with access to the difference of many heterogeneous others in an unconscious peopled and landscaped. The effect is a bisexuality and one affecting oneself as moving out to affect others through oscillation among the speakings of many male and female "unconscious" people.

Does this bisexual one of self-affection have no master? Jardine quoting Shulamith Firestone: "It would take a denial of all cultural tradition for women to produce even a true 'female' art."[5] I do not maintain a radically anticultural posture in this work, particularly in ways I have drawn from Freudian and Jungian traditions, and my "complicity"[6] with those traditions became the bibliography of each chapter, and yet that is not to say that those traditions became or allowed me to become the master of my discourse.

The dichotomies of metaphysics are not sexually neuter (Cixous):[7] the under, the inferior, the nothing, and therefore the castrated has been female, and if the erection model and its Big Dichotomy (presence/absence: what about the biologistic essentialism behind so much of the Western

---

[2]Jane Gallop, *The Daughter's Seduction: Feminism and Psychoanalysis* (Ithaca, N.Y.: Cornell University Press, 1982), p. 127, and particularly 149–150.

[3]Cixous and Clément, *Newly Born Woman*, pp. xiv, 55–57, 84–87, 146.

[4]Irigaray, *This Sex*, pp. 132–134.

[5]Jardine, *Gynesis*, p. 54.

[6]Ibid., pp. 63–64.

[7]See Cixous, "Sorties," in *Newly Born Woman*, pp. 63–132.

philosophical tradition?) collapses, what happens to our exploration of those "under/nothing" spaces and are they still inferior? This project is the result of what occurs when a woman explores the unconscious, that is, the improper, empty, dark, silent, mad spaces of another (the other) woman.

Jardine quoting Jean-François Lyotard:

> To the obsolescence of the master narrative device of legitimation corresponds notably the crises of metaphysical philosophy, and that of the institution of the university which depends upon it. The narrative function loses its foundations, the great hero, the great perils, the great quests, the great goal.[8]

To write the unconscious of a narrative in order to write the unconscious is to let the narrative break down: John Reed no longer villain, Rochester no longer hero, Miss Temple no longer unmoved mover. The end no longer the end. Many voices, characters speaking where before there was only implied speech in silences; emotion contrary to or unexpected from the emotion of the text. The narrative has broken down and the unconscious is *not* translated to a paternal structure of thought or legitimate authority, not reverted to Big Dichotomies of another transcendental metaphysics.

Great Hero Father falls. Brontë's text itself anticipated all that I write here in this "Introduction" and even anticipated the crises of metaphysics and the authority of legitimization. For she was exploring the "under/nothing" spaces of mother–daughter symbiosis, love between women, death between women, madness and rage of women, while sitting right there under her father's blindness. And finally Patrick Brontë has fallen—if he had not, this present work would not have been possible. Now with the detumescence of the Father (not his death per se, for that would keep us cavalierly within the erection/castration, presence/absence model upon which the Western patriarchal tradition is based), does an entire metaphysics fall limp?

What are the implications of the fact that I found so much pertinent material on the female unconscious in a woman's text written over a century ago? The fact that the figures of Brontë's imagination continue to inform now a post-modern culture is itself a statement that some sort of metaphysics is at work, or at least requires comment. Is the suggestion one that John Reed or Miss Temple are "archetypes," do they require a metaphysics of a neo-Platonic domain?

---

[8]Jardine, *Gynesis*, p. 65. See Jean-François Lyotard, *The Postmodern Condition: A Report on Knowledge*, trans. Geoff Bennington and Brian Massumi (Minneapolis: University of Minnesota Press, 1984).

We can deconstruct Platonic and neo-Platonic metaphysics, but we still have to negotiate the figures in our dreams at night, a "conscience" which often speaks outside our intentionality, a vision which does not always correspond to literal seeing. How can it be understood that Brontë's figures have implications for an "unconscious" which was not even found or named during the time she wrote, that the structure of the John Reed metaphor, for example, informs an understanding of the modern symptom bulimia? How do we account for the fact that the obsessive-compulsive syndrome (not delineated until after her death) is elaborated upon by the analysis of Brocklehurst, and that a particularly female form of it, previously unnamed yet which is corroborated by my work with patients, is described from the analysis of Rochester?

Does the ontological status of the figures of Brontë's imagination need to be placed in a metaphysical realm? My sense is that they are formal and not bound to a specific historical culture, yet their manifestation is affected by and even configured by the particular culture in which they both appear and are studied. Brontë's imagination infused and became implicated with that of Jean Rhys, and we have not so much a "modernist" version of that imagination but more a manner in which that imagination becomes manifested in modernist culture.[9] Likewise this work is another manner, another "style"[10] in which that imagination becomes manifest in post-modern culture.

The post-modern culture, in which I write the imagination which is implicated with Brontë's, requires putting the authority of my own discourse into question, there is no master here, and the only authority becomes that of the "unconscious" figures and their landscapes themselves, all of which have persisted longer than Brontë or Rhys (and will persist longer than I do). Is it that the figures have the last word? Is there a last word when narrative itself breaks down in this crisis of modernity? How do "I" understand the process of putting my own lyrical-analysis discourse into question, the dismantler dismantling herself? J. Hillis Miller speaks of oscillation as dismantling.[11] I would say that the oscillation not only between lyric and analysis, but the oscillation of the two figures at the "end" of this book became my own dismantling of myself and my discourse.

[9]Jean Rhys, *Wide Sargasso Sea* (New York: Norton, 1982).
[10]Shoshana Felman, *Writing and Madness*, trans. Martha Noel Evans (Ithaca, N.Y.: Cornell University Press, 1985), pp. 131–134.
[11]J. Hillis Miller, "The Critic as Host," in *Deconstruction and Criticism* (New York: Continuum, 1985). He amplifies "parasite/host" as a way to conceptualize intertextuality in ways that are interesting.

What is left after such dismantling? A language of the unconscious which is one of many "feminine discourses."[12] Heterogeneous figures who speak. Beyond the face of things are the figures differentiating, speaking, feeling through the gaps and silences of the text to claim once again their place in a culture. The moment the authority moves to the heterogeneous figures now speaking yet once unconscious is where deconstructive criticism and Lacanian psychoanalysis intersect with Jungian thought, which first posited the autonomous discourse of unconscious "others" distinct from an "ego" that must be relativized by them.

These figures remain as the authority, yet since they continue to speak the inferiority of "our" desire, can we claim them as authority, make them and their relations into a new "science"? My sense is not that the unconscious and its study must include or preclude science, but that it would require a "radical" science (more radical than phenomenology's human science),[13] not a methodology of qualitative structures but sequences of relations between figures, between figures and "ego," proportions between figures and degrees of their manifestation, symptom as their inability to interlocute, data base as symptom. But we are speaking here of a "new" Father, and we recall that explorers of the unconscious have always grasped for him (in neurology and physical science, alchemy, linguistics and mathematics). First we have to survive the passing of the old. Any talk of science or a broad schematic structure now is nostalgic. Or a frenetic grasping when no one is left in authority.

And what prevents chaos here? The Frenchman said the unconscious is structured as a language. He then immediately darted into modern linguistics.[14] The unconscious has its own language, its figures speak and their

---

[12]See the third section, "Exchange," in *Newly Born Woman*.

[13]Cf. Amedeo Giorgi, *Psychology as a Human Science* (New York: Harper and Row, 1970); *Duquesne Studies in Phenomenological Psychology*, vol. 1, eds. A. Georgi, William F. Fischer, Rolf Von Eckartsberg (Pittsburgh: Duquesne University Press, 1971).

[14]Lacan's statement is: "the unconscious is structured in the most radical way like language, that a material operates in it according to certain laws, which are the same laws as those discovered in the study of actual languages, languages that are or were actually spoken" (*Écrits: A Selection*, p. 234). I can work from the first phrase of this statement, yet disagree with the rest. For Lacan, the unconscious is "transindividual, that is not at the disposal of the subject in re-establishing the continuity of his conscious discourse" (p. 49). And what structures it are not archetypes (p. 234) yet structures which reside outside the experience of community and personal history "in which his place is already

integral relations persist, and when we find the meaning of their language (which is not to translate that language to the linguistics of the languages of our conscious daily speaking) that meaning precludes chaos or babel.[15] To let the images of the unconscious speak in their own tongue, and inform us

---

[14]*(continued)*
inscribed at birth, if only by virtue of his proper name" and determined by "permutations authorized by language" (p. 148). In my view, Lacan's return to the language of the unconscious, in an attempt to recover the primacy of the unconscious for psychoanalysis, is an important one, yet the unconscious does not speak in the language of mathematics (if it did, we would have equations and formulas for dreams), which is not to say there is not a mathematical and logical base of the unconscious (which Pythagoras knew and from which music derives), but one must return to the language endemic to the unconscious to determine such a base.

I believe that the Lacanian application of contemporary linguistics and mathematics to the unconscious is not a determination of the language of the unconscious. For the unconscious speaks nightly, and that occurs in images, in the discourse of figures traversing specific landscapes of their own design. It also speaks in slips of words and behaviors which are linked associatively to memories and images in the reservoir of consciousness. My sense is that Lacan's use of linguistics as the language of the unconscious is related to his devaluation of the Imaginary. When image is no longer Imaginary in a prejorative sense, and also no longer relegated to "preoedipal" territory, when Oedipus and Father's Law are no longer the standard to which the base of the unconscious falls short, then we will be closer to the language of the unconscious. An approximation to which this project is one.

[15]I am referring to the plurivocal discourse of the unconscious which entails a search for internal relations between images of the text. The syntax of the unconscious would then consist of "archetypal" images. See Kugler (*The Alchemy of Discourse*) who discusses (using Wilden following Benveniste) how Saussurian arbitrariness does not lie between signifier and signified but between signifier and object of reference. I claim that what still is necessary is an exploration of the relation of signified to archetypal image. Kugler demonstrates how particular sound patterns (signifiers) are nonarbitrarily tied through phonetic parity to clusters of archetypally related meanings (and he refers here to Jung's *Symbols of Transformation*, extensive etymological analyses of archetypal themes). Kugler recovers Jung's sense of archetype as invariant relationships determined by form not content, the emphasis on formal relationships instead of substance, and discusses the similarity between that and Lévi-Strauss's and Lacan's later work. His main thesis is that symbolism in an archetypal sense does not reside in relations between signifier and signified but that there is a symbolic (archetypal) level in language that is nonarbitrary and pertains to sound-to-sound relationships. However, the approach scrutinizing sound components too easily could avoid not only issues of the signified but also positional, sensate and emotive qualities of the image as well as its discourse other than that of its "proper" name.

of their position, intention, desire, language and meaning, is to affect the way we think about metaphysics. It refers to a metaphysics which is not nostalgic for the father, a metaphysics which is not logocentric, univocal, phallocratic or oppositionalistic, and, above all, not transcendent. Images not barred from but which consist of meaning.

What are the meanings of Brontë's images, with what are we left after all this dismantling? In Afterword II, what is summarized, from each of the lyrical-analysis chapters, is a theory of, or actually within, the female unconscious that takes as its baseline mother–daughter symbiosis. Within various levels of this symbiosis, various male figures appear in different possessive and dialogical relation to the daughter. Also, each encounter of the daughter with the emerging male figure pertains to various requirements and intentions, and refers to a female continually shifting conscious referent (Bessie, Miss Temple, Miss Fairfax), as well as a female unconscious referent (Helen, Bertha). We are left with the beginning of a tentative theory of the alteration of the figures of the female unconscious, their differentiation, language, ability to interlocute with the ego, distance from and proximity to the ego (and the effect of that upon specific "symptoms"), their relation to various landscapes, and the relation of landscape to metaphors of female anatomy, all this without even speculating on what may be *beyond* determining this movement. One cannot say, better not say. Father limps.

There are other ways in which Brontë anticipated the crisis of phallocratic models. The landscapes of her novel metaphorically follow female anatomy more than they inform any developmental fantasy of linear growth. That is, the territories which the "heroine" Jane Eyre traverses previously have been read according to her (and thereby a woman's) psychosocial development, enough so that the novel has been discussed as a female *Bildgunsromane*.[16] What emerges from my analysis is the way each "fictional" place—Gateshead, Lowood, Thornfield—becomes an index of a portion of female anatomy describing not only the dimensions and parameters of the space but also who we are when we live according to it, and how it manifests through whom others see ourselves to be. Also, each landscape refers to another relation of "ego" to "world": ego corresponds to world differently from the red-room of the womb place, from the corridors of temple regions, from the mad-laugh view of the third-story leads.

---

[16]For example: Karen E. Rowe, " 'Fairy-born and human-bred': Jane Eyre's Education in Romance," in *The Voyage In: Fictions of Female Development*, eds. Elizabeth Abel, Marianne Hirsh, and Elizabeth Langland (Hanover, N.H.: Dartmouth College, 1983).

Therefore, Brontë conceived of female "development" not in terms of linear progression but as an uncovering of the unconscious related to body in a passage (the eyre) circulating up and down that body. She was close enough to the unconscious to register what we only have been discovering this century: that the unconscious does not follow deterministic laws of the physical sciences, nor can it be translated into those laws; its movement is spiral, it repeats and echoes, its speech is ambiguous and fluid, its figures heterogeneous and very much interactive with the landscapes in which they appear. The "heroine" of Brontë's novel never would have reached Thornfield (or been hired by it) if that mansion did not have the crimson drawing room mirroring that from which she Gateshead started. Each landscape is included in the next which draws from it in further delineation of its properties; progression through regression is the movement of the passages here.

Brontë also anticipated Freud which would not have surprised him.[17] We see in the passage from Gateshead to Lowood to Thornfield various aspects of the psychoanalytic states — oral, anal, latent, and genital. However, all refer to the daughter's negotiation of the various male figures emerging from the symbiosis with mother. Also, we do not find any indication of the typical Oedipal patterning. The daughter's encounter with the paternal figure cannot be separated from the space of mother–daughter symbiosis within which she resides when that encounter occurs and which in fact is necessary for it to occur. That encounter is not based on an erotic drive as much as it is subtended by a desire to extricate from the more antipathetic levels of the symbiosis.

We also find that a "genital sexuality" is operative only when the daughter has become differentiated enough within the (now "sympathetic") symbiosis with mother in order to pass, through the erotic male figure, back to (and through) the mother–daughter shared madness. That a woman cannot entertain a genital sexuality without returning (as differentiated) to the mother's madness (which attracted her to the erotic male figure in the first place, he is "married" to what it looks like), is how Brontë "founded" a female psychology before either Freud or Jung were born.

---

[17]Freud, *S.E.* IX, p. 8: "But creative writers are valuable allies and their evidence is to be prized highly, for they are apt to know a whole host of things between heaven and earth of which our philosophy has not let us dream. In their knowledge of the mind they are far in advance of us everyday people, for they draw upon sources which we have not yet opened for science." Stanley Cavell refers to Freud's statement of being preceded in his insights by the creative writers of his tradition (yet does not cite the reference from Freud) in "Freud and Philosophy: A Fragment," *Critical Inquiry* 13 (1987), 386–393.

Brontë's placement of the unconscious in regard to the ego and its passages through the body also differs from much work in depth psychology that places the unconscious below or behind that which is conscious. She conceived of it around: on the edge of interior and exterior (Gateshead windowseat), below (red-room vault), above (red-room lightbeam), within (Miss Temple's chamber), and upstairs (Thornfield's third floor). This raises some interesting issues: if the unconscious is "around" us, what does that imply for our understanding of "capping" it, keeping it beneath, riding it, mastering it? What does it imply for our sense that we can rise above (the bar separating it from consciousness) through symbol or metonymic links of signifiers speaking Other's desire?

The use of the metaphor of female anatomy in delineating passages of the unconscious returns us to critiques of essentialism: that the inscription of the female body only ascribes to the reigning (phallocratic) binary system. My sense is that once we move out of the anal and phallic approaches (active/passive and presence/absence) of polar opposition, there are various ways to explore gender differences not according to such oppositionalism. In the viewing of difference as "essential" to a study of the unconscious, I have been very much encouraged by the French feminists with the respect they have for gender and its relation to the unconscious, genderized landscapes of the unconscious (Wittig),[18] and the possibility of female languages of the unconscious. Although I am an Italian-American working on a British novel, French contemporary theory often confirmed my intuitions on the necessity of what it was that I was attempting by supporting my methodological attempt not to place any grid of depth-psychological systems upon the literature or use the literature as data for theory and to enter the subtext with as much detachment as possible from masters of discourse.

The importance of such inscription of the female body, without limiting it by determinism or fetishism, is that it led to insights on the unconscious and its workings which would otherwise not have been available. For example, the "madness" of women is not that they are of earth/womb (and finally in 1950 have risen with Mary), cannot sublimate as much as men, or

---

[18]See particularly Monique Wittig, *Les Guéllières*, trans. David Le Vay, (New York: Avon, 1973); and *The Lesbian Body*, trans. David Le Vay (New York: Avon, 1976).

have deficient superegos,[19] but that they sublimate often too far and do not know their way down (through body)[20] and out (to world). This is why the French feminist question—how does female *jouissance* write itself—is so important.

Therefore, I am suggesting that the unconscious figures *themselves*, their intellectual, sensate, and emotive discourses are what prevents chaos in the exploration of domains other-than-conscious. Jardine states:

> New figures must be found beyond theocentric representation. The *technē* has been threatened from the interior and exterior by a language it may have produced but which, in any case, it cannot seem to control. Freud heard that language, as did Nietzsche; and they both could only, if in different ways, *represent* it as the unmediated violence of Mitra, the Great Mother.[21] (Italics hers.)

To that I would add, of course, that Jung heard that language,[22] and so did Charlotte Brontë, begun perhaps as "mad" third-story laughter.

Whereas Jardine sees modernity's task (to name this unnameable space formerly in the shadows) correlative to the ending of metaphysics and Judeo-Christianity,[23] I see it more as modernity's struggle to let the unnameable *name itself*, which is correlative to the ending of the exclusive metaphysics of Judeo-Christianity as it is a summoning of a metaphysics necessitating a radical reformulation of not only secular yet sacred dimensions and boundaries.

---

[19] On Jung's discussion of the relation of women to earth and body, and the relevance of the papal declaration of the Assumption of Mary, see *CW* 9i, pp. 107–110. On deficient superego: Freud, *S.E.* XXII, p. 129; on incapacity to sublimate: Freud, *S.E.* XXII, p. 134.

[20] Due to a fear of the "desire" of their own wombs which includes hate and the articulation of that.

[21] Jardine, *Gynesis*, p. 81.

[22] See particularly C. G. Jung, *Memories, Dreams, Reflections*. Interestingly, in another context (*Gynesis*, pp. 141–142), Jardine discusses Freud's renunciation of mysticism ("For Freud, any conceptual system that valorizes that maternal space, the *Id*, is mystical.") and the resultant battles with colleagues valuing Mother more than Father, his "maternalistic Others," including Jung. She then states that the lesson of the late twentieth century pertains to the impossibility of living without an experience of the sacred. Yet she does not develop this idea and states that women theorists in France have not either.

[23] Jardine, *Gynesis*, p. 81.

Transference/Countertransference

Beyond the formalism of structuralism and semiotic narratology, Peter Brooks summons an "erotics of form" to return formalism to more human aspects of literature.[1] From the close analysis of the formal relations of the *dramatis personae* of *Jane Eyre*, a formal-erotic language has emerged in my work. My sense is that permeating my own lyrical-analysis are issues (issues which Brooks also discusses) of transference/countertransference that concern my relation to the text.

Lyrical-Analysis: The Unconscious Through Jane Eyre rests on the assumption that the constellation of figures in a work of literature and the dynamic organization of their movement over specific landscapes corresponds to the figures of the unconscious and their operational patterns. This premise directly relates to the theory of C. G. Jung that the unconscious is polycentric, heterogeneously peopled, and that its *dramatis personae* become the drama and narratives of literature. Although more psychoanalytically inclined, Brooks also works off such assumptions "that there ought to be, that there must be, some correspondence between literary and psychic process, that aesthetic structure and form, including literary tropes, must somehow coincide with the psychic structures and operations they both evoke and appeal to."[2]

Mary Watkins takes it a step further, a different step, presenting evidence from writers of literature on the intrinsic relation between the personifying that occurs spontaneously in the unconscious (issuing, she feels, from formative dispositions explored by Jung and his followers) and the personified characters of the literary text. In her view, depth and specificity of characterization, degrees of animation, and complexity of perspectives are indices of a psychologically advanced human as well as a "good" novel.[3]

The need to return the *dramatis personae* of either the unconscious or a literary text to a monocentric system, e.g., the Self, has been questioned and revised in post-Jungian thought, with its emphasis on polycentricity and circularity, as well as deconstructive/rhetorical criticism. The differ-

---

[1]Peter Brooks, "The Idea of a Psychoanalytic Literary Criticism," *Critical Inquiry* 13 (1987), 334–348; particularly p. 339.

[2]Ibid., p. 337. Brooks's statement of the assumptions underlying his study: "Freud works from the premise that all that appears is a sign, that all signs are subject to interpretation, and that they ultimately tell stories that contain the same dramatis personae and the same narrative functions for all of us" (p. 336).

[3]Mary Watkins, *Invisible Guests: The Development of Imaginal Dialogues* (Hillsdale, N.J.: The Analytic Press, 1986).

ence between the two relates to "bracketing the human realm from which psychoanalysis derives."[4] Brooks discusses how deconstructive/rhetorical criticism too often remains in the linguistic realm, bypassing the difficult and necessary issues in poetics that are pertinent for the passage from formalist to psychological interpretation.[5] Gallop would agree with him, and also states that our own unconscious (its desires and defenses) must be implicated in the investigation; she cites the work of Schor and Kahane for instances of critical self-implication.[6]

What does one want to claim, Brooks asks, in showing that the structure of a metaphor is equivalent to that of a symptom?[7] Perhaps one wants to claim that both are languages of the unconscious (certainly Jung knew that) which corresponds to the fact that symptom is also metaphor. The metaphor in a text, therefore, would be a different (healthier presumably) metaphor than that of the symptom for what the unconscious wants to be speaking. Brontë herself moved from symptom as metaphor to metaphor in narrative which became the beginning of her novels. Since *The Professor* is written more from the stance of Crimsworth, the "Heger figure," my sense is that *Jane Eyre* is the first self-analysis Brontë wrote. She put down the pen of her symptomatic letters to Heger and picked up the pen of a self-analysis, finding a narrative of the working of her unconscious, its *dramatis personae*, its conflicts no longer her "hysterical" grasping for the manipulating Belgian, yet now a revival of memory, Brontë her own analyst, her text an analysis, a recalling through metaphor of what had been repressed instead of repetition compulsion from that past in the present (Heger letters).

Most would agree that *Jane Eyre* as narrative discourse is a more adequate rendition of the unconscious past than were Brontë's symptoms. August 1846 in Manchester was the crossover from symptom to narrative discourse, Brontë the analyst of her unconscious. The result is the delineation of her creative imagination and the first thirteen chapters of *Jane Eyre*.[8]

---

[4]Brooks, "The Idea of a Psychoanalytic Literary Criticism," p. 337.
[5]Ibid.
[6]Jane Gallop's essay "Reading the Mother Tongue: Psychoanalytic Feminist Criticism," in *Critical Inquiry* 13 (1987), see p. 321.
[7]Brooks, "The Idea of a Psychoanalytic Literary Criticism," pp. 340–341.
[8]There are many intersections between the first thirteen chapters and Brontë's life: the similarity of the one brother and two sister constellation of the Reed, Brocklehurst, Ingram, and Rivers families with that of Brontë's siblings, and the characteristics of those sisters—Georgiana as a representation, in my view, of the "underside" of Anne, Eliza of Emily. That there was, in fact, an aunt, who

From chapter thirteen on, as Jane develops the erotic relationship through courtship with Rochester (something Brontë never passed through in life with Heger or any erotic male person), there is not an unconscious past corresponding to the novel's events which became more a rendition of what Brontë would have wanted to occur, in fact, a "subjective figment" or fancy. My own study of the female unconscious working through Brontë's inscription of that unconscious (as creatively imagined instead of fancied) leaves off at the thirteenth chapter and then ends itself.[9]

To this text through which Brontë was the analyst of her unconscious, inscribing a more adequate rendition of that unconscious, I have been both analyst and analysand. I intervened in the text by the act of reading and

---

[8]*(continued)*

was a stepmother of sorts, in the Brontë home, is a point unnoticed or uncommented upon by the biographers I read. Here was a rigid, Calvinist aunt who more than likely did not want the pressures and burdens brought on by these children placed under her care. We do know that this aunt did not like the climate of Haworth, that she did rule over the children strictly, and that her money was necessary for their future. Branwell was her favorite, and next came Anne. The aunt easily forgave Branwell's delinquency as John Reed similarly was pardoned.

Biographers often do note the point-by-point correspondence between Lowood and Cowan Bridge, Maria Brontë and Helen Burns, Reverend William Carus Wilson and Brocklehurst, and Mary Ann Evans and Margaret Wooler (with whom Charlotte did teach and spend evenings) together composing Miss Temple. Other nonarbitrary correspondence: Thornfield with Ellen Nussey's house; Heger with Rochester (Heger's letter to student Meta M. indicating his mentor-seducer role with younger women); also, the mad woman with the Leeds' story and Charlotte's anger at Mme. Heger. John Reed, Brocklehurst, and Rochester are elaborations and differentiations of the Zamorna and Northangerland characters of Angria.

The point here is not that Brontë's unconscious, and its manifestations in her narrative, is reduced to her literal life, but that when that unconscious manifested itself through configurations of her literal life as well as her narrative (for which her life was used as channel to the unconscious) that narrative has a relation to the unconscious which the narrative based more on subjective fantasy of a potential outcome either does not have or has differently.

[9]Edward Casey's discussion of the distinction Jung made between fantasy, " 'a subjective figment of the mind,' " and imagination, " 'an image-making, form-giving creative activity,' " is pertinent here [Edward S. Casey, *Imagining: A Phenomenological Study* (Bloomington, Ind.: Indiana University Press, 1976), p. 213]. Also see his discussion of Coleridge's distinction of fancy and creative imagination, pp. 184–185; as well as his article "Toward an Archetypal Imagination," *Spring* (1974). Also, I am indebted to Jane Gallop's use of "Interstory" and "Postory" in *Reading Lacan* for my usage of Restory in "ending" this book.

continually reexamining the text, particularly reading it through dream interpretation. My countertransferential desire to interpret (master?) the text resulted in the analysis, the latter term of lyrical-analysis.[10]

The lyrical result was the manifestation of myself as analysand, my transference to the text, as well as to Brontë. This transferential effect allowed me to explore landscapes and figures in the unconscious through a mode of submission otherwise unlikely, and relates to Cixous's sense of "inhabiting."[11] The bulimia in Chapter 1, the incest in Chapter 2, the girls' school in Chapter 5, the death between women in Chapter 9, the ward in Chapter 11, and the runaway in Chapter 14 are not part of the fabric of my literal history, yet as analysand and as a result of my transference to Brontë and her text, the unconscious of the text became revealed: her text became more my dream, and those aspects of the unconscious became more accessible to me experientially and theoretically than if I were exploring them "masterfully" instead of lyrically. My therapeutic work with patients of course contributed in these areas, as it did to every page of this work, but intimacy with the detailed image and feeling and meaning of the place came from the submission to Brontë's "authority" there.

The more I submitted to (became patient to, and therefore patient with) the text, associations were enhanced which then permitted more hidden signification of the text to emerge. The lyrical process therefore produced more text, more subtext, and from that place more significance of the main text opened, more analysis, that is, the analysis became more precise, made me master in the ways Cixous and Clément speak of (and relating to the mastering Jane learns in chapter seven), more masterful than if I had

---

[10]See Brooks, "The Idea of a Psychoanalytic Literary Criticism," p. 343. Also, I profited from Shoshana Felman's Lacanian perspective on transference and its relation between reader (Freud) and text (hysteric) in "Turning the screw of interpretation," in *Literature and Psychoanalysis: The Question of Reading: Otherwise,* ed. Shoshana Felman (Baltimore: John Hopkins University Press, 1980), see p. 118. Susan Rubin Suleiman discusses the relation and difference between Felman's and Brooks's perspectives of the transferential model of reading in her fine article "Nadja, Dora, Lol V. Stein: women, madness and narrative," in *Discourse in Psychoanalysis and Literature,* ed. Shlomith Rimmon-Kenan (New York: Methuen, 1987), see p. 127.

The foundational papers for my views on transference/countertransference include Freud, "The Dynamics of Transference," *S.E.* XII, p. 97–108, and Harold Searles, *Counter-transference and Related Subjects* (New York: International Universities Press, 1979).

[11]Cixous, *Newly Born Woman,* pp. 148–149, her "transference" to Dora, and Cixous's resultant interpretative and creative work from that is an example of the transferential effect which I am discussing here.

retained a master-relation to the text, if I had not yielded to the effects of its unconscious and the necessary alterations in syntax accordingly.[12]

Brooks describes Freud's view of "the relations of analyst and analysand in the transference as one of struggle — struggle for the mastery of resistances and the lifting of repressions," and Brooks likens that to the struggle between reader and text.[13] It is true that in the process of opening up my resistance (to the unconscious revealed through the text), Brontë's text often became my resistance which I had to work through in order to get to an unconscious which necessarily included my own.

Jardine discusses Philippe Sollers's "erotic merging at the interior of language." This is how I experienced the lyrical mode of approaching the text (being analysand to it); yet she continues that Sollers does this "through a radical dismemberment of the textual body, a female body."[14] I did not experience the struggle with the text as a struggle for mastery (as in master over it) affecting such a dismemberment. I felt instead that what I needed to know about the unconscious was in the text and what mattered was the perspective (oscillating between lyrical and analytical from which the final lyrical-analysis emerged) I took to it. I found a precise form emerging from the erotic merging, which left the text altered. Although the eroticism with Brontë and her figures was at times quite active and even aggressive, my sense is that her text was not dismembered.

At the beginning of the project, there was often a struggle, "dialogic struggle,"[15] between myself and the text, myself as analysand wanting to drop even more deeply into the unconscious of the text through the lyric mode (sentimentalism would push me out), and as analyst incisively wanting to pull out meaning from some aspect of the text (aridity would pull me back in). So the dialogic struggle Brooks describes became an oscillation resulting in a novel form of discourse.

Brooks's critic asks: "How can there be a transference where there is no means by which the reader's language may be rephrased in coherent and manageable form by the text-as-analyst?"[16] The rephrasing of my perceptions over the years of dialoguing with *Jane Eyre* is evident not only in the plethora of drafts and the perpetual breakdown of discursive syntax across

---

[12]Cixous and Clément, see the third section, "Exchange," in *Newly Born Woman*.

[13]Brooks, "The Idea of a Psychoanalytic Literary Criticism," p. 344.

[14]Jardine, *Gynesis*, p. 246. This entire section on Sollers, pp. 238–246, is illuminating.

[15]Brooks, "The Idea of a Psychoanalytic Literary Criticism," p. 345.

[16]Ibid., p. 346. The question was posed by Terence Cave in a review of Brooks's work.

drafts, but also in the way the form of lyrical-analysis slightly alters: some chapters opening themselves more to the analytical mode, others more to the lyrical, others holding the tension in a more reciprocal way, all depending on the content of each chapter. And the converse of the critic's statement holds as well: the text (as analysand) changed, rephrased its language, as I analyzed it; it changed to the extent that going beyond chapter thirteen was impossible, and a restory necessary, which then in its nascent form affected the rewriting of the lyrical-analysis of chapters 1–13, and this in turn altered, more than once, the Restory.

Chapter 1

Windowseat

There is no walk this day of wintry wind and slashing wetness. The child is relieved, she is not large enough to keep up with the cousins, John, Eliza and Georgiana. She hangs behind on the walk from which today she is grateful not to be returning with nipped fingers and a heart darted by chidings of the nursemaid returning to the mother, that Mrs. Reed, drawing up by the fire beside her three children. The sofa is not for this smaller cousin. Mrs. Reed has ordered her to keep a distance until she becomes more the natural child, the sofa welcoming only young ones contented. Jane, this mother says to her, you have not an attractive manner, not sociable, until you become of a lighter disposition, Jane, you are not of us.

The child wants to know what it is she has done, the aunt scolds the question demanding a distance. Jane withdraws into a room adjacent she is crawling into the windowseat, drawing the scarlet draperies on her right as there on the left the clouds bearing down their ceaseless rain. Protected by the windowpane yet not separated from those November elements, she opens the book of birds today drawn to the sea-fowl of a haunted terrain of the Arctic Zone.

From these pages: a lone rock upon billowing sea, broken boat on desolate coast, 'cold and ghastly moon glancing through bars of cloud at a wreck just sinking,' solitary churchyard with headstone (she sees as haunted), two ships becalmed (she sees as marine phantoms), there is a fiend and thief (she passes in terror), and then the 'black, horned thing seated aloof on a rock, surveying a distant crowd surrounding a gallows.'

In her own way she is happy with these images evoking stories vivid and mysterious as those of the nursemaid Bessie who while ironing and in pleasant mood would tell the ballads, the old fairy tales. She is happy until that occurs the most feared: the interruption, a voice—Madame Mope—the cousin John is calling. Weak in vision and conception, he cannot find her yet the sister Eliza points out the windowseat then leaves as the brother enters fully stout ordering subservience. He wears a dingy skin, thick lineaments and limbs, fourteen and only four years older yet so fully larger. 'He gorged himself habitually at table, which made him bilious, and gave him a dim and bleared eye and flabby cheeks.' Heavy limbs not holding much affection for the mother who indulges him or sisters, yet Jane he hates. His physical blows to her arrive many times a day, these attacks for which there is no appeal. The servants do not stand up to this young master and as for the mother: even when they occur in front of her, she never sees his blows.

'Habitually obedient' Jane follows his command to stand before him whereupon repetitiously his tongue thrusts in and out. Terrified of the blow forthcoming, her body withering yet not avoiding a look upon him of disgust. (He sneers) This is for your impudence with mama (he strikes her) for hiding behind the curtain, for the look in your eye like that of a rat. As she totters, he is demanding to know her exercise behind scarlet drapery. A book, he wants to see the book and as he grabs it he calls her dependent, how dare she rummage in his bookshelves for they are his as it will be his home soon; stand by the door, he is telling her to stand out of the way of any glass. She is clearsighted but she cannot see his intent. The book hurled through the air hits her and with a cry she falls, her head striking against the door cuts. The blood bursts forth with its sharp pain.

She calls him slave-driver, Roman emperor. 'I really saw in him a tyrant: a murderer.' He lunges at her, grasping what is a desperate thing now, a frantic flailing one—bellowing he says rat! rat! Cousins running to the brother's aid, calling mother. Girl child flying in a fury at a young master. Mother orders this ' "picture of passion" ' locked up in the red-room.

Raw coldness and bleakness desolation of a motherless child sees the mothering of other children; sofa-maternal warmth available only to others. She is not the natural child. Inferior, awkward, she cannot keep up, lags behind, the hands get nipped, frost-bitten fingers clutched. She is chided, she retreats; this the "depressed" child, isolated, cut-off, out in the cold, on the windowedge of outer and inner, in-between, marginal, forlorn child.

Sombre, solemn and tender, she crawls into the imagination. Sharp edge of rock surrounded by billowing waves, nothing holds her here; the vessels are broken and sinking; she goes into the depths of the dead at the churchyard finding then a fiend and thief and gallows witnessed by an aloof 'black, horned thing.' Promontory and dangerous descents with no containment: this landscape is cragged, icy, desolate, what life there is appears black, phantomlike, demonic.

Here is the rejected child; residing within reflections of isolation offer the solace. It is a frozen landscape. Lapland. Iceland. Arctic. Vast black space of whiteness; isolation absolute of no sound, without color, touch nothing. The silence abrasive, jagged rock edge sprouting only the dead twig broken descent. No voice, no help, no comfort: there is no mother here.

There is no mother but a rejecting (step) mother when the child is unnatural, preternatural, not sociable, does not fit into the society yet is marginal, of inferior other worlds, from worlds of otherness, heterogeneous. How the child lags behind, is not the natural child, is that attempt at an alterity the mother rejects.

Stepmother demands a distance from (rejects) child's desire to be unnatural, to be of what is not of nature, and also not sociable, not of society, not of the natural daily social world, yet child of inferior, lagging, recessed place; mother rejects child's desire to manifest more from what is other-worldly, unconscious, her unconscious desire. Stepmother's rejection sends child away, out of the drawing-room, out of sight, into an alcove, repressed.

It is the "schizoid" child on the windowseat, recessed into a sanctum of arctic elements. The stepmother has turned; the space between mother and child a vastness becoming demon and phantom. Child rejected to the demand of a mother's recess; the mother turns from this child to escape the windowseat forces herself. The gallows, fiend and thief, sinking and phantom vessels are as responsible for the stepmother's distance and scolding as does that distance send the child to those gallows. Mrs. Reed fears the place of this windowseat child as this place reflects her own petrification.

Windowseat child sits between scarlet drapery and winter storm. The elements bear down upon her, she is on the edge between exterior and interior worlds. The child sits where exterior becomes interior, that is the windowseat understanding where she is not separate from any elements, no difference, no difference between herself and any beating element, undifferentiated within (step) mother's recess. Symbiosis.

Undifferentiated from stepmother is not that the child is identical with her or identifies yet stands within and thereby for stepmother's unconscious, which makes child appear alien, non-adaptive to what is conscious and therefore revolting. This alterity into which stepmother pushes child back binding to the realms rejected.

Child retreats when stepmother orders it. Stepmother's demand for distance becomes child's frozen retreat behind some scarlet covering. Rejected, the child sits in stepmother's order which is an Iceland recess covered by scarlet. Symbiosis: within stepmother's demand is child's desire for the unnatural placing her in a recess undifferentiated from the death forces mother rejects yet holds child within.

This rejection binds child to mother's unconscious, is a failed attempt at separation, keeps the child recessed/repressed in the very (unnatural/nonsocial) place mother shuns. The Ice Realm is not displacement of a desire for a sofa-mother yet is unconscious desire of mother to be thrown back to the origins, re-jecting child, throwing back child to the sources of other consciousness, unconscious desire. The Ice Realm is also child's desire to reside in the unconscious of mother which is the windowseat recess of the sofa-mother.

"Cold rejection" of the stepmother, what looks like space between mother and child, is actually child's retreat into the recess of mother's most feared, unnatural desire, frozen, becoming criminal. Antipathetic symbiosis: the child's retreat into the recess of mother's criminal desire keeps that child upon some undifferentiated edge of no movement between interior and exterior, still windowseat with no parent of a human comfort or guide buffering, instead a stepmother's face now ghastly moon and wreck.

Elements slashing outside also the scolding inside. The child sits protected yet not separate from both in the windowseat containing the forces of a turning mother as ghosts in realms of death, no pulse here of feeling, the child sits suspended, breath held, unmoved. Undifferentiated space of a windowseat without movement: nothing moves the child here, psyche in a vacuum. When the child is most undifferentiated, not separate, she is protected by a vacuum, schizoid protection when nondifferentiated becomes vacuum suspension.

The schizoid retreat, windowseat moment, when inner is all one wants of the outer, out of relationship, out of touch, all devitalized where churchyard of grave, the sea its phantom, the black one is aloof and horned.

Out of a windowseat comes a text, images and verbal accounts of those marginal regions and her place within stepmother's rejection is to examine their delineation, configuration.

The universe of the windowseat, its 'death-white realms,' is demarcated by the child yet never solidified through signification, nor does the child ever herself become solidified while demarcating that universe. What could have been mother has reverted to threshold of a death realm whose objects are non-objects, cracked, aloof, sinking, fading, decomposing, and they do not require, even preclude positing Jane as an initiating human being, more deject, with no object, desire for non-object, longing for permanent residence in a place of no object and no subject, no being.

"Pre-narcissistic" place of windowseat threatening the eradication of any human, happy in the place of demons.

For Jane is happy in her windowseat. The temptation here is complacency in a place of demons. We have been humanly alienated to a degree where suspended between interior and exterior we are secure with the demons keeping us in the mother's circle without touch. Frozen place of intimacy: it comes with a complacency in haunted retreat, this is the windowseat temptation.

We avoid this Jane, child inferior and rejected, we despise this face reflecting gallow and granite edge. We run from Jane at her windowseat, we run to be more the natural child on mama's sofa, we are shunning the other cousin. She is not to know fireside chatter beside a mothering protective, more this awkward one lagging behind becomes content in her Iceland retreat.

'I was then happy: happy at least in my way.' She wants no interruption and this is when she is called by the bilious son of the stepmother. With the demons she has dropped to the depths isolation on the windowseat and here she becomes addressed by John Reed. He has been looking all over for her. He is not discerning, he gets the overview, but he is tenacious in his searching. He wants to find her.

His voice comes to us joking and with malicious sneer: Madame Mope. It comes to us snide and cruel. It comes to us, catches us in its hate for all we are. It is a voice without, a call, Jane is called. John Reed's interruption is part of her calling. Madame Mope. John Reed mocking her retreat which draws her out.

John Reed comes out of her landscape with its fiend and horned thing himself as tyrant-murderer. She is sitting in a psychic vacuum, inner as outer undifferentiated from mother, recess attracting fiend and thief. In the vacuum of the windowseat is also the beating rain from which she is protected yet not separate. Vacuum and invasion mutually attract. Within the order by the stepmother to vacuum recess is the drop to the ice edge rock bottom completely alone as she is assaulted by the demonic son.

What Mrs. Reed had punished was Jane's question back later termed impudence: what did I do? Jane's question posits her as a differentiated person in Mrs. Reed's presence requiring interlocution. Her question is her presumption that she is separate enough to be Mrs. Reed's interlocutor even as she resides within that woman's rejection and inferiority. It presumes that the child can dialogue from another viewpoint with whom has alterity and the stepmother returns she cannot, the push back (in) by the stepmother is the stepmother's turn away binding them.

Asking Mrs. Reed the question about what she has done indicates that when snapped at Jane does not easily capitulate, returns instead some spark. And it is this spark the stepmother would extinguish, cannot meet, wants away, removed not entirely yet on windowseat periphery, scarlet curtain, and it is to this that her explosive son attaches.

Mrs. Reed's punishment of Jane's "impudence" is also how the stepmother is blind to John's attack. John attaches to a scarlet curtain side of which Jane already is a part. Jane has her own red but it has been humanly alienated and become demonic, attached the demon Reed, in the face of the stepmother who cannot face it.

The scarlet curtain side of Jane to which the son attaches, through which he sees with his sister Eliza's sharp sight, is Jane's extension out from the recessed, marginal, inferior place. The curtain which implicates her with the natural world, is to what John Reed attaches.

The tyrant who greedily gobbles mother's baked pies takes us back to the world. He is the other side of the window retreat. Here is the red "burst" always threatening to break through the secret citadel, that explosion every schizoid lies over, closing eyes to, holding off, locking up. John Reed is the manifestation of the rupture from which Madame Mope continually defends. When John Reed bursts, Jane moves out of the schizoid place more to the borders of a lived world, now of the borderlines.

He wants her to show him the book, the text of the windowseat terrains, and it is her calling to bring that out. When John Reed bursts through the antipathetic symbiosis within mother's unconscious, Jane is compelled to carry out the text of that unconscious.

When there are not yet the words, we do not yet know a language to delineate these unconscious figures and their landscape into which we have been unconsciously placed by the stepmother, the unconscious expression becomes bodily possession: the John Reed seizure. Repetitive thrusting tongue and sudden blow.

He is our tantrum. He bursts out from a tremendous appetite, a gorging. He is inflated, the skin everywhere bloated the heavy limb; he is the grandiose exhibitionist. When there is the tantrum also here is the arctic retreat, schizoid child beneath. Arctic retreat covered by scarlet attaches a grandiose, craving son which draws us out to the breakfast-room.

When it comes, the burst seems to come from outside ourselves from someone despising us. Yet it extends from our isolation which leaves itself through outburst, outing, exit, sortie. John Reed claims that Jane's book on the Ice Realm is really his own, that she is not alone in it and even must emerge from her recess to return it to his world. Arctic ghosts desire a breakfast-room delineation through the John Reed possession.

Arctic ghosts first make their appearance in the breakfast-room: before we have learned the language of their expression, or how to mediate their entry, they emerge through appetite. John gorges at the table habitually and at school his mother sends him what in his schoolmaster's opinion is an overabundance of cakes and sweetmeats. Jane and John do not dialogue from the place in which she has been, not interlocution yet onslaught, cruder appetite, primary need, possession.

It is his book. The rhythm of his language a rage and greed a grasp of what is world. In the tantrum here is seizing, incorporating, taking back; a lashing out in order to feed, take in, absorb, become and have it all. His is a demand for an appetite to be satiated and more to a bloating, craving. His text is absorbed, consumed by appetite. John Reed's relation to the borderline regions is the demand for incorporation as possession, not delineation; the text which would configure and delineate becomes used as weapon, unmediated contact precluding inscription, covered with blood.

Since the ice region in which we sit is undifferentiated from John Reed and his cruelty — it is his book and we sit in daily fear of him — his demand moves us. His energy crude of a dingy skin, heavy limb, bleared eye, flabby cheek, his lineaments are thick: his flab and inflation are our lack of differentiation.

He orders her to approach and stand before him and she does 'habitually obedient.' The John Reed force perpetually recurs: 'He bullied and punished me: not two or three times in the week, nor once or twice in the day, but continually: every nerve I had feared him, and every morsel of flesh on my bones shrank when he came near.' Insult followed by blows, he strikes. When this force comes, we are taken in by it: 'Accustomed to John Reed's abuse, I never had an idea of replying to it; my care was how to endure the blow which would certainly follow the insult.'

Repetitiously we do what John Reed says because of his sheer brute force which arrives when we have sat happily too long in the Ice Realm. Our acquiescence to him pertains to being surrounded by Iceland demons alienated from all human relation and too complacent in that. What then erupts is a tremendous need cutting across all human proportion and natural boundary, forcing us along. And that need is our own as it is also that of Mrs. Reed.

  œ§ Perpetual recurrence of the same thing: repetition compulsion. We have done what she has said to do, we live in her rule, we have left the room in her order and this has placed us in the realm of demons and we are happy there since it is the only way she holds us. She sends us to the place of her utmost desolation and then it is we must face the continual ravenous and bilious form of her hunger, her need, her unmet, unfed, now greed, after us, wanting our life, wanting all that we have touched. Daily attacks of us as she is blind to it is her windowseat, it is her son, we are desperately isolated and when he calls we obey 'habitually obedient,' it is his grandiose force that demands it and also we obey to get closer to her only life unconscious, we obey. „

Child recessed in mother's unconscious, when the desire of the unconscious is too recessed the child is assaulted by a tremendous craving, an appetite for an instant satiation, gorging, bilious, passing through mother and possessing the child. What removes her from the windowseat is John Reed's call to possession — his house, his book, his servant. The unnatural desire (too unconscious) hers as that of the stepmother, erupts to world as his gorging need, attacking, possessing her.

When our desire is to remain in the unconscious 'death-white realms,' when our desire to live out of the underside has been too long unconscious, what arrives is the craving. Need and craving emerge as the enactment of unconscious (unnatural) desire. Gateshead is where the first manifestation of unconscious realms is of impulse reaction, blood text permeated, and his flesh overwhelms us.

It is his book. Cruel master of Ice Realm he draws her out through the scarlet curtain, reminding her of the human scarlet side of the winter storm. There is no mother here yet a mother who has turned and that mother's son who interrupts within the mother's turn, bringing the child into the world with a smash, thud, blood trickling the pain of a severed head.

When we cannot yet speak the text of the recess to which mother sends us, cannot delineate the hate, stealing, death-dealing aggressivity and vacancy of that place, we become it in reaction to her son and her son's only language is curse from eruption at us. The ice-bottom engenders its own enflamed devil humanly manifested by John Reed who screams: you are dependent, you are not enough, you do not belong, you are a rat.

When he comes he beats in our heads all day, we hear his curse over and over, gradually bowing under in an inferiority we turn on ourselves to a burst. We find it difficult or impossible to hold any ground when he arrives. On the borderline, we have not a demarcated room, balancing on the windowseat and we totter when he hits.

John Reed comes through a stepmother's recessed windowseat where we do not have a differentiated place, have lost all balance, no sense of what is ours, dependent. John Reed comes when we have lost all sense of what is our substance, without any solidifying substance the John Reed attacks are merely repetitious shatterings. Primarily the movement of rejection, we sink back into windowseat recess, flesh on bones shrunk, only to be called out daily, mocked, struck.

Only motion of rejection and scission of the unconscious itself manifested daily in a John Reed scene without anything solidifying until the head open cracks and this day we strike back. When we have never replied to his abuse the day we do it is in the same manner we have been accustomed to receiving him, we lunge consumptively, becoming of his substance perhaps we think that solidifying.

The book hits, gash, and we lunge a tremendous gorging, we grasp. Flailing we seize for a consumption back. John Reed's possession of our text of arctic death images has become our possession by John Reed. We distend in appetite. Our habitual obedience to John Reed turns finally into lunge and the appetite now is ours: addiction.

We lunge back and our head breaks open, repetition compulsion becoming addiction. What could be scarlet force generated within mother's (unconscious) desire to become delineated now addiction.

᪣ Slave-driver. Roman conqueror. He inflates our need we want we have stepped out of some place sitting frozen vast-

ness to take in order to burst sever he fills to crack open.
Filling, no hold totter swirl what is this tunnel plunge to fill
in turn she turns and our gorge expels, incorporate for expulsion we vomit him out oral burst, for others his inflation that
moment to absorb for shattering recurrent release, anal
burst. And those who yet the very act on his demand only to
be filled, have stepped off the windowseat to fill the infinite
space before it happily smacks let it crack bleeding genital
burst as he whispers all through this night of the many lovers
he is whispering of our dependency. For the slave driver,
Roman conqueror, out of which on us her turn, expulsion
within incorporation, bulimia. ॐ

We destroy ourselves on his command as we despise our need. It is his
book, his assault is an embodiment of arctic demons. His attack and possession of us through his possession of the text on them indicates his relation to
the arctic forces as that attack carries us off the windowseat of their realm.
They will possess us bodily if yet not to be spoken through speaking with
us.

These demons do not want to keep us windowseat recessed, we are called
to carry them to daily life. Mrs. Reed's alterity made manifest. Yet as we
cannot be Mrs. Reed's interlocutor (undifferentiated from her), we cannot
through language carry out the windowseat unconscious within which we
are bound to her.

Our lack of differentiation from her is the impossibility of speaking
them, carrying out their text. As we cannot dialogue with Mrs. Reed, we
cannot dialogue with the figures of the Iceland recess, only subjected as
complacent object to their nature until he screams at us that torture, non-
dialogically which is possession.

When John Reed calls we begin emerging out of recess more to
breakfast-room, and his mode is of literal seizure, scission and compulsion. Broken boat, sinking wreck, broken cemetery wall, marine phantoms, fiend pinning thief's pack, gallows become his crack, seizure and
our lunge back. His cruelty and mockery draw Iceland demon out of what
was suspended now embodied through our lunge within his possession.

Tyrannizing as excessive, when John Reed calls we become addicted to
thrust back. This bondage has been invisible, no one has responded to its
tyranny over us. The servants see the blows yet do not speak and Mrs.
Reed does not notice, is completely blind to the extent of his perpetual
violence in attack which only emerges through her turned back,
unconsciousness.

John Reed is part of Mrs. Reed's unconscious that attempts to sever the child out of itself, by having her embody the scission and mortification of its forces into what is breakfast world.

A false sense of self-sufficiency subtends the John Reed bondage. We say no one will believe us, no one knows the windowseat place. Inflated as he strikes we say we will retaliate. His presence necessitates the isolation out of which we repetitiously attempt to burst through his presence. Jane is alone with him and she cannot summon a human assistance.

Part of the John Reed inflation, and the general force of the Ice Realm demons, is that we think ourselves powerful enough somewhere to go it alone with him. A grandiose part has taken over without containment for we have yet no way to signify in mediated forms the possessing forms. Grandiose with no one with whom to bond, and we find ourselves in bondage to a cruel master of our worse appetite.

The book is hurled and when it hits the child is possessed. She flails. Servants say: picture of passion. John Reed is our passion in a possessed state. John Reed is our passion as we break the unconscious arctic forces out of a scarlet curtain side and we are possessed. He even possesses the book and there is no articulation of where we have been, only bloody incorporation of those violent and marginal forces. This is to have no perspective outside his will we obey habitually lost to his sheer force.

The book is coming toward her hurled by its demon. Demon fiend of her secret citadel now fully embodied in the room here attack. She is hit, going under, the blood sticky crimson stream of a neck as she lunges back. The tantrum attack: sometimes with the servants, we fail to see that she is hitting back.

John Reed emerges as fully bodied from the death realms of non-objects, required by mother's blindness, requiring to manifest the fissure and deathdealing seizure within the unconscious of mother's breakfast-room. And in his severance, splitting, scission, split head scission no longer of ghosts alone he binds her to life, life's blood, focus on another while bleeding, his possession requires her arrival to some sticky crimson current, undercurrent of mother's desire which crashes, explodes, cracks open.

The annihilating force rises after being shunned on the margin placed where no interior or exterior, neither subject nor object, threshold of unnatural force complacency, shadow of a rejecting mother holding in isolation the inferior desire breeding greed. Undifferentiated sitting in a windowseat recess of demons becoming our most primal hunger exhibitionistically flaunted.

A one-sidedness is the "evil" of John Reed, he comes where there are no other voices, no dialogue possible at all. Allowing the book to be possessed by John Reed is to forego language. The head cracked open cannot express design. Possession of the windowseat retreat: her passion consumptive in its lunge becomes the possession where she signifies only through thrashing, bodily seizures, herself now the (out)burst.

Bibliography

Freud, Sigmund. "Beyond the Pleasure Principle." *The Complete Psychological Works of Sigmund Freud*. Vol. 18. Trans. James Strachey. London: Hogarth, 1955.

Guntrip, Harry. *Schizoid Phenomena, Object Relations and the Self*. New York: International Universities Press, 1969.

Jung, C. G. "Anima and Animus." *The Collected Works of C. G. Jung*. Vol. 7. Trans. R. F. C. Hull. Princeton, N.J.: Princeton University Press, 1966. (Hereafter referred to as CW.)

_____. "The Syzygy: Anima and Animus." *CW* 9ii.

Kohut, Heinz. *The Analysis of Self*. New York: International Universities Press, 1971.

Kristeva, Julia. *Revolution in Poetic Language*. Trans. Margaret Waller. New York: Columbia University Press, 1984.

von Franz, M. L. *Shadow and Evil in Fairytales*. Dallas: Spring Publications, 1980.

Winnicott, D. W. *Playing and Reality*. London: Tavistock, 1982.

Chapter 2
Mirrored Phantom

Thrusting her on the stool in the crimson chamber these maids threaten to use a garter to secure but she stills, no longer completely in the thrashing as that ' "mad cat," ' never has she been so out of herself. Their voices, a singsong also din: she is dependent on Mrs. Reed, she is not equal to the cousins, so be useful, pleasant, be humble, then she would have a home, they say, Jane, if you are passionate and rude, there will be no home for you here, and what if God himself in the middle of one of your tantrums strikes you dead, and so if you don't repent, something bad, very bad, coming down this very chimney, it will come Jane and fetch you away.

The door locks behind them. The room is awesome and dreadful. Entirely of mahogany and crimson except white pillows and mattresses of the 'tabernacle' bed, white chair that 'pale throne' by the bed's head. Mr. Reed's last breath in this room a death spell precluding intrusion. Solemn, lonely chamber of grandeur. She is returning to her stool after trying the door, indeed locked, crossing now the looking glass with a fascinated glance she involuntarily explores. Facing her the white arms and a face with its glittering fearful eyes, here is the effect of a real spirit, half fairy, half imp of the dells of Bessie's evening story.

Superstitions with her as she returns to the stool. Rush of hot blood in her head beating the charged thought: why was she singled out in suffering, the accused condemned child? Headstrong Eliza respected; the golden, spoiled Georgiana indulged; and John never accused with his fiercest tyrannies: twisting pigeon necks, killing pea-chicks, breaking the buds of the earth's fruit, reviling his mother's flesh as he spoils her silk dress. To that mother he is still the darling, indeed, no reproach for John striking her. Unjust! Escape: run away or else it must be not to eat and not to drink. To that tumultuous stool child, it is the Older Jane, with distance of years, saying she suffered at Gateshead because she was a discord, heterogeneous, alien, also contemptuous of them in her own way.

Daylight is leaving the room chillier now. 'My habitual mood of humiliation, self-doubt, forlorn depression, fell damp on the embers of my decaying ire.' Wicked, she had just thought of starving herself, now she sees the death vault, is it not the uncle placed there, that uncle who took her a parentless infant and when dying required a promise of care from his wife for that infant, to rear as one of her own children this one, the alien one also noxious, the one that wife could not love.

She sits still watching the bed, a fascinated eye to the mirror occasionally, would not this spirit of an uncle rise to avenge the oppression of his sister's child? Ah, this grief may 'waken a preternatural voice' to pity, she stifles the desire, sits boldly upon the stool. Yet then a light gleams on the ceiling; adult Jane later conjectures lantern yet child sees 'herald of some coming vision from another world.' Heart beating a rush of wings, head on fever, presence there oppressing, bearing down a suffocation; she is letting out the wildest scream and now she is shaking that lock of the only door.

The maids rush in at first they believe the child must be ill. Mrs. Reed, cap flying, marching down the hall smells trickery. The child begs she cannot endure it, let her be punished some other way, she will be killed in there. In the aunt's eye there is only a 'precocious actress' of 'virulent passions, mean spirit, and dangerous duplicity.' Abrupt thrust back in the room by the impatient aunt, the locked door closes as does a fit upon the child settling in unconsciousness.

We flail, dart, spit, never have resisted so entirely. Resisting we are taken. To resist John Reed is to be taken by him. Our possession by the force of him becomes our resistance to its (driven) eruption. When our only possibility of delivering the arctic elements off the borderline becomes unconscious blatant action in the breakfast-room, we are out of ourselves.

Projection of hate, incorporated expulsion is to be that son, possessed by what appears objective psychic violence. No one sees or speaks when sees.

No one sees or speaks when sees, the articulation of it will not come from outside ourselves and we are beside ourselves, out of ourselves, outside our selves. Entangled in him we give ourselves, what self for which a book aimed yet gashed, over to him, and left to himself he expands.

The rush as she is most out of herself she is himself as he is that violent gush literalized for which there is not yet word or limit. Resisting all limiting, all the way resisting the maids' confinement, she is heel scraping floor, twisting back arched, she hisses.

Placed in the room, forced on stool, the maids are saying her imprisonment has to do with something she is supposed to learn. Standing over her, they bark, it has to do with learning humility, something of repentance. She does not understand for she is the mad cat, she thrashes.

The maids are called forth by what her lunge resistance at John Reed was attempting. She tried to resist his violent enactment of emerging unconscious force. The maids arrive to sever her from that incorporation: thrusting tongue hurled book blows now her lunge at him from which they separate.

The maids come to tell us, in the possessed state, that we are mad. They hold our constitution as we are most out of ourselves. They feed us voices from more human, ordinary aspects; they carry our person in mind. These maids have never entered the Ice Realm nor seen our place within that death terrain, instead their view of us pertains to human affairs, garters, daily life requirement.

As John Reed has been the failed attempt at delivering out in articulate form the unconscious forces, this failed attempt evokes the maids. They will not have us reactively acting out forces once unconscious. They prohibit the (non-human) form in which we have been provoked to exhibit them, no home if mad cat.

Failure at the delineation which would constitute child as agent, narrator mediating psychic forces, becomes the maids' collective morality. For the morality of the maids' barking is collective: you will go to hell for your tantrum.

Our culture's handmaids do not guide us through the possessing forces of mother's recess, instead they moralize, and their collective morality wants to break the possession, sees an indulgence within the tantrum. Their human speaking is forthright, definite, collectively understood: they present God's proscription as a replacement for our failed inscription of unconscious force.

God's design of the otherworldly, collectively understood, arrives in order to break the John Reed possession. The maids of a collective standing drag us away from the territory caught enflamed madness through a speaking of God's retribution, some Father omnipotence. The maids' comprehension of God relates to the contiguity inherent within the John Reed possession itself, immediate reaction in either case.

Some Father's regimen an attempt to lock up the child a lesson of limiting the incorporated unconscious force. Retributive move to lock the burst (outing itself) away (back in); no one speaks to the child inside the possession, the maids locking her up do not see they lock John up with (in) her: isolation temptation of the John Reed possession.

As we resist externally imposed limit in the process of resisting his seizure which defies limit, our animal is maddened, and what comes are maids with binding garters speaking of God's punishment. Their response to the possession is not to educate us about John, or to instruct us about forms of his expression, or where we are going; working for Mrs. Reed, with a vengeance they fear the fit, any eruption of unconscious force to be locked away.

Maids use God's name to extricate us from bodily lunge. God is who is high to insure the unconscious not delivered nonhumanly as human blind incorporation Father prohibits. Sit still stool punishment in God's name justice done, let there resume an evenness and conformity.

In God's name the maids' barking comes from a vital fear of the nonhumanity of this mad cat resistance. Not approving of the form of our delivery of otherworldly realms, preferring us in conformity, they draw upon otherworld God-Father to urge adaptation to this world.

When we are in a John Reed possession, maids appear urging adaptation to a conforming stance through a God-Father proscription (' "you should try to be useful and pleasant" '), and this results in our being forced to a further recess in the room most remote. To forcibly attempt to even out the eruption of unconscious force drags us further into what is unconscious.

John Reed ruptures all boundaries, asks for severe limiting, the most isolated room in the house, large and solid, to hold the blast. The red-room has its stately qualities. Mahogany and damask, massive and shrouded, the uncle died here. A room of passage to beyond seldom visited by human, room of a passing to the more unseen forces not behind scarlet curtain yet through what permeates scarlet.

Child returned further recessed into the room never trespassed. A room so red.

A room so red, heavily textured crimson damask curtains hanging the bed and large windows of drawn blind, the carpet as scarlet as the cloth of the table at the bed's foot, the walls of pink blush. The father died here, a red-room in which the father is extinguished. What could be the structures of a father cannot survive in this room and the God-Father's strictures of the maids' bark do not limit the possession here which instead increases.

Here is a room not of the human, passage beyond the human, enhancing the child's preternatural faculties. She passes the looking glass, her glance is fascinated, half fairy, half imp attached to and peering out of her. Now her blood sucked out, given over to the Reed force, skin cast white, glittering frightened eyes, dazed as piercing, each in its own direction, her form a phantom air-suspended.

Mirrored phantom: she cannot recognize herself as identical in the mirror, no person to identify in mirror, no signifying human when dependent on the mother's recess within which the phantom she is. The red-room is where the other who reflects her is non-being, no longer is she excluded child, she is no child, no mirroring possible of her as human being, instead fairy, preternatural in possession of human body this the mirror reflects, this mirror reflection of the not-I, beyond-I, before-I.

The maid Bessie who locked Jane up also returns through a mirrored memory in the red-room as the storying of imp and fairy. Bessie has told the narrative for that which Jane cannot narrate yet instead has become. When the one who tells the narrative locks up the child, when the narrative told is locked up, then the person becomes imp.

No longer child listening to the story, while locked she only can recognize herself as the object the story attempted to impart, yet the story referent remembers once she was a listening child.

We have engaged with a thrusting son arising from the Iceland place, as he attempted to pull us out of the realm we have given ourselves over to it, a projection on that devil, and now we are infected, we touch a place first of animal and then of imp and phantom, and the room which reflects our preternatural counterpart is red, large, stately, its glamour scintillates.

John Reed's possession returns Jane to the phantom realm out of which that possession arose: the imp facing her mirrored brings to her mind the Bessie evening story as did the windowseat figures. Their mutual association indicates the homology of the mirrored red-room and windowseat phantoms. Now in this further recessed room, Jane is what she on the windowseat had only perceived.

Far from removing her from the windowseat phantom realm, John Reed's driving lunge and maid retribution pushed her further (back) into fusion with those preternatural forces.

She is charmed, held by the inspiring terror. Through a demonic son possession, Jane has entered realms of spirits seen through herself and she is fascinated by the mirroring glance. She has tried to overcome John Reed and now she is enticed by the nonhuman extent of the grandiosity.

After the mirrored glance, Jane sits down and an envy of her cousins turns in on herself. Mind beginning gyration: how is it others have the advantage, she is caught and condemned; they commit error and crime and are rewarded, she has not the fault and is attacked. She feels the unjustness of things, becomes argumentative and convoluted in thinking.

When who could be initiating agent is threatened—in a mirror we have seen phantom appearing through us—no person, nonhuman-being, and an envy calls us back to some human dimension: why do they get and we not presupposes person. The envy, as Jane pities herself, is an attempt to locate a human in the (red-room) place of preternatural.

Yet envy's resentment places us only closer to the evil spirits, animosity, evil spirits now in our heads convolute, cacophony. Here is "complex" talk: the brain in tumult, in the finest detail it accuses as it complains, but it does not suffer.

Her brain in tumult, snarled, her bad temper feeding on itself, still feeding John Reed's incorporation yet now in her head. Animosity of the head snarled. Animus of head. John Reed inside her head. Repetitiously attacked and even bleeding yet there is not present any human feeling for pain. No capacity of suffering, instead she whines.

Whining as the (unfelt) pain of a nonhuman attempting humanity. Suffering more requires the human touched. Out in the cold, on the windowseat edge of non-being, mad cat to phantom now a red-room of fascination, ghosts are herself, without a mediating human or touched humanly enough to suffer.

We are sitting in the Red Room. Seized by a grandiose, thrusting force, and the tyrant is beating, hurling and cursing, tongue as whip repetitious lashing. He is bloating us, we see our body inflating, we feel grotesque and about to burst. The blood breaks out, we lose our blood, we pale, and the stepmother orders us to a terrifying red-room locked.

Mother orders us to a locked red chamber which bears death, locked womb shattering into its blood flow saturating every textured tissue. Locked womb not bearing life yet life's decease.

Fit possession taking us through this red-room begins our initiation into bloody caverns of mother's dank, insidious, and morbid nature. Further within mother's recess now bloody cavern. Puberty ritual at the breaking of our blood. Hermetic vessel holding the rupture nightmare. Red-room return to our rupturing within locked womb of mother's body. Red-room as modern menstrual hut.

He enters us inflating, we incorporate him driven need, bloated attempt to express criminal and death force, what are the voices, articulated images of that other world, we incorporate him, bloated to burst them forth spilling of the blood returning to interior red chamber asking who are the spirits of our fate/face mirrored.

The red-room question where we face in detail his demonic aspects: he is tearing apart the bird and poultry, breaking earthly fruit, reviling his mother's flesh.

Severing, crushing, bursting, returning to a memory of that pure demonic aspect of nature pulverizing all nature: the landslide, avalanche, flood, hurricane, wildfire turning nature over to its underside, underworlds, otherworlds. When we sit in a blood cavern following his burst he is our question of that inflated demonic force pulverizing all nature, of nature, how is he of our nature for we have been blamed as he has acted up.

     ◅§ John Reed. As we have witnessed his action, picked him up walking in this world on its edge of annihilation we have claimed he is not of the female; this rape on every street, not discerning he has an overview, daycare repetitious raping and children playing on plastic clown now bullets in chests, curbed glass car crash, thief of a capsule poisoned. But we know he comes in our dreams, configured by men the tyrant-conqueror lighting the furnaces of concentration camps, incinerating Hiroshima, napalming Vietnam, and the deploying of ballistic missile; pulverization of animation, we have found him in our dreams as men how is he in our nature yet in the blood chamber perhaps in the bleeding monthly his action our regard. Bloated we hold him PMS, addiction and internal family violence, we are blamed for his cruel action. §►

The red-room has its temptations which would attach us to a continual incorporation of this John Reed force. The first we have seen as fascination; we are charmed suspended by the grandiose effort of overcoming him and its result in phantom mirroring. Another is anorexia. We have attached to Mrs. Reed through the one reviling her, her tyrant, yet then she locks us further recess.

We sit alone, the rapacious attack has gone on in the main part of the house, and in this solemn, remote room he is beating inside our head. We realize we cannot overcome John Reed and she still loves him better.

He still her darling as the anorexic moment of his tyranny where we sit on red-room stool, constricted further recess, becoming a turn of killing force upon ourselves as the ultimate prohibition of him which is to be most constricted no outburst possible as possessed by him we will starve ourselves to death. He demands so in her love for him.

The anorexic movement to literalize deathworld is the desire within the John Reed possession to live from defilement, loathing, the tyrannizing and revolting while locked up by the (step) mother's order. The John Reed incorporation takes its second form in this more remote room.

Pre-signifying, when we cannot yet delineate the figures of her recess, John Reed manifests in breakfast-room as expulsion lunge and in red-room as skeleton, the corpse within the tyranny. Grandiose form of escape from the John Reed oppression is to be most possessed by him in the red-room place where the outbursts are no longer, only the petrification of literal death, yearning skeletal manifestation.

Anorexia requires a metaphor of death world. The anorexic brain is 'in tumult,' hyperactive: 'revolted slave,' 'bitter vigour,' 'rapid rush of retrospective thought.' Head aching blood from the blow still brain in tumult when we will to literal death starve. What cools, what arrives in what cools, is the narrator.

Older Jane speaking from the distance of many years: 'now, at the distance of—I will not say how many years, I see it clearly.' The one who narrates the story can speak to the child of her marginal aspect. When there is no human within the possession, fit too closely with what drives demonic, best to go to the human we will become, the one who sees apart, narrates the drama of the heterogeneous forces once unconscious.

The narrator posits the possibility of a differentiated signifying body: 'I was a discord in Gateshead Hall . . . a heterogeneous thing, opposed to them in temperament, in capacity, in propensities.' The narrator perceives our relation to what opposes, to whom we are noxious, describes the drama of our cast, the effect of our indignation, our contempt for who are the other characters.

Narrator's distance cools to stone the anorexic place goes to vault, sees through, sees below, distance of the narrator moving anorexia to see through itself to the Father's vault at its base in the red-room locked in by mother.

Jane cools, embers of ire dampened by the familiar depression this time holding a vault. Dead ancestor rising while she is sitting still in the room of Mrs. Reed's punitive rule, father spirit entrusting her to good care, now in all his wisdom would avenge.

We call on the larger ghosts to break the hold of malevolent others. The John Reed explosions have within them the death of a father.

As we sit in the solemn red-room following the breakfast-room outburst, we remember that John Reed comes from a place of deep loss, and that death has to be arrived at, layers peeled, compulsions to tumultuous brain to starvings to sitting still, cooling ember, find the vault.

The father is dead, and in the room of his dying we are asked by our mothers to sit and know some devastating blood powers scintillate, preternatural forces through body. The mother has not known these forces herself. We are sent by her into the majestic cavern of blood-depths to know the forces when the father is dead.

But we cannot sit here unguided and alone any more than could she, we cannot sit within Mrs. Reed's loss, her forces unheeded and only projected she thwarts us. As we have not been able to know her in our distinction, we cannot suffer the loss.

The father is dead but we cannot face it, for we will see him as that light above, we will look up to him instead and we will say bless me father, give me your power. Power of the dead, idealized father to make her love us in our place inferior. When we have not been able to differentiate enough for delineation of where we reside unnatural, preternatural, as a last resort from the assault of demonic sons, we call upon the larger ghosts.

    ◦§ And we have looked up and said give us your word, father, power avenge. Looking up to him when that mother shunned us to her windowseat where we are met by her son bilious and thrusting, and she put us in a room of grandeur isolated to learn the constriction, the father died there, she honors him, it is now the only way to make her love us because he is on our side, where is he, he is above in a light crack the room is dark but the light cracks a door opened he enters. This is wrong but we do not know another way of getting to her but to look up at the one she has admired our father who art in heaven he is descending it constricts our throat, he will not let it be known, our mouths are silenced as we scream we are penetrated. And the fathers continue to take the advantage, our call for their word becoming immediate entry, entering from above they put their hand on our mouth and they say it is all a part of it and not to tell and we give one first scream in a throat choking we tried to tell her, we begged her, please please Mrs. Reed I cannot endure it—' "Forgive me! I cannot endure it—let me be punished some other way!" '—but she did not believe us and she pushed us back in, refusing to see the years also her silencing. And we thought we had doors, that our openings could be closed that we knew those hinges existed but now there are no doors for he broke through them all, splinters everywhere. Blood secular initiation of mockery now crude violation. How does this blood relate to the other monthly of where are our mothers in these horrifying seizures of dilation of constriction. ঌ

Father is of the word. The father we look up to, in order to escape the red-room and also the son's recurrent attacks, is the father whose word to care for the child makes the stepmother promise. The father is of the word expected to hold our fate from a distance. He leaves his word as Law and departs. His word is mediation of our care, of the passage of our history, word as symbolic mediation.

In the red-room, his word, we look up to it for distance from these ways of oppression, collapses, his word broken, collapsed his symbolic function in the red-room of Gateshead Hall where we are infiltrated inside crimson chamber.

Father's refusal to remain above, to hold the distance through promise word, his word does not separate us from the damask secret chamber when we want to use that word to escape his son, the urge of hate of hunger; also when his word is not mother's desire.

Father not to be an escape from son, father relates to son. Nondifferentiated from mother on windowseat, in red-room, her men of no appeal, John Reed comes from the rage ordeals, Mr. Reed more the pure terror ordeals.

Related forces, father and son: the red-room has its white mattresses, a white throne by the bed's head and in this place Jane passes from John's red raging to his father's white ghost seizure. Entering the stream of blood, forced by the stepmother to enter the stream of blood recessed between them, here the God is white winged power of savior, we had incorporated John Reed until submerged in blood-depths we face our white God first thinking ourselves immune.

Dilation. John Reed, human mimetic of nonhuman forces, his grandiosity becomes our red heat, arms flailing, eruption at every cavity. He infiltrates until we burst out/open with his driving pressure. He enters every vein and is exploding out of us, inflated sonorous thrusts. This mode of being possessed pertains to swelling and dilation: our muscles inflate, the blood vessels dilate, all is of turgor, reddening, seething—our mouths open as the hunger becomes roar we demand to be fed.

Constriction. In the wake of John Reed arrives his father's spirit, terrifying. First there is an awe of this father we apprehend as spirit, 'herald of some coming vision from another world.' Sunken vault to overarching light we reach beyond ourselves to extremes eliminating any human negotiation. We would like his help in the form of avenging, but we will not address him directly in fear of his preternatural properties. He takes us beyond the human, his word a promise of power to separate us from the oppression of son's drive, to remove us from within her recessed desire, yet we cannot speak, we give ourselves under him, borne down by him, held in place.

He bears down upon us no longer seething as we are depressed beneath him, he comes closer, looming over, we try to shrink, hold back, turn in on ourselves, implode. This mode of being possessed pertains to deflation and constriction: our muscles contract, blood vessels constrict, all is of pallor, coldness, we petrify. Winged almighty, descending, pressing down upon us to infiltrate. If we speak any of it we are a liar. Overwhelmed, mouth open as silent screams our mind given over to him we fall under.

        ◆§ Mr. Reed mentoring. His door always of the many locks. Books shelved floor to ceiling. He sits concentrating, head's spark caught by the only skylight. He opens the door if we bow our heads, this entry takes a shyness, it takes some terror. We are crouched in the corner with his image. Through our ears we receive him first the voice booming. Head bowed, we must not look at him yet draw him in our every sinew snapping with his circuit. We use our mind for him. Wanting to ask for guidance yet terrified instead we produce that outpour quenching somewhat the thirst of his only son the one from whom we run toward the beam of our reflection eye of the father. He holds us still. He is opening our skull to investigate the spark of synapse, his instruments sound their metal in our head. We know the cry of pain would betray him; we sit boldly on our stool. Drilling the tools to their finest point then he moves a nerve we forget our name. He has found the dendrite of mystery; gleaming, he reaches for its source. Stitching later with the black thread he undoes the last row, cutting back the thread and stitching again this time a row more perfectly aligned. The terror has inspired, we are charmed, our head is bowed, he is standing over us, hand on our head a heralding. We tremble to a quaking, we fall under a fit. ॐ

At first we are inspired, we think we can escape his son and the red-room through him, yet he bears down too heavily, depresses. 'My habitual mood of humiliation, self-doubt, forlorn depression, fell damp on the embers of my decaying ire.' He comes out of the "depression" following the John Reed exhibitionistic and "manic" bursts. Omnipotent pressing down a sadistic aggressivity which at times we prefer to the thrusts of his son.

Stepmother's rejection propelled us to realms unnameable requiring delineation from a windowseat ledge. Hierarchies of psychic forces arrived in various sizes requiring different modes of relation once called mysteries of initiation.

Different forms of seizure. John Reed is grandiose yet his base is human, Jane could attempt to lunge at him, project her hate onto him she was possessed. The terror she felt as he approached turned to disgust and a rage as she tried to overcome this one who began more on her level, attacked her horizontally. He starts out as stepbrother.

John Reed as that enraged deathdealing force which emerges from and pulls us out of the Ice Realm, off the windowseat edge back into breakfast-room; through him we return to the daily room, screaming and flailing. We begin to hear our voice and at last others hear us. This attempt to separate from Ice Realm through enacting its cruelty richochets: the literal contiguous action of criminal force not a delineation mediating dialogically a return to daily world, yet we plunge further now into the unconscious, locked inside what is mother's body, locked womb of mother's interior body.

The uncle-spirit is distant, her idealization of him is how he comes from quite a distance. 'Tabernacle bed.' 'Pale throne.' He resides outside of Jane's personal history, outside her age and size, beyond human dimension. Emerging from earth bowel as well as the illuminated height of a stately chamber, vertical axis impersonal level. He descends constricting with a rush of wings, he is not of the human or a human base, appears to her as preternatural the almighty spirit these generations has been of Father.

He descends as she remembers he had stood by her as an infant. His arrival a possible red-room delivery; she would like him to carry her back to a better daily world, severed from the oppression by Mrs. Reed's John. She requests the distance of his word through the mode is power.

Temptation of power-manipulation, he involves us in deals, in plotting, manipulation by power when most fused within the womb also of mother's body here the maneuver. Plots for power when new vision herald from the unnameable may move us out of the red-room, sever from any of her recess, lift us father, use your word to keep this red chamber unnameable, forbidden object.

When through manipulations by power we try to bypass or objectify the hold of Mrs. Reed and her son, the plot suppresses, further fall into recess. Descending Mr. Reed is no longer of the human, so abstract that to address him requires complete loss of consciousness when we want to escape that most unconscious (secret forbidden) place of her red depths.

The maids' manipulation of power, working in the service of Mrs. Reed, to constrain the John Reed possession with God's strictures, did not serve to sever Jane from the possession yet deepened it further recess. Likewise, uncle's word of promise does not deliver yet descends.

Again we become seizure, Reed seizure: he sweeps down as a large-winged presence, she collapses in convulsion, limbs of lightning. Overriding each convulsion here an omnipotent Father pressing down. We are caught beneath, circuits firing as invaded from above to a constriction further into non-being: the other side of the John Reed possession.

Father's refusal to stay above, his word of promise that we be cared for does not stay above and sever us from the damask chamber when we implore it as escape, displace us father, and also when his word is not the mother's desire.

For Mr. Reed has 'required a promise' that the child be mothered as that mother's own child. His word was to guarantee cozy sofa embrace excluding windowseat excluding red-room to guarantee against alien, preternatural forces of rejection, the criminal, deathdealing of scission, explosion.

Yet mother's desire has been not to care for yet hate this child, has been that the child reside in the realm of revulsion and rupture, which has been the place this child has met even been possessed by mother's (unconscious) desire. From that domain child has beckoned word to separate her out instead it lowered touching.

Care for one cannot be required by another, and Mr. Reed never consulted that mother of her desire. He did not consult Mrs. Reed, instead he faded away. And in dying out he said to the mother: look after this little one, care for her, she is special to me, keep the word, make the promise. And fathers have left the mothers even as they demand care for favored daughter, attached to a daughter while leaving the mother then must shun that daughter.

Father's attachment to daughter returns his word to mother's (unconscious) desire, to those blood death-depths where she desires daughter reside. When our position in the red-room calls on Mr. Reed who descends, no longer is language symbolic function constituting itself at the repression of (severance from) blood relation to mother. Instead incest with father becomes predicated by that with mother from which daughter attempts (unsuccessfully) to be lifted above.

The moment father's word touches mother's secret chamber (in which he once extinguished) becomes our shattering. Too close, immediate contact without mediation, word not delineation of the damask chamber yet familial incest, incest with father while inside the blood womb where he died, faded away, returning for our delivery, too close and nothing gets delivered, nothing even spoken, throat choked constricted we fall under.

Gateshead as that place of contiguity where word touches the blood depths to which we have recessed: the text became covered by blood in the breakfast-room; omniscient, omnipotent Father lowered in the red-room and his word became silenced, no word, all word covered by further recess fit of depth. Gateshead is the place of unmediated presence, presignifying, familial incest, the literalization of his word entering her womb through our channel choking us, in a word—hysteria.

Hysteria as that moment when father's word will not be separate from the desires of mother's blood yet has not been able to delineate that red chamber. Not hysteria as the search for maternal fusion, yet as that place already fused within what is also mother's body into which father descends.

Hysteria as the attempt to let the father's word appropriate to itself the maternal chamber. The hysterical moment is when the word refuses to be any longer mere sign above warranting mother as severed object, and becomes the passage of father's word into the desire of mother's blood through daughter when there is not yet a way to delineate and as a way to attempt to delineate this familial incest.

What subtends the red-room scene of hysteria is the requirement that word descend into mother's blood and that become specified to serve what has too long been mother's secrets forbidden.

We cannot use father to escape mother and mother's son, the hysterical moment demands it. For at Gateshead, father and son revert into one another. Father's symbolic function, word holding promise, word as release of non-being death force through signification, or even the paternal metaphor of need's eruption, does not occur when father's word we try to keep separate from mother's desire, no delivery of unconscious image to a daily world in fact lightning crack.

His visit overwhelms us, too weighted, we have held all we can of him, to crash. We have come from the threshold of the unconscious, through the John Reed force laden with a rage not knowing its limit or constriction; we face the challenge of the larger ghosts and we begin to sense a human limit. Gateshead as that place of contiguity, infiltration, no mediation where the crash shatters the red-room's fascination, numinous archetypal breakdown.

Father and son Reed revert to one another. At the base of the John Reed bursting inflation is the death vault of father (anorexia: dilation to constriction). Then the father's prohibitive word's requirement becomes our flailing as of his son: again we are in seizure as the promise father becomes our violent thrashing (hysteria: constriction to dilation).

We become possessed, they infiltrate, inflating and deflating us at their will, and this form of attachment to them is our bond with the rejecting mother, an effort to signify forces of preternatural desire to and of that mother. Possession by each Reed a failed attempt to delineate unconscious realms to her for instead of signification, there is blatant act, seizure, deed, fit.

The violent, omniscient and avenging aspects of yet unnameable realms articulate themselves through us in possession, becoming bodily seizure when we cannot mediate them through language delineating their images. Signification of the contradictions within unconscious: the tension and interplay there, dilation and constriction of its forces require articulation, the specification of their differentiation.

Stepmother's rejection sent Jane to the preternatural realms unconscious yet that symbiotic rejection also precluded expression of those unnamed regions which became the child's possession. The child incorporates what has possessed, infiltrated, as expulsion when there has been no mother holding at all, no human mediation provision from impingement.

At Gateshead there is no language at all, no Reed asks our speaking but instead maids' sing-song monologue on our dependency, God's retribution, and we do not speak of or to that which grips.

Only contiguous there, presences immediate contact we project, act-out, possessed in fit. Swept away and the red-room stay is locked. She has been locking us in with the violent infiltration of these forces. Our menstruation is a part of it.

At the first blood we are no longer daughter to a father. We know we have a violent pulsation within our pelvis and that if we worked off this power it might debilitate him, that he is weakening, the father is deceasing, decreasing, and we have this tremendous force stirring in our veins, womb, and pelvis.

Our mother does not want to know it, as she has not wanted to sense her forces only unconsciously remaining subservient to them. Our mother does not want to see it, once the blood stirs in a vagina, we are no longer her extension, she curses us for having our own womb, the impudence of the singular way we encounter dilation/constriction forces beyond conscious life she can only call false (our experience in the red-room is a lie) and we blame her for delivering us such a body (that she forced us into the red-room).

With the coming of the blood arrives the question whether we give this force over to him (repressing it by escaping through his word) as she has her entire life, or do we recognize through it that he is deceasing, we are stirring with a vital force, he is deceasing and our mother will not see it.

With the coming of the blood, we are left with no father and the curse of a mother. Mother is abandoned, she has no love; she is tortured herself, strained, resourceless, continually worn down, crippled, harried, and mean. She has tried to cover it with the promise of Father's word, but instead curse. We are left with deceased, descending father and the curse of a mother through which we begin death passage to regions yet unnamed.

It is not like the ones of which we have heard: males entry to monster's belly, threats of vagina dentata, a swallowing and rebirth. In our perilous initiatory journey through death regions there is a hurled book, pointed attack, swooping visitation, a rising from a death vault to then lower, the threat not of being swallowed but of infiltration and invasion.

He gets in our veins in various ways firing out a death in a fit. Each male force another initiatory ordeal at Gateshead taking the form of possession. John and Mr. Reed ordeals to differentiate the psychic depths of her rule: can we cross through to the side of otherness (male forces) to signify the broken boat stranded on desolate coast, fiend, churchyard, gallows, as well as the son's thrusting tongue and revilement of mother's flesh; that phantom mirrored and the dead father vaulted rise to a descent what is the language of the specific death images of these recesses, what is their desire.

Mrs. Reed orders Jane to a locked red chamber bearing death. The child is thrashing when she enters, sits still long enough to find herself as phantom and is invaded by unseen preternatural force. Mrs. Reed does not believe Jane, thinks the child is faking, that here is an 'artifice' of a 'precocious actress.'

The mother indulging son's greed while unconscious to his cruelty, mother living out her hungers blindly in the gorging bilious and raging son, cannot see the fit of the possessed child as anything but false. Child as actress, child a figure in the drama of unconscious forces; child has itinerary, configurations of *dramatis personae*, drama of the heterogeneous psychic forces, repetitive plots. Child passes through the itinerary of her psychological drama, daimonic fate history. Child as actress in the red-room scene of *dramatis personae*.

It is this 'artifice' statement of the mother which accompanies the fit itself. An aspect of Jane's reality cannot place her stepmother's ghost husband, thinks it superstition. The child and Mrs. Reed have not been able to let metaphorically configure through their nature these voices calling from beyond that which is adaptive conscious stance. Father-spirit of the word is descending. The mother does not know how to delineate the differentiation of death forces and their interplay in the blood. Deceased Father descends,

mother does not know. Before we can know we have to go through some
ordeals.

    ·§ 'The room was chill, because it seldom had a fire; it was
silent, because remote from the nursery and kitchens; solemn, because it was known to be so seldom entered. The
housemaid alone came here on Saturday's, to wipe from the
mirrors and the furniture a week's quiet dust; and Mrs. Reed
herself, at far intervals, visited it to review the contents of a
certain secret drawer in the wardrobe, where were stored
divers parchments, her jewel-casket, and a miniature of her
deceased husband; and in those last words lies the secret of
the red-room: the spell which kept it so lonely in spite of its
grandeur.'

    Mrs. Reed. Over again she strokes. Hands to those parch-
ments, thumbs rubbing frame, miniature in a frame. Her silk
dress has been torn by her son and it is sinking in some
water. Chin squared skin aged thirty-six years old she manages the household. Her hands are lean, long-fingered, large
knuckled, aging stroke of his picture. Blood pushed through
his heart then aorta pulse portrait perfect she knows him
better this day, turning she looks upon the red tabernacle bed
she hears his requirement makes his promise she wants him
to leave. Never was he with her in this grandeur crimson
chambered before the sickness and he never felt her contractions, the mirror's phantom through her contractions the way
her blood pulled back, pale cheek he never saw her pale
cheek. He dies afterall leaving her a waif. And the girl
knocks on the door yet the woman screams only one of us
can be in here at once never will I wait with you child in
layers of scarlet damask for you would seek in its every fold
the oily dust of cracks no housemaid's hand could reach. The
screeches of my children pull me out with no interest to enter
this jewel-casket but when my long finger taps the parchments here also the child Jane knocking Jane it is inevitable
now knocking.

    Miniature husband, I stroke your miniature, you remain
wisp even reappearing within this frame, I cannot find you
concrete evidence. My body constricts around your memory.
My womb cramps always menstruating and yet when I sit in
this room with you husband the scent of my discharge creases
your framed visage until all blood stops. It is the moment

you cease breathing no oxygen and I harden more than you
always were the softer. In this room, some optic nerve urges
atrophy. My iris by you never seen. The arm with which I
do not write numbs. My ankles are crossed and the gap
between my knees still frightens me. Sturdy black shoes want
to tap to some love music instead I shun you husband were
more interested in my eyelash on the pillow, make a wish,
yours that I remain with waif, what is red crusted, this lid is
granular, the curtain crimson folds I do not notice, I have
not stopped spotting since you left. ৯

Bibliography

Elaide, Mircea. *Rites and Symbols of Initiation*. Trans. by Willard R. Trask. New York: Harper and Row, 1958.

Gallop, Jane. *The Daughter's Seduction: Feminism and Psychoanalysis*. Ithaca, N.Y.: Cornell University Press, 1982.

Guntrip, Harry. *Schizoid Phenomena, Object Relations and the Self*. New York: International Universities Press, 1969.

Hannah, Barbara. *The Problem of Women's Plots in "The Evil Vineyard."* London: Guild of Pastoral Psychology. Pamphlet No. 51, 1948.

_____. *Religious Function of the Animus in the Book of Tobit*. London: Guild of Pastoral Psychology. Pamphlet No. 114, 1961.

Honey, Margaret, and Broughton, John. "Feminine Sexuality: An Interview with Janine Chasseguet-Smirgel." *The Psychoanalytic Review* 72 (1985): 527.

Irigaray, Luce. "The 'Mechanics' of Fluids." In *This Sex Which Is Not One*. Trans. by Catherine Porter. Ithaca, N.Y.: Cornell University Press, 1985.

_____. "Is Her End in Her Beginning?" *Speculum of the Other Woman*. Trans. by Gillian C. Gill. Ithaca, N.Y.: Cornell University Press, 1985.

Kohut, Heinz. *The Analysis of Self*. New York: International Universities Press, 1971.

Kristeva, Julia. "From One Identity to an Other." In Leon S. Roudiez, ed., *Desire in Language*. New York: Columbia University Press, 1980.

Lacan, Jacques. "The Mirror Stage as Formative of the Function of the I." *Écrits: A Selection*. Trans. by Alan Sheridan. New York: W. W. Norton and Company, 1977.

_____. "On a Question Preliminary to any Possible Treatment of Psychosis." *Écrits: A Selection*. Trans. by Alan Sheridan. New York: W. W. Norton and Company, 1977.

Lange, Carl George, and James, William. *The Emotions*. New York: Hafner Publishing, 1967.

Miller, Alice. *The Drama of the Gifted Child*. Trans. by Ruth Ward. New York: Basic Books, 1981.

Oesterreich, T. K. *Possession*. Trans. by D. Ibberson. Seacaucus, N.J.: University Books, 1966.

Rapaport, David. *Emotions and Memory*. New York: International Universities Press, 1971.

Rush, Florence. *The Best Kept Secret*. New York: McGraw-Hill, 1980.

Schwartz-Salant, Nathan. *Narcissism and Character Transformation: The Psychology of Narcissistic Character Disorders*. Toronto: Inner City Books, 1982.

Todorov, Tzvetan. *The Fantastic*. Trans. by Richard Howard. Ithaca, N.Y.: Cornell University Press, 1975.

von Franz, M. L. *Shadow and Evil in Fairytales*. Dallas: Spring Publications, 1980.

Chapter 3

Apothecary

Is this a nightmare from which she is emerging? Here red glare crossed with thick black bars. The voices swirling are muffled. Slowly she is being lifted, it is an arm behind her, tenderly supporting her to a sitting. Resting safely against it, red glare now nursery fire. The nursemaid Bessie with a basin in hand at the foot of the bed and the gentleman behind her, he is not related to Mrs. Reed. She is immensely relieved that he is a stranger. It is Mr. Lloyd, not the physician whom Mrs. Reed calls for herself and the children, but the apothecary, called when the servants are ill.

This man is asking her does she know him. She pronounces his name giving him her hand which he takes smiling. They will get on well he is saying and he is instructing the nursemaid that there are no disturbances for the child that night, and now he is leaving with a suggestion of a return the next day. Yet the shelter departs with him and a great grief falls upon her as the door shuts behind him. Bessie is afraid of this sickness of the child, she is asking the other maid to sleep with her in the nursery, and so it is that Jane hears them discussing her ' "fit" ' with its passing white figure and trailing black dog, the tappings on the door, the light over the uncle's grave, all in the child's screams, now that child lies in dread.

The narrator Jane notes that to the day she feels the shock of the red-room, yet addressing Mrs. Reed she says she ought to forgive the woman: 'while rending my heart-strings, you thought you were only up-rooting my bad propensities.'

Now the child is wrapped in a shawl by the hearth and the tears on her cheek they are those silent tears and even with the cousins being out with their mama, even with Bessie beginning a kindness, now without reprimand or flagging, still the nerves are racked, nothing soothes.

Bessie's attempt: here is the tart on the painted china plate with its rose-buds nestling that bird of paradise Jane always admired could never touch and here now too late. Bessie suggests book. Jane asks for the favorite it is *Gulliver's Travels* more of interest even than the fairy tales whose elves she could not find though she looked beneath leaf and mushroom, yet Gulliver's diminuitive and tower realms she is sure they are located on her earth and so today she turns to the favorite book. Yet no charm instead the giants and pigmies turn malevolent and this Gulliver resembles 'a most desolate wanderer in most dread and dangerous regions.' The book is placed beside the untasted tart.

Bessie begins to sing a ballad of an orphan child, Jane begins to cry. And so it is when Mr. Lloyd returns in the course of the morning, he asks whether she has been with tears, whether she is in pain. Bessie claims the child cries because she could not go out in the carriage that day with the Reeds. The man responds she is too old for that pettiness. And Jane wounded by the false charge is saying the tears have nothing to do with the carriage, she hates the carriage, she cries because she is miserable.

The eyes of this man attend her. Steadily while upon her she sees that they are small, gray, not very bright but now she would say shrewd and looking at her he asks what it was yesterday made her ill. Bessie replies, the child had a fall. Fall! The man is exclaiming this one is no baby she can walk easily enough. With mortified pride the child's words: I was knocked down but that did not make me ill. The dinner bell rings, the apothecary sends Bessie down.

Ensuing dialogue she says she saw the ghost of her uncle while shut up without a candle in a room no one else would enter at night; and also she is unhappy for other things.

Gently he inquires whether she would tell him the other things.

She is moved by the request yet she pauses in the first moment she has been asked to speak. After nervous hesitation, she is telling him she has no father or mother, brother or sister.

He suggests she has a kind aunt and cousins.

But the cousin knocked her down and the aunt shut her in the red-room.

The house is beautiful, it is a fine place to live.

The maids remind her that she has less right to be there than a servant, and she would be glad to leave it.

What about any other relatives?

Possibly there are low relations, with the name Eyre.

Would she like to go to them?

The child reflects, sees the ragged clothes, fireless grates, the manners that are rude. She declines saying that poverty is analogous with degradation and crudeness, she is 'not heroic enough to purchase liberty at the price of caste.'

Would she like to go to school?

Images from Bessie's stories of the back-boards, the discipline, and John Reed's hate of it but then more of Bessie's story: young ladies and their paint-ing, songs, French books. It would be a separation from Gateshead. Yes, she would like to go to school.

At night she overhears the nursemaids' talk and learns that Mr. Lloyd's recommendation of school was accepted by Mrs. Reed. And then the maids are talking about her parents and for the first time she learns that her mother married a poor clergyman, the match being beneath her, she was cut off by her father. While visiting the poor, the husband contracted typhus fever, mother caught it and they died a month apart. The nursemaids are agreeing the child deserves a pity, yet her suffering would be easier to take if she weren't such a ' "little toad," ' were more a beauty like the blue-eyed long-curled cousin Georgiana—the image of whom whets their appetite for dinner, they fancy a Welsh rabbit with roast onion.

Red barred by black the hollow sounds, rushing wind, whirlwind. The nightmare ends, our senses still devoted to it, we awake to its shades. Glaring red we sweat and the black bars jar us.

Leaving the possession on the same path she entered, Jane emerges from an unconsciousness through the red glare of the nightmare carrying her to the fit.

Nightmare's red scorching until shielded nursery hearth, the arm holding her is neither terrifying nor winged, instead very tender. Black bars a grate for a fire now hearthed. The upperside of the red textured horror is nursery fire barred. Red-room reverts to nursery as the arm uplifting is of a stranger. She wakes to the strange apothecary, gentle stranger, unfamiliar and therefore welcome.

He lifts her and supports her in a sitting position, stranger support. He raises her, all the stranger that one should lift her tenderly out of what is not yet conscious, glaring recess of secrets crimson chambered. The guardian supports her rise to a sitting position, no longer flattened as shattering seizure beneath a lowering deceased Father, yet sitting, facing servant with basin figuring the ground of nursery fire, resuscitation to daily chamber.

Strange apothecary, human arm her rise, gentle other unfamiliar, heterogeneous thereby protective, not a Reed, what lifts her out of unconscious glare, the glare of the silence, the blindness within the Reed family, gap in the family as glare she went under when asked to face his word in her blood seared to glare; the return is through this one not of the family.

And what is at her feet a servant of basin, the maid who locked the redroom door now nurse wiping out her fit in return to nursery bed: we leave the possession on the same path we entered, unconscious and conscious realms transpose.

Here the nurse is maid and he is the lower physician. Lower than physician, not of a high class, called for the servants, closer to the base, of base minerals he knows the combination and he soothes what ails, his hands in the oils of roots, herbs, gums, his hands of the oils touch our baseness, inferiority, where we ache he touches, soothing ointment.

Physician of the lower regions where lie our shame, humiliation, our unnatural desire, physician of servants, he touches what is inferior, kept down, below, behind (the dead ancestors, our shadows, what is revolting, ugly, freakish in quality) he sees through our symptom to its lower interior wound.

He tends to servant, he tends to who handles daily care physicality, domestic chore, the simple human requirement, here a human base. The apothecary is outside the Reeds and their forces, distance through human base his arm is able to ease her out of the charred hollow of what was seizure. How he is heterogeneous to Reed is how he touches and heals the inferior; he meets her where she has carried for the family the heterogeneity and gives it a human lift.

Within the Reed possession, sojourn to unconscious forces, gone to death margins where our throat clutched, swallowing breath as we smashed against a human limit, unspeakable rupture. For that place of holding the tension between the inherent contradictions of the blood (inflation/constriction) and his symbolic word has shattered.

We extended ourselves through a grandiosity to limits of a crash returning us to someone human. For that mirror had reflected phantom as well as fascination, we may have stayed in the remote room of death as preference or lowered ourselves to the literal death of its vault until the seizure.

Stepmother locked us in until deceased Father descended until we know now his word could not survive his death yet requires this embrace in her red chamber. Through mother's order we realize that father's word will not remain disembodied, requires human base to which we awake.

The father lowered and who raises us is who touches inferior confirmation of where we have gone under the father's descent, Mr. Lloyd, lower physician.

We have extended ourselves through a grandiosity to limits of a crash returning us finally to someone human only now ready for what can be human arm supporting it is not a Reed we had gone through the Reed to death demons now we only want to be here with who has his hands in the earth elements, apothecary.

For a long while we have been complacent with those phantoms, happy in cragged terrain we became of the demon and gallows, not privileged in any human relation with who is mother we were of her ice realms fragmented as comforted there until the son burst us to rise to a father of a word power numinous seizure we convulsed in a writhing fit. We tried to run and we were shaking that locked door, shuddering.

Lying in the memory of the seizure, we shudder again while waking in some human encasement. Quivering of this skin, sudden quivering to the skin of who is human, quivering skin as first definition here a human. Sent to the limits of some unconscious realm and this shuddering dread begins a sense we are human even as we return from what has been preternatural. We are ready to have an human arm backing yet not before we begin to shudder.

Within Mrs. Reed's turn, spirits of the psyche take us away from everything profane but not without offering a way back. At first it may seem unrelated to that which seized us. He is not the physician of the family. Mr. Lloyd is that moment of human shuddering relief after possession by the more unconscious disturbing forces.

He first asks, ' "Well, who am I?" ' He is who locates his name, has a stake in her identification of him, will not be fused with the glare place. He slices through the possession not through reprimand or a further isolation yet through identifying his human substance and asking her relation to that. Simultaneously, he preserves her humanity against encroachment, provides the space in which she can locate herself without infiltration, injury.

> ◄§ Mr. Lloyd. Consistent tweed. Writhing body's blood
> sparks may have been chasing him we thought we saw it yet
> instead he sits still and the red scorching now ribbons encir-
> cling some magic protective circle encloses screams subsiding
> we are not within her sight or embodying what is her blind-
> ness. Spices, myrrh and aloes, boiled lemons and he also
> recommends a soup of garlic; thickly skinned hands smelling
> of leather have caressed the oils do not enter instead the arm
> backs, clock's chime he leaves on schedule protective guard-
> ian his instructions say no disturbance, shielding us from
> further invasion his tweed consistent. In his carriage he car-
> ries a shelter. §►

When he leaves for the night, shelter departs, and the emergence to human after a residence in regions of the dead, depresses. We return naked, exposed, empty, no longer at one with demon-son and his Father-God, after the stunning shock of otherworlds, our humanity is inadequate, cowering in dread as Mr. Lloyd departs.

The emotions accompanying the descent have been a disgust, rage and terror. Those rising with us in the return are shuddering dread and despair. The child lies in dread sensing the ways she has been visited by a white figured relative of the dead, the maids are whispering it was accompanied by a black dog.

We are enough apart from the red-room that we can dread, there is a quivering skin which separates ourselves from phantom though an ambivalence pervades this dread, will we return afterall, or has the seizure taken? Bessie is afraid to be alone with the child in the echoes of realms not of this life, the child may die she says, asking for another maid's presence alongside, extra dosages of human in room of death-child.

'Ghastly wakefulness' when the spirits of the dead are too close and our skin is young, we had been seized, and the only shield for the night has departed. In asking our relation to his human identity (named), he posited our humanity (named) not possible in the windowseat/red-room possessions and still tenuous becoming ghastly dread; if we stay awake, we are.

She is marked. The visits of figures from the unconscious through who is mother mark. There is no physical sign of it yet reverberation of the nerves to this day shocked. This violent agitation of nerves: the deceased Father's word can no longer cover the repressed desire for union with her unconscious body; the impact of the stepmother's unconsciousness making Jane consubstantial with the death Father jarred the nerves to this day, further shattered. Some say "nervous break," it has been a shock.

From within the night dread of the child, the narrator speaks to Mrs. Reed of the shock. 'But I ought to forgive you, for you knew not what you did: while rending my heart-strings, you thought you were only up-rooting my bad propensities.' Heart-string rent, stepmother wrenched, she did not want this heart a unity she ripped its string, violently torn, cleaved to the heterogeneous heart.

A heart which now knows the contradictions: the expulsion within incorporation, the pull blood penetration of up-lifting word of promise; heart of the hysteric who knows that the Father she addresses is dead and descended; our bad propensity to want a homogeneous heart without contradiction, she cleaved our heart our mark.

'You knew not what you did.' Cruxificion when one has humanized the numinous Father. A human is speaking what once was unseen Father's word unspeakable. Our mother as Pilate's ruler desires to keep the Father invisible, omniscient his word not to speak blood contradiction.

Narrator Jane addresses Mrs. Reed, stepping outside the text. Outside text the first person addressed by the narrator is Mrs. Reed, the teleology of text is an interlocution with Mrs. Reed: to become narrator, to see the heterogeneous figures and their plot is to find a differentiation within what was unconscious and thereby have a perspective to Mrs. Reed, address her without possession.

Emerging human from unconscious glare anticipates the narrator who speaks a time when the possessions have been negotiated, the "masters" mediated, when we may emerge as dialogic narrator, meeting the unconscious desire of the text, arising from the rupture within the first chapter of the impossibility of interlocution with that stepmother, reprimand sending child to unconscious.

(This address of the narrator also suggests an homology between Mrs. Reed and the reader who, perhaps like the stepmother, may have turned from the unconscious in which Jane resided, read the surface only, dismissing this narrative as pubescent fantasy; reader too may need to read the text of the unconscious which from the perspective of the narrator is now the text [Jane Eyre] herself.)

The shock tore Jane out of the red-room fascination, but the senses still are not hers. The sweets do not soothe; after residing in realms unconscious, of otherworlds, the earthly world looks and tastes even reads differently. Blandness and a desolation, insipid world now in comparison.

Her appetite has been altered upon return. Where she once knew its drive, now it is alternative, the sweets do not soothe: visits from dead and deathdealing figures affecting her "instinctual drives."

Everything around appears faded, ugly, dreadful. There are objects which once held a delight, they would catch her eye: now they are plain and they recede, she has not a taste for anything, only a faint pounding in a head which does not want to collect anymore, no flavor, no nuance, nothing in the world beckoning, all sits gray and there is no animation.

Here is what appears as "despair." It is not that she is absent in life or that she is in despair, as much as she is entirely present to death while attempting to return to life. *Gulliver's Travels* had been a favorite tale because she expected she could find its lands of Lilliput and Brobdignag on her earth. But after the red-room seizure, some (childhood) belief in the worldly translation of otherworldly forces is no longer possible, there is not to be merely literal (re)placement. Her survival of the red-room posits her necessity as mediator between, a speaking of the figurative translation of unconscious to world.

Our calling has been to bring out the text of the unconscious, windowseat possession by John Reed has said that incorporation and blatant action is not the text emergence yet further recess. Red-room possession by Mr. Reed has said text may be symbolic function but cannot be severed out from (sever us from) mother's desire.

We have met the Father's word as descending figure in the mother's unconscious, asking what is the figuration of the unconscious, we know now it cannot be located in a point for point correspondence on earth, and we have a choice to die to it incorporating and possessed by it, or impart it, carry its metaphor out. This child has been to a place precluding literal translation to natural world and she lies suspended between death realm and lived world, not yet able to speak figurative mediation.

Unlike the threshold place of the windowseat, she is not happy here. Collision with numinous (archetypal) Parent shatters complacent collusion with mother's unconscious: the naive hope that we can both resume knowledge of that omniscient, universal Parent through that unconscious place as well as be delivered from it by him.

Orphan is where we relinquish fusion with the unconscious forces, no longer windowseat complacency, we find ourselves desolate only slowly learning to reside in a human sense. Recognition of ourself as orphan requires human orientation. We mourn for the passing of archetypal Parent in this discovery of a mortal human body, we cry as orphan for we have been alone through hell, felt the pulse of the dead, returning hollowed the desolate wanderer.

> ◄§ Despair. Burnt umber and an olive green also chrome green deep alongside a burnt sienna coagulating chest. The world out of these eyes gray to all affect. No Reach. They need company to guard against us. Looking at us in a side glance they whisper of a black dog trailing. We see only a lone tree as we pass and even this glance we cannot hold. Having been shocked we are disinterested. Hands offering to us only mirage of some longing in a chest clogged sienna burnt. §►

Hollow after the fit, after the fit we are hollow, lightning shot through limbs and this jolt cannot be sweetened away. The tart no longer appeals; too late for the china bird of paradise; Gulliver a desolate wanderer in regions of dread; the child sits under shawl by hearth crying for the orphan.

Bessie singing an orphan child ballad. Of lonely moor and gray rock the orphan saying ' "Ev'n should I fall, o'er the broken bridge passing,/ Or stray in the marshes, by the false lights beguiled,/ Still will my Father, with promise and blessing,/ Take to His bosom the poor orphan child." '

Yet no Father Heavenly full dove bosom, word of promise that blessed one descended, we looked up, red-room child beseeching an aid, Bless me Father, instead of bosom reception uplifting he penetrated to a seizure suffocating more isolated only return we cry too late is this maid's tale.

Orphan despair is where we can no longer find the protection for our unconscious experience through whom was Omniscient Parent. Orphan is when we mourn the loss of uplifting through word of Father which was to deliver us. Nothing can express where we have been, the old ballads and tales no longer recount it, and we do not know the form or meaning of unconscious realm desired.

The call of John Reed has carried her on a perilous trip through a red-room hell and now more than ever at Gateshead she is alone, not even ghosts for company. As we approach a humanity after the fit, Bessie is kinder, she has held the basin, offers treat, sings a song, yet this caretaker still sings of Father with promise and blessing, there is no mother's voice speaking more accurately our passage and the room swirls without such mother now here a motherless bland swirl: long-waved echoes of unheard sound pulling us in their tide.

After the shock, shuddering we know ourself fully as orphan and for the first time we suffer it; interpenetration of unconscious with conscious becomes our orphan suffering, for when we are identified only exclusively in either extreme we whine. Beginning to offer a recognition of our humanity and loss of Savior Father as we return rent (by her) is the return of Mr. Lloyd.

Mr. Lloyd stands in the interstices of unconscious and conscious realms while clarifying his human identity. Child's shuddering skin as first definition of a person non-fused accompanies Mr. Lloyd's return the next day. Child was broken apart in fit; the fit an essential dismemberment resulting from the inflating fusion with the bursting son and with the potentially uplifting word of Omniscient Parent. This mourning loosens, dismemberment becoming suffering, allowing the child to move the possessions through her, return to a humanity, the arm she awakens to is humanly tender and when he returns the next day, he inquires upon her crying.

Each possession requires something of us; as we pass each through us we relinquish some of our preter-human size which requires assuming more a human size speak in language those forces, human condensation, configuration.

With Mr. Lloyd's return, Bessie tries to make surface excuses for the orphan pain. The Bessie input at this juncture is a denial of the realms from which we are being lifted. Bessie is who will not accept our residence in realms beyond the natural yet instead reduces our state to the infantile. Even as we summon Mr. Lloyd, a Bessie part does not want the revelation of the landscape lying at the core of the child's misery, instead packages it in daily occurrence, thereby negating the essential horror of the death journey as well of the necessity of signifying that.

Bessie is that moment when a return of consciousness occurs only through repression of unconscious seizure in naive honor of the Father's continual omnipotence/omniscience, that all word stay distant from redroom secrets.

And Bessie's surface accounts (the child cries because she could not go out in carriage, had a fall) are precisely what provoke Jane to a 'mortified pride,' 'self-esteem being wounded by the false charge,' allowing the child to begin to express what subtends the suffering of where she had been.

Bessie's is the position against which we push off when our pride and self-esteem want to be located in the unconscious where we have resided, not wanting merely to translate it contiguously to natural occurrence, reduce it to infantile state, and let it be forgotten. There begins a self speaking in the contradiction to the Bessie repression.

After the red-room, we are larger than Bessie's account and it becomes a matter of self-esteem to speak from the depths of where we have been is the base of who we are, esteem for that rent, heterogeneous heart.

Bessie is who would have us rise out of the red-room too fast without negotiating that death chamber back with us. 'But how could she divine the morbid suffering to which I was a prey? In the course of the morning Mr. Lloyd came again.'

His eye shrewd, Mr. Lloyd peers, he sees through Bessie's contrived surface account of Jane's distress. The lower physician assisting to carry the vision of the dead back to life does not fall for the simplistic Bessie cover. His arrival statement is ' "What, already up!" ' – that we cannot quickly rise above it, covering over where we had been. His arrival signals the articulation of the messages within the sickness, the direction within the fit, the word of her 'morbid suffering.'

Apothecary seeing through the earth's minerals, her materials, peers through them to their transposition to healing quality, death property; an alchemist, does not treat literally yet extracts from the material its figurative significance to cure. He refuses a literal reductive interpretation of the child's symptom, instead, physician of inferiority, he meets the wound behind, beneath, where in the lower regions we have been wounded he shrewdly sees through to that profundity, does not infantilize Jane yet tells the maid the child is too old to cry for not going out in a carriage, too old to fall down.

Child says: I was knocked down but that did not make me ill. Mr. Lloyd sends Bessie down to dinner. Carrier back to humanity, to carry us back he knows of otherworlds they have seized. His mediation is what lowers Bessie so the child can speak from the base of things, dismissing silly childish mishap to hear outcast child cast out to preternatural realms marking.

If the maid had stayed fixed in her position, had not gone down to dinner, there would have been another sort of possession. Bessie's requirement for consciousness through red-room repression implies another seizure: if no one had lowered to listen to the underlying meaning of the red-room, Jane would have had to reside in a hysteria, flailing a continual pleading for the recognition of the reality of those phantom forces attempting delineation.

At Bessie's descent: ' "I was shut up in a room where there is a ghost, till after dark." ' The beginning of acknowledging that the forces another calls unconscious are real is the beginning of a differentiation from Mrs. Reed and the Gateshead perspective that the forces of our seizures are not real therefore must remain unconscious.

Mr. Lloyd begins mirroring her through language: she says she is unhappy for other things, what are the other things? Reflecting and following, he gives her stance and voice a space, a sounding. He asks for elaboration. His concern is with the human, her human pain, holding her through language mirroring. Mirrored human.

The one who lifts us up asking to impart unconsciousness to consciousness, mirrors. Extension of the red-room mirror, he was hired by Mrs. Reed. The stepmother does not require a literal death, she called the lower physician who mirrors the child out, mirroring through language provides a space for the delineation of the secrets of the blood chamber. Mr. Lloyd is an extension of the place where Father lowered, humanized to (unconscious) desire. Mr. Lloyd humanly wants Jane to speak her desire and his human base is what Mrs. Reed hired.

An extension of the mother's unconscious blood desire is that the unnatural child begin to speak from the depths of that blood, finding its meaning, its translation not to be provided through a son incorporation or a repression through the Father design, speak from the depths of that blood, womb of blood find the figures of its desire of unconscious speaking when the father is dead. She hired Mr. Lloyd who asks what makes the child so unhappy, when Bessie goes down.

Phantoms of that mirror operate even as a human is here mirrored: the red-room pull back urges a silence. Jane pauses, a 'disturbed pause,' critical moment.

Whispers of red-room fascination lingering call us back, desiring only in itself we remain of phantoms, silenced human. To speak of them humanly would preclude the return eternal return remaining undifferentiated, condemning any otherness, not in relationship.

Denial of all depths is the Gateshead human consciousness, therefore to speak of unseen force there requires a non-human-being. Split now it is a choice, to speak humanly relate we fear loss of damask mystery.

She begins to locate herself through his mirroring, which precludes her fusion with him. His continual mirroring return to her allows a differentiation between them becoming the emergence of language which places her places.

The windowseat and red-room possessions occur repetitiously when we have never been asked to speak them or when we have refused to speak when asked. Blood ordeals not signified incorporate. What is language when word is not severed from or identified with the unconscious realms, yet speaks through them, is language of the unconscious, possession is placed humanly differentiated through such figurative language and this attempt is Mr. Lloyd's mirroring.

We often remain silent after the red-room experience in fear of breaking our bond with eternal powers, for we were one with that winged descending Father afterall; if we word it humanly we will lose its unnatural terror and beauty and our immortal fusion with that. If we speak to this mortal man we sacrifice the eternal forms of no dying and if we remain silent of those recesses we never will die.

The discrepancy between the grandiosity of those forces and our human (inferior, servant) selves accounts for the contradiction we first experience between the red-room and Mr. Lloyd.

She is saying to Mr. Lloyd that she is unhappy for other things. ' "What other things? Can you tell me some of them?" ' Mirroring through language, reflecting recessed figures — ghost, cousin knocking down, aunt shutting in — by interlocution. Figures of what previously was unspeakable when we face whose presence is asking to receive them.

'Children can feel, but they cannot analyze their feelings; and if the analysis is partially effected in thought, they know not how to express the result of the process in words.' No words in the red-room or through that mirroring, post-red-room through his human lift to consciousness mirroring she knows relief is through impartation.

By his mirroring she reflects on her unhappiness, its meaning, 'the analysis is partially effected in thought,' now its speaking the meaning in analysis of what underlied her seizures is that she has no family. To speak from the unhappiness is to differentiate the depths from which she had been knocked down and locked up. Her location takes shape in this mirror through analyzing the fragmentation not through illusory, childlike (Bessie) unity.

Speaking the analysis of unhappiness provides definitive ground, no longer windowseat edge of another's unconscious realm but some room upon demarcated ground, here her property, here her definition, analysis of unhappiness, she does not have a family, she was hit and locked up, she is treated as a servant of the house.

Speaking to Mr. Lloyd of who was the human in the red-room, who was the human in the red-room and what is the meaning of this Gateshead life for her and eventually she is not only what occurred in the red-room. She is no longer blood ordeals yet does not abandon them altogether through simplification in a Bessie fashion.

The ordeals of Gateshead now analysis having impact on his human sensibility. The red-room scene is what carried Jane out to Mr. Lloyd and he is the natural extension of it as he opens himself to engage with its effect.

The advantage of the uncle's shock descent is the residue caution of travelling through death regions uneducated. Some of the grandiosity has been negotiated. She speaks to the apothecary.

First she says she has no family. Analyzing the meaning of the red-room arrives at the death of family. At the break of the hold of archetypal Parent, there is no family. No family is her property. Instead of returning to the windowseat, she speaks from the windowseat. At the base of possession by unconscious forces (Reeds knock us down, shut us up, ever exposed as penetrated), there is a profound separation, scission, fragmentation, dislocation, no family, presupposing the undifferentiated bond with a stepmother.

What results from Mr. Lloyd's mirroring is the speaking of her fragmentation which is the analysis of the meaning of the windowseat and redroom, that they are the landscapes prior to a mirror human image, properties for a rent self.

She says she has no immediate family yet she could not live within the poverty of her Eyre relatives. Less than a servant in Gateshead's wealth, yet the Gateshead value still holds her: she claims the poverty of her relations and from her Gateshead stance that appears only degradation.

She claims the poverty of her relations. 'Fireless grates, rude manners and debasing vices,' human relations of her name debasing, kin too lowly. Low relations called Eyre, to relate humanly lowly beneath Gateshead, beneath red-room grandeur, is to err. Errare: to wander from the truth, to be mistaken; errer: manner of progressing, or to make an error, err. To relate humanly is lowly, is to err, to be of errant, deviant, wandering, stray to astray, to be erroneous in conclusion, 'synonymous with degradation.' She would prefer the Gateshead tyranny over the poverty of her father's family.

To know herself as eyre is also to have itineration and find the justice of that. Eyre: circuit rode by itinerant justices appointed to it. Justices in eyre. What is justice, how to proceed. She may have to wander to find her circuit to learn the justice, where there is justice, what is the correct way to proceed. The right of passage. She prefers Gateshead tyranny possessing.

The Gateshead (material) wealth holds the worth so demon/divine arrive as seizure there. Jane is held within the same view necessitating Mrs. Reed's perception of the falsity of the uncle's visitation, that is, that which exists and matters is grossly material, exclusively.

Gateshead tyranny preferred. Here she is held in place by being prohibited a place, there she would wander. She would not be a beggar to know her family which is the Gateshead perspective ushering in the outraged and inflated John Reed in the first place.

Either a grandiosity or poverty in relations, she cannot imagine a worthy relatedness outside Gateshead. Some of the deathworld horrified fascination still appeals more than what is human relation, to relate humanly is to eyre, within this first interlocution of relating humanly to eyre is lowly, degradation.

To relate humanly is also to learn to hear, through eyre, let another in, interlocution, which is to relate not in seizure, she is humanly located by who is the first to hear her and who she first (likes what she) hears.

When Mr. Lloyd hears she is not ready to know human relation, finding her suspended relative to unconscious, he inquires of school. John Reed hated his school, wants no part of the figurative translation of explosive force to what is society.

> John Reed at school. Their smile for the teacher, pet of teacher, they smile I will rip it off until the blood underneath. They prance. At recess they prance holding careful beneath arms the milk jar squeaking clean so they could put in the precious seeds. Their teacher's lesson on seeds and those green plants. Milk jars prancing with the sand and the seeds. I am hiding behind the tree until I see them and then I charge. I charge and aim for the jar. It explodes under my foot I love the sound of the seed cracking. I grind my foot into the ground so it can eat up every bit of seed. Then they are crying so I pull their braids and I take the ribbon and throw it to the ground to make a grave for their dear earth. The girls with their perfect smiles, perfect frocks, perfect arithmetic and here am I in the corner of the dunce. My grin is wet, my shirt is hanging, the skin on my knee is torn apart and I watch the mud in the ripped skin, mud and blood and the blood is getting hard to a crust, crust on my bread the best. And I am sitting in the corner they call it the discipline. I pick the scab.

Mr. Lloyd is an extension of the red-room fit, he sees the forces with which we have been struggling and suggests a discipline, not Reedian, more a Bessie story, we imagine learning French, we imagine the art class, hand's craft the minded hold of that force, school. Our way back is similar to that of our entry: Bessie's story inscribing otherworlds draws us.

In the dialogue with Mr. Lloyd, he follows her, they each have a say, he does not talk at her, speak more or louder. He begins with another viewpoint, of another, not a Reed, but gradually he yields his viewpoint (it is a beautiful place to live) to her singular discourse with a level of empathy. He is that aspect which is the potential for her developing empathy, through which she would begin to enter the perspective of another placing her outside Gateshead offsetting John Reed's inflation and rage.

Mr. Lloyd does not exercise by authority, interpretation, or any sort of seduction. Neither grandoise or patronizing he does not attempt to supply an education or take care of her himself. He does not reappropriate Jane's red-room experience into his own design, his structure of (masculine) consciousness or another paternal law.

For that Father's word lowered, law of omnipotent/omniscient Father sunk to mother's blood which became a Mr. Lloyd assistance of Jane to articulation: can you tell me some of the other things making you unhappy? Mr. Lloyd is not an extension or replication of the Father's Law overriding mother's desire, yet that moment Father's law descended through daughter into mother's blood desiring impartation.

Mr. Lloyd is that moment of condensation into language of the contradiction within realms once unconscious. His mode precludes phallocentric authority; he is not master, the red-room descent, heart now rent heterogeneous heart requires that the one arriving be non-authoritative. Yet Mr. Lloyd also is clear: he provides precise questions, firm in his identity, never losing his definition of self or his position towards her throughout he knows himself solidifying substance, cohesive identity. Clear and non-authoritative, he does not operate an univocity (that there is only one way for her to proceed now which he knows before she does), yet explores the plurality of possibilities.

Mr. Lloyd is where our clarity is not also univocity (for in the Father's Law of past they were contingent) which is the effect of the red-room seizure, Father's crash. His resiliency and openness to the effects of Jane's unconscious is the beginning of her differentiation of the heterogeneous figures of that unconscious which is the start of her desiring to know the selves, her properties, go to school.

His focus on the specificity of her discourse (heterogeneous to his own, his own perspective) involves the risk of loss of his position, identity, loss of himself, death. He does not attempt to adapt her to his viewpoint or order and thereby he risks unsettling his own position, risks his own unconscious plunge. The ability to meet another's psychological heterogeneity risks one's own death; Mr. Lloyd is inferior enough for such risk, already knowing the inferior, underside.

He does not insist on her education in a masculine mode, in the dialogue with him what gets imagined is a Bessie school. Not a Reed school where one beats up, where the eruption of John Reed even beats up master, but Bessie school where what is mastered is a plurality of crafts.

Mr. Lloyd sends us to the place where girls learn to read, write, speak, sing, draw, impart the story. Woman not of materia, passive, inert commerce exchange between men as in the Gateshead possession by son exchanged for possession by father. The masterful possession of Gateshead implied the right to exchange the female yet Lloyd assisting her passage through Gateshead, arranges to send her to school not as commerce exchange, he gets nothing from it.

Through the interlocution with Mr. Lloyd, the meaning beneath the Gateshead possessions becomes delineated as the lack of family and denigration of human relation; the articulation of specific figures as ghost, cousin, father's poor family; and what then emerges is the (unconscious) desire to go to school.

He is that mediating passage for us to go to a girls' school to learn what is the language of the locked crimson chamber. School of languages toward which we begin a movement yet only when he gets Mrs. Reed's permission. What to be learned is the function of Mrs. Reed's desire, post-red-room school of language and craft is based on/by her desire.

Not the authority, inferior physician he mediates horizontal crossings of temporal, spatial, class dimensions. He mediates her movement through preter-human realms to the human to a particular caste and then out of Gateshead, spatial movement, change of place in what will be now is directed toward a future, temporal horizons broaden. Enlarging her dimensions of time, place, class, he stands outside/beside the Gateshead manor/manner of continguity/contiguity, immediacy.

Empathy is the transmission of his mediation. He takes on her unique perspective, and he mirrors her location, her property. His empathic level does not pertain to the acquisition of what was her experience; he has never had similar red-room experience yet he peers into, approximates who she is in what was seized there. His mirroring her location (temporal, spacial, societal) is a recognition of her heterogeneity to the place, that she belongs in a different place to learn a new vocabulary.

He has not had our experience. Introject to project accurate mirroring of location and property all the intimacy we can (with)stand after residence in Gateshead's corners.

Archetypal forces strike and we hit bottom and inquire on our family. Where lies the wealth? What is caste? How to avoid the ancestral traps? His mediation passes through temporal dimensions, she finds a past. The tart and plate no longer please, Gulliver not any longer the favorite book, and overhearing the maids are speaking who were her parents. The parents of a past, some family was tangential now is in our overhearing, we hear overall a parental death.

After the Mr. Lloyd interlocution we learn of parental limit. When we are no longer of the gods or phantoms, yet in relation, we hear our parents die, our parents' limit, our parents abandoned us also to a meagre human mortality. Parent not Father's law or Mother's magestic chamber, inflating/deflating, yet parent is human and dies and is dead not even ghost and we will die.

Sacrifice of the immortality of the gods who were parent, sacrifice of their godly, omnipotent quality is Mr. Lloyd's entry and speaking to him of our unhappiness our human property. When we speak our unhappiness to who mirrors, we identify our human requirement of human parent, hear for the first time our parents' story, which is to begin to sense the plot of the drama in which we are one figure, locate ourselves in a storyline reaching beyond our personal history, one figure in the drama of many, *dramatis personae*, our property.

Overhearing the maids: it was a marriage of poverty which estranged her mother from the Reed family. Mother left the wealthy family of gentry for a poor minister. Her mother knew the poverty of Gateshead but substituted for that a literal poverty with one who saw the wealth only in a divine unseen, and it killed her.

Jane has seen that the divine unseen has body: it suffocates, it arrives with a black dog and stirs the wind with the rustle of its large wings penetrating to a fit body seizure. From her mother's history she knows that the way to leave Gateshead is not a literal move separating from the Gateshead site of seizures to a word of spirit, severance from reactive impulse becoming debilitating poverty. Yet here this Lloyd is mediating a move from Gateshead through a Reed permission and how may that include body?

Hysterical, choking fit, the hysteric recognizes that Father's law (which had been bodiless, its impartial philosophies and mathematics relieving us from corporal matter of density and desire) has body; recognizes that beneath Father's law, word of his spirit, has been a desire for body, blood of womb body. Through Gateshead she has known body only through alternating unmediated seizures precluding interlocution; what is the father's word of this body and its mother's blood chamber, and how to find her speaking the desire of unseen forces within a protection more embodied?

> ◄§ She left us to die with him, die from her body of us. She left to leave her body this Gateshead mansion all she knew of body for his ministry. She severed from her mansion to find a spirit in him pulling as it did toward the house of death. We do not want to understand her choices, we want her breast, we want to pull at its warm milk even sour spurting we do not want to hear of her choices of a ministry word of spirit she followed the paltry father to parishioners on fever, none can take that heat with no body, leaving her mansion only the fever returned to her not enough body to take the heat of spirit, she left us. And the other-mother abandoned remains only kept in mansion body her spirits they are demons becoming ours as we sit on her edge shunned. She left us not to die with him. §►

Learning the ancestor's drama, plot of drama of which we are extension, takes us to school. Mediating her configuration of plot residing beyond the

Gateshead contiguity, he orients her to her fate, the call from the dead, enraged/enlightened male forces of a mother abandoned.

Many are possessed repetitively by John and Mr. Reed yet few go to school to learn the vocabulary and figurative value of their seizures, carry those seizures to signification.

Marginal child has been possessed by the more malevolent forces. It is not that we have to learn to become less marginal or avoid the emerging unconscious forces and voices, for they come as our design from all mothers, coming through (antipathetic) symbiosis with mother in various ways marking us, even leaving messages requiring translation to a human symbolic.

We can hear the voices from the unconscious and engage with them, learn to hear them without possession. The possession is our ignorance of a mediated relation to them, how we can speak them in a language, speak through them in a language, speak a language through them, which is not the possession by them which is madness.

The dialogue with Mr. Lloyd is prototype for an interlocution with the possessing forces themselves: it suggests that she has to go to school to learn to identify herself clearly and open an ear to what is their message, listening to the call of those voices surrounding mother's rule, listening to their promise, their curse, their requirement, mirroring that while asking what makes them unhappy, what do they want?

For these "evil" voices arrive with message: madame mope, you are dependent, nothing. They arrive to tell us we are stuck on her windowseat where interior is all we know of exterior, too complacent in the ice realm, somewhere only frozen. If we do not let some of the "evil" come before us and know it as our own, we stay forever on the windowseat, floating then frozen, as always situated in a mother's fearful rule, never attaching to the earth, never can hold forth on this earth.

To learn how some of the "evil" coming before us is also our own desiring articulation of what was unconscious is to begin a differentiation not to be absorbed by mother's rule.

They arrive as evil and dreadful voices concomitant with our attempt to be wrenched out of her recesses. Yet we find that John Reed, though he removes us from the windowseat, sends us through a crash to a more remote chamber; and Mr. Reed, though he promised red-room delivery, sends us through a fit to further recess unconscious.

These forces ultimately pull us further into her recess, we are not to sever from the unconscious into which she has unconsciously ordered us. Their messages of severance do not imply extrication from her depths yet differentiation within those depths which is to speak them out analyzing their aspects: it is John Reed's book, bring out the text of the ice realm delineating its specific properties, its drives; it is Mr. Reed's word, speak the contradictory forces within the red-room, fervid to dampening ember to vault, is delivery.

Differentiation within recess is what is required in the translation of unconscious regions to the human, which implies separating from Mrs. Reed's immediate rule, which constitutes school.

Learning to let configure the contradictory forces — dilation and constriction — (the expulsion of incorporation, the incorporation of disembodied word's fit) — without being possessed by extremes of inflation and deflation is the lesson of marginal forces.

For we had been clutching desperately to mother through her recesses, preferring possession since she alienated us, outcast child extension of her dread as desire requesting interlocution (what did I do?). Fused, we were floating in her realms unconscious eternal images as she alienated us. They arrive as "evil" voices when we too long have been humanly undifferentiated in a symbiotic alienation.

They offer a promise of delivery from her hold yet ultimately return us further clutched as we go under, for they have told us we are nothing, we are dependent, we are a rat, they swoop down in seizure to show us that using their possession is not the way out of her realms searing and shrivelling us, only pushing us further in, nothing her most cragged cavity.

They arrive as father and son possessing us first as we sit antipathetic symbiotic within recesses of the alienating mother. For generations we have been alienated from these mothers so remaining secretly bound with the unconscious of she who values more father and son.

And she has pushed us away, no cozy sofa merged mother bliss instead her arctic thief, learn to steal for her love. We clasped beneath and her demons came to rupture us within her every recess. Heart rent. They were severing, tearing, delivery and we were seized under in extrication attempt from her eternal most horrific depth.

Mother's unconscious requirement is that we let son and father pass through us as we take their forces, expansion and constriction, life forces, blood forces of her recess, carry them out differentially translated which is to become humanly differentiated recess not possessed.

Differentiation within her depths: to ask who are the forces, what do they desire and how do they configure in our ancestral plot is the meaning of our analysis. Can we reside within realms of which she situated us, can we reside there differentiated human and carry them back, imparting.

We need an education in differentiation to translate their messages of severance to an analysis within the eternal images with which for long we have sat. We are talking now to a person with eyes shrewd and kind not violent. We need an education in a differentiation through discourse which is not abandonment to incorporation, symbiotic alienation.

> ⋅§ Apothecary-condensation-alchemist; 4 a.m. vigil, diplopia, paresis, contractures, paraphasia we will not speak it and there is not your question 'who am I' the room is empty empties. Devils in head exhort silence at father's constriction we have no word only foreign language and not even that prayer works for the devil's head is on fingernail as father expires until we choke and a Breuer man receives the emission talking cure. Talking cure for thirsts and repulsion to thirst, skeleton frights, desire to dance to that music playing through the dying man's wall. Glare to hearth a bar subtends chimney sweeping with him fit converts to word condensation to an indecent charge until some school social works. §⋅

Chapter's ending open-ending. Chapter's end not a definite event, this conclusion does not finish as did the others of a passion lunge, of a convulsive fit, remains open, the suggestion of school accepted but not yet implemented, the maids' appetite expressed yet not yet satiated. Not a chapter pushing forward a momentum to definite closure, more an unfolding, opening to what desires who she is and the appetite is delineated yet not demanding a consumption.

This unfolding is Mr. Lloyd's mediation. Appetite is mediated, named, imaged as blond curled cousin desire, not seized, and such mediation identifies Jane: crying beneath shawl, once favoring book and treat and plate (her past aesthetic, her taste), her unhappiness, her parents, that she is a toad.

Mr. Lloyd's methodology of mirroring identifies her heterogeneous to the family, her contradictory sides (she wants to leave Gateshead but not go to her father's family) and her desire to go to school. His mediation of the Gateshead mode of immediacy and closure of what is appetite allows unfolding desire, perhaps desire the needs of Gateshead cover.

Compared to blue-eyed Georgiana summoning the desire of Welsh rabbit, Jane is the unnatural, freakish child. The servants say toad. Her mother's death taught her that severance from Gateshead body for love in a poverty ministry means literal death. Taken from the natural mother's arms unnaturally early, Jane was thrown to the land of the dead, region of ghosts, imps, a desolate wanderer, a horned black bird, a demon son of greed and an uncle savoir who seized her in a fit. In carrying her back to this world to educate herself, Mr. Lloyd asks about her family, she faces the poverty of her family. She wants to go to school.

Bibliography

Breuer, Josef and Freud, Sigmund. "Studies on Hysteria." *The Complete Psychological Works of Sigmund Freud.* Vol. 2. Trans. James Strachey. London: Hogarth, 1955.

Edinger, Edward F. *Anatomy of the Psyche.* LaSalle, Ill.: Open Court Publications, 1985; Chapter 7, "Separatio."

Eliade, Mircea. *The Sacred and the Profane.* Trans. by Willard R. Trask. New York: Harcourt, Brace and World, 1959.

Freud, Sigmund. "The Dynamics of the Transference." *The Complete Psychological Works of Sigmund Freud.* Vol. 12. Trans. James Strachey. London: Hogarth, 1958.

Gallop, Jane. *The Daughter's Seduction: Feminism and Psychoanalysis.* Ithaca, N.Y.: Cornell University Press, 1982.

Herzog, Edgar. *Psyche and Death.* New York: G. Putnam and Sons, 1967.

Hillman, James. *Healing Fiction.* Barrytown N.Y.: Station Hill, 1983.

Irigaray, Luce. The "Mechanics of Fluids." In *This Sex Which Is Not One.* Trans. by Catherine Porter. Ithaca, N.Y.: Cornell University Press, 1985.

Jung, C.G. "The Development of Personality." *The Collected Works of C. G. Jung.* Vol. 17. Trans. R. F. C. Hull. Princeton, N.J.: Princeton University Press, 1954.

Kohut, Heinz. *How Does Analysis Cure.* Chicago: University of Chicago Press, 1984.

Perera, Sylvia. *Descent to the Goddess: A Way of Initiation for Women.* Toronto: Inner City Books, 1981.

von Franz, M. L. *The Feminine in Fairytales.* Dallas: Spring Publications, 1979.

_____. *Shadow and Evil in Fairytales.* Dallas: Spring Publications, 1980.

Winnicott, D. W. *The Maturational Processes and the Facilitating Environment.* New York: International Universities Press, 1965.

_____. *Playing and Reality.* London: Tavistock, 1982.

Chapter 4
Black Pillar

Daily waiting, no word of school, more marked is the separation between her and the family, she sleeps alone small closet, meals alone all time in nursery. Aversion so rooted in Mrs. Reed's eye the aunt will not endure for long this child yet no allusion to the school. Cousins avoid her, once John attempts a chastising, Jane is leveling on his nose a blow, he runs to the mama now ordering her children never to associate with the smaller cousin.

' "They are not fit to associate with me." ' It bursts from the bannister. Though a stout woman, Mrs. Reed nimbly she is rushing up those stairs a whirlwind flinging the child into the nursery, crushing her on the crib's edge, daring her to rise, to speak. A voice speaks through the child uncontrollably: what would Mr. Reed say? The aunt's look a fearful wonder is it child or fiend who continues saying: uncle Reed and papa and mama know, they see you shut me up in the nursery, you wish me dead. The response a boxing of ears.

For an hour Bessie does the homily: I am the wicked and abandoned child. November and December and now half of January passed, Christmas and New Years were the usual festivity, excluded, I witnessed Georgiana and Eliza in muslin and ringlet descending to the music below, the glasses clinking the good cheer, I would sit on the stairhead the hum of conversation beneath, doors opening and closing. I did not want to be in that company, would have preferred Bessie in a kindness in the nursery, yet she is in the livelier kitchen, I remain alone; there is my doll. Sitting doll on knee, fire lowering, tugging at strings of the clothing undressing to the bed with doll nightgown folded, 'cherishing a faded graven image,' I fancy it with sensation as we lie in bed and listen to the company departing, occasionally Bessie would come with a bit of dinner, twice a kiss.

15th January. Eliza and Georgiana not yet summoned down. Eliza preparing to feed that poultry of which the eggs she sells to the housekeeper, then hoarding the money received also from the gardener for the flower-roots, she ties up that money, she would sell her own hair for it, for its security she entrusts it to her mother's keeping with a high interest recorded accurately.

Georgiana on her high stool, artificial flowers and feathers adorning her curls, she commands me as I assist in the cleaning as Bessie's under-nursery-maid not to touch the furniture of those dolls. I was straightening them at the window, now I sit breathing on the frost flowers dissolving to a carriage arriving, it is more the hungry robin who catches my 'vacant attention,' and I am tugging on the window's sash to deliver the crumbs of my breakfast.

Now Bessie is pulling me out of pinafore, scrubbing my face with the coarse towel, for it is I who am being summoned below. I am standing before the breakfast door, so unused to any territory outside the nursery, fearful, who would want me, I tremble. 'What a miserable little poltroon had fear, engendered of unjust punishment, made of me in those days!' Ten minutes of 'agitated hesitation,' neither able to return to nursery or proceed to breakfast room until a bell from the latter clanging now I must enter. Who is it beside Mrs. Reed here I look up at a black pillar appearing to me 'the straight, narrow, sable-clad shape standing erect on the rug.'

Mrs. Reed signals approach; he is asking my age and name and then whether it is I am a good child. Impossible now the affirmative, I am silent. The aunt replies for me the less said on that the better. We shall have some talk then, he sits in a chair drawing me up to him the face of the great nose and mouth, the teeth so prominent! He wants to make sure I know that the wicked go to hell and burn, that I know I must repent ever being the discomfort to a benefactress. Benefactress! Now the Bible, he is wanting to know my fondness for this book. I reply my pleasure is in the Revelations, book of Daniel, and Genesis, and Samuel, bit of Exodus, Kings, and Chronicles, and Job and Jonah. He hopes I like the psalms. No, Sir. Shocking to him. I say they are not interesting.

Proof of a wicked heart! I must pray to God to transform that heart from stone to its flesh. I am wondering on such operation when Mrs. Reed orders me to sit and carries on the conversation herself. She tells this Mr. Brocklehurst she wants my admittance to his Lowood school, but those teachers upon me must keep a strictest eye because I have a tendency to deceit and she wants me in this hearing. Cruel wound for I had always strove to obey, please her strenuously and now heart cut by the accusation in front of a stranger. She can only spoil this 'new phase of existence which she destined me to enter . . . sowing aversion and unkindness along my future path.' Transformed now only to the noxious child.

All liars are in the lake burning with fire and brimstone, yes, the teachers shall watch her. He is assuring: plainness prevails to the point of poverty, habits are hardy, ' "humility is a christian grace" ' as is consistency above all desired by Mrs. Reed. The proof of success of the mortification of worldly pride his daughters remark on the plainness of the Lowood girls acting as though never before had they seen a dress of silk. He leaves but not before handing Jane the Child's Guide recounting the sudden awful death of a child addicted to falsehood and deceit.

Mrs. Reed and Jane are left alone. The silence in which the woman sews becomes the surveillance of her by the child seeing this woman possibly 36 or 37, square-shouldered, strong-limbed, stout not obese, the under-jaw is solid, low brow and eye 'devoid of ruth,' skin opaque with flaxen hair, she runs the household thoroughly, dresses well, is never ill, cleverly manages with an authority only derided at times by her own children, her attire is handsome.

Sting of her words to that mind becoming 'passion of resentment,' her eye on mine and she orders me out, to the nursery, back. I walk to the door, then back across to a window and then right up to her. I must speak a turn of being trodden: speak I am saying if I were deceitful I would say I loved you but I dislike you more than anyone except your son, and this book you may give to your daughter Georgiana for it is she Mrs. Reed who is the liar. Her hands have ceased their sewing, eye of ice upon mine, what more is there I have to say? asks she as though to adult. Shaking throughout, 'thrilled with ungovernerable excitement,' I am telling her she is of no relation, I will never again call her aunt or see her and I will say to any asking it is with the most miserable cruelty she has treated me.

How dare I affirm that, she asks, and oh aunt, how dare? how dare? — you think I have no feelings, that I can do without love, you lacking any pity, you violently thrust me back into a locked red-room though I cried have mercy have mercy aunt Reed, punished because it was your wicked boy struck me for nothing, I will tell all, you are not the good woman yet hard-hearted, *you* are deceitful.

My soul expands in a triumph: 'It seemed as if an invisible bond had burst, and that I had struggled out into unhoped-for liberty.' For that woman has a look frightened, hands raising, rocking herself, her face twists. She wants to know why it is I tremble so violently, would I like some water, she wants to be my friend, she had to correct my faults. '(S)avage high voice' crying deceit is not my fault! She wants me to lie down, for I am passionate, send me to school I say and her murmurs that she indeed will send me to school soon she leaves abruptly.

First Victory. On the rug where Mr. Brocklehurst had stood, victory of my hardest battle yet that it was such an uncontrollable fury now the remorse begins after a short time a silence tells me 'the madness of my conduct, and the dreariness of my hated and hating position.' Aftertaste a vengeance a sensation of poison.

She reaches for the book of tales Arabian does not cease the swimming thoughts, she is walking out toward the ground sequestered the trees silent fir-cones fallen, leaning against a gate into the empty field where there are no sheep feeding, short grass nipped, gray day of an opaque sky, wretched she asks: what shall I do? — what shall I do? — A voice calls: Miss Jane! Where are you? Come to lunch. Once she would have seen as cross this Bessie coming now down the path — naughty thing come when called — yet now she responds more to what in comparison with her brooding seems a cheerfulness; this child is no longer after the breakfast room scene interested in the maid's transitory anger instead heart lightness, come Bessie, don't scold.

This action pleases the maid saying Jane, you should be bolder, you are the ' "little roving, solitary thing." ' Bessie is to cook and prepare her for school, the others are away. No more scolding asks Jane and Bessie responds then of a good girl and do not be afraid, saying that if the child did not start at any sharp speaking, her fear provokes the reprimand. Used to Bessie, not to be afraid of her again, but at school new people to dread yet the maid states if you dread them they'll dislike you. As you Bessie? No Miss, of you I am fonder than the others.

I tell her she does not show it, she calls me the sharp little thing, asks from where comes this new venturesomeness. The scene with Mrs. Reed is what passes through and yet I remain silent on it and Bessie is asking am I glad to be leaving her and believing my response too cool asks for a kiss. Mutual embrace. Comfort of an afternoon until enchanted story of evening, sweet song of hers a delight to me, gleam for the outcast.

After we have spoken out, emergence out in Mr. Lloyd's ear our alterity given voice the stepmother will not hear, not bear, yet adverse she shuts it in. She keeps us out sent into the nursery holding in, isolated yet accessible, outcast available.

Pre-school, we want a language in wanting all we know a blow; a blow to the son's nose, no longer Father's prohibition of that burst of impulse still driven blow to nose when not yet word of school.

We have something she is not ready to have, another perspective of its own temporality, its own spaciality, another perspective would require interlocution she forbids, she wants it out of sight, yet not gone entirely, in reserve, the back-room, nursery after we had burst out of that red-room womb.

She pulls us back in nursery kept only for her desire where there is no mobility, no speaking possible. If she let us out, arranged a move out to school, she would lose the one behind a scarlet covering who had seen the thrusting son within what was blindness, and the one who then negotiated her locked red-room. Desiring through us she cannot let us out, nursery return, rejected as thrown back to a regressed nursery state, just as we had begun to speak of what was damask.

How she desires to see what she cannot see, what is locked away, is how she desires our closeting fears our learning to speak any of it; no word of school though we await day after day, losing all temporal sense, days meld regression.

Living together, we hear her every movement, we are close enough to her and her household to hear all that passes, their daily exercise. Regular sounds mark the day, we know the time by the angle of shadow. She is ever intimate eye adversion-filled has filled us in this nursery place as we stay alone, complying.

Her adversion, the very way she opposes us pulls us further into her hold, her adversion, push of a contrary direction, is what still binds us, antipathetic symbiosis of the nursery now we are living together in close union bonded yet we are in stasis as she is of the holiday animated cheer.

‮§ Obesity. Nursery stay, often for decades, even through the bearing of our own children we stay in the nursery kept. We move our family to be closer to her adversion, her calls arriv-

ing daily to criticize our household managing, we wait for
them. We direct every aspect of our being toward her, toward
her contrary direction, set up crises with her to engage violently; the nursery is where we desire this violent holding
suspension. Not in her body but not separate from it
either. ॐ

Mr. Lloyd's mediation and we have a location even with past, and we
have begun to pass the Reed possessions through us they speak us; we are
stronger, message to that mama we are stronger, lunge back at son. We
send that John Reed running back to his mother. We will no longer carry
him covertly for her. We do not yet know how to speak through John Reed
or see through to his meaning, yet we now hear him speak through us at
her: ' "They are not fit to associate with me." '

They are not fit to associate with me. They have not the fit to associate
with me. We have a past, we have met some family, we see how we are not
of the family, here through John Reed speaking we begin to enunciate
ourselves, extolling ourselves we begin to speak our place in the son's voice,
a grandiose shout declaring our scission from the family.

The shout sends Mrs. Reed reeling. Unmediated action reactions,
Gateshead contiguous acting-out: the stepmother cannot face the daughter
with John Reed speaking through her, cannot meet such speaking scission
in relation. Instead mother in her own fit; mother in her own John Reed
burst. In Gateshead, mother hates the John Reed speaking back of the
daughter as becoming the John Reed force herself.

She is crushing the child beneath her on a nursery crib. Crushing
mother with a mouth distended, daring the child to rise to speak, swirled
the wind whirls holding child under her full blast. Daring child to rise or
utter, stay in place, sit in place, forces her to sit in place, postum sedere,
possession. Mother in her own John Reed burst, where formerly John Reed
through mother's unconscious had possessed the child, when child dares to
face stepmother with the son speaking through, mother is in her own
possession, crushing child on crib.

The nursery is where, after Mr. Lloyd's exercise in language, we have
emerged from her interior chambers a speaking being, yet as yet only
speaking the forces met when possessed in those chambers: we have differentiated out of Mrs. Reed yet not differentiated from her. The nursery is
where we name ourselves separate body yet this body is connected unmediated to hers, crushed beneath hers, a crib place where there is not yet any
space between us though we are no longer within her.

We are crushed beneath her, threatening she bears down upon us. We
witness her release as we are held by it. She who is now the embodiment of

what daily was the son's invasion is on top of the one she has punished for once becoming that embodiment.

Stepmother and daughter bodily unite in the nursery place where John Reed speaks through one while the other incorporates him. Their pact is still his blatant exhibition in a mode purely reactive, Reed, when neither have yet mediated his force through interlocution, with relation necessitating differentiation.

We had called for the Omniscient Father when confined within mother, he lowered to body fit and now he speaks out of us while we are pinned under her. He speaks through us surprising both Mrs. Reed and ourselves: '(I)t seemed as if my tongue pronounced words without my will consenting to their utterance: something spoke out of me over which I had no control.'

The larger spirits who have the purview speak through us to keep her distant from what she is in possession (once her unconscious desire) and how she pins us in place is the embodiment of that which the nursery represents. The nursery is where mother's once unconscious desire becomes more manifest: not to put the child to bed in nursery crib but crush and strangle child there.

John and Mr. Reed are speaking out. We have been with Mr. Lloyd finding some continuity of being, becoming a being, speaking being; when we are no longer within her yet nursery cribbed we are speaking however not initiating. The Reed men speak through us, however still unmediated as we are crushed beneath her, yet this allows a reflection back of them to Mrs. Reed, making her more conscious of precisely what we had to carry in her unconscious.

Making her more conscious of what she was unconscious: the way the Reed forces seized us once her unconscious now these forces speaking at her through us becoming conscious, becoming her conscious seizure of us. Making them less unconscious makes her seizures more conscious. She bodily seizes and crushes us, two bodies becoming one.

We have the son and father speak out of us to her and she crushes us one to her body. The crib scene, unmediated connection to her body, is what subtended the Reed possessions all along, as they had been infiltrating us we originally at base were possessed by her.

On the windowseat and in the red-room, recessed to and into her body chambers, the Reed forces bodily entered us, we became the physicality of them. After Mr. Lloyd's mediation, we emerge from Reed possessions to a speaking conscious being in the nursery, which is to be no longer her interior but not yet differentiated will consenting, which is an intermediate seizure.

The father and son speak out of us when we are her release on the crib which pins us beneath her. When she attaches us bodily we are neither interior nor differentiated she releases herself yet will not release us as the Reed men speak through us back at her.

We experience her so singularly bearing down upon us emphatic voice, she owns us exclusively in her privileged, punitive bind which we hear is actually multiple, constituted by the many voices. For it has been a match of males. John Reed speaking through us becoming corporated by her bursting reprimand to which Mr. Reed also speaks through us. Within this mother's possession is a multiplicity of voices requiring a mediation (narrator) which is not possible as we remain literally under (placed by, possessed by) her.

The father–son explicitly speaking through us without our mediation (consenting will) is also our naiveté in a nursery crib where we are yet premature, even infantile, pinned by her precluding any of our motion or speech. For we have not yet been educated in the ways to speak the father and son, speak to them, and speak through them which is to be in relation to them so their emergence becomes figuratively placed through us, which is different from their speaking us.

After Mr. Lloyd, the possessions become verbal. He placed language at Gateshead, yet he was only an insinuation of, could not himself teach us, mediated relation. The first nursery step of our speaking the forces once unconscious is in the Gateshead contiguous, unmediated mode: they speak through us directly, only way they can have utterance from those rooms.

Through the brief interlocution with Mr. Lloyd, we received some distance from — temporal, spatial, and class perspective to — the Reed family, which became the space for the nascent speaking of what was once only the unconscious of that family. We begin to learn the language of the unconscious forces, and by imparting that in their preliminary speaking through us we are still possessed, placed beneath, unrelated, uneducated in the Gateshead nursery.

Their speaking us (nursery) is a psychological advancement over our embodying them unconsciously and being taken by them (windowseat, red-room); and with their speaking us begins the manifestation in her presence of our continuity of being, self-referential property.

But their speaking us does not serve to differentiate us, pinned beneath bodily union (nursery now), we are not yet speaking ourselves in relation to them yet literalizing their speaking, keeping it in her place, placed by her, which is not to find our place through them, which in fact keeps us further locked in: boxed ear to a Bessie homily.

For we have not been educated in the ways to speak the father and son: what is the language of the drives and the desires of her blood and to us what relation. Instead unmediated we let them have their say through us, word blasting apart from her no mode of differentiation, further pushed in nursery kept.

Mr. Lloyd himself could not perform the operation of the Gateshead extrication. Interstice messenger, first interlocutor, he instructed a speaking, this word of desire becoming desire of school's word. Mr. Lloyd is where we awakened to the possibility of mediating unconscious desires, enunciating figurations.

Mr. Lloyd initiated the possibility of Jane learning to speak for herself yet he does not speak for her. These first blast speakings to Mrs. Reed are not yet her own initiation, yet speaking the literal voices of son and father adds some distance, more separate from the family now, more autonomy she can take her own meals, sleep as she wishes, though as kept.

The naiveté of the nursery regression is also that attempt by Jane to keep the Father and his word above, attempt to use the Father's word to prohibit mother's possession. This attempt also negates the red-room where Father's descent required word enter blood possessions. To attempt to keep Father above (in a post-red-room denial) is to continue to be beneath Mrs. Reed, possessed and further crushed, for the red-room lesson is that the possession is not to be prohibited yet spoken through, finding the configurations of its meaning.

Keeping the Father's word above constitutes a boxed ear, homily to which we realize we have not the ear, cannot listen, has no effect on eyre, keeps us mute requiring a further nursery isolation. Small young coal kindling in the nursery shadows descending.

It is almost completely dark in the room, we have begun tugging the knots of our clothing, undressing. The party continues below as it has every night of this holiday. We sit wide eyed taking in, hearing all yet not wanting to be there for we shirk from that society.

Schism. Her eye adversion filled keeps us out, we would not want to be there, do not want to be in her company anyway, and we hear everything. Two in one home, not speaking, refusing contact as aware acutely of the presence of the other, passionately involved with the antipathetic other absent. This passion of schism is the counterpart of the possession and we have touched her red secrets his word will not prohibit.

Apart as completely engaged. Cleaving to in the cleave apart. She returns us to the nursery where no one is present, return to what attempts a split apart while kept within a monocentric universe, one mother crushing us locked up not within yet not differentiated: schism as the attempt to split apart a unity has us kept, to find relation to multiple voices when a unity is demanded, and our attempt to speak the multiple voices stays within her possession.

   ⟜§ Nursery daze numbness, we do not feel or imagine and
   no ideas here we lose our skin-touch or else we feel a skin

everywhere sinking into layers of the flesh folds. Clouds set in, our eye becomes veiled, a band stretches in our forehead and all is vague, room losing its definition, vision lowers will not be insight yet stops at the eyelash veils. Cloud speak of the nursery in and out of days unmeasured. ৡ

A desire for a Bessie begins yet Bessie is not possible yet. We have our doll, one doll of this monocentric world, on which we dote all our sincere attention; we hold in, we collect, reserve. We eat our meals alone, night after night fed by ourselves, we feed off ourselves.

She is hugging her faded doll before the dying fire. She is collecting and she is silent. What is she doing by the fire night after night with her doll imagined alive? This doll is the one for whom she cares, with whom she sleeps, which soothes her to sleep, tender and 'graven image,' sensually stroked.

When we were confined in her womb redroom womb there was a Father-God above but now we have realized the Omniscient Parent is no longer, now human design, in her nursery our God is in transition, transitional object, non-human to human for we have risen from our unconscious bond nondifferentiation with her, non-human to human shape yet not animated yet imagined alive, doll when the Omniscient Parent with whom we are no longer one has lowered to human and in this start a difference, nursery isolation yet just as kept, intermediate the God is doll, 'graven image.'

> ৳ Graven Image. "Thou shalt not make unto thee any graven image, or any likeness of any thing that is in heaven above, or that is in the earth beneath, or that is in the water under the earth." (Exodus 20:4). "To whom then will ye liken God? or what likeness will ye compare unto him? The workman melteth a graven image, and the goldsmith spreadeth it over with gold, and casteth silver chains. He that is so impoverished that he hath no oblation chooseth a tree that will not rot; he seeketh unto him a cunning workman to prepare a graven image, that shall not be moved." (Isiah 40:18-20). "Behold the voice of the cry of the daughter of my people because of them that dwell in a far country: Is not the Lord in Zion? is not her king in her? Why have they provoked me to anger with their graven images, and with strange vanities?" (Jeremiah 8:19). "Every man is brutish in his knowledge: every founder is confounded by the graven image: for his molten image is falsehood, and there is no breath in them." (Jeremiah 10:14). ৡ

93

What is she doing by the fire night after night with her doll imagined alive? This doll is the one for whom she cares, with whom she sleeps, which soothes her to sleep, tender and 'graven image,' sensually stroked. She is tucking this one in the nightgown's folds, she wants the cloth child to be happy, sleep well, the tucking evoking a kindness in mothering herself. She is preparing, this sincere doting on her doll, for a better mothering, human mothering.

This practice for a better mothering, what soothes her is how she can be a better (human) mother of this doll extension of herself than how she has been mothered, is her also receiving a better mothering. By the fire nightly with this doll, she stores. Unconscious storing, unconscious holding itself, doll imagined alive is her happiness protected and in reserve. She is regressed to a place not of the holiday world. She sits still in the shadows, autoerotic.

Doll of the intermediate nursery place: not where interior is exterior yet the transitional place of learning what is not subjective and where we are no longer fused within the mother's body is the doll which can stand for something else, what soothes continually persevering, and as such is the possibility of figuration, mediating function, extension of ourselves yet not inner not outer, potential relation to mother differentiated. (Only potential for standing for something else since it is the nursery where she is kept and possesses her doll as she is kept.)

Bessie arrives occasionally with bun, not scolding. The better mothering evoked has summoned this maid yet only occasionally. Bessie begins to arrive in this nursery place of pause between the fits, silent resting place, where we are ever aged as regressed, alone in bed, no God above as when we were at one in mother, instead doll in nightgown folds.

There is no Bessie story in the nursery because we have not found the new way of speaking the unspeakable regions where we have been and have not yet found the way out of the place demanding we not speak.

Who appears externally, who goes downstairs when the rejected child is nursery shut, are Eliza and Georgiana, split sisters. Ringlets and muslin they proceed into that world of the ladies and gentlemen. Extreme offshoots of a Mrs. Reed self-sufficiency: they care for themselves yet only on the surface.

Eliza withholds, hugging profits closely to her chest. Stingy, she holds back. Nothing gets out of hand. Anxiously every penny marked she tabulates her accounts, would sell her hair to better them. Georgiana is sitting a decoration of elaborate curls with the artificial flowers brought out of an attic's chest. She gives out. Effusive side of costume and drama, she performs, an acting-out.

Literal sisters often split into Eliza and Georgiana as distinct expressions of some attempt to cleave when one is most nursery bound. Also one person splits into these two when most shut inside the nursery: using Georgiana to flaunt for an attention sorely needed but then we must reserve, hold back, withhold, repress, here is Eliza to warn and scrutinize and we never can let go in feeling, never fully greet another. This enticing woman carrying the split-sisters flickering, we are intrigued, as much as we go forward into the attraction, adorning feather, we are reduced, held back, accounts tabulated.

Eliza and Georgiana are external manifestations of the one who has not yet traversed through the mother who runs the household. They accompany one another, are sisterly cycles, and at the base of them, that to which each spirals down, here is the nursery child sitting still pinned down as alone.

Hungry sisters Eliza and Georgiana each in their way hungry. No mother to feed us while kept in Mrs. Reed's nursery, no "breast" outside for a feeding, we are in the recesses of her possession as one body so to be fed by her is to feed off ourselves, kept inside regressed no feeding from without possible.

Our schism with Mrs. Reed is the other side of her possession of us requiring we cleave into the worldly "false selves," Georgiana and Eliza, either giving out for a bite or hoarding what resources there are, hungry split sisters. They occur when we are in the nursery crushed by mother not fed from without.

Eliza and Georgiana are Mrs. Reed's daughters. Each ostentacious in her way, daughters of a mother petrified of insight. Their mother will not look in the nursery, refuses all interior, invested in surface. Surface daughters, daughters who emerge to the surface self-sufficiently repress and act-out while widow mother keeps inferior child shut-up, repressed as acting-out.

The nursery temptation is to continue feeding on ourselves which becomes an overextended feeding out to others. We dote on our doll, feed the robin, become the under nursery-maid tidying up others' affairs while shut in.

Overextended giving, sign of being pinned beneath her in a nursery, feeding on ourselves as off of others. Inherent in such overgiving is the cruelty interlacing Mrs. Reed's treatment of Jane: to feed out indiscriminately is to feed ourselves the delusion of doing good, giving to others as an indulging of an autoerotic self, indiscriminate love contains a cruelty homologous to the cruelty of Mrs. Reed locking child's interiority.

We are vacant in such overgiving, vacant attention, breath on frost flower melting a carriage drives through what was frost flower we do not notice, let it steam vacant attention, we do not notice the carriage driving up, habitually we are feeding out and feeding on ourselves only.

Our loyalty to this nursery possession by her is our vacant attention out of which arrives the black carriage to which we do not pay attention. Sitting in a vacant attention we see a little hungry robin and begin feeding it the breakfast crumbs. We were not expecting a carriage arriving when we are most vacant, completely subservient in a nursery possession for which there is no enunciation since kept too close. At first we do not know we are being summoned out.

Afraid to leave, terrified of that which awaits outside, other rooms now abysmal. We would rather stay inside her possession preferable, the days of their own regularity, we sensed her in our every pore we prefer to stay under afterall, pace at the breakfast door questioning this call.

'What a miserable little poltroon . . .' The narrator's exclamation arrives in the midst of Jane's 'agitated hesitation' at the breakfast-room door. Crushed on crib we become craven. To open the breakfast-room door, to announce ourself as the one summoned, to announce in a breakfast-room entry is not to be poltroon. Threshold at breakfast-room door evokes narrator's exclamation, what will acquire the narrative voice, out of her possession with perspective, needs to go through the breakfast-room door threshold.

What summons us out of the nursery, rings for us through even our trepidation to leave that place, is mother's black pillar. '(S)traight, narrow, sable-clad shape standing erect on the rug.' Here is the call by mother through an erection, the 'stony stranger' who measures and compares, evaluates critically.

He looms over us yet is within reach, pulls us forward within his reach, his features are prominent, he places us in front of him, eye to eye. He scrutinizes, he questions our moral standing: are we the good child?

He stands erect for a differentiation through opposition. Good or not. Good or not, differentiate ourselves through speaking in front of mother he stands for erecting opposition he will pass judgment. The first opportunity at interlocution in mother's presence comes through her black pillar. He distances us through a scrutiny opposition questioning of enough distance so we finally can speak in front of her.

Morality standing good or not who are we, morality differentiates us out of the nursery numbness. Morality as the rudimentary opposition following, relieving, possession.

Through Jane the Reed forces spoke back to that stepmother, a biting back more than mutual speaking, biting when interlocution not yet possible, as an attempt to find a mother without, vital connection without herself. Biting-back stepmother shut Jane further nursery isolation as it also provoked this rigid black and white oppositional response from stepmother.

When we first dare to "bite" back at mother, she "reacts moralistically." Brocklehurst arrives.

He is not here for Eliza and Georgiana, only Jane has gone to the chambers of mother's unconscious to hear of hell judgment. Evil is the child who has been possessed in mother's unconscious, intimately knowing its windowseat, red-room, nursery.

We have witnessed a multiplicity of voices there, contradictions, the red-room descent and not just mother but daughter received his penetration, also the father with access to two wombs in one. Antipathetic symbiotic and incestuous family has shattered family necessitating heterogeneity of desire, how we are not of the family our desires impart when a black pillar speaks monotheistically all else evil constituting single frame of reference yet we have witnessed multiplicity.

Brocklehurst is the ability to rebound through the violence of rejection (interlacing fusion) to a beginning self-referential enunciation in Mrs. Reed's presence. Through his oppositional viewpoint we stand distant enough from Reed, distance out of nursery bind allowing now enunciation.

His is a test of hell, does she know the effects of wickedness in an afterlife? Unlike the Reed forces, he is grounded, columnar, asking her to speak herself up to some grounded pillar of strength no longer craven.

We provide the way for mother's moralistic black pillar when we have been poltroon in the nursery so long that we cannot say we have an inherent good. Brocklehurst bears down questions on whether she is a good child and Jane cannot answer affirmatively.

Her inability to speak her inherent worth in front of Mrs. Reed indicates how she is still possessed (evil) and this constitutes a black pillar emerging from an intense fear of the stepmother's contrary view. Jane has resided within aunt's contrary view, which was the aunt's adversion to Jane's alterity, more than Jane has resided in her own alterity: what of an inherent good makes her alter. Her fear of Mrs. Reed's contrary view when she is addressed as finally someone other provokes the Brocklehurst moralistic black pillar.

Jane cannot stand for herself contrary opinion in front of this mother, will not betray the view of the harsh mother which is to not betray the possession: all words must be returned to the ownership of that mother. Out of her loyalty to possession emerges Brocklehurst's assertion of the child's wickedness, hell's fire awaiting.

    ◄§ "For with priests *everything* becomes more dangerous, not only cures and remedies, but also arrogance, revenge, acuteness, profligacy, love, lust to rule, virtue, disease — but it is only fair to add that it was on the soil of this *essentially danger-ous* form of human existence, the priestly form, that man first became an *interesting animal*, that only here did the human soul in a higher sense acquire *depth* and become *evil*—and these are the two basic respects in which man has hitherto been superior to other beasts!" Nietzsche ৡ

Hell is what comes when we will not begin, have not consenting will begun, a differentiation within the recess of mother's possession. He lectures us on hell. His teeth are prominent, he bites back. The child attempts to stand up to his prominent feature in opinion, through opinion she can begin to state a difference in things not of herself: in her view, the psalms are not interesting.

Black pillar, here is not a Mr. Lloyd mediation, for this one in Mrs. Reed's presence, brought in by her to interview us, has not arrived to hear what Jane has to say. Monocentric, univocal, in asking her the biblical preference, he wants a special answer.

He requires a special answer in a paternal authority, yet we have become heretic. For we have been through the red-room, now heretic, Father's Law weakened a descent to body blooded word, rent strings heterogeneous heart, no unified doctrine of Psalms to a Father's Love, yet multiple configurations of revelations, dreams of Daniel, serpent of genesis desires.

No Father authority unified doctrine and mother's retaliation now a patriarchal black pillar, speaking on hell, pronouncing the child's heart as stone. Black and white, his monocentric desire to fit another into a cast already set, he does not bend.

When we have been locked in mother's nursery too long we turn to stone, we petrify, a rigidity sets in, we get critical, controlling, see something according only to its measure erection, we compare and we compete.

Brocklehurst is the resort to opinion when we cannot stand for our worth and he is the (only) way we can converse with the stepmother. We are shaky, symbiotic fidelity we have believed her more, and the only way we can speak in her presence is through opinion, sounding like the stony stranger. We do not know who we are outside the nursery yet we know the psalms are not interesting.

We collect who we are by proclaiming our opinion when speaking to Brocklehurst in the presence of Mrs. Reed. Here is a beginning differentiation, assertion of our difference, within her recess. His critical distance, oppositionalism, morality judgments, and monocentric thinking are necessary for eventual differentiation out of the nursery first being spoken as opinion.

The woman is speaking forth her opinions emerging charged and focused, pointing and darting. She is opinionated. Beneath is a nursery child never before speaking through the recess and petrified of entering any other room in the house. Within each opinion here a secret kernel of who we are in what is our individual drama: the one who is drawn to Revelations and Daniel differs psychically from those preferring the Psalms.

      Critic Ordeal. Severely he speaks of universal punishment. Knowing only his own principles and opinion, his own direction, he is hard. Never relocating at another's stance, he installs the other in front of him, desiring a correct answer. He arrives rigid columnar out of a vacancy. His speaking is an interview for leaving the nursery. Our mother is ordering the exact folding of our clothes in a drawer. We tuck in the corners of our bed at the precise angle, insure the lines on our socks are completely parallel, we tell the younger siblings the prayer must be learned by the morning or else they will be in a hell of fire. At the first communion, we are posing in the white dress starched. We do not move or smile, not wanting to wrinkle dress or face in any manner. The sun tearing beneath our clothing provokes a sweating. We stand perfectly still and straight staring into that sun, daring its further advance, attempting not to blink.

The mother is alone, untouched, not spoken to. Her own vacancy becoming so vast she seizes and crushes the child beneath her. That one bursts with the pressure of what the mother will not have or see to which she will not speak, child stored further in a nursery until the numbness a vacancy through which mother calls him. He is erect and formal. Critical distance. Prominent, he speaks of universal punishment.

      Mrs. Reed, in abandoning you, the father of spirit left you much to carry, and where is your mother to buffer you from this anxiety the dust rising a household to mend, to manage? Your children ridicule and scorn, no solace back, to whom do you speak? I have stayed in your backroom for long but your pillar drew me to this encounter of intimacy drawn close 'square and straight before him' I too erect as distant to him as I have been possessed by you.

The critical distance he demands in drawing Jane close to his prominent feature is the distance required for any interlocution with Mrs. Reed. No speaking is possible in seizure, when we are symbiotic antipathetic one body feeding off of or becoming another precluding all speech. No speaking possible on the windowseat, in the red-room, in the nursery, each in their own way a seizure, yet in the breakfast-room his distancing criticism the beginning interlocution with Mrs. Reed necessitates.

Wicked is how we are proclaimed different. Jane is pronounced critically different through her wicked heart. Not only a bad child yet wicked, evil, headed toward fire and brimstone. Evil as possession in a mother's unconscious perceived from without, that place where we are carrying the unconscious finally perceived by conscious perspective (he is grounded in conscious reality, is pillar) becomes evil.

Evil is that moment we have taken a step differentiating ourselves within her home, have even considered leaving it, are being interviewed for leaving it, and the possibility of differentiation becomes a proclamation that we are evil.

Evil is the moment that the unnameable, numinous forces of recess come face to face with, become interviewed by, a conscious perspective, pillar of righteousness, when it is now right to have conscious perspective, even one monocentric, as we are delineating a continuity of being, we bring the places we have been kept to a breakfast-room speaking (breaking the fast of how we were kept unconscious) and what is upright condemns our marginal existence calling it evil.

Brocklehurst as black pillar, firmly grounded, emerging from the ground, thrusting up to heights while having a base at the blackness below ground he looks down from his conscious perspective righteously into the black hole the child has been kept he sees black holes her eyes to eye of his mouth proclaiming her evil.

Still not to extricate completely from that stepmother: Brocklehurst in a first speaking interview for leaving the nursery proclaims Jane wicked while Mrs. Reed places the curse preventing any of Jane's further speaking by making it lie.

Brocklehurst cuts the child out of nursery haze as stepmother provides the curse through which she must follow the child to any other life. Curse is what guarentees the schooling be differentiation within an unconscious also mother's not as a complete extrication from it.

Stepmother's curse is that child lies, that the red-room occurrence was a lie, that Father's word did not descend seizing body, that body with its blood rhythm desire cannot begin to speak its word will lie.

Brocklehurst is the witness to the accusation that the child lies since his authority must judge from an omniscience, proclaiming word of God as above. Brocklehurst is the authority through which Mrs. Reed speaks denouncing (denying) the child's vision that the Father's authority, word as Law, fell, crashed into body.

That body with its blood rhythm desire cannot begin to speak its word will lie, is also his proclamation that heart is stone. The stone heart has no strings for her to rend the red-room seizure was false anyway.

Stepmother dictates through Brocklehurst that interlocution with the child is aborted, possible only speaking at child as lecture, contemptuous accusation, homily. Bessie's homily followed the bed-crushing scene, it was the verbal analogy to that seizure, and Brocklehurst in effect continues it. When who was unconscious finally begins speaking, the fear of its eccentric and numinous property, for what if the unconscious depths spoke, this fear will not let it have its say, calls it evil, a lie, will let it in the breakfast-room by questioning it only talks at it.

They will let her out of the nursery only by insuring she will not speak from the heart of the matter, heart of unconscious regions must not be a speaking heart; what is the heart of being with shades, ghosts, imps, where is the language of our blood desire in those (unconscious) regions? They proclaim nothing speaks through a heart of stone.

Brocklehurst talks at the child and within his ministerial condemnation arrives stepmother's accusation which 'cuts' the child to the heart.

Curse is her desire of our heart, she is in our heart, rending its strings still, cutting us to it demanding we see it in this exposure of our marginal existence, she knows the direction to our heart and can cut right to it, heart leaving her must remain with her in part, her curse that we must not let her go as we go through her.

Jane's survey of Mrs. Reed's person, after Brocklehurst leaves, is the result of the Brocklehurst (morality) differentiation. After Brocklehurst speaks and leaves, Jane has enough distance for the first time to see her aunt, her body, her physiognomy, the way she dresses and manages the household, seen with an objectivity not before possible.

Objectively we look, we set her before us, throw her against ourselves, throw her into the opposition Brocklehurst dictated. His black/white focus gives a distance she is far enough, we can throw to her in what is distance, we pace it to insure, there is a space between us, not beneath one body yet two bodies and one is pacing back and forth to the other bringing her up before, objective stance, we walk it.

We are looking this stepmother over for the first time, her features of a solidity, firm stature, not a softness the jaw hard. Once she sees we have enough distance, we are even walking it, enough distance to set her before us, objectify, she immediately orders us back to the nursery, rejecting. She will not let us view her apart, signifying the loss of who knows what lay behind the scarlet curtain she cannot keep us unconscious desire if we are viewing her this way objectively.

Her order his authority, we will not be influenced by his authority for we felt its lowering in the red-room and now there is more to say and she looks strong enough.

We speak back when Brocklehurst is no longer in the room yet his morality judgment has begun a self-referential differentiation in her presence which the nursery of her order would occlude. He has shown us how cruelty spoken is a way to differentiate where we have been, who we are within her mansion. It takes a cruelty speaking resentment which is a passion.

Passion of resentment. Animosity. Passion of animated forces of her rejection. In her throwing us back to an original state as if unanimated, her male forces have animated us, John Reed, Mr. Reed, Brocklehurst, where we were no one, lost as possessed nobody on the windowseat, red-room, nursery regressed. Her animus spirits have animated us to this passion we speak now a cruelty back.

Our passion of resentment that she runs the entire household but has lost her appetite to the unconscious blastings of a son, preference to pillar authority; how we have been forgotten in her fold she then reaches us through the folds with that sharp-pointed that large-toothed black and white he is righteously cruel her aim through our numbness in which we had been going under cuts to our heart.

The stepmother's attempt to send Jane back to the earlier state, the rejection to a nursery, is spoken with an 'extreme, though suppressed irritation.' The rejection, being thrown back to the earlier, original place, always has been interlaced with a suppressed irritation which now becomes extreme in the breakfast-room. When we have some distance we walk it to insure we are not her irritation suppressed instead we passionately speak our own resentment.

To speak the passion of the resentment, her resentment of our passion also hers which she locked up, for which she locked us up, is not to return to the nursery. Nursery return is the locked up passion which accompanies her resentment; locks up the way passion is also resentment. To speak back the passionate resentment implicit in her possessions of us is not equivalent to the possessions speaking us.

We take off from Brocklehurst's monocentrism giving her back a self-referential comparison. Discrimination through comparison: Jane dislikes Mrs. Reed more than anyone except John, and Georgiana not Jane is a liar. Differentiation within her recess, passionately speaking dislike of her mansion, cruelly incisive, Jane cuts apart.

We erect ourselves through comparison speaking dislike. What more do we have to say, her ice eye upon ours, asking as to an adult for we have earned this right to speak back to her, negotiating her unconscious forces, grown to an age speaking ourself in comparison; Mr. Lloyd had provided for our speaking saying we were no longer baby, no longer fused, now we fire back.

'That eye of hers, that voice, stirred every antipathy I had.' Our pathos, our suffering, how we have endured in her keeping, suffered, suffer, passio, passus, our passions are turned against her, antipathy, we release the passion against her that we had been keeping locked up for her.

Passionate declaration of our righteousness, her wrongness, after we have obtained the Brocklehurst oppositional distance we have alterity, we are differentiating an erect being apart from hers, to whom she is no relation. We are so different we will never visit yet will speak of her cruel treatment.

We differentiate ourselves in Mrs. Reed's presence through antipathy, when we speak with the passion she had once locked up with a violence. Speaking differentiated saying we have feeling needing love whereas she does not have a pity, instead rough and violent thrusts, no mercy, thrust into the red-room without pity when her wicked son knocked us ' "down for nothing." '

We are shaking with the passion to which her rejection sent us back as we tell her she does not relate those passions suppressed in her lack of relation we express.

We passionately speak back the possessions, red-room, John Reed's knock, differentiating who we were in them even when we were nothing is to be no longer possessed. Jane is finding the narrative of what was once fit and rampant seizure, locating the images and metaphor of Gateshead events. She is beginning a mediation of her own Gateshead history which is the extrication from Gateshead.

First she declares herself apart and then she tells the story of her relation to the place: where she fits into the Gateshead plot, even as a nothing, knocked down for nothing. By finding the ' "exact tale" ' of the Gateshead figures and her place there, she finds too the metaphor of the tale: a heart of feeling differentiating herself primarily from the aunt's hard heart.

The aunt's curse cut to the heart and locating this heart in the tale and differentiating it from the heart of the aunt is the final move out, a heart of feeling is not a hard heart: Jane delivers herself by finding her unique heart of the tale. She does not speak directly from the unconscious places (windowseat, red-room, nursery) where she had been, yet speaks through them from a feeling heart, enough mediation in the Gateshead place, differs enough from the Gateshead mode of contiguity and acting-out to extricate her from that mansion and its family.

Their hearts differ, they are no longer fused, Jane not confined in recesses only unconscious, a heart beats passion through resentment, feels and feels differently.

Brocklehurst provides the manner of first speaking back to the aunt. One-sided, more as lecture, Jane uses his accusatory condemnation and monocentric position to refer to her own goodness and from a distance judge the aunt as cruel and hard-hearted saying she will retaliate by a public speaking of the tale. The text Brocklehurst left with her is a public account of the sudden death of a child ' "addicted to falsehood and deceit." ' The Brocklehurst mode publicizes and that is his form of severance; words as weapon, images of our tale slices us apart from her, we see her objectively and have narrator perspective, potentially publicized, our narrative slices us apart.

> ◆§ Mrs. Reed, your acute brow arched eye of ice, you have thrown me back to the weapon which finally turns on you, becomes the speaking you nursery silenced, rigid weapon of righteousness, columnar speaking hell fires. I face you and the speaking fires out, I am shaking uncontrollably you say violently, offering me a cooling of water, a rest, for I stand at a distance to burst that bond with the claim of my goodness, narrow and straight pillar of excellence, weapon of a military right, I pronounce myself as against all you are. Together we are shaking the passion you resented. Mrs. Reed, you have twisted: contorted face, hands no longer in their duty have risen to this trembling. Your own curse has carried me to this encounter I aim for your chest the heart is stone I will disengage this reddening blast each of its particles stinging every wall of your solid mansion. Black columnar one has us both now, returning to you the Brocklehurstian curse, I challenge you to this red and black this violent and critical intimacy, but you do not sit in it. You leave the room abruptly which is my move beyond your need is stone heart without releasing what curses us both. ଛ

Speaking as Brocklehurst is different than speaking as the others because here there is a distance (this possession afterall is not by a Reed and follows Mr. Lloyd's human mediation) so we are not in her back-room recess yet standing full view in the daily breakfast chamber. The Brocklehurst possession is a way to differentiate Jane's qualities from those of Mrs. Reed's, in a moralistic and oppositional manner the extremity of which is proportional to the pull of the nursery bind. Brocklehurst pertains to articulated differentiation within the premises, quality comparison to her face, not a move outside, which the earlier possessions by Reed forces more were attempting.

The result of differentiation within her premises, how qualitatively their hearts differ, is severance. Jane's passionate statement differentiates yet the soul exults *as if* an invisible bond had burst.

Jane has said it is the other woman who has treated her cruelly, she claims she will never call the woman aunt, says she is no relation. Jane is saying she will live a lie here and in this sense she is caught already by the aunt's curse, fulfilling it by vowing to speak the lie that Mrs. Reed is not her aunt which is not to see her own relation to the aunt's deceit which is herself to be deceitful.

As if an invisible bond had burst: we think we have broken from the stepmother through our blast back which actually is to fulfill her curse remaining with her. If we are no relation to Mrs. Reed then we have not been in her red-room, not witness to scarlet locked secrets also our own, and that word once Father's authority has not descended to this blood chamber, ours as hers, which is to say the red-room incident did not happen which is to lie.

To blast back Mrs. Reed, reverse of homily of crushed crib nursery bind, is not to speak through unconscious forces, figuratively place them and their desire (since Brocklehurst is still a possession as were the Reeds), yet it does serve to extricate us to go to school to learn such speaking, a discourse of what is recess.

After the beginning interlocution of Mr. Lloyd's visit, the possessions began to speak through for our benefit, some person began constituting resulting in Brocklehurst's moralistic critical distance affecting a self-referential speaking of narrative, a heart violently differentiated with a passion once suppressed by her rejections.

To show the stepmother back the passion she has used us to repress, which is her cruelty, her stone heart, is to break out of her nursery finally stand exterior to her.

The discharge of our speaking back the once suppressed passions, each of us trembling, makes explicit the incest base of all her possessions. Learning the language of her "animus" forces, negotiating them, and directing their words literally back to her strips us to the scene of the essential fusion underlying them all, now not as baby, we reflect back to her this passion is one incestuous.

Brocklehurst's chastening implicates Jane's unchaste nature, her unchastity, in-chaste, incestus, incestuous. For in each of the possessions there had been a familial incest: with John Reed, with Mr. Reed, and it is in regard to them that Mr. Brocklehurst is summoned to corrent, chasten her.

When we take on the Brocklehurst mode we make explicit, demonstrate as well as condemn, the incest implicit between us. We have the distance to afford an articulation of the passionate resentment within fusion, now as if adult to adult but not, is incest. Incest spoken now public statement releasing us.

To demonstrate the passion once implicit in Mrs. Reed's unconscious, make her face it, is to make visible the un-chaste bond, antipathetic symbiotic. To break out is to threaten a publicity: for if we speak it even in condensation we are no longer one with her unconscious, not locked up, and can move out to school. Yet as we have been Brocklehurst possessed throughout our demonstration, we are still possessed by her, the severance is cursed, severance without releasing us entirely, as if.

Mrs. Reed's inability to respond to Jane's speaking is how the education of interlocution and differentiation is precluded in that mansion, their exchange still unmediated.

The woman is no longer stone, she rocks, she shakes, the twists even placates, says ' "there's a dear." ' Where once an eye of ice she now offers water to the 'lighted heath' burning before her she will not have it tremble through her too and her need to douse it, put it to rest, is also her need to keep Jane in scarlet recess locked to a nursery numbness, which is the aunt's abrupt leavetaking as Jane is passionate and says she will make the tale public.

'(A)s if an invisible bond had burst,' for a time we think ourselves free from her entirely.

> ◆§ Brocklehurstian victory. On the rug where he had stood,
> 'conqueror's solitude.' Victory as if bond had burst with her
> we carry the black pillar out all the while believing we have
> severed from her we hate. Our invisible bond as if burst
> becomes invisible union with her severity, a passionate criti-
> cal exchange taking the form of a tidy arrogance: obsessional
> qualities of a rigid nature, superior moralizing of other's
> indulgence, a fixed view preached to others who must con-
> form while our eyebrow raises. §◆

'(A)s if an invisible bond had burst.' What has broken is the antipathetic symbiosis resulting from fusion with the mother's body, the Gateshead contiguous and unmediated mode of connection, which permits our leave-taking of Gateshead.

She sends us off because she cannot stand this reflection back to her of the incestuous nature of our passionate resentment, its breakfast-room statement.

The ridge once lighted and alive is burnt, the possessions pass, 'same ridge, black and blasted' now the 'dreariness of my hated and hating position.' What was blasting, even intoxicating, now after-flavour as of wine, corrodes, as if poisoned. Black and blasted, hated position, poisoned, a cruelty here, evidence of what cruelty the windowseat, red-room and nursery concealed. Within the fusion has been a cruelty which this attempt at interlocution with Mrs. Reed made manifest, is now our poison.

The cruelty of antipathetic symbiosis is that the passion is subtended by an inherent violence and there is no relation. The connection remains essentially unmediated, possessing, defying meaning, cruel, crudelis, crudus, crude, undigested, not brought to a form to give nourishment, unripe, immature, incestuous.

The passion of antipathetic symbiosis is unripe, immature, cannot be digested, is too immediately an infiltration and then release, cannot be mediated to provide nourishment. The passion of antipathetic symbiosis is unripe, crude, contains a cruelty, even violence, which has not been mediated in relation.

The threat of a public speaking does not mediate the cruelty of Mrs. Reed's passion yet it does announce it in a way she can no longer remain unconscious of it and unconscious of Jane's relation to it. What was implicit in the Gateshead corners manifests through narration (as well as its threat) and moves Jane out.

We have blasted back, we have returned the blast, one-sided discharge demonstrating incest and what arrives is a displeasure. Victory pyrrhic, the heat of the passionate condemnation opens to a spaciousness soon becoming depletion, gray day, empty field.

For the Brocklehurst discharge was one-sided, has not taught us relation, now the depletion where nothing feeds and 'the black frost reigned.'

'(B)lack frost,' the frost was once flower, frost flowers of a nursery through which a black carriage drove, we know him now and what reigns is black frost, 'where no sheep were feeding, where the short grass was nipped and blanched.'

The depletion where nothing feeds, from once overfeeding out indiscriminately now nothing feeds, nothing to feed, depletion. In a sense, Jane experiences the effect of her own "evil" here. The mode of righteous and doctrinal defense which can be hell and which she herself has fired out is her gray day realization of the evil of her Brocklehurst possession now nothing within or without.

The elation of the as-if-burst-bond after the Brocklehurst encounter becomes remorse. Fires of hell through the black pillar have blasted back upon the red-room tyrannies, a way out. Lesson of the gray field is that one must not stop there.

Nothing feeds here she stares into the wintry field. It would be easy to slide back into the nursery bond invisibly ever more. She was our only intimacy. Speaking to and from Brocklehurst has cleared out a space, no longer possessed by, exterior to forces of a mother's fusion, is the gray field of an open question.

Here the nipped grass and stiffened leaf is why we remain bonded a lifetime with mother's invisible, absorbing the red and black possessions. Fearful of the vastness permeating hollowness of the gray field outside the nursery bind, we return to the nursery to feed on ourselves, staying home alone trapped eating more, becoming sloppy, becoming confused an unhealthily fatter ever invisible fusion with stepmother.

Gray field shadows differ considerably from those of the nursery. Both are places of stasis, yet the question echoing the gray field — What shall I do? — never emerged in the nursery where there was no initiating I.

Gray field contains a question positing Jane's existence apart from the blastings of mother's possessions. That she exists and has a fate within which she is an initiating figure is the gray day question never reaching the nursery in which "I" was doll and bed and clothes knotted and the nursery itself as mother's kept doll knotted.

After the immolations, we have been blasted and blast back a constitution of some "I," many run back to the nursery saying it was never meant.

Instead Jane stands, 'a wretched child enough,' asking the question now incantation — What shall I do? — and a voice (return) calls. First exterior to mother's body, and no longer pinned beneath or kept by it, outside the mansion, it takes a call and gray field listening, now a being continuous eyre hearing the calling.

The question (What shall I do?) announces the possibility of interior reflection which was impossible inside Gateshead when we were fused with the interior without the distance necessary for the perspective of reflection. Enough gray space distance now on stepmother's property to allow various perspectives introducing the possibility of interior interlocution establishing a questioning "I." The potential interior dialogue, nascent reflection, occurs while she stands upon her first exterior space at Gateshead and in this place Bessie's calling indicates school.

Sequestered part of the plantation with its silent trees, she is called again in a recess yet here is the first recess not within or kept beneath the mother, external to and removed from her though on her grounds. It is Bessie; the call is for lunch. Why doesn't the naughty child come when called?

Bessie is who has done the homily and now Jane can go forward to meet the maid's 'transitory anger.' After conversing with Brocklehurst in the mother's presence, Jane is less susceptible to the moralistic scolding from without. She embraces Bessie's scold; holding her arms out where formerly she would have cowered while projecting an attack. Now Jane's response is 'frank and fearless'; it pleases Bessie.

We are beginning to see through the unmediated forms of cruel passion, seeing through to the black and blasted ridge, corroded after-flavour. Bessie and Jane talk about the scolding, mediate it, analyze its meaning.

Some multiple vision accrues: ' "And won't you be sorry to leave poor Bessie?" ' the maid asks as if asking for poor Bessie, for that one who is poor Bessie to Jane. Jane replies, ' "What does Bessie care for me? She is always scolding me." ' Jane asks a question to Bessie about a third person who is also Bessie. She sees Bessie triply; here they see through Bessie's scolding arriving at three Bessies: the Bessie who is standing in front of her who is and who is not poor Bessie who is and who is not the Bessie who scolds.

Likewise, Bessie has multiple vision: she sees that Jane's lot at Gateshead is objectively difficult (that the child is ' "put upon," ' and Bessie uses her mother's perspective here, so her concerned mothering aspect sees Jane this way), but also that Jane provokes the abuse in subtle ways by her fearfulness and projection.

The dialogue between Jane and Bessie occurs when there is enough gray space for each to differentiate the other's (heterogeneous) qualities, which is analysis and which is fondness.

The dialogue also suggests that Jane is gaining perspective on the scolding one who also holds in place [And won't you be sorry to leave . . .] who is also poor, she is beginning to see through the contradictions within antipathetic symbiosis.

Bessie sees through her own scolding saying she scolds because Jane is a ' "queer, frightened, shy little thing" ' who should be bolder; and at the same time she actually is most fond of Jane than anyone.

Sometimes we are sent or we choose hard ones to make us bolder. ' "(V)enturesome and hardy," ' after the Brocklehurstian Mrs. Reed scene, Bessie notices it and it mitigates her need to scold.

When Bessie asks Jane what affected her becoming more steadfast and bold, the image emerges of the recent scene with Mrs. Reed at Brocklehurst's departure. Narrating the cruelty passionately which has been bound in fusion makes us bolder, external to it and we can remain silent on it.

Bessie calls in the gray field at the first trace of an initiating "I" to tell Jane that she is to pack for school. Jane had to speak her way out of Gateshead, each rebound from the violent rejections within the fusion with Mrs. Reed constituting an "I" serving severance. "I" comes with discerning in relation to another the heterogeneous qualities once unconscious.

At each step of Jane's negotiation of the Gateshead possessions, constituting herself bolder, Mrs. Reed loosens. As the possessions spoke through her back at that mother they affected Mrs. Reed: John Reed's voice grandiose proclamation ' "they are not fit to associate with me" ' had Mrs. Reed a twirling whirlwind; Mr. Reed's voice booming out an omniscience and that stepmother's composed eye became troubled with fear; a Brocklehurstian threat of public condemnation and the stepmother trembled to a placation.

At each negotiation of her unconscious forces we delineated more firmly our alterity, becoming differentiated, hardier and more embodied, while parts of that mother loosened, a trembling, allowing some sequestered gray space to open to better aspects of mothering.

Now the maid who used to scold sees through her scolding with the help of a concerned mother. The maid who used to scold in synchrony with the Mrs. Reed tyranny has softened, wants us softer, not as cool, asks for a kiss, is not afraid of our warmth. Mutual embrace allowing a departure of this Gateshead family, within this embrace is packing and departure, not possession.

Consensual embrace is not to remain in Gateshead where connection was antipathetic symbiosis, unmediated confinement and discharge. Interlocution, mutual exchange allowing the seeing through of one another's perspective, not one blasting followed by another, when the maid who used to scold in synchrony with the Mrs. Reed tyranny softens, mediates and enters the child's side as benign. The result is the pleasures, song and cake, enchanted story.

We begin reversing with the stepmother, obtaining the distance to face and finally speak to her, discharging yet a beginning speaking of an initiating "I" opening a space for mediating the annihilating and moralistic forces claiming her also our own. We do not know how figuratively to impart in life these forces yet. Awkwardly, we move through them to separate from her mansion to go to school and learn what she could not.

Bibliography

Cowan, Lyn. *Masochism: A Jungian View*. Dallas: Spring Publications, 1982.

Guntrip, Harry. *Schizoid Phenomena, Object Relations and the Self*. New York: International Universities Press, 1969.

Hall, Radclyffe. *The Unlit Lamp*. New York: The Dial Press, 1981.

Hillman, James. "Schism as Differing Visions." In *Loose Ends*. Dallas: Spring Publications, 1975.

Holy Bible. King James Version.

Jung, C. G. *The Visions Seminars*. Books 1 and 2. Zurich: Spring Publications, 1976.

Kristeva, Julia. *Powers of Horror: An Essay on Abjection*. Trans. by Leon S. Roudiez. New York: Columbia University Press, 1982.

Meigs, Mary. *The Medusa Head*. Vancouver: Talonbooks, 1983.

Neitzsche, Friedrich. *Beyond Good and Evil*. Trans. by R. J. Hollingdale. Baltimore: Penguin Classics, 1973.

_____. *On the Genealogy of Morals*. Trans. by Walter Kaufmann and R. J. Hollingdale. New York: Vintage Books, 1969; quoted pp. 32–33.

Winnicott, D. W. *The Maturational Processes and the Facilitating Environment*. New York: International Universities Press, 1965.

_____. *Playing and Reality*. London: Tavistock, 1982; quoted p. 92.

Chapter 5
Lowood

Her five a.m. candle has dispersed some of the shadows finding me nearly dressed. She has lit the nursery's fire, found me with no appetite for the biscuit then placed in my bag. She puts on my wrap and bonnet and outside Mrs. Reed's bedroom she questions my entry for a farewell word. No, that woman came to my bed last night, not to disturb us in the morning her message, remember the good aunt. I put those sheets over my face, turned. Missis has been only foe: Goodbye to Gateshead my cry.

At the porter's lodge, here is the six a.m. coach, the fifty miles long for a child the porter's wife comments. The coach is loaded, that door shut severed I am from Bessie and also Gateshead. A minute before I had clung to her neck with kisses.

Several towns, to me it is hundreds of miles and finally a stop at an inn, the guard suggests food, but there is no appetite. I roam the gallery, fearing a kidnapping, yet then the guard returns and I am put back in the coach, the towns become country hills, it is night and I am lulled to a sleep interrupted when the coach ceases its motion and it is a servant-like person inquiring on a little girl within, Jane Eyre.

I am in a parlour alone, two women entering, one impressing me immediately by her look, voice and air, the dark hair and dark eyes, pale large forehead, she is asking about my trip, saying I look tired, am I hungry and my name my parents if I can read, write, sew, now she is gently touching my cheek, she is saying she hopes I will be a good child. Then I am passed to a woman more ordinary and ruddy who leads me to the hum of many voices: the girls of every age on benches at tables with their pairs of candles and the hum of their 'whispered repetitions,' the next day's lesson, hour of study.

Supper trays are ordered, common mug, portions of oaten cake passed, still I cannot eat, even prayers and I am so weary now, I can hardly see these girls passing in their file to the bed-room this long room of its many beds, two girls to a bed. Gusts of wind and rain only barely disturbing a sleep finally broken by the morning bell ringing, bitter cold, girls are dressing, one basin to every six girls, Prayers. Form classes. Silence. Order.

I am placed in the class of the smallest children. Bell. The four teachers are in their place during the Bible read through the dawn's rise. Another bell. Breakfast, yet here the smell only sickening, weak as I am from the famine these bowls bring only repulsions, nostril turned: now the whispered words from the taller girls in front. Burnt porridge.

It is before the next bell rings, the girls in the classroom chattering their wrath over what none have eaten, the room speaks loudly the abuse until the

nine o'clock bell. Silence. To your seats. Ordered now the 'confused throng.'
We wait.

I look at these girls. Eighty motionless now sitting from youngest to oldest
they are wearing the same brown dress, woolen stockings, brass buckled
country-made shoes, plain locks of not a curl in sight. We wait.

Then in a moment the entire room springs up, stands and then seats.
Baffled I turn to the direction of other eyes. Here has entered the woman
greeting me last evening now surveying us. I take her in with awe: her eyes,
the cluster of her curls, her carriage, her complexion; I look at her this Miss
Temple, later learn it is Maria Temple, superintendent. Purple cloth dress
trimmed in black velvet, gold watch shining at the girdle.

She is giving a geography lesson to a class, she then teaches music to the
elder girls and this same one is saying now that it has struck twelve, to the
surprise of the other teachers she is saying that she has ordered a special
lunch of bread and cheese to make up for the breakfast they could not eat. It
is to be done at her responsibility.

And after this treat, to the garden. Walls preventing any sight out, in the
enclosure, I see each student has her own bed of garden yet now all in 'wintry blight and brown decay' toward this end of January. Here I am shivering
on the verandah in a familiar isolation, the rest are hardy, the rest romp on
the soaked ground except for a few of us huddled on this shelter and out of
the damp fog penetrating a thin skin a hollow cough. I am trying to ignore
the cold without, the hunger within, I hardly know where I am. I stare at the
church-like house with its latticed windows and here a stone tablet saying it is
a Lowood Institution, rebuilt by Naomi Brocklehurst, followed by a Biblical
phrase, it is Matthew glorifying our Father in heaven.

What could this tablet mean? My puzzlement responded to by that cough
again, I turn. The girl of the cough is reading a book its title *Rasselas*, I am
usually not so forward but her reading evokes a 'chord of sympathy' and I
approach. I ask her on her book, she hands it over for my perusal. It is not
as frivolous as my taste, more dull, here no fairies and genii within the pages
so serious; I dare to ask her now about the stone tablet. What is an
Institution?

The girl is reserved but I learn from her that the school educates orphans
and much of the payment comes by the benevolent ladies and gentlemen. I
learn it was founded by Mrs. N. Brocklehurst, her son now directing as
treasurer and manager, I learn that even the tall lady with the gold watch
who gave us the bread and cheese must answer to this man for it is he who
buys the food and clothes.

The girl is reserved. When I ask whether this Brocklehurst is a good man,
she says he is a clergyman, said to do good. I inquire on the other teachers,
learn their names, she describes them to me, she does not talk on them. But
surely, I say, Miss Temple is the best. The response is simple: Miss Temple is
very good and above the rest because she knows more than they do. I ask her
about herself, I learn the mother is dead but on my question on her happiness, she says too many questions, she wants to read now.

Called in for a meal smelling of fat rancid, 'indifferent potatoes and strange shreds of rusty meat'; lessons resume but what catches my eye is that the girl of the verandah is dismissed in disgrace by Miss Scatcherd, ordered as punishment to stand in the middle of the large school room. Why is she not humiliated? How can she bear it so composed? No weeping, not a blush. I would want to be swallowed by the very earth.

She is in a place beyond her punishment, she sees something else, is she in the place of the day dream? Her eyes on the floor but she is not seeing it, ' "her sight seems turned in, gone down into her heart: she is looking at what she can remember, I believe; not at what is really present." ' Another small meal of coffee and brown bread after five, I am left still hungry. There is a half an hour recreation, more study, the piece of oat-cake, prayers and bed, the end of the first Lowood day.

When what could be breakfast-room summon large-featured, demanding opposition our hell accusation of a distance through which we can see her objectively use it against her proclaiming our heart is different. Exploded to a final gray regret the way we reversed, we condemned her in reverse still a tyranny not reciprocity. But we have had an influence and we leave the next day. Goodbye to Gateshead.

To school to know who is a self the forehead was gashed to fit, the apothecary said it was not a baby, it had parents a past, once enjoyed the tart, the Gulliver tale, can begin to speak and when upon the Brocklehurst spot of the rug first address back to the aunt trembles and we turn away she is whispering goodbye speak well, our covers overhead.

She says to us the night before that she is the good aunt. She does not know herself. We want to know ourselves. We sever to school to learn some lessons, let Bessie put on our coat, a bonnet, walk to the coach departing. Goodbye to Gateshead. There would be a pull back to the one our step-mother and so we think we leave in hate.

Who packs our trunks, enters the five a.m. shadows dressing, hands us the last meal, walks us to the coach, Bessie medium, it was a last day dialogue becoming the leavetaking of the Gateshead place of monocentric perspective, univocality, tyranny. A dialogue prefigured by Mr. Lloyd yet not implemented until we spoke back to the aunt she loosened, softened to the Bessie reciprocal mode of relation, severing.

Bessie medium standing between the worlds, carried us to the narrative of the otherworldly we located at a windowseat, carried us into the red-room, carried us out, midwife at the foot of our returning bed she held the basin, and now she brings us to where we will travel to the next place.

She hugs us and cries after the coachman to take good care of us, yet she does not accompany. Perspective of gray day first outside mansion, prereflective with perspective, multiple perspectives, and this nascent autonomy is how we are travelling alone, solitary passage out of Gateshead.

We are moving beyond the landscape where unconscious only becomes incorporation of fit, blatant action, Reed reaction to impulse undercurrent, yet we cannot yet initiate a movement to the next place, we are taken. For we have only made it out to the sequestered plantation, still hers, and asked a question. Bessie's reciprocity gets us to the coach yet we do not know our ways through reflection to initiation, and in order to leave Gateshead we have to be carried and others are guardians.

'Thus I was severed from Bessie and Gateshead: thus whirled away to unknown, and, as I then deemed, remote and mysterious regions.' We are no longer Reed, other than Reed, but not fully autonomous, we find ourselves in contradiction to the Gateshead place placing us in a coach to unknown destination. We never know where we are going when we finally leave Gateshead, and our sense is that we are severed.

The next place is vague and remote, it is not the point, there is no point when we Gateshead depart except separation from the clutchings and addiction, the fits and the nursery daze of Gateshead.

We know when we have left, there are guards, coachmen, but we fear a kidnapping, do not know our way, and are not able to feed ourselves along the way. We leave Gateshead only with our name, is not Reed, is not to be Reed.

She had cast us into unnameable regions of imps and demons and white winged savior seizures without instructing us any language to carry it up, back, how to impart those forces, configure, speak through them even in breakfast chamber, and so we have bitten back severing from all her chambers and we are roaming in a gallery at an inn midway not knowing our route. In between Gateshead and the next place, a Bessie story remembered as fear of kidnapping, the way we suspect the familiar intrusion is how we are not yet autonomous, but the guard mounts his seat we are coached to the next place perhaps where how we will speak such unspeakable is no longer fable.

A woman is whispering, ' "Is there a little girl called Jane Eyre here?" ' We arrive where we are expected, who we are someone of a name on their ledger they await and meet the coach. We cannot arrive at Lowood until we have a name, have located it (Mr. Lloyd dialogue), and know it.

We were roaming in the inn, had been accosted many times in suspension within her fold still expect it: we may know our name yet still not knowing who is this person on which the woman at the receiving coached end inquires.

Jane is immediately met and she is lead to join the rest in their definite pattern. Strict holding discipline after the Reed separation, required by it we are disoriented, having been seized and burst. Gateshead leavetaking requirement a clear structure without. Schedule.

The place which draws us post-Gateshead is run by women for women. Closer to our nature. We know we are distant enough from Gateshead when we can see who greets us, she stands without us. Instantly appealing through 'voice, look, air,' she greets us upon first arrival. The next place is where our senses gain access to another.

Upon the Brocklehurst rug we had looked over Mrs. Reed for the first time, feature by feature, our perception a sign of our differentiation within her bind, senses a way back to what we distance as we are leaving as if bond burst, becoming the fine detail perusal of the gray field, our perception refined and moved us to Lowood. The next place is where our senses gain access to another.

Nurturant (are we tired, we must be hungry), she attracts in outreach, we are drawn to her impressed by her voice look air and she is distinct, to get to us her arm must reach out, a mother discovered without, she puts her hand on our shoulder are we tired.

Interstice. Between two landscapes, about to enter the unfamiliar. On the threshold of the next, liminal space, and we look up to what has bearing, presence, gentle touch, drawn to as we look up, awe in this evening dawns.

She speaks desiring an estimation of our hunger, our past, our quality. We meet at limen a reciprocal exchange, desire of our perspective she stands without which draws us to her.

The Lowood entry is where the Brocklehurstian oppositional stance on good girl and hell is not necessary for the distance required by initial meeting, yet the Brocklehurst opposition has distanced us to where we arrive that goodness is spoken from one exterior with a touch gently on the cheek.

Forefinger gently to our cheek she hopes we should be a good child. Our goodness is her forwarding desire. Her bearing is erect. She has her own erection yet it is not his of Mrs. Reed. Where he moralized, she desires.

The Lowood place of order operates through a consistency and uniformity — plainness prevails in dress code, strict exercises of the Bible, scant meals and certain lessons dictated by clock and bell. Bell. Basin. Prayers. Form classes. Bell. Bible. Bell. Breakfast. Bell. Classes. Recess. Bell. Classes. Dinner. Study. Supper. Prayer. Bell. Bed.

Jane is not required here to define herself from the exterior as object, not a splitting off for an arbitrary external design, yet instead she is asked to enter what already is programmed, the uniform, they have all the same exterior and what she hears first are the hum of whispered repetitions.

Rules and an order marshalled by the spinster. Everyone at Lowood looks the same. "Clinic" following breakdown, how we are shattered broken apart without unity semblance, yet no diagnosis or case at Lowood more convent. We join the rest, not outcast, all are orphan, not part of family, not part of whole, apart, there is not an outcast here for being apart all are a part. We are one of the rest none are a whole and none are ashamed to be here.

Consistent repetition, uniformity tames what was black and blasted ridge. Daily regimen orients to human proportion. En route post-Gateshead, between two disparate psychological landscapes, we feared vestige of Gateshead, kidnapping, yet here protected within canopy of structure, senses ordained.

Within such canopy, uniqueness in person becomes explicit. Each girl has her own seat, her specific class, bed in the garden. Finer discriminations made within similarity. Locating uniqueness in commonality makes any difference explicit: we begin to notice difference as all reside in sameness.

Everything exterior is expected and that calms. No sudden breaks or interruptions. Not a possibility here for blatant impulsive action, Gateshead compulsion and reactivity. The porridge is burnt and the girls angrily chatter, speak the abuse to one another even teacher nods of the 'general wrath: doubtless she shared in it.' Room engaged between meal and lessons, 'glorious tumult.' Release, chatterings of complaint, articulations of wrath, are allocated to their restricted time and then when the bell rings all resume the silence.

The spinsters give orders here sternly yet not violently. A retreat but not of the nursery room which was still within the grip of mother's madness. In the nursery, Jane fed off herself, feeding out to others, unable to know the dimensions of her own hunger apart from mother's unconscious. At Lowood, scheduled frame and rules preclude intrusion, she is not tied to anyone else's hunger, and for the first time she realizes how hungry she is and her hunger's dimensions.

Unmediated connection to as within mother's body and out of that unconscious rose a greed crushing Gateshead outcast: she was in contingent relation to the impinging forces there, vigilant attempt to avoid the next blow, never could sit and know her appetite.

To be severed out of Gateshead, we have to go further in, further to a retreat of low wood recess yet not one of fusion. It has a regularity, order, formality distancing, all in place, detachment. Lowood is Brocklehurst's Institution, related to the moral righteousness of stepmother's black pillar which began our severance, breaking bond. What resides at Lowood is severe, that severity Mrs. Reed demanded through Brocklehurst, yet another side of it a discipline female.

Retreat from untamed bursts of spilled hunger, from torrents of fearful mothers have lost their voice, only whisperings in the occult crimson linings, Lowood we travel to it from mother's out of mother's punitive extremes, but it is of another order. Each person has her place within a boundary, limited parameter. Lowood is the place of a possibility of detachment from the impact of impressions which was Gateshead while retreating further.

Brocklehurst is an extension of the attempt to constrict the inflated sonorous thrusts, yet now it is a school. The isolation in the Lowood garden at recess is familiar. Yet at Lowood, what leads us, what precedes our recess, is not punishment, severe crack, yet desire, edge of what crevice once closed edges open and what responds is our 'organ of veneration. . .sense of admiring awe,' reverence, venus, veneris, our love in awe, our desire an awe, fearful still a wonder our desire an interstice, dawn of rose, pencilled of long lashes round, 'tall, fair, and shapely.' Purple cloth and a gold watch at her girdle.

Miss Temple is a detailed and three-dimensional figure for Jane who is aesthetically and erotically moved by the woman, finds her beautiful, is attracted to her.

Detailing Miss Temple, her size, the irids of the eyes, how the lashes are pencilled, the shade of the front, the way the hair curls at temple and the cloth and trim of her dress the gold watch shining at the girdle. 'Let the reader add, to complete the picture, refined features; a complexion, if pale, clear; and a stately air and carriage, and he will have, at least as clearly as words can give it, a correct idea of the exterior of Miss Temple.'

When she feeds us at her responsibility, fed from without, she feeds not according to her own hunger, fed we move into the Lowood garden, the place behind, more secluded, occluded, where the hidden growth beneath our conscious world is wet can flourish.

    ◄§ Maternal as desire, desire and maternalism conjoined and this love must include a woman. Friedrich on Sappho: "This crucial set of poems to daughters and daughter-like girls has, in turn, to be taken together with her erotic work; the meanings of Demeter and Aphrodite, or the complexes of sexuality and maternalism, are partly conjoined in Sappho, who is quite definite about the analogy in at least two fragments (82, 142); the latter runs simply, 'I've flown to you like a child to its mother,' and the former comes near the end of a strongly erotic Lesbian poem. . . Many of Sappho's poems deal with the affection, love, passion, tenderness, infatuation, and other feelings of a woman for one of her own sex. . . Some of the fragments seem unquestionably carnal and erotic. . . The Sapphic grouping, on the other hand, based on the woman as the sine qua non, derived from and was consistent with Sappho's vision of beauty and creativity: creativity and beauty require a female principle as a necessary and a sufficient condition. . . Sappho's goddess is often golden, as in 'O golden-wreathed Aphrodite' (9), as are her companions, the Nereids, the Graces, and the Muses: 'But the golden Muses gave me true wealth, and when I die I shall not be forgotten.' " Bowra on Sappho: "She was the leader and chief personality in an institution which trained young girls, but owing to the customs of the time this institution had a special character. It was, as she herself calls it, a *moisopolon domos*, a house of those who cultivated the Muses. . . and Maximus of Tyre was not far wrong when he compared the relations between Sappho and her pupils with those between Socrates and his disciples. But while Socrates held his young men together by his personal influence and the glamour he gave to the quest for truth, Sappho was bound to her maidens by ties which were at least half religious. . ." The arousal of desire and maternalism within the intellect lesson conjoined is temple. ❧

Who carries the muse is familiar, we recognize her from the night before, Lowood is where muse becomes familiar. Our desire is aroused, bonds between women in a community marginal, set apart, liminal venusian, and we begin to feel it bodily, organ of veneration.

This garden recess is highly walled, we are protected from seizure. Its 'middle space divided into scores of little beds'; each person with her own plot. Who we are that our unique plot is inscribing begins in the Lowood recess, insular place where ours is divided, differentiated in what is recess at Lowood has a plot. Differentiation within recess, what the Reed possessions had been attempting after we have negotiated them we find the possibility in the Lowood garden.

Post-Gateshead Jane takes Lowood in with her senses, sensually. There are no names, no overview, not a cognitive mapping possible. She takes Lowood in with her senses: tall and shapely woman in the purple dress with black trimming, the burnt porridge, the wintry air of the walled garden, clamoring bells marshalling the marching pupils.

There has been a severing and we are not one of the hardy ones romping on the ground drenched by yesterday's rains, we are with the ones more frail wrapped on the verandah, huddled, we are alone once more, we pull our cloak around us. Mist penetrating, Gateshead only a wisp now yet nothing appears definite in its place. We are hungry. Liminal on the verandah between school and recess, what is the lesson of the recess we have come to school to learn it. Our reflections, we lean back and we are watching them, are fragmented, they float.

There was never a possibility of reflection with the Reeds. To detach oneself from the impact of impressions (Gateshead) is to reflect. To reflect is to have a place of detachment in which to stand. Here is the Lowood verandah. Yet we still know not the language, text of recess. We cannot at first record the reflections.

Our reflections are fragmented cannot be recorded when where we have been fades away and we do not yet know where we are, huddled. We lean back and wonder where we are in this new place when a stone tablet says Institution. The new school signs itself, as we begin reflecting a sign appears. We are not intruded upon here instead we want to move out.

Pondering the words on this tablet and the response is from one also huddled on this sheltering verandah, a cough.

The effect of the Lowood austerity and discipline, no embellishment, is a stripping, we strip to the garden in the midst of the low wood where a mist penetrates to the rudimentary 'hollow cough.'

How we stand within her hollow cough is the beginning of our reflection which is a way to locate the sign of the recess. The cough announces something. It announces head bent in book. Her reading, her text, is what accompanies our reflection. The cough is as hollow as the verandah isolation encasing us within.

Stone-tablet says rebuilt by Naomi Brocklehurst. 'Convent-like garden,' latticed windows of the schoolroom and dormitory 'which gave it a church-like aspect,' and her name is Miss Temple. The women are of some sacred body to receive us formally yet this stone-tablet in front of us declares let men see ' "your good works, and glorify your Father which is in heaven." – St. Matt. v. 16.'

And in our severing from mother's womb, the place which receives us glorifies a heavenly Father. In mediating us closer to our autonomous nature what speaks to us is a nurturant woman of authority to whom we sensually attend yet the place still says that Father is overhead, would put him up high, here is the Lowood stone-tablet which is where we know we are no longer where we had been yet do not know where we are.

The way we have thought to leave her has been through glorifying the Father even as we had been crushed to fit beneath his descent. The way we still think He may be responsible for this distance from her is Father in Heaven the stone-tablet has said so. Yet as He is the sign of the place it also signifies that a woman rebuilt it. The Father's works a woman rebuilt.

The stone-tablet names a woman while a venerated teacher has made the hunger decision, Glory Father contradiction, she is an employee of Brocklehurst yet the lunch arrived on her (awesome) authority. Contradiction within recess. The inherent contradiction between Glory Father (human sensuality prohibited as access to Temple) and our sensual adoration of Miss Temple is the Lowood place.

Glory Father the only way we thought we have attained distance, formality. This garden is a 'wide enclosure,' separate student beds, space of detachment, separate from intrusion and distinct from one another. Yet Father signing our Lowood entry to recess only occurs through a rebuilding mother and all within the new girl's cough is what announces something.

Her cough announces head bent in book. We had a calling to bring out the text from our windowseat recess where we resided and this looks familiar. In the strange place of a familiar isolation, we move toward likeness. Head bent in book, here is a 'chord of sympathy.'

But the book is different. It is the strangeness of the title we find attractive. Lowood makes difference, cuts boundary, impersonalizes through formality and we have the space here to move out, be drawn, find another attractive. Not a book of fairies or genii, to us it is dull. However awake our senses will not be dazzled in this post-Gateshead school place.

Something to learn in what looks dull: as our senses gain access to what is distinct it does not dazzle and we no longer are in a Reed place as possessed merely reactive, we move toward what is dull. Dull is the moment at the start of locating a worldly sign of the recess after arriving from the Gateshead place of addiction to possession by otherworldly.

The girl-of-likeness emerging after the immolation has a new book. Differentiation within sameness: at Lowood we are reflected, fragmentary moment, in likeness, she has head in book as we have had, yet this allows us to find the difference, we are not taken from without, her book is different.

> ◄§ *Rasselas.* " 'Human life is everywhere a state in which
> much is to be endured, and little to be enjoyed' . . . 'Perpet-
> ual levity must end in ignorance, and intemperance, though
> it may fire the spirits for an hour, will make life short or
> miserable' . . . 'Let us live as men who are some time to
> grow old and to whom it will be the most dreadful of all evils
> to count their past years by follies and to be reminded of
> their former luxuriance of health only by the maladies which
> riot has produced' . . . 'I have found,' said the prince at his
> return to Imlac, 'a man who can teach all that is necessary to
> be known; who, from the unshaken throne of rational forti-
> tude, looks down on the scenes of life changing beneath him.

He speaks, and attention watches his lips; he reasons, and
conviction closes his periods. This man shall be my future
guide. I will learn his doctrines, and imitate his life' . . .
'Whether perfect happiness would be procured by perfect
goodness,' said Nekayah, 'this world will never afford an
opportunity of deciding. But this, at least, may be maintained: that we do not always find visible happiness in proportion to visible virtue. . .All that virtue can afford is quiet-
ness of conscience and a steady prospect of a happier state;
this may enable us to endure calamity with patience, but
remember that patience must suppose pain.' . . . 'Pleasure in
itself harmless may become mischievous by endearing to us a
state which we know to be transient and probatory, and withdrawing our thoughts from that of which every hour brings
us nearer to the beginning and of which no length of time
will bring us to the end. Mortification is not virtuous in
itself, nor has any other use, but that it disengages us from
the allurements of sense. In the state of future perfection, to
which we all aspire, there will be pleasure without danger
and security without restraint.' " ℬ

' "Is your book interesting?" ' we ask, we are making the first move
forward. Drawn to another. The text binds at Lowood. Verandah interstice
between school and recess and here the text to which we are drawn, we
want to learn the inscription of what differentiates in recess, she looks like
us, head in book interior, yet we can borrow the book which is different
than any of ours and it allows us access to one distinct yet related, not us yet
like us.

The walls surrounding the garden are high, 'so high as to exclude every
glimpse of prospect.' Lowood is not outlook. It has not to do with looking
out, anticipation. It settles us in a wood heavily protected, its high wall
precludes vista, prevents fusion. Separate plots here and we learn of boundary, where ours ends and what is hers begins. Sympathetic chord drawing
us to her arrives at difference: what divides her from us, split other in base
of likeness.

The high walls do not allow in foreign elements easily. The place is not of
the daily social world, insular space, more of church our bible speaking
spirits, yet not allowing in foreign element. The girl behind the book is
reserved, this one is private. Her response to our eager advance is with a
directness, succinctness. She does not entertain us or talk to us, also she
does not let us pry.

Alone in the sequestered gray field Jane asked ' "What shall I do?" '

Bessie's call prepared her, initial dialogue, for school at which her question—Where am I, what is this place?—from the vagueness of this verandah place became answered by the coughing girl-with-book.

This girl is the privacy of detachment within subjective likeness and through her Jane learns about the Lowood place: who is a charity child and who supports them there, who manages the place and who teaches it. This questioning of the girl-with-book is the frame of Jane's reflection, the ruminating, questioning self.

This girl-with-book is the divided self allowing Jane to reflect. Here is a private one of the studious close-print, not the old one of fairies and bedtime story. This girl does not speak her animosities or the gossip ensnarements. She is self-possessed yet not withholding. She answers the questions yet knows her limits, wall of propriety. She will not answer our question of her happiness here. She treasures knowledge. She simply says to us that Miss Temple is above the rest because she knows more.

The one who holds the text on the verandah interstice, this place we stand between perception and reflection, returns us to our awe, whom we have venerated, for whom the organ of venus is the mind, head, temple. Miss Temple knows more. When she enters the classroom, the students stand, she surveys. Commanding a respect she does not dictate and we begin to reflect on the place on which we stand through the girl looking up to the one of temple.

As we move to where the place has regular frame, to where we are boundaried, perceive another from more than one perspective, our sense of difference within the sheltered place of sameness becomes our dialogue on the verandah which continues the gray field self-reflection and which is also Lowood's depth of characterization: Miss Temple fills out as no other, she is animated, multidimensional.

Perceiving Miss Temple in her multiple dimensions sends us to the verandah where our dialogue with another perspective, different text, reflects the place to us. In Gateshead of one perspective the figures were stereotypic, abstract as personal, uni-dimensional; the dialogue with the verandah girl is presupposed by Miss Temple as the first detailed and three-dimensional figure of any landscape yet.

Miss Temple is a detailed and three-dimensional figure for Jane who is aesthetically and erotically moved by the woman. 'Let the reader add, to complete the picture, refined features. . .'

We want the reader who reads the text of who is Jane Eyre to see the complete features of this one, insure the full delineation for whom veneration organ expands, our first venusian desire is when we want to insure 'correct idea' for the reader of our text. Lowood, place of propriety and education where our desire is also to have a correct idea, temple is correct and has an aesthetic, erotic body.

She feeds the children bread and cheese when the porridge has been burnt; she knows more yet not at the expense of the human being. She does not let the excesses of burning rule at the expense of the human child. She is who can break the code of uniformity for human hunger and its singularity; her mode prevents the Institution from an order autocratic, dictatorial Brocklehurst non-reciprocal.

She locates herself firmly in the bread and cheese decision though it surprises the others. That it surprises the others is how she breaks regimen, conscious order, to use her authority discriminately, discriminating something unconscious desiring manifestation. She is close to the appetite of the students which the regimen prefers to leave unconscious.

Miss Temple is close to unconscious appetite. Appetite, the unconscious of it, has a place at Lowood in Temple and this is our amorous bond to her. This employee of Brocklehurst, not at the expense of appetite, will not keep it unconscious, will be accountable, appetite to Temple, sacred body, body of what is sacred fed singularly.

We have found from without who mothers with knowledge and an arousal of desire, can see her body from every angle, not possessed we are human ourselves to know how hungry we are yes we want that bread and cheese she offers. Lowood privacy and detachment designates fed from without. Newly discovered mother where her feeding us is to be accountable is not in order to feed herself.

Mrs. Reed's punitive and critical nature has sent Jane to an exacting place where the consistency heals and which houses an appealing woman-teacher. Brocklehurst is the stepmother's unconscious attempt to bring Jane out from the nursery shadows, judging to a severance. Standing his stance on the rug, Jane spoke of her different heart bond burst through the fusion, Brocklehurst a boundary lesson.

He is a cover for Lowood. Getting past our mother's Brocklehurst, to get past our mother's Brocklehurst is not to be caught by him a turn of him upon ourselves. Getting past our mother's Brocklehurst, his speaking through us the critical judgments and opinions darted to hide the fear, fear of fragmenting further, fear of twistings our features too prominent, caught, manipulating, we criticize, we moralize, we speak of hell.

Once past Brocklehurst, saying no more, no more the screeching back at a mother who cannot notice, no more the harsh condemnation back she is trembling, cannot see us, we have lost her, Brocklehurst and his hell fires only an attempt at a false intimacy with that mother who we have loved, have lacked, we have missed so dearly in our abandonment.

She has only called us out through Brocklehurst, and so we think he is the way back to her but finally we know we have lost, the victory pyrrhic, too much burning, when burned enough we leave that Gateshead with a maid's help, we sever. We go past Brocklehurst, we refuse to stop at him, we go past him through his cover and we find on the other side we find Miss Temple, the place is run by women, the spinsters have an order it calms us, and in the midst we find a desire for she wears a purple dress, her hair curled around the large pale forehead, eyes lined by the large lashes, she has touched our cheek, we stand for her, we watch her teaching, she feeds us at the off hours and she knows more.

On the other side of stepmother's "moralism," an awesome woman resides welcoming us an education. What is it that Lowood wants to educate? The verandah girl-with-book has access to a world of which we know little: when punished the girl does not react an impulse against the external impact, she does not look upon immediate surround, instead active inner vision. The girl mediates the ignominy which could cut to the heart through a vision interior: ' "her sight seems turned in, gone down into her heart." '

The heart which was the metaphor allowing us to articulate our difference from that stepmother the heart the way out of Gateshead lands us at Lowood where the teacher moves us the girl sees from her heart.

Jane wonders about the daydream. She is watching this girl drawing from realms publicly invisible while publicly disgraced. In the presence of punished Helen, Jane speaks to herself, interior locution; her reflections are now vivid enough to be recorded, her interior thoughts get quoted as part of the text. At Lowood, inner regions become mediated forms of exterior actions, and these interior realms take their place alongside narrated event, descriptive action.

The punished girl's stand as disgraced here is a composure, a sight turned in, insight, allowing her not to be possessed, not taken. Reflective stand precluding possession. The attraction to an externally invisible, intangible place mediates, the girl stands does not flail, and as she is of daydreams we realize we are still hungry, our hunger for dreams of day, interior mediations, the girl stands does not flail, the order of the day resumes.

> ◂§ Lowood. I wake up charred. Charred skin flaking its
> dried sweat. Any motion now stiffened I lay for a long while
> fearful before I see her. At the corner foot of the bed, her
> hands on the post. Her head is down, she must have been
> waiting all night, I thought I saw her once in my twisting,
> her colors of purple and gold. My hair is snarled as I stand
> before her she is touching my cheek and now I want to wash
> like the rest. She sets me on my schedule. We begin cleaning

where the spirits had not been lived well have damaged. We
are on our knees together and we are scrubbing off that floor
traces of common misuses, our elbows working in unison.
She does not let much time elapse between the projects.
Studying these scriptures we are learning older ways of handling more difficult demons. There is a knock on the door
she does not answer. The small portions of food define my
stomach's motion, she tells me to eat as regularly as she exercises my thought. At the recess I am cold, I know my hunger, some mist is penetrating, and she tells me to listen for
the new voice. Great girl with a daydream. There are many
others here all female. I see I am part of who convenes in
plots, clearly walled, we turn the pages together in unison we
hum in distinct, the definite repetitions. ❧

Bibliography

Bachelard, Gaston. *The Poetics of Space*. Trans. by Maria Jolas. Boston: Beacon Press, 1969.

Bernard, Mary. *Sappho: A New Translation*. Berkeley: University of California Press, 1958; Bowra quoted pp. 98–99.

Burckhardt, Titus. *Alchemy*. Trans. by William Stoddart. Baltimore: Penguin Books, 1971.

Friedrich, Paul. *The Meaning of Aphrodite*. Chicago: University of Chicago Press, 1978; quoted pp. 109, 112, 114, 117, 107.

Johnson, Samuel. *Rasselas*. Woodbury, N.Y.: Barron's Educational Series, 1962; quoted pp. 55, 75, 77–78, 106, 181.

Silberer, Herbert. *Hidden Symbolism of Alchemy and the Occult Arts*. Trans. by Smith Ely Jelliffe. New York: Dover Publications, 1971.

Townsend, Sylvia Warner. *Lolly Willows*. Chicago: Academy Chicago Limited, 1979.

Chapter 6

Helen Burns

Whipping north-east wind that night children shiver in the beds while the water in the pitchers turning to ice prevents the morning 'ceremony of washing.' I sit the hour and a half of Bible weak from the cold and then the scanty portion of porridge finally arriving, not burnt this day, I wish it had been more. No longer only spectator, I am participant in the class, these lessons are long and the frequent changes from class to class bewildering.

Finally at 3:00 I am given a muslin to hem, told to sit quietly in the sewing, and so I am overhearing Miss Scatcherd's class on English history and there is the girl-of-the-verandah whose place at the top of the class is slowly diminished as that teacher criticizes this girl called Burns the way she sits, holds her head, the girl now is sent to the bottom of the class.

I am sewing my full attention on these students who close their books and Miss Scatcherd examines them on the reign of Charles the First. The difficult questions most are unable to answer except this Burns who knows that answer to every question and yet no praise forthcoming instead the teacher cries out Burns, you naughty girl Burns this morning I see you never cleaned your nails.

I am sewing wondering on the frozen water in those pitchers and why the girl Burns is not explaining on it. Instead she is being ordered to gather from the book-closet a bundle of twigs used now Miss Scatcherd is striking her on the neck a dozen times. I pause with this scene my fingers quivering; here is Burns' pensive face not altered. Miss Scatcherd is calling the girl hardened, she is saying nothing, nothing can correct her of her slatternly habits. A tear there I see as the girl puts away the rod.

Here now the rest period the girls laughing in their groups the tumult of their merriment I am alone yet not lonely as I look out this snow falls fast, I see the window's drift of it, the moan of the wind also suggesting the sadness of this moment I would feel a great regret in it had I a family missed, left a home loving. No family, as orphan these elements speak to me now their excitement, I feel the fever even I long for the wilder wind, and inside this very room a clamour of more fervor, yes, I long for it.

And I am jumping over the others to the fireplace there kneeling is Burns I find absorbed in the book still *Rasselas* she just now is finishing; I wait for its close asking then her full name. It is Helen Burns. Does she want to leave here? No, she is here to get an education. But that Miss Scatcherd is so cruel to her. No, that teacher is severe, disliking her faults. Oh, I say I would have seized that rod, broken it if I were you. No, only an expulsion then, better a patient endurance than the hasty action spreading evil consequences to all around; the Bible saying return good for evil.

Helen Burns speaks to me of bearing what one is required to bear, forbearance even to one's chastiser, I cannot understand this 'doctrine of endurance.' But she seems so good and sees, I suspect, by a light invisible to my eyes, yet 'like Felix, I put it off to a more convenient season,' and I inquire what are her faults. She is telling me now the correctness of Miss Scatcherd's view: that she is slatternly, has no method, she is careless.

A smile now at the mention of Miss Temple's name for I have asked her if that teacher is severe to her, a smile and she calls herself wrenched that even with the gentle reminder of that good woman of her faults while praising so her accomplishment, she has not developed a carefulness. But Jane, she says to me how she sees it is easy for me to be careful and attentive for she has been watching me in the class. While she during the lesson she is in a sort of dream listening to the visionary brook by her home in Deepden and she cannot then reply in the lesson, and the correct answer to Charles the First mere chance, she respects the ' "poor murdered king" ' who could not see further than his crown's prerogative.

With Miss Temple (I have asked) her thoughts never wander, it is as I suspected, so I tell her of course: she is good with Miss Temple since the teacher is good to her. When struck we must hit back and only a goodness to those whom to us do good, I tell it to her clearly. She calls me a little untaught girl, for it is neither violence nor vengeance overcoming a hate, read the New Testament she is urging a scrutiny of this Christ, love the enemy.

No for it is impossible to love that Mrs. Reed and her son John and because Helen Burns asks I am telling her the story, releasing the painful tale in its rhythm of resentment 'bitter and truculent . . . without reserve or softening.' Is not, I then ask, is not Mrs. Reed the most hard-hearted, a bad woman? No, Mrs. Reed is unkind because she dislikes your character as does Miss Scatcherd mine, Helen is saying, but what a ' "singularly deep impression" ' Mrs. Reed has branded on your heart, how minutely you recall every detail of her behavior and comment. Forget, she is telling me, do not exert so in ' "nursing animosity." '

She continues and it is almost as a prayer a meditation on the time which will appear when we drop our burdens, debasement and our sins with the corruptible body of flesh removed only spark of spirit remaining returning to the Creator to pass in its gradation through human to seraph only . . .

' "Surely it will never, on the contrary, be suffered to degenerate from man to fiend? No; I cannot believe that: I hold another creed; which no one ever taught me, and which I seldom mention; but in which I delight, and to which I cling; for it extends hope to all: it makes Eternity a rest—a mighty home, not a terror and an abyss. Besides, with this creed, I can so clearly distinguish between the criminal and his crime; I can so sincerely forgive the first while I abhor the last: with this creed revenge never worries my heart, degradation never too deeply disgusts me, injustice never crushes me too low: I live in calm, looking to the end." '

She is sinking in these her own thoughts as a rough monitor rushes in and bursts the meditative silence now commanding Helen order her drawer or else it will be to Miss Scatcherd. Sighing she obeys, 'reverie fled.'

The Lowood water is not fluid, not flow instead ice, dry ice, this place is cold and dry. What is served here is less than we want; after Gateshead where we go curtails, tempers, subdues, diminishes, contracts.

And as we sew our lesson, who is on the top of the class, who rises knowing every answer her mind's height then becomes diminished. As we sew we see who is top diminished; ladder to bottom descent. The girl Burns has come from the sky here Scatcherd lowers her says hardened, slattern.

The one who excels the mind knows the answer, is slattern as Jane learns the lessons. At Lowood, who burns and rises to some height shines knowing the king's answers, vapor magestic, and then cools, hardens, solidifying descent to a body can be ignored, has been neglected, is careless, dirty nail, does not care to attend, is slovenly.

At Lowood, the solidification of who rises in intelligence is twigs on the neck, this head has wanted to fly from its body rise, body burned to vapor ascends the red welts remind of neck here is a body not to neglect.

As the whipping wind ices the water for washing, Burns is whipped by a severe teacher. Harsh turn in the elements she knows in a woman who bears down on her, criticizing, flogging. Burns withstands the whipping mother, that mother of another character.

> ◄§ She is sitting sewing the muslin to the drone of each class
> in their lesson overheard as on her cheek a warmth from one
> across the room shines each answer the dirt nailed beneath
> and the twigs crease her neck their red mark while pinned
> down above her the flaring aunt as held in a room reddening
> not to flinch not to flail one tear glistens a cheek shines. §►

The elements have turned on her and she cannot enter the morning's waters, the teacher whips her for the dirt in the wrong place, matter out of place, Burns's material body does not know its place for body in her consciousness is off, out of itself, misplaced. For Burns, body is preferred unconscious.

Beneath the ascent to kingly intelligence is a flogging teacher. The twigs whip and the neck burns. A burning body both continually sublimates, vaporizes the lower processes, sublimis, up high, as well as remembers them, brings through the neck knowledge back to body's lower members.

The flogging teacher indulges in snapping, whipping, thrashing, giving the red passions over in order to chasten. At Lowood what is red passion, even concupiscence, becomes vaporized through chastening welt which in a sense keeps the girl disembodied.

Burns does not give out or become porous and depleted when the teacher whips. She stands it pensively while Jane quivers it. Burns becomes firm, holding, localizing light within. Jane is who shakes bodily for the other's withholding, for how Burns does not lower to the teacher's chastening of misplaced material body.

The first Lowood lesson is that Scatcherd whips Burns yet does not appropriate her. Burns takes an individual stance, she sees from perspective. Lowood is where we are drawn into another's potential seizure and then see the difference. Burns has a Miss Scatcherd whipping but with a difference, does not pick up that woman's force unconscious possession. Burns is individual withstanding, not windswept, not bent, not flailing back reactive, whipped yet not Reed.

The rest are playing in a tumult, excited, jovial, play-hour; Jane is alone by the windowpane, here would be the loneliness if there were longing for the family, but without family she enters the elements, and now she longs for their wildness.

Burns's vaporization at Lowood opens to whirling elements, this ascent from concrete body (neglected) and we have left family enclosures, tangible body and family no longer frames yet as orphan we burn elevating to wild element. Familial love binds us inside, confines, refuge now confinement too safely from the more extreme elements.

Jane has given up her longing for the wrong family. Once we step outside, have moved out of, up from, the longing for a binding familial (kept where that family needs us a family which we have used to keep kept) we are back at the windowpane, on the margin threshold where the fever of the wind's fervor is within snowdrift, where a whipping resides in the morning's iced water, the burning elevates to light shines knows the answer yet these heights are cool.

Witnessing Burns's flogging, how that other girl attracts then withstands the teacher's friction, draws Jane to the marginal pane. Jane leans on the window alone yet not lonely desires entry to elemental wildness.

Burning at Lowood is not fit or seizure yet elevates, is part of separating, rising, knowing difference. At Lowood, Jane knows the difference between the moaning outside and the tumult within: 'putting my ear close to the window, I could distinguish from the gleeful tumult within, the disconsolate moan of the wind outside.' She 'derive(s) from both a strange excitement.' Yet after the Gateshead extrication, she knows the difference between them. Whereas at the Gateshead window interior was exterior, the Lowood pane distinguishes one from the other.

This way that the Lowood pane distinguishes is the way Burns can withstand the flogging, remain individual, ' "hardened." ' What draws Jane back to the classroom hub from the windowpane margin is not an outburst — the elemental force personified inside as outside — yet the girl Burns sitting still head in book.

Lowood is where we have solidified enough to differentiate within stepmother's antipathy to begin to find the text, through Burns, of the elemental at windowpane.

Head in book is the counterpart of elemental forces exciting. Jane is not lonely by the window since she recognizes the elements and sees them reflected as contained by Burns sitting by the hearth reading. Burns's reading body is the concrete analogue at Lowood of the tumult within, moan without.

This moan and tumult stirs us, stirs our desire for its intensification, and 'reckless and feverish' we carry this desire to Burns. Whereas at Gateshead Jane was reactively propelled from the windowseat by the son bursting without, here she is active jumping over and creeping under to Burns, desiring further black night whirlings and clamour let those students' sonorous rise the whipping wind relentless wind howling its siren cries summon to realms unknown she wants to know this elemental stir that she has sensed possible here in this very schoolroom and she turns and finds Burns.

At Lowood the elemental excitement is not embers of ire or a burning ridge yet leads to a fire-place where a silent girl 'abstracted from all round her' reads.

Whereas Jane was caught in a Gateshead arctic void between winter gust and scarlet curtain, where a burst called her out; at Lowood Helen stands (withstands, sits) for a place where the coolness (winters' drift, iced water) has its own heat, raises an excitement, aloof cool girl absorbed in her book quietly burns.

&§ Helen Burns. The noise, the chatter the girls' joyful clamour submerges in surround dimming only outstanding these words of this page. First I gaze lovingly and my eyes begin their caress, stroke the page, eyes coaxing it all the while to allow an entry, meeting each sentence, familiarizing, and the sentences let me closer, I am forward, the page is shy, holds back until the stroking, the coaxing a kind persuasion in kind and we open together and we are holding one another in suspense of what comes next. I move even closer, eyes opening now the mind penetrates with a sensitive chiselling and when it touches a certain word the pattern of a sentence unfolds and we have struck a recognition and we smile within the embrace we are shining in this its light is precise it shines from a distance and a prism struck shatters to its colors now the fine pointed tip of a petal whose tissue undulating mind's pulse palpitating, we are smiling within the embrace. Book struck. Each page offers a further entry to these recesses she is letting me turn her pages rapidly now I am met in the crevices of every petal's shape we recognize. And all around the chatter as I am reading alone, my skirt is crumbled beneath many an hour, a leg asleep I do not notice as they do not notice me I read alone. ⪔

No friends flock about the girl who reads. Her companion, the one that attracts her, is her text. We are held by a book, we curl up with it, we take it in, it feeds us. Text is what attracts Burns, what she desires to be held by more than anything in the room or without, that to which she is drawn, absorbed, loves. Burns knows what text entails of love.

⪖ "(T)he text establishes a sort of islet within the human — the common — relation, manifests the asocial nature of pleasure (only leisure is social). . . we also have a body of bliss consisting solely of erotic relations, utterly distinct from the first body: it is another contour, another nomination; thus with the text: it is no more than the open list of the fires of language. . . .Does the text have human form, is it a figure, an anagram of the body? Yes, but of our erotic body. The pleasure of the text is irreducible to physiological need." Roland Barthes ⪔

When the others romp excitedly is when Burns reads, her reading is homologous then to the romping body, the pleasure of a body romping is her reading body. Burns's reading body stirs us to action, draws out our feverish recklessness for as she has penetrated the text and bodily resides with the lives of its characters, we move into the privacy in which her reading body has enclosed her.

⪖ "Perhaps the most fundamental value that the Novel, as a cultural institution, may be said to uphold is privacy, the determination of an integral, autonomous, 'secret' self. Novel reading takes for granted the existence of a space in which the reading subject remains safe from the surveillance, suspicion, reading, and rape of others." D. A. Miller ⪔

At Lowood, the elemental stir at the margins of community becomes embodied not through concrete body (or its bursts) yet the erotic body of text. The one to whom we find a likeness at Lowood has as her companion a text, and speech begins with Jane when the text closes.

When Helen reads, she is absorbed, abstract, does not speak, when she closes the text she speaks to Jane. Speaking to Jane is a way to move out from text to world for Helen. Jane is who extends bodily in the world the (erotic) body of Helen's text.

We move toward the one who is so abstracted we are drawn clearly out. Reactor and spectator at Gateshead, at Lowood we become actor the second day participating in the classes however bewildering and toward this ' "great girl" ' who reads we initiate an action, conversation. We ask her name and her place first, name and situate and then inquire on her friction it has been like our own that bad other mother.

The one with whom we speak at Lowood, who has emerged out of the moaning wind outside, bustling confusion inside, is abstracted and teaches us forbearance, no reactive flailing yet distance with overview can see the perspective also of the severe teacher. Patient endurance.

Endure instead of hasty action, our fate required to bear. Bible as crux of Helen's patient endurance. It is a light invisible to our eyes she is speaking faith, apostle, we are Felix want to put it off, have just arrived from Gateshead feverish here we are hearing "justice and self-control and future judgment."

> ◄§ "After some days Felix came with his wife Drusilla who
> was a Jewess; and he sent for Paul and heard him speak
> upon faith in Christ Jesus. And as he argued about justice
> and self-control and future judgement, Felix was alarmed and
> said, 'Go away for the present; when I have an opportunity I
> will summon you.'" Acts 24:24–25 §►

The one to whom we speak has a body above the other concrete body, her body of the text is lit with a light invisible to our eyes, views over all overview has a patience which is to be careless, not have a method: her thoughts wander, she replies only if the subject interests her, she follows as inclination guides, making no effort.

We stay and listen because she knows her fault, careless without method, and we never could say our fault from the Gateshead place. Lowood patient endurance: when something exterior concurs with Helen's interior images, thoughts and language, she responds, which differs from the Gateshead unmediated reactivity to exterior stimulus. Lowood primacy of interior life.

What resides in Helen's interior world is a little brook running near her home through Deepden. From the depths deepest den of her origins runs the water sources to which she returns interior. And also there is a dead king. He did not have the vision, the overview, though conscientious and with integrity this Father could not look to the distance, fell myopic. Helen pities the ' "poor murdered king," ' feels strongly that his enemies had not the right to kill him.

For Helen the king has fallen, she would have wanted him remaining up high abstracted, as far as she is with sight to distance yet the king is dead. Dead father and whipping mother and we are drawn to her 'doctrine of endurance.'

When the king is dead, Miss Temple teaches at Lowood. Where we have gone through the father's death we hear this teacher knows something new there. Discussing Miss Temple is what precedes and follows Helen's account of the figures and landscapes of her interior world and also provokes the discussion of the place's creed.

Jane's creed: strike when struck. This ' "little untaught girl" ' has a Gateshead creed, resist those who wrongly punish, love those who love. Helen speaks another which her Christ has said: love your enemies.

> ◆§ " 'You have heard that it was said, "An eye for an eye and
> a tooth for a tooth." But I say to you, Do not resist one who
> is evil.' " Matthew 5:38–39 " 'You have heard that it was said,
> "You shall love your neighbor and hate your enemy." But I
> say to you, Love your enemies and pray for those who perse-
> cute you.' " Matthew 5:43–44 §◆

There is an intense, careless girl at Lowood who has a creed. The psychological landscapes through which we move each have their own creed. Gateshead's creed eye for eye, power and might. Mighty greed in Gateshead is an affluence and reactivity one strikes when struck, is good only when responded to well. Lowood has its scanty food portions, pitchered ice-water, and a young girl seeing by a light invisible to Jane's Gateshead eyes.

We hear for the first time the Lowood creed and we find we begin submerging again into the Reed possession, we are lowering into that elemental rage. Helen with overview listens, Helen's ear from the closed text allows us to find the text, narrative of the elemental at windowpane of the last place.

Somewhere in our mothers, those who lash, who hate furiously want to catch us in that hate called son, somewhere in our mothers is Helen desiring to instruct us pass through it do not get possessed by John Reed. Mrs.

Reed sent Jane to the place of Helen and talks of eternity; through her moralistic Brocklehurst, Mrs. Reed sent Jane to a Helen distancing, sublimation, mediation through and from those very Reedian annihilating possessions.

Within Mrs. Reed's moralistic rigidities here is an antidote for compulsive possessions in the form of a messy girl carrying a message of the love of Christ. Mrs. Reed has a virginal Helen: mother who bursts a chaos whirlwind also has hidden a cool side look to angels.

Helen's admonition of distance emerges from being within the stepmother's wrath, for she also has been whipped and blasted. Severe Scatcherd and Helen hold out to and from one another. Perhaps stepmother would want Helen to traverse her (their) own madness. Helen perhaps needs that madness body welts, concrete body yearning notice.

What would it mean to move out from the nonhuman elemental stir at window's edge and not fall into Mrs. Reed's (unconscious) animosity, now self-loathing, we are doing it again in a new domain and this one beside mediates though we are resentful even speaking savagely we rise to her ear our narrative here at Lowood she hears through gradation we rise, mediated do not stay possessed.

Differentiation within what moans, clamors, could possess us. Impatiently we ask: ' "Is not Mrs. Reed a hard-hearted, bad woman?" ' She replies over-viewing, names it we are ' "nursing animosity," ' bleeding our milk over to that animus, for animus has passed through that hard-hearted stepmother successively of many forms, we shun it daily as we feed it a consumption of ourselves. Nursing animosity. Nursing stepmother's animus.

> ⊷§ Sublimation. Hate sears stomach truculence, we suspect
> him, we will tear through his chest bending those ribs
> crunching and our hand to his heart we are compressing this
> heart until the dried dust of his dessicated blood pours out
> streaming.
>
> Ceasing our 'feverish and reckless' run at her legs are
> crossed a head at book prays to the text of what we cannot
> see yet moves her moment is when he shapes himself in mind
> interior, letting this shape himself before us and we feel what
> was hating and frazzled pass through to this shaping of him
> we hold it before ourselves: all we have done which would
> remind us of him, how we have used him to stand between.
>
> Letting go we fall upwards the trace around its edges per-
> haps blue and purple relief. Below bowel surges those sources
> unknown though she finds their words glory gradation we

know once we have seen him and passed beyond he is not
gone yet behind pushing us to what is spacious where we
have met her textual sister enspaced purple lining sister. ࿇

Lowood's listener of Jane's 'bitter and truculent' speaking of the
Gateshead narrative suggests a move from fiend to seraph, and, in doing
so, interlocution becomes meditation, interior reflection: 'I saw by her look
she wished no longer to talk to me, but rather to converse with her own
thoughts.'
How our Gateshead events are held by Helen's ear at Lowood moves the
narrative through bitterness and truculence projected without to an interior
resounding, meditation, place of creed, distinction of criminal and crime, a
mighty home.
Through a love of temple some insight cools where we have been
branded. Helen's coolness is to burn off passionate feeling branded, burn
off, rising refined. Interlocution at Lowood is with one who hearing our
hate does not entangle herself within our flaming bowel. At Lowood the
other one burns cool does not catch the fiends though they are contagious
which is why we have flown across the room to her because we have seen
even in our elemental turbulence that she is sitting closest to the fire what
stirs abstracted the air is cool.
In Helen's creed body is branded passionate emotion churning bowel
body is corruptible shall be put off. Her burning interior light a creed. Hers
is a flame unlike the Gateshead compulsive flare-up, her burning insights
the corruptible body will fall from us leaving 'spark of spirit' which is:

' " — the impalpable principle of life and thought, pure as
    when it left
the Creator to inspire the creature: whence it came it
    will return;
perhaps again to be communicated to some being higher
    than man —
perhaps to pass through gradations of glory, from the
    pale
human soul to brighten to the seraph!
Surely it will never, on the contrary, be suffered
to degenerate from man to fiend?
No." '

࿇ Plato. *Phaedo.* " 'And is not purification really that which
has been mentioned so often in our discussion, to separate as
far as possible the soul from the body, and to accustom it to
collect itself together out of the body in every part, and to
dwell alone by itself as far as it can, both at this present and
in the future, being freed from the body as if from a prison?

'By all means,' said he.

. . . 'This is much more likely: If [the soul] is pure when it gets free, and drags nothing of the body with it, since it has no communion with the body in life if it can help it, but avoids the body and gathers itself into itself, since it is always practising this—here we have nothing else but a soul loving wisdom rightly, and in reality practising death—don't you think this would be a practice of death?'

'By all means.' "

Plato. *Symposium.* " ' "Next he must believe beauty in souls to be more precious than beauty in the body; so that if anyone is decent in soul, even if it has little bloom, it should be enough for him to love and care for, and to beget and seek such talks as will make young people better; that he may moreover be compelled to contemplate the beauty in our pursuits and customs, and to see that all beauty is of one and the same kin, and that so he may believe that bodily beauty is a small thing . . . Whoever shall be guided so far towards the mysteries of love, by contemplating beautiful things rightly in due order, is approaching the last grade." ' "

I Corinthians 15:51-53. "Lo! I tell you a mystery. We shall not all sleep, but we shall all be changed, in a moment, in the twinkling of an eye, at the last trumpet. For the trumpet will sound, and the dead will be raised imperishable, and we shall be changed. For this perishable nature must put on the imperishable, and this mortal nature must put on immortality."

II Corinthians 3:18. "And we all, with unveiled face, beholding the glory of the Lord, are being changed into his likeness from one degree of glory to another; for this comes from the Lord who is the Spirit."

Plotinus. *Ennead* III.6.5. "But if there is turning in the other direction, to the things above, away from those below, it is surely (is it not?) purification, and separation too, when it is the act of a soul which is no longer in body as if it belonged to it, and is being like a light which is not in turbid obscurity."

Implicit in Helen's creed is linear gradation: fiend to human soul to seraph. Attachments, attackings, addictions (called corruptible body) are lower. From the Helen perspective, body is compulsive reactivity of passion and spent fury, Gateshead is body.

In order to arrive at our first perspective on Gateshead we look down and judge Gateshead concrete body inferior. Possession at Gateshead becomes body corruptible. Gradation lesson is a necessary step in extrication from Gateshead body which is possessed body.

The first mode of differentiation from Gateshead body when the stone-Tablet has said Glory Father in heaven is the Lowood lesson of leaving "body," putting it off as corruptible, as it has been of our Platonic, Christian and Neoplatonic teachings. Leaving the corruptible, leaving possessions (nursing animosity) defined as body, what Lowood's Helen finds as she sublimates body becomes reading body, her love imaginal as ideational, love of text, Miss Temple's new ideas, essentially an erotic text body uplifting.

Miss Scatcherd is the Lowood element wanting to teach that body is not only criminal, that care of one's nails and drawer also is prayer. Helen has left her physical body and belongings to her creed. She is slatternly, sacrificed body's care through her mediation of the stirring elements to a place sublime they become love of text of wisdoms Miss Temple can add new reflection brings out a lovely smile, erotic reading body; Miss Scatcherd wants to whip that body back to physiological dimension.

Miss Scatcherd whipping a premature return to concrete body too soon after the Gateshead extrication and while just learning Lowood ascent for differentiation within recess.

We had been almost annihilated by our mother's John, and this Lowood domain is of consistency, order, celibacy, high walled propriety in the hollow of which appears Helen Burns saying not to be branded rise. Jane never knew she had the choice.

Choices of proximity. Helen speaks from abstract atmosphere, her text shines light is higher than we know, we can refine, vaporize to the high grade, and Helen tells Jane the story of Charles the First who could not see beyond the perogatives of his own crown, his vision too myopic and without the larger sun-sight he is murdered.

Lowood strips as we extricate from Gateshead. Singed layers for we have been branded now strip, cool down spacious left to our own yet within a consistency, repetitive protected, we begin to sense spark of spirit, unattached. We attend to the chaste/chest friend with the inner burning; the intense, clumsy girl sitting by the fire, absorbed, meditative—her hair is stringy, dirty, the way she sits badly crumbles her skirt.

Confession of faith in creed. We never see what Helen looks like. The tangible world is not of her creed. Her tangible body is her dirty nail, crumbled skirt, untidy drawer, slouched shoulders. The (interior) river in Deepden and Charles the First, here also are her earth and body.

Her creed of severance through love and she does not return a love to that concrete body, does not care for herself personally. In order to sever from the Gateshead body, our first step is to differentiate through abstraction, reflection, mediation as sublimation, love as severance from body as corrupt, neglected body, first step out is gradation up as the Lowood lesson of differentiation.

Helen as speaking subject — the gradation lesson occurs through a beginning Lowood interlocution — gradation is dialogue with whom is interiorly based, has overview and reflects difference. Interlocution with Helen is the beginning of interior reflection which rises us from what was Gateshead possession. Interior reflection in the place of elemental stirrings when pane separates instead of shatters.

A rough monitor interrupts Helen's meditative silence. After the eloquent expression of her creed a personal care continually calls her back. Helen sees the necessity of the Scatcherd whipping, she rushes to the call without honoring that drawers of this world belonging.

&§ Albedo as sun. We have awoken and have seen we are locked in the bowels of the earth and there is a fire raging here, this fire wants to eat off us, wants what little spark of life there is to enrage us to only its own we are trapped within the bowels without escape, no air, no light but the starving flame and we are open we are alone and we desire and so we engage it and we are burning we feed off ourselves until finally we convulse for that guide that grant that god until the flame begins to lower while we begin the suffocation now numbing we can no longer feel anything taste anything the senses blur and we are veiled numbness we are going under until we fire our last shot sickened this the only way we know we fire that shot, sickened we leave those bowels and we are weak, we follow the order of a new place some say Institution, it is of the women, they tell the new order. We wait here until we are noticing her she is besieged also by the same searing and yet here is a light as the sun and she burns in the sky this one of a distance, treasure inward ever white ever light burning light her sight is precise she reflects through the shadow discerning the worth of every mother severe not cruel and she speaks her mind a dance of its light to burn now fever a mind's sight mind sparkling the ethics, hers is a philosophy of love. &•

Bibliography

Barthes, Roland. *The Pleasure of the Text*. Trans. by Richard Miller. New York: Hill and Wang, 1975; quoted pp. 16–17.

Cowan, Lyn. *Masochism: A Jungian View*. Dallas: Spring Publications, 1982.

Edinger, Edward F. *Anatomy of the Psyche*. La Salle, Ill.: Open Court Publishing Co., 1985; Chapter 5, "Sublimatio," and Chapter 6, "Mortificatio."

Freud, Sigmund, "The Ego and the Id." *The Complete Psychological Works of Sigmund Freud*. Vol. 19. Trans. James Strachey. London: Hogarth, 1961.

Holy Bible. Revised Standard Version.

Jung, C. G. "The Relations between the Ego and the Unconscious." *The Collected Works of C. G. Jung*. Vol. 7. Trans. R. F. C. Hull. Princeton, N.J.: Princeton University Press, 1953.

Miller, D.A. "*Cage aux folles:* Sensation and Gender in Wilkie Collins's *The Woman in White*." *Representations* 14 (1986): 107; quoted p. 116.

Plato. *Great Dialogues of Plato*. Trans. by W. H. D. Rouse. New York: New American Library, Inc., 1956; quoted pp. 470, 485, 104–5.

Plotinus. *Enneads* III. Cambridge, Mass.: Harvard University Press, 1967; quoted p. 231.

Chapter 7

Natural Curl

The first quarter at Lowood: the severe cold cuts through the shoes, swelling the feet already raw, enflamed each night, agonizing force back into the shoe in the morning. The other students hastily steal favorable places in front of the hearth after an afternoon paralyzed from the cold of the church service. These 'famished great girls' provoke, even menace the younger ones to give over some of their meagre portions of food. Finally back after the long service, bitter wind of the exposed road 'almost flayed the skin from our faces,' we were frozen on that road walking even the teachers dejected except Miss Temple actively encouraging us on as the ' "stalwart soldiers." ' The Sunday evenings are spent by heart repeating 5th-6th-7th chapters of Matthew and listening to Miss Miller's long sermon as the young girls here they are falling in a slumber, we have to prop them up.

Sitting with slate in hand one afternoon, I am puzzling over a long division sum, and the long (he is narrow) figure of Brocklehurst passes. It is the same black column, the ' "Coming Man" ' I have feared as awaited this one who would carry forth Mrs. Reed's curse, 'brand me as a bad child for ever.' We all rise.

Brocklehurst speaks to Miss Temple:

Only one darning needle to be given out to each pupil.

The black hose should be mended better.

The extra luncheon of bread and cheese—by what authority was it introduced?

Miss Temple replies: She is responsible. She could not let the pupils fast until dinner time after the burnt porridge which they could not eat.

Allow him an instant!—his plan for us as ' "hardy, patient, self-denying" ' none of this ' "luxury and indulgence" ' he is saying: ' "Should any little accidental disappointment of the appetite occur, such as the spoiling of a meal, the under or over dressing of a dish, the incident ought not to be neutralized by replacing with something more delicate the comfort lost, thus pampering the body and obviating the aim of this institution; it ought to be improved to the spiritual edification of the pupils, by encouraging them to evince fortitude under the temporary privation." '

Now he is exclaiming on the martyrs and how it is a starving of our immortal souls if bread and cheese substitute burnt porridge it is a feeding of the body vile.

Miss Temple hears this gazing straight ahead, her face a marble cold and fixed, mouth and brow settling into their 'petrified severity.'

Brocklehurst suddenly gives a start: hand shaking the cane is pointed

toward a girl and he is asking *what* is that girl with curled hair? Miss Temple
quietly states the girl's name. He asks why in his establishment is her hair the
mass of red curls. Even more quietly, Miss Temple responds that her hair
curls naturally.

    Brocklehurst: ' "Naturally! Yes but we are not to conform to nature: I wish
these girls to be the children of Grace: and why that abundance?" ' Cut
it, the hair only modest, plain. He is ordering a row of girls to stand
and turn around: he will survey their plaits. Involuntary smile curls
Miss Temple's lips now covered by her handkerchief.

    I am leaning back further to witness the looks and grimaces on the girls'
faces their comment to him with their back to him, no, this man cannot
alter the inside of who they are.

    His verdict: cut off those top-knots of a vanity.

    Brocklehurst pursues, Madam, he says, ' "I have a Master to serve whose
Kingdom is not of this world: my mission is to mortify in these girls
the lusts of the flesh. . ." '

And he is pronouncing against the embellishments of a female nature when
the three other visitors enter. They had been inspecting the dormitories and
now they reproach one of the teachers. Velvet, gray beaver hats, ostrich
plumes, the false front of French curls, these the wife and daughters of
Brocklehurst to whom Miss Temple gives seats of honor.

    Jane's slate drops, it crashes to the floor. Splits in two.

    Brocklehurst recognizes her, he almost had forgotten; he calls her to come
forward.

    Miss Temple is whispering to me as I pass that it was only an accident; I
am pierced by this kindness: ' "Another minute, and she will despise me
for a hypocrite," thought I; and an impulse of fury against Reed, Brocklehurst, and Co., bounded in my pulses at the conviction. I was no
Helen Burns.'

Now he places me on a stool before all with those waves of plummage
beyond of his ladies as he announces me an agent of the Evil one, for I am a
castaway, alien, not of the fold, interloper, I must be scrutinized, even
excluded from their company if necessary since I am a—liar (a pause of ten
minutes, the Brocklehurst ladies take out their handkerchiefs) and I would
have contaminated the home of my pious benefactress, I am diseased to be
healed I was sent to Lowood.

    Imploring the teachers ' "not to allow the waters to stagnate round" ' me,
he leaves with an order I remain on the stool for half an hour longer and no
one is to speak a word to me the remainder of this day.

There was a time I thought I could not stand the shame of standing in the
room for all to see, and here I am exposed on 'a pedestal of infamy.' No
language for what arises in me now stifling my breath, constricting my
throat, and yet here is a girl passing and with what a strange light in her eyes
the ray of which bears me up, extraordinary sensation through me, 'I mastered the rising hysteria, lifted up my head, and took a firm stand on the
stool.'

After a brief question for which she is chided, Helen Burns returns to her seat smiling at me again as she goes by. 'What a smile! I remember it now, and I know that it was the effluence of fine intellect, of true courage; it lit up her marked lineaments, her thin face, her sunken grey eye, like a reflection from the aspect of an angel.' Her exercise blotted wrongly, condemned to a bread and cheese dinner by Miss Scatcherd, this girl passing wears the untidy badge on her arm. How the teacher focuses on her defect, cannot see what she inspires, 'full brightness of the orb.'

Spark of spirit, her speaking was fervent. Gentle brilliant guidance of a great girl and an awesome teacher, and perhaps we have begun to ease, ease into what is of women surrounding us. Then all we know is that everything again is freezing. We expect Brocklehurst, daily fear him.

Not yet an entry to Helen's Lowood. Sent by Mrs. Reed to learn punitive constriction that severs, a prohibition; yet this girl speaks severance through love and at a hearth we have bent toward her word. Mrs. Reed's Brocklehurst has led us to another order, female aesthetic intelligence; our touching to it returns Mrs. Reed's fear of that nature we await him.

Mrs. Reed who raised us to know his moral opposition stripping us from our nursery haze. With his erection she slit through our numbness splitting us out of Gateshead has he more lessons. Sensing him always possible in this Lowood place, we await the ' "Coming Man." '

As we feel his presence imminent we have difficulty in the entry first quarter. We observe, we pick up sensations, but all appears rote and very cold. Our life becomes routine. We feel outside ourselves. Cold only rote behaviors.

Gateshead had its privileges. It seized us and we were in the sizzling heat at times we thought we were well fed. Here it is very cold and we have trouble entering, our enflamed foot does not fit comfortably into the frozen morning shoe.

Used to outburst, we do not trust the motion in this Helen landscape, used to hell's fire explosive, how can this cool white light stir us? Here it seems too still. We were one with the Gateshead reaction and there is no violent motion to follow here. Austere, the spirits are not moving in the frozen pew, the church service does not warm us, we sit rigidly, stingy allotment of cold meat and bread, we still have the bitter walk back two miles we sit paralyzed, ears frozen shut the same drone.

Only Miss Temple musters an urging seems foreign and we cannot join, we cannot find that soldier of whom she speaks, stalwart soldier. No entry, nothing stirs, we await the Coming Man.

Our fear of Brocklehurst is also our desire of Mrs. Reed, a desire after all to return to that family, the familiar mode of explosive prohibition fires.

Reedian outburst all we have known of desire is familiar. We fear this closeness to the women in this new place. Our fear returning to hers of us, the way we crimsoned before her saying stand mother within your own red heat now our fear that is also hers, awaiting him.

Gateshead had its compelling forces. Here the other teachers are dejected, frozen themselves, and in the evening the younger girls slump, fall under during the sermon too long, too cold. We are not moved, we await it from the outside but all appears routine, asleep, ice still.

We have carried Mrs. Reed's Gateshead curse here, awaiting Brockle-hurst to proclaim it. And we see that a great greed arises in this place of the cold, hollow hunger. The larger girls are famished, they push their way to the front of the hearth. They make us divide and relinquish our bread slice, eagerly they consume much of our coffee the closest heat of the day.

Years isolated interspersed assault, when we have been touched ever so lightly upon our cheek, another girl has heard our bitter narrative, reflecting alongside, bending back, and then a great hunger erupts in us. Great greed from the deprivation of Gateshead's gorgings unfed, and the way we oppose this hunger a resistance which is Brocklehurst whom we expect while we cannot enter the Lowood shoe.

She would not want us comfortable here, bending to the fold of young girls. These women have openings, eloquent speakings, and we may want to fold into them. She would not want it, sending instead the son repetitious to a Brocklehurst prohibition.

Hating our place of her desire she ensnared us. Becoming all we could for her, entangled body, this collective female body can ensnare we fear as did she, ensnare is our fear he will arrive speaking condemnation soon, our fear of blending into the female nature becomes a paranoia he will 'brand (us) as a bad child for ever.'

We do not relax and let go into these great girls. Instead they take and we give it over to them. Still feeding out is the Gateshead curse. Our portion to them as we refuse to bend toward the long sermon, here the women are convening and yet it becomes petrified as we watch out for him living her curse.

We understand these chapters of Matthew, the wisdom words shepherd of authority spoken the beatitudes we are blessed as meek, as mourning, as merciful, as persecuted and hungering for righteousness we will be heard, satisfied. No eye for eye instead not to resist the evil one, and of those who boast their prayer, blatant their gifts of alm, who fast to be seen these are hypocrites, instead a secrecy the shepherd whispers secrecy, he says so with an authority we listen: as above so below, on earth as it is in heaven, judge not here and so not judged, measure given out is what is gotten, ask, seek, knock, beware the false prophet, these words done will be the house of rock, in any flood firm foundation, winds blown and beaten.

Then the teacher gives a sermon yet there is no movement, that woman is not carrying the shepherd has not made it to the woman, we are women listening but how do we as women live those words: can that shepherd lead us to our mother for we are orphans, and it has been such a long day in the cold, the younger ones fall under in their slumber.

We have come to Lowood to learn not to react in a blind groping blatancy, we have come here to learn a secrecy, what is hypocrisy.

The Lowood place of teachings is based on stripping the pride, hubris, of the collective body entangled, we have arrived to learn of severance, differentiation within recess. Severed from Gateshead, on our own after years of impulse and implosion, explosion, left to our own, it feels like nothing, frozen hard too still.

We are learning long division at Lowood. We see the differentiated parts and how they stand on their own. Dividend contains its divisor the number of times as quotient. Dividend within bracket collective body. We want to begin to differentiate within the collective body, know the unit by its specified and related parts.

We want to begin to differentiate within the collective body. We know we are still tied to her will always be related though we are attempting to deny that relation, split off from it completely since she was consuming us using our motion only as her own until we had to burst out for her, impulsively discharge to sever she would not feed us distinctly.

How to divide. At Gateshead, division as impulsive discharge, blatant discord until a gray field interior where someone asked a question, speaking subject, someone here a subject of our question, her Brocklehurst had given us the distance, we could see her contour as we found speaking subject: beginning self-referential differentiation yet still not in relation. In the Gateshead mode, either we are hers completely, fused within her regress/recess, or completely split, irrevocably unrelated and we have screamed it.

At Gateshead one is not different and related. The division on this Lowood slate, the parts stay related. Here division has its inherent pattern indicating the relation of specific parts to collective body, the design of its patterning inherent in the division. As divisor and as quotient differentiated out of the bracket yet still related.

We want to be stripped of Gateshead embellishment, that inflated madness impulse, know ourselves outside the bracket, standing rock foundation not shattered, we want to divide. In the long division lesson, the long way to know division, it is slow and this slate is cold; in the long division the first lesson is splitting. Before we learn the relation of different parts, we first split divisor out of dividend.

The only way we have known splitting is when we did not want to leave that nursery, still our desire to be held within her body, pacing outside the door when summoned, the only way we have known division is through splitting in condemnation, Brocklehurst. He has to be passed through first in our lesson of division. Our freezing fingers are writing long division sums on a dark slate upon which the long shadow of the narrow minister falls.

His rigidity is at Miss Temple's side and we expect as fear she will be influenced. Paranoid, we hear him whispering, his arrival is to immediately whisper to the woman we most admire, how we have looked up to her he will have her look down at us. 'I did not doubt he was making disclosures of my villany; and I watched her eye with painful anxiety, expecting every moment to see its dark orb turn on me a glance of repugnance and contempt.'

He is whispering to the woman who has met and touched us, begun to feed during the privation, we had begun to feel an attraction for her, return with desire and here he is denouncing. We experience his entry as paranoia: our fear that our desired one will turn is our fear of that desire.

We were trying to settle in yet have been unable, wind flaying face's skin, he is the way we will not fold into this female nature. Denouncing, he defends against any comfort, demanding strictest minimum. Comfort as excess, excess as sin against which he splits with severity: darn, restrict, starve body feed soul restraint of a privation.

The shepherd had advised not to flaunt our prayer, to know ourselves stripped as holy invisible, yet this minister turns the words of that Christ to torment our visible body, what could have the comfort once it was touched by her, only vile.

He says it to the woman who has met and touched us, begun to feed during the privation, we had begun to feel an attraction for her, return with desire and here he comes and he denounces, fear of the origin of such desire is his denouncement.

    ❧ The body only vile. We have opened our legs and
expelled what remains entangled of our bodily fluids even
attached through stem it is a daughter. This baby is all in a
mess, oozing the liquids, brown masses continually, also the
vomit. Nothing stays put in what is her every cavity demanding our full. Food swallowed not digested globular in its
motion down the chin smearing. Summoning our entry yet if
we enter her massive waves, body movements, we return we

step back fall back the waves capsize us to when there was
only absorption and expulsion as need with no restriction,
she excretes we remember a mother recoiling, fearful of
drowning she seized Brocklehurst and we severed to a thud.
He was schedules of abandonment. She claimed it dirt, mess
only chaos to her a germ it will spread this chaos of being.

At the other end of our stem, offshoot, sprout, germ, she
is our germ, she will look like us and she returns us to our
origins, germs as waves summoning us both indistinguish-
able, loss of any self, whether birth whether death.

Perfection in cleanliness, we do not want one flake of
excrement to remind us, return us to this primordial age
rolling in the unnameable grief of our mothers, sorrow waves
of their mothers no mother could ride all women recoil from
the daughter returning them as infant abandoned by a mother's terrified grief.

We will clean every morsel of this daughter's excrement
and regurgitation, the way she has expelled and spit back to
us luring and deathly waves we become afraid even this morsel may spread. We see it moving from the diaper to the
rubber pants to her legs and the changing table and now to
our hands, now to our slipper and everything we have
touched that day we are frantically cleaning all we have
touched every contact we disinfect. It will spread and we will
be swallowed primordial of mothers where no mother there.

He comes to prescribe against this nature. In his name we
shun our body restricting its foundations. We say only one
darning needle, do not wear the colored stockings and do not
exhibit those swaying breasts, the friends walking you around
the corner they are instigators, hold back. We prohibit her
entry to where we have not known there could be inherent
form, cautious design. We prohibit: clean the rim of that
sink, beneath the metal clean that grime with a toothpick
sharpened. We say save, constrain, hold back. The body as
vile. ৡ◈

Lowood has its own regulation yet we are too frightened of remaining in
it long enough to know the design, its natural and long division. Mothers
fearing waves, femaled body, flooding, drowning, have not known a holding, what orders there, or what could shore, the words of the Fathers never
spoke to what is the natural and long division within these waves of collective body.

Our mothers left uncontained in their own nature so we too shun it. We have been touched by a discovered mother and we recoil, resist. We hear Brocklehurst whispering, curse of mothers.

Paternal authority of the Institutions have said split off what could wave, what could enhance, proliferate, embellish is waste; what it could not see the waves were our practice of distinguishing, the way we have expelled matter to know what is this frame remaining, separate, what is the scission, the rupture, bowels tearing, mouth expelling what it will no longer take in what it is not, positing that it is without what it is not which is being expelled.

Generations passing terror of these waves the preacher condemns says split we have not realized it was only the first lesson. The preacher condemns. As we listen, we confuse him with those scriptures and we are splitting from our collective body, we seize Brocklehurst first, women to women convening, Brocklehurst arises first.

The temptation of the Lowood place of collective female body where we begin to learn of differentiation, severance through love, propriety, the erotic coolness of our nature, is Brocklehurst's rigidity where the cold becomes prohibition.

Possessed by him we become obsessed with our alienation from others, desire becomes a paranoia. He stands us on the outside and superciliously looks down upon us. He is where there is only an exterior shutting out, condemning; he puts us on the outside which is our nascent knowledge of ourselves as distinct but as we remain out he wants no human touch, sterile. Brocklehurst is when learning a loving severance becomes punished for being touched we prohibit.

֍ When the dust begins its cover on my wooden floor often the broom is not enough. I get down on my knee with a large cotton cloth I rub those boards until the cloth's hand print becomes clearly visible, for the floor it is practically a polishing. I prefer all my tiny glass figurines in an exact angle on their table, everything aligned according to the order of their finest regard as the even proportion of towels arranged by color and size in the bathroom pleases me. But it is a Thanksgiving coming those children, nieces and nephews crawling they will be under my feet and rolling and scratching they will be crawling so I will have to walk a foot above my own polished floor no longer in its cleanliness the hands of those children carrying the grime of all ages settling into each of this floor's crack. And my figurines what will they look like on that highest shelf there they must be seques-

tered four days from the curious hands of children groping
they will reach for my ankles most likely I shall have to
pinch.

My cousin will be in my bed, I will remove my favorite
sheets, she sleeps so wildly, the crumbling, in the bathroom
her bag of makeup will disarray, she may put her tooth's
brush very close to mine, forget, wrongly reach, use mine
instead, so I must insure to check the degree of its wetness,
scrutinize before, if necessary sterilize. After washing her
hands streaks of dirt are left upon the soap.

The child will call me aunt she will reach up at me with
those fingers grasping, she will want my hold, my food, my
purse, I will not give a thing for it would be pampering. The
older will bring in the latest essay written at school, the water
color, I will simply nod as withholding the praise so desired
would swell her head. ॐ

Brocklehurst contaminates as he fears contamination. His supercilious
stance implicates us, makes us feel guilty, we become polluted through his
gaze and in this way he spreads, indeed is the source of, pollution. He
infects through his prohibition and its inherent accusation, spreading pollution, dirtying through contact.

When he possesses us, we want to split apart from what would be our
endemic nature. He possesses us to scrutinize then alienate from the
woman, if the other catches him from us, then the splitting multiplies. The
way he bears down in pleasure aiming to cut into what would be our fault is
his sadism arising out of the great fear of being locked in the nursery place.
The splitting out proliferates sadistic cuts alienating. His splitting proliferates becoming disease.

Miss Temple is who is not contaminated by Brocklehurst. She sits as
marble. Hard, off-white stone has definite boundary. Do not resist evil. She
does not absorb a word of him as he is spreading himself. She does not resist
as she does not absorb since she knows the tragedy of a woman Brocklehurst possessed who superciliously precludes all contact becomes a dirty
contact.

'Coldness and fixity' of her marble: his word not part of her teaching. If
she had lent him ear of the bowed head, if he entered the slightest crevice
who would depart this one she serves of her temple and turning Brocklehurst on herself all appetite loses.

For his demand is to eradicate nourishment any increase of life cell he
suspects multiplication. His suspicion is contagious and in fact multiplies.
We have absorbed him when we do not trust our appetite or any internal

motion defining. Brocklehurst's definition cuts against, cuts off, is at the expense of nourishment. Not multiplication of life cell related to human nature, yet multiplication of life cell through splitting by renunciation of all nature.

When his prohibition force arises, it suspects, it infects, his moral law therefore increases guilt, the more we listen to him the more guilty we become. Yet he speaks while a teacher sits by, he appears in the company of who does not take on his contact. He raises in full regard, in sight of, his antidote.

Miss Temple does not engage with Brocklehurst because she stands for her decision of appetite, she holds it, is held by it. Prohibitive and punitive, Brocklehurst would sever us from a woman's hold, that one fearing appetite only blind to her son's compensatory concupiscence.

At Gateshead, Brocklehurst's severance, that form of Mrs. Reed's sadism, and we discharged to a distinct interior voice ' "What shall I do?" ' bringing us to a place where our senses can sense outside, we sense exterior, and here when Mrs. Reed's sadistic form of severance arises, it does not have an effect on who already perceives herself as distinct, firm encasement, boundaried, who has not even attempted to appropriate us.

Off-white marble, 'petrified severity,' her severity is as hard as stone, that limestone metamorphic to stone severity keeping her severed which is the Lowood austerity Brocklehurst's sadism has lead Jane to in the first place. The stone of Miss Temple severs without cutting, yet wards off, she does not take his recrimination, and her severity is the lesson to which Brocklehurst's severance was aiming yet hers is without sadism, she separates herself not by cutting off/up another a pleasure.

She does not submit, does not engage, does not retaliate. Marble white hard the surface texture is silken stone infinitely durable, still as the sculpture impenetrable, interior life swirl protected. Marble refined and durable stone of beauty accompanies what would be Brocklehurst temptation.

When confronted with the moralistic voice of law demanding we eat a burnt porridge, a turn to marble is being in the temple place, becomes a sacred endeavor, and resides beyond that paternalistic word. The Bible has said conformity to Paternal Law (and its prohibitive strictures on food, the female body) allows us access to the holy place of Temple. Yet at Lowood conformity to Law is not of the Temple place and here is our lesson in learning our natural division yet how we are still related to Mrs. Reed, her red-room and femaled collective body.

Learning long division, his was only the first lesson of splitting, and his temptation is, once outside the bracket, to repudiate that collective body, split entirely from that nature, that femaled body. When the Temple place is to stand for the appetite of the collective body, he is deflected.

Unable to infect Miss Temple, he is deflected off her surface. Left to his own device, he begins to spread, to bring himself out in a way ironical and finally comical. He is deflected off Miss Temple to the girl of the red curl.

The Brocklehurst belief, that which extricated us from the Gateshead body, is that nature would infinitely curl and embellish, nauseating morass, suffocating abundance. He believes it is up to him and those of his discipline to prohibit such natural growth as moral Law, here a human intervention to prevent an overwhelming by those most primordial waves and their deathly multiplication. He pronounces: we are not to conform to nature. Split off that curl.

We were beginning to learn division in the collective place of women when he entered. We use him for the first splitting, divisor out of dividend, sense of an alterity arriving us at Lowood, but the only way he has known this severance from collective body is through condemnation, one side only superior, we meet Brocklehurst and suddenly we begin thinking not horizontally out of bracket yet oppositionally in a way hierarchical.

After his splitting, something contemptible becomes useless and it pertains to our nature, our appetite, some parts no longer matter, are disgusting, disgraceful. Indulgent v. self-denying. Physical pampering v. spiritual edification. Vile body v. immortal soul. Nature v. Grace.

Splitting too rapidly while detesting that body, split cells splitting too rapidly, not a long division but proliferation wanting eradication of that collective body, cut it apart as vile is the cancer.

Once we learn our long division, however, we see that divisions do not preclude indeed even necessitate a multiplication which stays related to collective body. They require that quotient and divisor multiply and move in and out of the dividend collective. Multiplication a requirement within division and not an excess: division has a place for all the parts, suggests heterogeneous body, necessitates multiplication, no outcast by annihilation or contempt. Division has a place for all the parts.

Remaining possessed by Brocklehurst at the initial splitting stage precludes learning the natural order of long division, how multiplication is inherent in division, how differentiation is to be within collective nature. We can learn from nature. Nature cuts back herself, even tears herself asunder. She strips herself of her own overgrowth.

Nature has her own mortification, resides through contranaturam, evolves in and out of her own decay, putrefaction.

Through the cold, the precipitation, the wind, nature cuts back, separates, shatters, severs herself from herself, ourself from ourself. 'At the close of the afternoon service, we returned by an exposed and hilly road, where the bitter winter wind, blowing over a range of snowy summits to the north, almost flayed the skin from our faces.'

Nature as the teacher of long division, all her parts always matter. We enter our nature to learn division and inhibition in a way that all distinct parts still matter.

He says we are not to conform to nature. Yet nature will not let herself be stripped or eradicated (insulted) by a figure who ministers outside her in this way. Her laws are also our moral law (on earth as it is in heaven), her desire to be cut back, trimmed, pruned, often asks the human to assist in such inhibition, naturally.

Indeed, nature cuts back (and off) herself especially in her more "reckless" turns on herself, but she will not let herself be mortified by human prohibition. Brocklehurst attempts to eradicate the natural curl.

As minister pronounces curl and braid the sin with cutting the penance, the lips of the teacher curl, the girls' features bend in grimace and curl. Naturam expellas furca, tamen usque recurrent. Nature will not let herself be eradicated by a figure who ministers outside her this way.

> ◄§ Curl bending toward some heat. Bodies as ribbons we
> curl into lovers' arms the animals encircled at hearth. Soup
> stirred the vegetables spiral their flavor. The petal convolutes
> its backward bending towards sun's favor. Curl of the slope
> now a woman's outline gentle curve of breast, of stomach.
> Tear trickling down the sloped lash. Baby's fingers grasping
> our own. Hands freckled with the age spots wrap around
> cane's curl old woman ready to return to all nature's bend
> back into herself. Bowels coiled rhythmic relief. Our mouths
> open tongues curl searching, sea-searching. Swirling in that
> ocean's undertow our long hair plaited with seaweed looping
> around our bodies' flow. Whorls of a spiral shell. The tend-
> ril's helix. Hair kinked the mainspring ready uncoil: curl as
> nature's most potential exclamation. Always the turn back to
> itself, curl's unfolding never bursts, crest wave ride we are
> buoyed or rolled never jetted. Curl becomes wave, plait,
> wreath. Curl's swirling force containing a most vibrant inhi-
> bition. §►

Jane arrived at Lowood to learn severance, formal schedule and marble discipline, distinction from the mother without losing or condemning the mother as our only desire, decentered desire of what was mother. Natural curl needed at Lowood: curl allows us to learn division within the Lowood place without splitting accusatory. After extraction, divisor curls back into dividend to differentiate quotient. Curl defies splits.

Curl infolds, cuts back on itself, inhibits without condemnation. The power of the curl is as secretive as the edge of a smile. Curl serves as antidote to the rigidity setting in Brocklehurst's splitting, prevents teachings of severance from becoming sadistic, autocratic.

Teaching severance requires a bending or else a cracking into hypocrisy ensues because even as she divides herself nature will not cease her curl: the Brocklehurst ladies enter.

Deflected from the marble of Miss Temple, deflected by the girls' curled lips, Brocklehurst's prohibition does not catch and gets caught in its opposite. The prohibited parts split off return becoming members of his family. Aim of the inflated preacher deflates before each student's eye with the entry of the Brocklehurst women in plume and ringlet.

False front of French curls, he dresses up his women as he preaches on the vanity of the curl. When we absorb Brocklehurst, our obsessions become extravagant, huge dramas of prohibition. Our attempt to keep the baby clean warrants a hugh cast of housekeepers and a vigilance on every germ we chase that germ in an excessive drama.

The Brocklehurst ladies are the "hypocritical" sides which even as preaching an ascetic moralism must flaunt: every prohibition's effusive underside emerges in performance, publicly displays itself. Soon the entire room is in a flourish of that which we would prohibitionally strip. Brocklehurst himself is split: he supports in his female that which he ministerially denounces.

He is who came to separate us from Mrs. Reed through a sadistic severance becoming then its opposite: tying us to her even more for he will carry her curse carrying us back to her. His prohibitions sound like battering in our heads through which we hear Mrs. Reed's retaliation, and we are very close once more to that rejecting stepmother.

Splitting necessitates desire for the lost part, Brocklehurst is Jane's split from Gateshead, abrupt cut where she is not divided in fact is actually still fused as alien (her marginality at Lowood is yet her allegiance to Gateshead), and within her split lies her desire still of the Reeds, Gateshead luxury and its arbitrary discharges, her Reedian hold where desire is hot burst requiring prohibition, love only as possession.

What could be long division becomes merely split apart in Brocklehurst's presence. In this split he says: one part is not to be; and, if it appears (as it must, alongside), we speak of hypocrisy. Yet in long division, all parts decentered have a place, none are feigned, if they appear they are.

Brocklehurst would keep Mrs. Reed's curse the dominant motion. He does not facilitate the way Mrs. Reed can be one figure, one voice, part of the multiplication within the division of the psyche. Instead, in his oppositional way he bears down upon us, he keeps her exterior, univocal, monocentric desire.

We feared him all along and when he comes (as he must through our potent fear stemming from a desire for the stepmother which draws him to us) our long division slate splits. As Brocklehurst appears, we face our splits.

His battering is the curse of our return to her as we see behind him (what backs Brocklehurst) the mother and two daughters pompously they are taking seats of honor: we hold on tightly to Gateshead by his splittings.

Jane has needed Gateshead at Lowood for who are these women touching her in what could be love, even love of enemy, and what of their internal heat, no, it is only cold here and she expects the fires to come at any moment from the outside only for that is how it always has been and that is all there ever was of desire.

Brocklehurst arrives when she is at Lowood living still out of Gateshead, holding closely, unconsciously, to that which she has denied, split-off. She has arrived at Lowood suppressing her pulse, listening how impulses of fury yet may be uneducated.

She has been very cold here while awaiting the Gateshead fires. All splits doom failure, crashed slate, must always expose its hypocrite. Brocklehurst summons her and she walks forward about to comply in the outburst, hell's fires, lost to his possession returning her to what was origin.

Anal Eroticism. She had told Mr. Lloyd she wanted to leave those Reeds but not for lower relations. She has tried to split from Gateshead in not recognizing those Reedian forces also her own, says they are not her family. Yet she hungers in the cold and poverty at Lowood, wants to be fed from without, resists, she had not wanted a lowly life and she is starving, and, as in Gateshead, is ready to discharge for their pleasure her pleasure, the only way she knows of getting heat.

She will discharge at her own leisure, will not withstand relating lower, the superior splitting is her own but she has been blind to it, yet in the Lowood starkness it emerges out of two fragments of a cold slate—and it humiliates her. The slate crashes and she has to face her splits. She is summoned forward.

Miss Temple's kindness cannot help now for when possessed by Brocklehurst we see her aligned with him, all mothers as one univocal desire, she too will brand as hypocrite. Jane's first response is impulse of fury against Reed, Brocklehurst and Co. She is no Helen Burns. Gateshead returns fully visible now the underside which she feared for which she longed.

On the stool we are humiliated, our stool is how we are branded servant of Evil One, castaway, and alien. It is where we are what we are is waste repudiated.

Brocklehurst is the (paternal) form is Mrs. Reed's sadism placing Jane on the stool as other, he is the way Jane begins to know her alterity from

Mrs. Reed yet still within an autocratic rule. Brocklehurst is the sadism of moral (paternal) law demanding we sever from Gateshead body (unity with Mrs. Reed's demand) as he also provokes our impulse to remain fused with her. If we resist Brocklehurst, our discharge against his sadistic thrust, we have become Gateshead.

Our expulsion (at Gateshead) had always been within bodily seizure, there the experience of separation through expulsion had returned to our attachment, and we will return to that now. Yet contained in one spot (stool, throne of stool) within the audience view makes our potential discharge more conscious and visible, and now we have a luring pleasure/displeasure of discharge while held in one spot.

He is who holds us in one spot requiring we know our difference. We can see ourselves from our audience perspective more than we know our private selves and now what always has been most privy becomes public, becomes our increasing sense of otherness through humiliation.

Her rising hysteria is the way her inflated discharge will not be constricted, announcing this way of stricture is prohibition not containment.

Contaminating what is purity (he says) the waters must not stagnate around her. The way she is still fused with Gateshead is the way her stool at Lowood marked by Evil One is constricted throat 'rising hysteria.'

We are no Helen Burns. None of what is occurring is known also interior, there is nothing within, no interior light, no way to articulate or even hold the moment, we are no Helen Burns, we will flaunt our resistance, demonstrate in a hysteria which is a plummeting between our own splits while screaming for her, we had begun to enter a private flock while learning division, he has come between branding us alien, ' "not a member of the true flock," ' our alterity only as a public splitting off denouncement humiliates.

The moralistic Paternal agent repressing our Gateshead sensations is not containing, the stool is too public as it precludes articulation, results in a hysteria, rising sensations stifling breath will burst through what constricts throat.

' "My dear children," pursued the black marble clergyman, with pathos, "this is a sad, a meloncholy occasion; for it becomes my duty to warn you, that this girl, who might be one of God's own lambs, is a little castaway: not a member of the true flock, but evidently an interloper and an alien." '

The only way he says we can know difference is to be agent of Evil One. He puts us on a stool for this to be seen bodily. His strikes: ' "(B)e on your guard against her," ' ' "shun her example," ' ' "shut her out from your converse." '

He is fixed, his marble is black, and his speaking pathos, it is for our own good, the occasion is melancholy, it becomes his duty. At each strike he is wanting our confession, we are marked, devil's mark, mole the dark teat, he whips for all to see a public inquisition. Grand Inquisition.

Sadistic public humiliation. He is flagellating us. We are outside ourselves, most split we condemn and are condemned from the exterior as we redden. Vulnerable and disgraced and simultaneously we worry about our public view. The Gateshead concern how it looks becomes our humiliation, this way we now perceive from the outside our worry of our public prestige.

Difference only to be object discarded, to be seen is to be excluded, that she is seen as being servant of the worse unseen which makes her the stool carrier of what must remain unconscious, she will hold it so the flock proceeds.

Brocklehurst is the critical agency which prohibits her being seen yet demands she reflect to the group their underside split. He stool places her so his Lowood flock see the reflection of what they shun, castaway.

As Brocklehurst is to carry the Gateshead curse forward, we here also must stand for the interior rejected. Nonsocial unnatural desire once her unconscious is here seen stool agent of Evil One. Servant of evil is their secret knowledge that father descended (their looks and grimaces with their back turned) which he says they have to split off, see reflected and shun.

We had begun some lessons in the house of women convening privately yet the way we were her unconscious desire returned us to his sadism this way we of her desire have the paternal Law striking us when we do not know how to hold the difference within this desire do not yet know the Lowood division.

He is beating and we cannot see the lesson. Just as we were about to blend into flock, fold, he came through our mother's terror he entered infecting our discharge wanting its pleasure the old way.

Split from our nature, cursed as we are flaunting, inflated against constriction. We rise for a public eye at his order, he proliferates is that we will retaliate. We can no longer locate the temple woman when we rise to him. Since he preaches opposition and is two dimensional eventually we flip to the other side, under side, split we go under.

The audience must see us as split off Gateshead castaway, unconscious desire of Mrs. Reed which is evil, alien, interloper; we have to stand for that before we find a relation to her divided, a decentered desire.

The shadows cast by Brocklehurst are of a flagellating man as well as the wife and daughters abundantly arrayed. Such shadows emerge from the naive optimism within a Christianity not promulgated by Christ himself, that we must conquer and ourselves mortify the natural.

As he strikes us, the only women we can see are three wearing an excess of animal fur and feather. We can no longer see Miss Temple. Three women caught in the master's scorn and denial of all they have made themselves up to be for him, three women caught by and dressed for his scrutinizing eye of hate. The hysteric screams.

The hysteric's scream pronounces loss of temple Helen creed while grasping a drowning in depths rising to a throat constricted as the stepmother seized a paternal solution the sadism of which became the return to remain possessed.

She has touched desires women decentered (even at the hearth the girl spoke gradation and a multiplicity of angel) regions of unnameable, and then he came thundering from high, resistance to any articulation of natural divided desire, whipping her split, to be evil marked she became frightened, lost herself, split and no word to rise wave worry on the public retaliation view while what only passes through interior are inarticulate waves submerging, the hysteric screams.

When the hysteric screams, the witch is being tortured, public accusation the condemnation of who would divide within, articulate difference within unnameable we have touched it here as collective femaled body, we become marked and the way we stay loyal to Mrs. Reed is his erection striking us in public demonstration.

Bodily flail those secrets of collective body is not yet to articulate their differentiation from within not yet affordable becomes his sadism.

When the hysteric screams,the witch is being tortured, public accusation the condemnation, and three women are bonding yet in service to the Father a competition as form of what would be lessons of inhibition, of differentiation not yet of their nature.

An attempt to get it right, how to divide within collective body and carry the quotient up articulate the differentiated parts. To speak the unnameable there are "right" ways, it takes an ethics which is not the same as his moralistic word prohibition negotiating which becomes our practice, our attempt to get it right.

Three women are acting in an unison feigned as they scrutinize us, one must not get beyond the other, be given more, one must not surpass the other. They act in feigned unison, illusion of our unison, beneath suspicion envy tears at those bowels, long coils of fur wrapped.

They have been scrutinizing the rooms above and they return to castigate a teacher in the Father's favor. They act in unison, in accordance with his view, in his regard they turn on the other woman, continue his reproach in order to stifle any singular voice or view, what sees from the interior does not speak, remaining unnameable.

Three women bonded as they serve the Father, and alongside the hysteric screams, the witch is being tortured.

She has gone to a school of women and finally she has begun to learn of a natural inhibition, gentle curbing force here spoken as creed, women knowing their containment in convent, curl. Beginning to learn the lessons, but there have been the long Gateshead years, three women still in an autocratic rule of a Father, self-sufficient only desire their own advancement.

We cannot enter Lowood until we are mortified of some of the Gateshead layers. The humiliation summons such mortification yet we resist it in the Gateshead mode: we will slap the other back.

Brocklehurst is when we hurt as we sit in an inferiority, and in his presence instead of stripping we strive for the opposite, refusing the hurt, we fire out, we judge, will forever hold that grudge.

With his striking we rise for a public eye. Public eye of horrified delight. Everyone sees our shame, the vile result of our desire, we cannot stand it, we thrust back to gain a superiority, for upper edge we thrust, will crack that male tyrant now preacher back.

Brocklehurst possesses us when we pompously preach, take on the word of God as our own, we preach edification, mission, fortitude, when we oppress below to strive above, never yield to loss.

On the stool we are no Helen Burns, we do not know how to begin to describe what we are experiencing, no light shed on what would be interior to language it even as we begin to know we exist distinct entity.

The woman's hair is shorn, she is being racked, she is being burned publicly, searing because she does not yet know the language of decentered regions were only unnameable. He is pronouncing us alien from all other women and now all know our disgrace, we redden and cringe in a public display to condemn he calls us liar for he would have the paternal of high take the place of unconscious desires, our red-room is a lie.

When Brocklehurst announces our mark, we are liar, our Father's descent has made us the Evil One, we are on a stool. There are no differentiated words for what would be interior so it rises thundering waves constricting our throat, choked scream flailing arm and we remember when we before sat on the stool within the secret linings of her interior chamber and we were marked.

She had put us in the red-room to learn a restriction, paternal authority not to discharge yet constrict, paternal authority to replace to remove us from what would be mother's unconscious desire, and then it was the Father lowered, let word differentiate desire by entering it not repressing, yet he crashed, his repression our hysteria, our word choked we were stifled and our mark is how silenced we have seen him lower.

Father not Law which derives from repression of desire for mother also is mother's, instead Father shattered in her womb pushing us further down until we spoke out of it which took us to where we are told our desire is yet uneducated.

She has a creed and for her the rising sensations from marginal regions are not unnameable.

Learning through repetition, we are again on the stool and he is bearing down on us, 'What my sensations were, no language can describe.' Our eruption threatens yet another suffocation as we are going under the waves are formless have long waited articulation.

We do not think we are ready to give him up. We may prefer his superior splittings since we know the familiar reaction from without (we are in their superior view of us inferior we writhe for them out of ourselves), never need to know the interior, yet merely two dimensional only that we repress the red-room. Glory Father in Heaven. Keep him up and we are seen reddened from exterior familiar again rising sensations stifling breath we can flail back.

'What my sensations were, no language can describe; but just as they all rose, stifling my breath and constricting my throat, a girl came up and passed me: in passing, she lifted her eyes.' When we think we have no language to describe what rises she comes up and passes us with a ray sensate as it penetrates it holds.

Jane on stool is mortified, she is being flayed, she knows she may shatter, break open. The stool is the place of holding tensions, inherent contradictions (the red-room is not a lie, I am here because it is a lie) where what can no longer be discharged according to reactivity impulse can hold.

The stool is the place of not discharging impulsively (immediate gratification) yet it is the desire of discharging not according to the previous ways, and that decenters desire from gratification which becomes the realization of the contradictions, interior divisions, in what waves through us.

Holding our stool discharge is decentered desire which is Helen's moment that possibly there can be language mediating this experience not repression of desire to derive word yet differentiation of our desire through word. To not discharge impulsively is to hold the violence (splittings) at the root of the discharge which her intelligent ray sees and penetrates.

Our humiliation has indicated we are distinct body, we see ourselves from the exterior as their inferior, we no longer need impulse discharge to establish an experience of separation. Yet it threatens to act-out for the public view, confirming it, confirming that the only way we can be separate is to carry their negative reflect it back to them, ashamed.

Divisor out of dividend through the Brocklehurst humiliation but threatens to go under in the same way and not divide through to quotient and remainder fraction. What her gaze now communicates is that we do not have to know ourselves only from exterior acting their castaway to separate and perform the Lowood division.

The way the waves of rising sensations could rend could shatter she holds in her gaze back our body differentiating.

Helen is who holds our heterogeneous body in the stool moment through a gaze that shows understanding of the shattering. Her gaze is not an unification of our rupturing or a demand of its coalescence in any way, yet it imparts to us that the violence inherent in the currents rising to our constricted throat can be messaged.

For Jane sitting on stool is experiencing what she senses cannot be expressed, named, 'no language can describe,' her throat constricts what she cannot speak, what is beyond herself from otherworlds, deathworlds, windowseat red-room nursery all of it in the waves rising to submerge her back to them, threaten her very existence she believes cannot be spoken: that there is no solidifying substance to speak or a language through which it can be imparted.

The way Brocklehurst's sadism has allowed Jane to see her body as distinct is a preparation for Helen who posits Jane's substantial riding the violence inherent in the rising sensations. Waves of the accumulated possessions.

Substance of her own now can hold it upon the stool which is less impulse more buoyed until a refinement can condense; Helen is this possibility of refining the tumultuous waves unconscious. Letting them rise to gaze (back) reminding her the narrative can be spoken to another, not fused, in relation.

Helen's interior eye peering to the vista of angel and her Christ has emerged from mortified body. Mortified the pleasures and she lets the interior regions form themselves and she becomes heterogeneous body, not only of this world yet Northumberland and the regions of Charles 1st, no flooding necessary, she knows her mishap, locates her errors and lets them shatter her to interior realms. She finds there a natural inhibition, infolding temperance not submission.

Helen correctly (empathetically) perceives Jane's interior devastated state, the violences there, and she communicates that by various bodily languages of stance, smile, eye.

In Helen's bodily response and reflective gaze are the beginning articulations of Jane's interior world, and this articulation (wordless yet) allows the tumult to subside. Helen's gaze indicates that from the exterior, Jane's interior world (and its violence) exists, has a form which can be perceived and communicated back.

Helen looks at us but sees into us and reflects our seeing-into, insight. Hers is a gaze of knowing interior, more intimate than the phantom and

Mr. Lloyd mirrors. Mirror gazing. Mirror gazing: red-room phantom looked at Jane as object possessed, Jane saw it seeing her being it; Mr. Lloyd did not look at Jane (his mirroring was not exterior reflection of Jane) as much as he located her position in the household, reflected her a being there who did not want to be there then where.

The Brocklehurst Lowood flock looked at a reflection of what they shunned, she was their interior rejected waste reflected back to them so they could split from it. As Jane almost became (acted-out) the flock's (rejected) interior, Helen reflected Jane's interior. Helen's gaze is not a direct (mirroring exterior) reflection as it is a reflection of Jane's (potential) interior-seeing (calm, lit, intimately containing).

Helen is a reflection of Jane seeing inward; Helen is a reflection of the interior of Jane looking at what Jane looks like on the stool as she allows impulse to mediate to insight and be placed decentered.

Empathy passage of angels. '(R)eflection from the aspect of an angel,' Helen's mirroring gaze is through angels, angelos, those who emerge from primordial waves, beyond pleasure, beyond human, and linked to death and the mortification of who would fuse in collective body univocal, who are messengers to speak messages of those waves beyond life, not centered on the human, decentered human, which is to be bore up as human, not impulsive, 'firm stand on the stool.'

These sensations rising each a wave in its own right with message, distinct voices, are how her aspect is of angel reflecting. Helen stands at the place beyond what attempts to restrain the waves, more of angel, of 'effluence of fine intellect' knows these waves passing through are from marginal worlds closer to where we will be at death.

The otherworlds of nonbeing which infiltrated at Gateshead (reflected by red-room mirror) now we are a continuity of being, here on stool a human being (reflected by Mr. Lloyd and separated out through Brocklehurst), and the otherworld has risen to angel, sublime aspect of angel, and its ray penetrates, goes through us yet we remain sitting there and it does not take us.

She does not remove us from the stool since the stool is the way to move beyond temporary and impulsive discharge. Helen's presence allows us to sit as waves from without (unconscious) move within and rise do not submerge us yet rise through us, sublime. Helen's sublimation is not eradication of these waves which resonate off the impact of the Reed and Brocklehurst forces, yet mediation, refinement, rise to message possibility interior even of language.

Brocklehurst is a preparation for Helen if we do not stop with him which would be to split and discharge against him which would be to be ever fused with Mrs. Reed, still fused with that impulse (Reed, Brocklehurst and Co.) of that mother.

Helen is stronger than Brocklehurst because she has less fear than he of what emerges from margins unknown, nonhuman, and of what curls. Helen's gaze penetrates but it is not voyeuristic, objectifying, phallocentric, or sadistically possessive. Nor is her ray of vapor ethereal, it is sensational, sends an extraordinary sensation through us, penetrates our body filling it we are buoyed and shored; her refinement embodies us.

Helen as that interior gaze to Jane how Jane's interior containing impulses looks lit, smiles, offers an otherness yet not through sadism yet an otherness intimately contained. To have an occasion to see our interior intimately reflected otherwise is erotic.

We sit still, rising, what was unconscious, in the backrooms, of recess, is rising, and as it is a public affair it remains quite private between us, kindly she is meeting us in a touch of eyes, now smile's firm embrace and suddenly it is quite private and they do not matter, we have risen to this embrace gently thrilled, slowly remove our Gateshead clothes, those layers crumbling at stool's foot, we rise to this stripping now we take a firm stand on the stool and the breathing comes easier.

Brocklehurst's mode of repressing unconscious desires, prohibiting rising sensations through his Law, does not provide delineation of the unconscious from which we have emerged through Gateshead, to which we are perpetually in relation even after Gateshead.

In Lowood, the Brocklehurstian mode is depotentiated. Teacher even smiles, students grimace, his ladies flaunt and waddle.

The one would repress these desires, unconscious waves rising prohibited, is also who proclaims our red-room experience a lie. For he would have the agency of that Father high: Father's Law derived from the repression of (maternal) desires. Yet we were in there and we experienced that Father's crash, Father suppressed in Mother's red-room, stifling us.

When Brocklehurst is depotentiated, Helen passes by. Far from suppressing them, she knows these desires are uneducated, want articulation. Helen can pull through us, designate by the language of her gaze and her smile, that by which we are being gripped. What Brocklehurst denounced lie, Helen rises to a public view yet in metaphoric holding.

Helen offers signifying function for these (unconscious) waves rising, holds their message in her passing. We go through Brocklehurst to arrive distinct stool body. We cannot find Helen passing until we are stool separate we can hold these waves and their inherent tension would rupture through what was not solid containing substance.

The place where stepmother's Brocklehurstian sadism severed us to know our difference, boundary, in the Lowood place of high walled propriety, is where Father attempts to remain high, Glory stone-tablet in the name of Brocklehurst yet ultimately is where Father's word of Law fails to dominate split from repressed desire. Lowood is where Father's Law, Glory Father tablet, passes to Helen's reading.

In Lowood, she passes by, her passing a possibility we can remain on stool, demarcated not by impulsive release yet sublimated until what rises unconscious becomes message of angels, she knows our discord, the way we have ruptured even been shattered there heterogeneous body opening to realm of death interior life the home.

The way she looks for languages of realms beyond this life toward death, mortified, mortified the fused monocentric impulse, is our decentered desire which she holds, we see it in her passing it comes after his Law has once again collapsed from high and it buoys us up.

When the sadism has severed us apart but its Law makes no sense, makes us grimmace, Father has lowered his word entering our desire which rises to her ray and we feel an empathy at Lowood from the one like us who is different enough allowing us to see ourselves the exterior as polyvalent interior, and not go under.

Beginning an empathy for our heterogeneous selves, our many sides divided. After sadism we are divided and we see this other one with many sides her untidy badge alongside effluent visage.

We let Brocklehurst's whipping hold go as we are held by Helen's smile, penetrated by her ray, there are many sides to it. Held by Helen's intelligence at the same moment she wears the untidy badge, more empathetically we can see the differentiated parts as well as their relation: defect is of human limit, the angel as messenger through our defect, how the one of defect, bad girl, is also of angels, angelos, message of the badness, angel of the evil agent, message of our mark, how we are heterogeneous and not split, multifaceted nature.

Mortified we begin to see what natural division indeed resides beneath the Gateshead layers.

Hysteria is that divided nature not knowing or speaking itself trying to constrict itself back to place, back to a self, wanting its pleasure, one human self. Not held by a penetrating gaze to empathetically place its differentiated nature, instead of lowering to waves rising possibility of distinct language of heterogeneity the sensations choked a throat still of the Law said difference is evil interloper must be excluded, shut out, cut off, castaway.

Through her light, extraordinary ray, the effluence of smile, she reflects the passion of the stool place penetrating through us, im-passioning which is her empathy which holds us up. We begin to learn we can transmit the language of the waves, a language of unconscious.

Whereas her passing says let those desires rise to angels, there can be speaking, as yet we are uneducated. Only stopped at the splitting stage in the Lowood lesson of long division, we have only known the parts through a condemnation splitting then requiring exaggeration, flailing, pleading adornment above adoration.

When the hysteric screams, plea for another to find her stool, she is resisting a stool sitting where she feels most out of herself where she longs yet fears to be part of the flock, and when the only way to be distinct is out-of-herself humiliated, public eye disgrace.

When the hysteric screams, plea for another to look for the parts disavowed, whipped in accusation as she stands only exterior split herself, fear of those rising depths.

The temptation within the hysteric's scream is to remain with Brocklehurst, not marble to him yet absorbing his contagion in condemning her, contribution to his whipping petrified of the waves accumulating in every scream. There are many and they require words not of this convention yet.

To get tempted by Brocklehurst is to say it is an act, she is lying, it is intentional, deceptive dramatic, which would be to reduce it to a deliberate human will when she is flailing because with a nascent sense of distinct body she also finally is beyond where there is not any human centric gratification.

To remember through the hysterical scream what it is to sink with no air forthcoming only the crashing about what angels to inform what is the form, design each wave comes its distinct design, and we transmit this intelligence to the woman on the stool it cannot at first be in words since she is drowning the words cannot be heard, but our stance, our eye, this smile, sometimes our sigh or a low chanting from the depths of any ocean.

Marble to Brocklehurst and we know ourselves as separate substance so with her we hold the curl until she strips to where the splittings become the inherent relation of all the distinct parts.

Helen is divided from us, separate, yet she reflects our interior, therefore her passing signals we can know (empathize with) our interior divisions.

After Helen's passing, Jane is struck and bore up. 'What an extraordinary sensation that ray sent through me! How the new feeling bore me up!' The one who can see our divisions and how they have been based on violence is our divided self divides our self.

She knows how it is we can have a detached body of singular substance yet be drowning in unconscious rising from what is seen as defect she holds the product of our division and the possibility of its intelligent expression. She knows the product of our learning our long division.

Helen's holding does not gratify, it does not remove Jane from the stool.

Jane's stool space is to mortify into the divided parts without being stopped by Brocklehurst yet separating through him. Jane is on her own yet held.

Sitting in fragmented yet divided parts while held together by their inherent relation: Helen's passing holds both the differentiation (even shattering) as well as the inherent relation, and this holding of such contradiction becomes our humility.

Also in no way does Helen sweeten the stool suffering. Her air and light provide the refining passage so Jane can strip the Gateshead layers, sitting shameful becoming mortified, Jane is not rent but parting from Gateshead choices, into her own multifaceted nature, contained as dividing upon the stool.

Angels behind, around, even penetrating her, and she can take off the layers, divided let the depths of the mothers ever feared rise to this natural division, on her own as accompanied.

Helen's mode of humility, this transition of the Brocklehurstian humiliation to Helen's humility is not submission. Our stand is firm, no buckling on the stool, differentiated yet not unrelated.

Brocklehurst as master is depotentiated as we sit in our own defects, that inferior position when the unconscious breaks its waves through us and we feel fragmented, shattered, ashamed. As we sit in this place, accept it with Helen's passing hold, depotentiated Brocklehurst is our humility and is how we are master, the master collapses as we accept our inferiorities while holding on what was unconscious passes through which makes us the master, some Brocklehurst force negotiated: 'I mastered the rising hysteria.'

Reacting to Brocklehurst in a hysteria would have been a passive submission as active as it may have appeared. Helen of angels not a passivity, nor is a passivity the humility to which her passing invites us. Her ray penetrates; girl with sunken eye has a driving force penetrating.

Our humility has derived from Brocklehurst's depotentiation in front of students and teachers through his ludicrous attack on the red curl as well as the blatancy of his asceticism seen through the artificial adornment of his wife and daughters.

The prohibiting master also binding us to Mrs. Reed is let down as Jane sits in the midst of her own human fragility and a nature soiled: that she has been possessed and rent by agents of evil and she has lost her appetite. Her long division slate has been split. She sits amidst the fragmented pieces calmed and reflected by the light of the curl of a smile.

Bibliography

Cixous, Helene and Clément, Catherine. *The Newly Born Woman.* Trans. by Betsy Wing. Minneapolis: University of Minnesota Press, 1986.

Cowan, Lyn. *Masochism: A Jungian View.* Dallas: Spring Publications, 1982.

Freud, Sigmund. "Beyond the Pleasure Principle." *The Complete Psychological Works of Sigmund Freud.* Vol. 18. Trans. James Strachey. London: Hogarth, 1955. (Hereafter returned to *Standard Edition.*)

_____. "New Introductory Lectures on Psychoanalysis." *Standard Edition*, Vol. 22.

_____. "The Case of Schreber." *Standard Edition*, Vol. 12.

_____. "The Psychogenesis of a Case of Homosexuality in a Woman." *Standard Edition*, Vol. 18.

Holy Bible. Revised Standard Edition.

Irigaray, Luce. "The Power of Discourse and the Subordination of the Feminine." In *This Sex Which Is Not One.* Trans. by Catherine Porter. Ithaca, N.Y.: Cornell University Press, 1985.

Jung, C. G. "Psychology and Alchemy." *The Collected Works of C. G. Jung.* Vol. 12. Trans R. F. C. Hull. Princeton, N.J.: Princeton University Press, 1953.

Kohut, Heinz. *Analysis of the Self.* New York: International Universities Press, 1971.

_____. *How Does Analysis Cure.* Chicago: University of Chicago Press, 1984.

Kristeva, Julia. *Powers of Horror.* Trans. by Leon S. Roudiez. New York: Columbia University Press, 1982.

Lacan, Jacques. "The Agency of the Letter in the Unconscious or Reason since Freud." In *Écrits: A Selection.* Trans. by Alan Sheridan. New York: W. W. Norton and Co., 1977.

Rajchman, John. "Lacan and the Ethics of Modernity." *Representations* 15 (1986): 42.

Spignesi, Angelyn. "Verso una Comprensione Psicologica della Strega." *Giornale Storico di Psicologia Dinamica* 7 (1983): 44.

Chapter 8
The Seed-Cake

Finally the bell, the half an hour over, others go to their tea, alone I descend, face to floor wetting that floor, grief. What was supported dissolves, replaced by reaction. 'Now I wept: Helen Burns was not here; nothing sustained me: left to myself I abandoned myself, and my tears watered the boards.'

For I had meant to do so well here, earn respect, find friends, just today to the head of my class I rose, teachers' praise, Miss Temple's promise that in two months to begin the French and learn the drawing from her, pupils my age no longer molesting, treating me instead as equal. Yet now laying crushed, it is all over now and it is to die, I want to die mumble repetition then a start: the figure of Helen Burns approaching it is coffee and bread she carries me in the light of the fading fire. Come eat something. But I push it aside, would only choke, I cannot calm, perhaps she is surprised at this agitation I cannot help and I continue to weep aloud. She sits hugging her knees, silent Indian embrace beside.

It is my voice asking how she can sit so close to what all believe to be a liar. Only eighty heard it, she says whereas the world contains hundreds of millions. The eighty despite me. No, more it is a pity. But after the words of Brocklehurst? Not god or even an admired man, he never strove for our affection, had he singled you as favorite then enemies you would have here, instead now if they dared they would offer sympathy and if you continue to do well, the friendly feeling again will appear only now temporarily concealed. Besides Jane—Well, Helen? and I place my hand in hers, chafing she warms my fingers and begins in a low voice she is saying if all the world hated me yet my conscience approved me and absolved me from guilt then I would not be without friends.

No. I cannot tolerate it to be ' "solitary and hated," ' for to get an affection from her or Miss Temple or anyone who I truly loved, I would do anything, have my arm broken, let the hoof of the kicking horse smash this chest.

Hush. Too vehement and impulsive I am she says and I think too much of the love of human beings, for there are resources beside my ' "feeble self" ' and she begins telling me of another world besides this race of humans, invisible world of spirits watching, guarding, and if we lay dying with only scorn all around us, these angels see our torture, our innocence (if it be so and she knows I am innocent for she read it in my ardent eyes, my clear front), and with the separation of flesh from spirit the reward, life so soon passing over to this glory indeed the overwhelming distress not necessary.

Her words fall over me, now a calm mixed with an 'inexpressible sadness,' I cannot tell from where it comes this sadness; and now she is breathing quickly, a cough, I have concern for her and my head placed on her shoulder, arms around her waist, she draws me to her, we sit in the silence, clouds shift and that moon shining full moon through this window upon us in embrace as upon this figure approaching us, Miss Temple.

She wants me in her room, since Helen also is here, she may come. Threading 'intricate passages' and one last staircase mounted we arrive, and that woman sits Helen and then places me by her side: have I cried the grief away? Never, all will see me now wicked. Not so she says, it is more how I prove myself to be, continue to do well and she will be satisfied. And she asks my story on this Mrs. Reed, did she adopt me of her own accord? She wants to know my story without exaggeration. I remember Helen's caution on 'indulgence of resentment' also I am so exhausted that the story is more moderate, less gall, thus more credible.

Miss Temple hears, she says she has heard of this Mr. Lloyd, she will write, his corroboration will be my public exoneration, to her I am clear now. A kiss; she then inquires on Helen's cough, takes her pulse. Sigh low and pensive until rings for tea and toast. Toast however sent by housekeeper strictly within the usual portion — toast for one, not enough. The teacher smiles, she has it in her ' "power to supply deficiencies for this once." ' In a drawer unlocked, it is a seed-cake. Slices cut by generous hand, a feast 'as on nectar and ambrosia.' Then by the fire, each of us placed on either side of her there follows a conversation between her and Helen in its hearing I am privileged.

Always around Miss Temple is the serenity, 'refined propriety in her language, which precluded deviation into the ardent, the excited, the eager: something which chastened the pleasure of those who looked on her and listened to her, by a controlling sense of awe; and such was my feeling now: but as to Helen Burns, I was struck by wonder.' For the first time her cheek has color stimulated somewhat by the meal here with the instructress beloved but more through powers of 'her own unique mind' also shining in her eyes acquiring 'a beauty more singular than that of Miss Temple's,' a beauty 'of meaning, of movement, of radiance. Then her soul sat on her lips, and language flowed, from what source I cannot tell: has a girl of fourteen a heart large enough, vigorous enough to hold the swelling spring of pure, full, fervid eloquence?'

How many books they speak of and here are countries of afar and facts of nations time past and secrets of nature, and the language and authors of French. I am amazed and this amazement to its climax when Helen is reading Virgil for this teacher has asked can she recall the Latin taught her by her father. The bell. Miss Temple holds Helen longer, sad sigh and carefully follows her with an eye tearing as we go to the door and depart.

At the bed-room Miss Scatcherd is scrutinizing the drawers, Helen reprimanded murmurs to me her things were of disorder, she had forgotten. The next day a pasteboard bearing the word Slattern bound on her forehead. She wears it unresentful as though deserving yet the moment the teacher departs I am running to Helen and tearing that despicable sign and thrusting it into the fire: 'the fury of which she was incapable had been burning in my soul all day, and tears, hot and large, had continually been scalding my cheek; for the spectacle of her sad resignation gave me an intolerable pain at the heart.'

In a week it is Mr. Lloyd's response corroborating my account, Miss Temple clears me publicly from the charge, the class congratulates, kisses, murmur of pleasure through it. I set out to learn, work diligently then, improving the memory, advancing until one day in less than two months I am allowed the lesson of drawing and also French. That night it is not food as usual in my imagination, right before sleep not those cravings fancied but instead the future drawings all of my hand here trees, butterflies and roses, birds at cherries, wrens' nests wreathed by ivy these the feast. Lowood's privation feast never would I prefer the Gateshead luxury.

Her gaze gone what sustained empty, the room empties, without interior reflection: reflection by our interior. Without further interior reflecting what rose dissolves, we dissolve to reaction.

'The spell by which I had been so far supported began to dissolve; reaction took place, and soon, so overwhelming was the grief that seized me, I sank prostrate with my face to the ground.' Reaction taking place of gaze supporting is to sink prostrate when what was rising to articulate gets seized and reversed, back down to primordial wave sinking which is reaction.

Dissolve, our reaction is to inflate what is negation: we are nothing, all is lost. In the Helen absence, Brocklehurst negative inflation is the only thing we are is reaction makes us sink. His grandiosity becomes the hyperbole of our doom, repeated statement of deathwish: we are nothing, all is lost, never respect from others.

Without interior reflecting which was sensation rise sublime gets stopped and all is empty not to language it yet react which is to split again and see ourselves as nothing from the public eye, which is the Brocklehurst split is the Mrs. Reed curse.

We are nothing is to become the public eye viewing us to shun us outcast when what was interior that saw and promise of delineation is gone, we reverse to the Gateshead curse. His voice our sinking in ardent whining red-room wish to die.

We sought to sublime that curse, and perhaps in our shedding of the Gateshead impulse layers, we sought to shed that aunt. We were looking into the great girl's eyes, and we though we could leave that curse.

She leaves, he swoops back, curse catches us, our unconscious rising is a lie cannot be reflected and messaged, we totter, we fall off our stool, agitation of feeling locked in what is empty of human, we are shaking that locked door of the red-room again, stepmother curse, drowning in old regorging.

We are in some vacant room and we are shaking the locked door sound in our head frenzied descent. Curse of we cannot go forward without her and she proclaims unconscious lie. Collapsed, ministerial cracking whip self-torments, we return to a humiliation at the foot of our stepmother.

Our fall to the floor is our running to that stepmother, fuse again with her body to be a body only way we have known ourselves as nothing to be all of her especially unconscious.

Our fall to the floor is the running to that stepmother through her Brocklehurst, as we fall to the floor, tears to those boards, we are returning to her. As we return to her we are nothing.

Her male agents and our impulse reaction as and against them has always been the way back into her, and familiar now we grasp her Coming Man, Brocklehurst, we slip, seized we see ourselves from the condemning public eye is our reaction a dissolution.

We slip to these floorboards at stepmother's feet we are nothing. '(L)eft to myself I abandoned myself.' Our self is not self. Interior reflecting abandons is to abandon self. Nobody when the shoring unconscious rising sublime has not the further lesson of primary condensation, laconic translation to language.

For a moment, it was a light is that girl's eye, ray shot through us and we felt the sensations once unconscious as pulling down were rising sublime to her reflecting, it was not belonging to Mrs. Reed even as it related to her charge, it was a moment we unconscious existed apart.

But now is our reverse dropped and sinking into sensation reactive the same way through her Brocklehurst now tears watering.

The girl returns when he resides within what was most intimate. We start at her step and looking up we see by the fading fire that she carries coffee and bread. What allows her to come back, as we are losing ourself in his grip, is a suffering our loss of appetite. She remembers and carries a simple food back to us.

That she has held us interior in exterior absence and returns with a concrete manifestation indicating not only that she remembered who we are but what the place is like and what we may require in it.

She suffers it together with us without becoming our suffering, passions it together with us and her compassionate memory becomes presence which holds us for we have been sinking in an old regorging.

Suffering begins to bring us where we are low in. The Reed and Brocklehurst forces provoke reaction making change, burst from inertia, but do not transform through suffering: John Reed in our head within the red-room was self-pity, a whining when the capacity of suffering not yet possible. Lowood has Brocklehurst in our head an agitated worry of public view, public condemnation.

Submitting to the possession of these forces do not change scene yet all dissolves to reaction. Helen approaches with what would return those forces to our appetite.

With what would return those forces to our appetite accompanies a movement to suffer. Helen's presence and Jane begins to suffer, returns an interior motion of what is the stool descent.

His temptation of negative inflation keeps us under waves rising now exterior and crashing upon us. To receive Helen in this place entails risking a different relation to these waves, for we begin to see she has not returned to lift us away from them, yet more to let them through informing. Not falling flat in catastrophe yet slow companioned descent.

She is silent in this sitting beside descent. As she sat beside when the Reed demon spoke through us, again there is no false assurance. Rooted, ready for any of its form, Helen sits beside our grief. Suffering grief as the condensation alongside her not possession.

Because there is a presence there we trust who sits solidly, because she sits beside and though we have expected to surprise or worry her with our agitation, we find she settles into it, we still. And we see we can go further into this abyss the winds had been churning, tunneling descent, neck bowed and then snapped forward, rivers from sockets flooding lap, stomach pulling out its torrent and here she is there again, slower now, cries become a heaving grief.

This grief had been locked beneath the Gateshead outburst and seizure. With her alongside we sink into what had been covered by obsession or seizure exterior. She does not speak for us here, no coercion of what begins as agitation. No compromise or patronize of this place, nor a merged release, instead beside planted.

Helen sits down in it, silent as an Indian, she sits low with us in the deep dusk of the red-brown silence of soil containing the heavy muteness of ages, resonant enough to hold the moanings, the eternal chant of the most hallowed grief.

Helen's presence alongside allows Jane to descend not in the Brocklehurst mode, whining exterior stance, but through a grief well suffering it. The sensations had rose to her passing gaze, their language a rhythm of grief which becomes condensed not through impulse reaction yet suffering word related.

Jane speaks first wonders how Helen can sit so closely.

What would it be to return his critical stance to the unconscious forces, distinguishing their elements as we stay related to them neither split nor drowning. Helen returns and our words are this way we are different and yet still in relation.

Jane asks Helen: how can you sit so closely to one whom all believe liar?

Her question itself threatens the Brocklehurst doom: an inflation now negative (the underside of his pomposity, his split). Everyone sees her mark, everyone despises her.

Helen's response clear and distinct, cuts through the Brocklehurst inflation: eighty people, not everyone, not an entire world of hundreds of millions, eighty people who do not despise, more it is a pity.

The Helen mode is analysis, from perspective (her gaze of high, angelic) she trims, pares the flagrant catastrophizing and projection. To move through Brocklehurst, learn severance yet still remain related to recess, is to address the negatively inflated thought with statements succinct.

This is the way his word enters our desire, neither submerged entirely nor split off not repress desire yet rise from that very desire through which his word descended this word of what could be tumult wave sensations becomes Helen's address.

And in this precise addressing, Helen condenses. She says he is not a god. She takes us back to the human, saying he even is not a great or admired human. She takes us back to the human through a laconic translation which condenses as it holds, we give her our hand.

Coffee and bread in the hands same hand it holds our chafing heat soothing exchange through the palms placed one upon the other as fingers curl their touch elaborately simple. It warms, it says: my heat also yours, you are not too much for me and I too have something to impart.

The hand unique, a fate in its palm, a history in its fingers' spread, the knuckled lengths. Nails of our anxiety, our toil, this hand is of our shape, indicates our design, our motive, what stimulates, what attaches, toward what we draw, what distinguishes us from any other we are unequivocally apart it is the print of a thumb, as we are related we reach. Distinctive, never duplicated. This distinction of who we are and how we touch she holds.

Distinction. He had come to sever us from the natural forces through a collective morality, public the verdict and all must agree with his every conviction. Her form of severance is speaking to even through the force of these desires as distinctive voice, conscience befriending: if all the world hated, one would not be lonely.

When the forces seemed only external and beseiging tossed we had no sense of distinctive voice. Now she sits beside and speaks of conscience. We do not want to know it yet we want her hand chafing ours, we would be abused for her love, the love of Miss Temple.

Helen teaching us of the angels as she holds our hand and we feel its heat as she calls us too impulsive and vehement. She is speaking of realms of angels seeing our tortures, spirits abounding, through them our justice, later glory, look to the angel-friend, conscience as friend.

Impulse mediated through hand-held hear of angels; not paternal law another sort of agency regulating, friend a conscience.

It takes someone in our likeness, holding our hand and we find care can sever distinctly it is a conscience met as friend. Without the hand felt we lose the human touch in it, what those angels desire within our humanity, their secret nostalgia: yearning for us to embody their gift to us. Without their return through hand, embodied manifestation for which they long, even as we know those angels surrounding as guarding, something remains untouched, lost, 'inexpressible sadness.'

As Helen yearns for God's final crown after the parting flesh, she coughs and her body fails within what Jane senses is an inexpressible sadness. Jane draws closer, the two sit arms to the other's waist, Jane's head on Helen's shoulder.

When we took on the Brocklehurst lesson, did not use him to split off from our forces but moved through him to distinguish them, their long division, we found a great girl of all stratospheres, of heightened vapor. We were drowning and she condensed dryly, we began to learn of discernment within the blood forces apart from possession, and we dried to some distinction.

And now we begin to lend her the sweat, we reciprocate wetness of palm for her lesson of distinction, she has elevated too far from all flesh, and now she receives our warm embrace. Head on shoulder silence.

Our compulsion is being condensed by Helen now to conscience and when we return in conscience a concern for her body, downward teachings now, conscience returning embodied as a cloud shifts humid haze shows a woman walking toward our embrace.

The woman is inviting us to come further inside her chambers. Intricate passages. One last staircase and we are mounting.

Miss Temple is looking into us and asks: have we cried our grief. Her residence at the intimate grief's chamber she appears to take us through intricate passages to the heart of the matter, she wants to know what is the Gateshead story.

We speak our narrative clearly: we had been seized by the John Reed and the Mr. Reed forces, we have thrashed and we have been seized again. They have come when we were engaging in the recessed chambers often red also of our mothers.

Now this quiet chamber of a temple, mosaic echoes, less fear here, sanctified place where the edge of our story takes some resonance and does not turn back on us.

Miss Temple is where the heart has a capacity to understand that the aunt did not choose us of her own accord, we pass the story of aunt's revulsion for red-room child through us and we remain standing.

We remain standing as our story differentiates and passes through us. The chamber of Miss Temple is where we first become narrator, with an overview, not identified with any voice, and not exaggerated. Enough sublimation we have the distance, tumultuous forces refined to condensed words, we can see all the distinct characters and ourselves in relation.

No longer driven by our narrative we speak it, Brocklehurst's prohibitive strictures have been transmuted to gentle curbing force we locate the narrative interior temple. We become rather excited when we get to the red-room scene yet we let the force of it move through us becoming narrative by which we are not taken and we see she believes us.

Miss Temple and Helen are listening to Jane speak.

And we move through Brocklehurst and Reed in our narrative no longer liar, we say Mrs. Reed is our aunt, we are related, now neither inflating with gall nor splitting through denial, we are no longer liar. As we move the forces through our story there is some conscience listening alongside friend.

The hearing of Miss Temple of the red-room story is that the Father's word did descend into the red-room that womb of maternal it is not lie is how we are now wording what previously was unconscious. The belief of Miss Temple of our narrative is the possibility of narrating from our unconscious, out from that desire, not at its expense or repression. Our narrative speaking has an ethics the way we are in relation to it is how she judges the veracity, which is conscience, which is not paternal law.

This narrative speaking of what in once we were drowning is due to a Helen perspective presenting conscience. Father's descent not lie when we have discovered conscience befriended can hear the internal divisions; desires not impulse reaction yet dialogued with conscience counterpart, taking into account desires which have longed for designation.

Miss Temple arrived with an invitation when conscience is becoming and the law descending is no longer lie once it becomes, befits, suits, is appropriate to conscience.

This way the descent of Father's Law into the blood forces that were recessed becomes conscience in dialogue with the words, narrative, of that recess occurs through friend caring she sat by heart delivered us to temple with an ethics for the contradictions of where we have been rent.

Miss Temple says to Jane she will write to Mr. Lloyd upon his corroboration she will be publicly cleared; Miss Temple says to her Jane is clear now. Mr. Lloyd for higher agreement, the public exoneration. Who is the authority to which conscience resorts for public opinion. The girl alongside us coughs.

There has been some part that has been distant, guiding throughout, she has not become bound in our impulse or agitation, but stayed there alongside, soaring she was of her own flame, blue flame, rising however aloof always we felt her vision at heart from above she held.

Now she coughs. The teacher takes the pulse of this once desiring to return to angel. Miss Temple returns to her seat after taking Helen's pulse and with a low sigh is quite pensive before ordering tea.

    ◆§ Miss Temple's Sigh. Occasionally I would hear-her whispering to her angels. Hers is a fervent longing to return to them, just reward. Daily I notice in her walk, her stance and bearing that she is aspiring to them by leaving us, the cough resumes harsher. And I feel it come upon me, winged, rising in my chest and coming in folds falling down out of my mouth I release this Sigh. Angels not wanting the gift returned to them yet to know their gift through her flesh of this life, my Sigh. I will feed her, lower her to this body, tea and toast, this my plea my pardon. §◆

Jane and Helen sit at the table and Miss Temple serves them slices of seed-cake.

Mystic banquet, we were not expecting it. Just when we had named our Gateshead story and Helen offered her cough, these ways we have been marked, we begin a dialogue with her, open drawer and here she is offering us some seed-cake.

It has been a long toil in years before we had known her yet she hears it now: we had been beaten red welt repetitions, violating mock initiation to the death world, we offer our narrative without exaggeration and here a different sort of initiation she opens her drawer and we feast with her that night it is seed-cake.

Food of the feasts of the souls departed, for our ancestors seed-cake was the food of the feasts of the dead, binding the living to those dead, eating this cake they would hear the speaking of souls departed. Angels choralling through what is of grain substance. Seed in a cake, seed shattered now life extending to hallowed chambers and the dead they sing a new instruction.

Generous slices, a feast then as on nectar and ambrosia.

We are in a temple where through our appetite we summon the voices of the dead begin the feast of what is their secret nostalgia to return to us. We are very hungry when we arrive. From her drawer the nourishment is as nectar, and we find ourselves with gods speaking through. These invisible forces now secrets emerging through dialogue exchange feed us, our appetite satiated.

Her food feeds our body more because she knows this food carries spirits surrounding and fed we open ourselves to their breezes inspired now soul on our lips. Substance of the messages of all dead whispering chorals slowly penetrating until our lips move, some say creativity, more it is a matter of appetite, the one who is awesome also nourishes. Now we are fed by forces invisible even long dead as we have feasted in her temple.

Who is the ethical listener when we finally speak our narrative is who we adore brings out our gift. This listener of our narrative our adoration. The god is not the teacher instead our adoration of her evokes the gods, souls departed return soul on lips through the cake with which this teacher nourishes us.

Helen and Miss Temple have a conversation by the fire.

And then we can go further, pass through the most unlit chambers, ageless secrets, our imagination hungry and fed the seed-cake we imagine our way now the beam of that torch brighter. Our vision begins changing in her room, half-lit, illuminations offered and intuitions form themselves more readily. She is hearing the ancient language it forms in our voice we know yet not from where in her presence our memory is revived, breathing better in her chambers, we capture the breezes, carry them up for her.

Her sound, her smell, her bearing, the move of her wrist, the way her legs cross and this way she receives our articulation brings color to our face. There were some rhythms, we had not heard or caught them before but now we sense them in this atmosphere, circles surrounding, each in its own rhythm extending to her received sent back as she holds our gaze, we are held within these rings and we are stirred.

She stirs us to long lost beauty 'of meaning, of movement, of radiance.' We are recognizing the archaic designs and those radical chords and we bring them up for her.

We are listening while these two traverse this world's history to its margin of lost nation, ancient mysteries, dust as sheet covering chests the leather straps broken they are sounding the manuscripts of ages ringing through nature's secret struck in dialogue.

Their dialogue a prayer, shared divine service, love service, mutual submission to what is of gift, hidden treasure. Intimate disclosure, we hear two alternating voices stimulating one another to foreign country, lost nation.

Brocklehurst depotentiated to Helen's holding interior division she messaged conscience in whose hearing we become narrator becoming where we are listener to ancient secrets, once lost regions. Finding our narrative allows opening to where we can listen to what was once lost, unconscious, can be heard, foreign secrets once unconscious can be worded.

We begin to warm. Color rose. She has placed the china tea cup in each of our hands, the chair is comfortable yet straightbacked for she is a woman of propriety, does not incline to the ardent. Neither excited nor eager yet serene, here is a china cup placed in our hand. But our eyes catch the fire's glow as we sit closely to her and our hands begin trembling, the china sounding on itself.

We want to whisper to her: it has been of too many generations we had to worship you in Convent, untouched, proper, of all propriety, you were distant, we could barely sense you. Sometimes you carried yourself to us it was through a glimpse of another sister yet always when we moved closer not even dialogue permitted, years behind a blackened habit, only way of worshipping you in any service.

Now we wait, reddening, we want this one to meet us in full fervor. Here is the temptation to make what is being revealed here Miss Temple herself. We have always wanted to touch the mystery by touching the woman one external, we would smash a rib to do so.

Helen of another way she summons from what sources we cannot tell 'swelling spring of pure, full, fervid eloquence.' How we wonder 'has a girl of fourteen a heart large enough, vigorous enough to hold the swelling spring of pure, full, fervid eloquence?' Lost mysteries and countries of the margin become a language, unconscious sources spring dialogue when conscience here an ethics intimately befriended through a heart large enough to hold.

What passions as fervid in Helen is pure eloquence. Now that student is roused and stimulated those sources of a full cheek flush and eyes radiant of meaning a beauty more singular than that of Miss Temple.

Helen roused in dialogue with beloved teacher, has not made her gift that teacher's instead asking something from this one serene, from this teacher's propriety 'which precluded deviation into the ardent, the excited, the eager,' something asked.

Teacher and pupil touch qualities in one another which are yearning to be manifested in each.

Women speaking intelligence luminous not pedantic, two women speaking intelligence. Helen shines off toward Miss Temple in luminescence not incandescence, does not absorb that teacher's light. Helen shines toward Miss Temple and it comes as a sort of radiant beauty more singular than the teacher's calling that teacher further to manifest through the girl who loves her some intelligence fervor, imaginative ardor.

Two women dialoguing in intelligence, this teacher is allowing herself to be divested as master, secret conspiration.

Soul on lips, Helen challenges teacher in a radical shift to know beloved gift through who is student; what is required here is a reciprocity, worshipper becoming worship. Required here is that the teacher lower to aspire to that which speaks through student: through Helen appears this longing of Miss Temple for manifestation of what is ardent.

Miss Temple asks Helen whether she can read her father's Latin Virgil.
At what is the moment, our 'amazement reached its climax' witnessing
this conspiration, the teacher has been called by the light emanating by this
girl Burns and returns with a question does she recall Latin by the father.

◄§ Virgil. His was a soul blasted by the ancient rancor of the
Highest Queen while protected by a mother Venus who
would alight would appeal to many almighty gods for him.
With what begins "I sing of warfare and a man of war," he
was serving was served by Venus yet his service specifically:
Aeneas blasted by Juno on land on sea perilous howling gust
the rapid whirlpool gulping until Father prevailed over her
fury. Subduing, compromising her fury, subduing Rutulians,
the fates decree Ascanius will be Iulus to command Latium
in power thirty years the fortress Alba Longa.

And when a woman has desire, this Dido, hear Aeneas
from his high couch recounting the battles with Danaans,
Laocoon's coiling ensnarement a sign warranting the horse's
entry, and Dido's desire giving her no rest. Juno requires it,
that the Dardan captain would tarry in Tyrian Carthage. "All
to divert the future power from Italy/To Libya." Yet the Dido
desire a plot must be extinguished. Dream of a mercurial
figure saying do not linger: " 'Ha! Come, break the spell!
Woman's a thing/Forever fitful and forever changing.' "
Extinguished desire is the Iris extraction of Dido's spirit from
the self-destructed body.

Games and wars of this passage son of Venus: gauntlets
stained with spattered brains, Eurytion's arrow through the
dove plummets down. This way Venus appeals. Venus appealing to her Father Almighty, Jupiter King, all Olympus trembling at his nod, her appeal to Neptune, her appeal to Vulcan.
Father/son the passage, greeting Anchises in the world below
Sybil mediates son to father their " 'voices in communion' " and
they look eagerly upon Dardan future generations. Evander
later sees in Aeneas his father's voice and look.

Juno excites Allecto whose serpent to Amata's breast a
fever infection, whose torch planted below Turnus's chest
driving him wild wrath boiling of a caldron's foam, and the
Allecto intervention directs Ascanius's shaft of war-breaking-
out blow. Camilla, Metabus's offering to Diana, fierce war-
rior of Trojans, dying her last word admonition to Turnus.
While Lavinia, long hair aflame divine, never speaks, never

moves — "the cause/Of so much suffering, lovely eyes
downcast" — blushes, cheeks burn as her mother proclaims
never will have Aeneas as son. Lavinia never speaks yet facing her Turnus's desire becomes burning for battle, a last
challenge to Aeneas for which Lavinia the prize. Allecto,
Camilla, Lavinia: here another sort of temple.

Venus's dittany to Iapyx's herbs from Phoebus, the gifts
her son for war, man of war and Juno's wrath compromised,
Aeneas's blade sunk in the chest of Turnus exacting due.
Same goddess yet of another service, other temple. ᛒ

Jane's 'organ of Veneration' expanding at every Latin line of Virgil's
Helen read. The powers within Helen roused by 'something in her own
unique mind,' yet now she uses those in a Father's lesson and we venerate.

What organ of venus a love as worship expanding to this girl, fourteen,
fervid sources swelling spring when placed in the service of the father's
lesson we move our worship becoming excessive perhaps even an idolatry
upon her; and something of the spontaneous fluency adheres too closely
our devotion of her as a Father's lesson, and a bell rings.

Venus only for the sons the Father's lesson of what was secret designating
now only clinging too closely to her our devotion. Stopped, returning to the
door, a walk with Miss Temple's second sigh relinquishing the student
reluctantly.

Jane and Helen leave at the bell and Miss Scatcherd punishes Helen.

Now some older woman is lashing at her for untidy drawers. She had
been singing forth gifted intelligence and the teacher knew not how to take
the heat of that fervid spring, went instead to what was the Father's lesson
ending the visit to this specific temple.

Soul on lips. Language of soul, of what had been recessed, powers of her
unique mind kindling eloquent meaning. Fervid spring, the words spring
heated and when this ardor reverts Latin of Father something closes.
Vacant cough. Wrong forced friction.

When what was unconscious 'secrets of nature' becomes manifest, hear
the language, something heats, and this language desires now an ardor
exchange. Instead reverts to fathers and sons the girl coughs to the heated
reprimand of Miss Scatcherd turning on her wrong forced friction.

Revert to the Father: Jupiter consigns and concludes. When we cannot
bring a speaking out the radical design of what has been secret organ of
Veneration, the exchange remains between the men: Brocklehurst and
Lloyd determine and something of this chamber fades its privacy now does
not matter in what becomes only public through men exchange
determination.

We find the temptations of idolatry as we learn with women to conspire in intelligence. Jane's temptation of idolatry has been to locate the gift only upon Miss Temple and Helen as external others. Helen's temptation of idolatry has been to locate the gift only upon invisible angels, not knowing these qualities in embodied manifestation.

In Miss Temple's chamber, we are asked to see through our idolatries in arriving at a singular beauty. Jane witnesses Helen's brilliance roused through Miss Temple's presence without being located upon that woman. Yet Helen beginning to lower her gift to the human gets stopped.

It is a moment where our 'amazement reached its climax,' and in that moment we hear the words of an ancient man, they are very fine and of many truths, but they belong to other generations of past worship. What rings now a closing bell.

> ◄§ Virgil. To the younger girl I had been speaking of spirits round us watching and guarding and then she entered and invited us to her room. In her presence I felt those angels descend and my mind's worth ignited cool light I began to feel them through my lips and in what radiated as this body's heat. Here they were, beloved, warming my cheeks, caress- ing me, desiring that I finally hold them more closely to this their word. I was slowly persuaded. Perhaps I saw she had to submit to this holy vibration to continue also, and then she was asking of father's Latin. "I sing of warfare and a man of war." And in a far background I heard a great shattering yet would not turn to it for I preferred to follow her. I will say my Latin lines with flourish enhancing this moment's vibrant passing but as I lose her I rise only to be whipped back down by the one red-faced and rather flailing. §►

Gift stopped in a cough, her drawers awry. There was a moment when the girl has caught onto a mystery gift and it was lowering to her lips she was asking through the teacher's apprehension and acquiescing (a sort of service) to make such sources more manifest of what conspires between the women.

Teacher and pupil touch qualities in one another which are yearning to be manifested in each.

Miss Temple has not been able. Virgil instead. Something goes to an older place certainly deserving service yet not of this temple where the beloved ones have been of female tongue and conspiration between breasts heaving breasts of awe and stimulation not lacking nourishment, here another temple. Virgil brings on the bell.

But we learn in witnessing. Conspiring in this temple place we leave inspired after the bell. Imagination becomes a food and we craft its design satiated. What was unconscious hunger becomes designated through craft.

In places of Brocklehurst there have been bells stopping as we learn to enter this service of fervid sources: ardent dialogue with conscience bringing to language what was secret.

Of what we are yet unknowing: how to maintain distinction as we reciprocate and mutually submit. The bell rings and some Scatcherd power rage dominates.

The next day Miss Scatcherd binds a pasteboard bearing the word Slattern to Helen's forehead.

While Helen wears the Slattern sign on her forehead, Jane is burning with the rage Helen is incapable of experiencing. Jane finally runs up, rips the sign off and throws it into the fire. The two carry one another's lesson, but where Jane is taught by Helen to enter other invisible realms precluding impulsive grasp of the human, becomes conscience speaking, Helen has not been able to learn the friction permitting her eloquence its bodily design, neglected body spills to waste, careless, body of the one sublime now only slattern. Helen has not been able to learn Jane's downward lesson.

  ◄§ Miss Temple's Second Sigh. She closes the door behind
  them, stands staring for a long while at the vase on the table
  which has held the repast of a seed-cake.

   Their love for me is of the order, as it was through the
  love of my teacher for me. Bending she would look into my
  eyes, hers squaring mine, ores mined, I rose for her and
  together we would explore caverns long ignored. I became
  less frightened of myself, the crevices, and I too began to
  read fluently very early for her.

   I frame their eloquence. As she did for me, I catch their
  luminosity however slight and then I darken the night around
  them so they can see the forms of that glowing dark enhance.
  Merely I say: continue, unfold to the beauty it is yours
  already glimmering womb of it.

   She folds a napkin, takes off the gold watch chain. Slowly
  pins removed from her top-knot, hair falling its long plaits
  felled the softer trees suggesting tropics. White cotton
  drawers now nightdress. The chair is velvet and she sits
  alone.

   Soul outpour on lips moving tenaciously moving viva-
  ciously, I can mark their lesson, through me they are moved

to sources of their singular gift yet unnamed appearing in the dimensions required of each of them. I hear their history by heart evoked an angel I consult telling me to trim their exaggeration or pointing me to their wound, their lack, their malice, whether the girl has moved off, how to feed her. Yet I know not how to stop that cough.

In the chair's long hour alone the teacher walks the heart passage, eyes accustomed and she sees the unfamiliar woman upon the far corner's pillowed couch. Something dazzling she feels a shock, some shift of balance required, she can not sustain the impact and averts her glance.

Before my head turns away I see your hair of auburn thickly curled. The sense of recognition is very strong, it was during the discussion with Helen, her pallor so permanent, I cannot still that cough, the pulse low. Our speaking began of the many languages traversing continents of idea, discourse rapid exchange propelled and soaring to summit spired colors splintering into the shades previously unseen. Bending back to nature's secret caverns recovered by the light of these shooting star lights dipping I wanted to string the points scintillating hers most fine some cultured.

Yet I could not. Within and behind our discourse, through Helen's presence yours began to reach mine, red hue swirl encircles and something was asked of me of the vibrant instead I reserved.

I sought to remember the familiar verse of a Latin to recover what would be balance. The young girl with us in amazement yet I had by then forestalled the splendid stir and stopped there coming the cough I cannot stop.

I want to approach you yet I do not know the service, for what have you to do with my bent knee, your lap I desire it to encase this sigh yet I will not approach you are not of Mary for I had been accustomed to blue folds and the larger lap of a Mother Ann and a particular sweetness, not you so energetically awaiting every caution. I stand withholding, eyes cast, some bell rings.

For a long while she has been sitting alone in the velvet chair. Aching are the walls of her room. Out of drawer, wide paged journal to the table of one candle lit as flickering, writing she is all she can know for now. ❧

Bibliography

Corbin, Henry. *Creative Imagination in the Sufism of Ibn 'Arabi.* Trans. by Ralph Manheim. Princeton, N.J.: Princeton University Press, 1969.

Herzog, Edgar. *Psyche and Death.* New York: G. Putnam and Sons, 1967.

Jung, C. G. *The Visions Seminars.* Books 1 and 2. Zurich: Spring Publications, 1976.

Spark, Muriel. *The Prime of Miss Jean Brodie.* New York: New American Library, 1961.

Virgil. *The Aeneid.* Trans. by Robert Fitzgerald. New York: Random House, 1983; quoted pp. 3, 99, 116, 184, 348.

Chapter 9
Crib White Curtain Covering

Spring, air softened and swollen feet returning to themselves walk now pleasant recess through what are becoming floral paths. I venture outside the high
spiked Lowood walls and the wood receives me. This wood had been ravaged
by the wintry elements: beck whirling to a raving, now it slowly eases to its
gurgling. The wilder rain in its slashing had left trees only skeletons yet here
in May 'Lowood shook loose its tresses; it became all green, all flowery.'
Sunshine grounded in its wild primrose plant as these skeleton trees become
embodied 'majestic life.'

I romp with more liberty than ever since Lowood lying in its cradle of hill
and wood, fog of that cradle carrying the typhus, and many within more
than half the eighty girls have no resistance, through 'semi-starvation and
neglected colds' are struck by the infection, disease penetrating, institution
now hospital, teacher as nurse, they are packing up those girls with any
family could depart, while inside prevails the camphor and pastille, many
die, buried quickly and quietly as the days a more striking blue, tulips and
roses, the scent of sweet-briar.

They permit the few of us who are well to exercise fully all day away in
the wood we are the gypsies, and there is more food for us since all rules are
lifted, the Brocklehursts dare not approach, we carry our slices of bread and
cheese thickened slice to the wood. My friend there Mary Ann Wilson,
shrewd and witty, always flowing from her a narrative for which she has a
bent, she is older and she knows of the world, she informs me on what I like
to hear, while with my turn for analysis, I question, and in our wood spot in
pleasure we chat.

Yet where is the first friend Helen Burns certainly this Mary Ann is not of
that one's higher taste for in the wood she can only offer me amusing stories
and many a time we indulge in 'racy and pungent gossip,' had I left my
Helen for such? No, of many defects I am yet that first friend still held for
me the more sincere attachment 'as strong, tender, and respectful as any that
ever animated my heart.' But Helen is ill, not of typhus but with what they
call consumption and I am ignorant of such things, I am sure it is not serious
and she soon will recover.

We had strayed far away that day Mary Ann and I, gotten lost in fact,
and it is after moon-rise that we return seeing first the surgeon's pony, someone is quite ill probably dying. I decide to remain outside longer in the garden to plant the roots I have carried from the wood these roots cannot wait
until the morning, and I wonder what it is for the one there about to die.
And for the first time my mind tries to apprehend what it has learned of this

heaven this hell of what is death and my mind 'recoiled, baffled; and for the first time, glancing behind, on each side, and before it, it saw all round an unfathomed gulf: it felt the one point where it stood—the present; all the rest was formless cloud and vacant depth; and it shuddered at the thought of tottering, and plunging amid that chaos.' The front door opens to a nurse and a surgeon who departs and I go to that nurse and I ask how is Helen Burns.

She tells me not well, not here long. The day before I would have thought she was going to return to her own home in Northumberland yet now I know it in an instant, Helen is going to the 'region of spirits' and I receive this news of her dying with shock of horror, then grief, then desire: I ask what room. She is in Miss Temple's I hear I cannot go near. Instead to bed, it is two hours later at eleven all around finally slumbering so I climb out and negotiate those passages, I know my way and I grope now in the dark assisted by a window here and there, descent to the lower portions, closing two doors then mounting a staircase, and here is the room, door ajar for any fresher air.

I push the door back and fearing to find death I seek Helen. I see a nurse sleeping beside the crib placed close by Miss Temple's bed still empty as that teacher ministers in the room of fever. I am pausing by this crib's side, fearful to look inside its white curtain, is my friend dead? I speak first her name and she answers, pulls back the curtain, her face is pale yet looks so little changed my fear subsides, they must be mistaken. Can it be you Jane?—she is composed, she speaks my name calmly, too calm to be dying. I get into the crib, I kiss her, she is very cold but her smile is of old. She knows how late it is, heard the time strike, wonders why I have come.

I tell her it is to see her, that I had to speak to her. It is time to say good-bye then she says I have come just in time. I ask if she is going home and her reply is that it is her last home. My distress now tears and she is seized with her cough. When we both still, she notices my bare feet, tells me to lie down, cover myself with her quilt.

Her arm is over me and I nestle close to her, after a long silence she whispers that she is happy and I must not grieve, the illness is gradual not painful and no one will regret her leaving, her father is remarried, will not miss her, and she does not have the qualities to do well in the world, she is avoiding much suffering through this dying she tells me do not grieve. I ask her where she is going and hear it is to God who never destroys what he creates, she will be restored to him, God her father and her friend. In her whisper: she loves him and is loved by him.

I ask her whether I will see her when I die, yes, she affirms it, I too will be received by ' "the same mighty, universal Parent." ' She is dear to me and I do not want to let her go, my head tucked in her neck and soon she is whispering how comfortable she is and that now she can sleep and asks me not to leave her, likes having me near.

I will stay with her I say dear Helen no one will take me away and to that her question am I warm darling. Goodnight say each she kisses me I her we then sleep.

Strange movements and I am being carried in the arms of the nurse, no one reprimands me for having left my bed nor do they respond to my many questions yet it is a day or two that I learn how Miss Temple returning that evening found me in the crib by her bed, my arms around Helen who was dead while I slept.

For fifteen years her grave covered only by the grassy mound but now gray marble marking inscribed her name and ' "Resurgam" ' the word.

The heat from his scourge whose whippings settle into the crevice of our school. It comes with the fog. The vision is no longer of clarity, we have again become baffled, his regimen clouds us, he wants to cut us apart no longer differentiation lesson could provide distinction within collective body. Instead we divide from our body, begin to lose our sense of things and this comes as a fog breeding disease.

We have taken to the wood. It is filling itself out. No longer shades of the skeleton here. We are heartier than the rest, we have learned to pass through his punishment and deflect his disease, coming to a place we speak an ordinary discourse. We climb over the sturdy Lowood wall, we explore, we break through those old structures, break through to this wood which receives us.

It is shaking itself out, tresses, folds, frills, its layers enhanced and partially covered by the greenery: lanceolate, palmate, perfoliate, whorl.

We break through the old structures but the others have succumbed. He is highly contagious and his is a complete infiltration wants to possess the very marrow. The others have not learned the marble lesson. Everywhere around us these women are falling under in the fever, dying to the Brocklehurst condemnation.

For his is a foreign spirit, hostile and pathogenic, source of disease. 'Semi-starvation and neglected colds had predisposed most of the pupils to receive infection.' His form of severance, sever from all body, this neglect of body is what the body receives as infection, his form of severance has become disease. Whipping Lowood girls from their bodies how they carry unconscious through the body split off they have no resistance to hold forth and now they fall into a delirium.

They writhe in his fever. Quick and quiet burial. All around we see it: half our female population going under.

      •§ Typhus. He has not allowed a clean place for our desire
      and it has become asphyxiating, stopped, fogged, and now a
      fog breeding pestilence and this louse has a powerful sucking

mouth and with sharp teeth it grips our skin through which it
cuts with its pair of stylets. And it begins to suck our blood
injecting into it its germ its microorganism these rickettsiae
have been living off, inside the body of this louse as parasite,
the louse transfers them to us, and they pass through our
pharynx, they invade cells of our intestinal walls, multiply
there until after a few days the cells burst and the rickettsiae
are released and they are filling now all intestinal canal. He
is in our entrails he who does not want a speck of dust of dirt
who says the body is vile only feed the soul he has had only a
collective understanding of us and never fed never cleaned us
overcrowded only one piece of clothing the body is vile and
now the body is infected and in a fever he has not wanted
our heat and in whipping it out of us we have lost our blood
to his parasite infecting and this fever our delirium we die,
populations of us die writhing and frenzied. When he has
spoken of logos spirit not in our body the host has become
human, we are the women now human host to his louse. ह

The witch at stake flogged, the convulsing hysteric couched, the hyperactive anorexic tyrannized: he has come as inquisitor, analyst, psychiatrist
and his is a foreign spirit. The fog settles and they have no resistance,
flailing in a feverish death. We see this population of women going under.

But we have had the lessons and we break through the walls now. Once
when we had been infiltrated by some compulsive forces would annihilate
until these walls enfolded and protected us, we sought the safety and she
taught us when the elements whirl threatening impingement threatening
ensnarement she taught us to rise, mediate compulsions, rise differentiated
designation desires mediated to temple overview of our narrative we speak
its divisions. We learned to move through the Brocklehurst ordeal and we
did not go under his possession.

And now we break out. Here the scourge, Lowood shakes loose its
tresses. Trees round themselves in a green softening, beckon. The flores-
cence in the wood draws us in its scent.

We will not stay in this fog cradle of disease, disease of severing us from
these bodies, female body, we will not be trapped in it. We have moved
through his splitting to our natural division, divided self-reflection becoming conscience befriended, we do not remain split and his rickettsiae do not
cut and invade: we divide out within the larger ground.

We have built our resistance which is not to resist him and become
possessed. We have rooted ourselves, stripped older layers and rose until
speaking condensed while held by her throughout. We built up our resis-

tance. We can reside alongside and not go under and not come up against his fever instead we take the enormous energy and break out.

    ◆§ Spring as hate. We will not stay in this fog cradle of his disease of severing from these bodies the scourge makes us delirious while fogged, we will not be possessed in it. And it takes an enormous energy to break out. The buds shoot, green darts tear out of this brown soil, they rupture through the heavy morning mist. The limbs of trees divide open and we marvel at what hate it must take not to stay hidden blasted by the wintry forces yet instead construct carbohydrate, the cellulose, the cell wall, divide to it. He hates our body its movement yet it is a matter of using the force of his hate and with our hate we transmute it to crack, to shoot, to rip forth and deliver ourselves new divided body. Forest and field take the whipping forces of the ferocious winter and transmute them in air and light to the cellulose of these teeming life plants not cowering not obliterated but using what heat comes off the slashing storm to break out, hate now the melting spring. Spring as hate. ε◆

We go where we see this hostile force now as shooting leaf. For we have been involved in our own transmutations. Mediated by Helen to Miss Temple's chamber we learned to move through his condemnation, marble to his disease while passage for that force previously impulse reaction we used it to strip our Gateshead layers, soar and then condense, differentiation of our narrative in her chamber, we are no longer possessed yet differentiating within recess in what is dialogue with conscience.

Held by her, rooted, his force could not crack us as we stripped to what heterogeneous what once only unconscious now whispering its words through our body feeding in her temple.

These forces, surging fluids up through heterogeneous body, no need for him to sever us, prohibit us from body its curl of desire waves. Letting them up, now knowing their design builds up our resistance, we are not receptacle for his disease. Moving through the force of his condemnation we transmute his pestilence to our food, our romping in the wood.

We transmute his pestilence recalling our Gateshead hate. Scatcherd reminder way to leave Miss Temple's chamber is embodied not slattern body, not neglected body. Recalling appetite, this body romps, a way to bring out the lesson from her chambers and not become diseased.

We do not pause to wonder why we have gotten free when so many others are possessed and killed by him. We do not let him stop up our canals. We keep ourselves well fed our cell walls are hearty and they will not be invaded by the parasite. We take to the wood, way to move out from the temple is to the larger body not without it.

We know our liberty pertains to having entered Miss Temple's chamber, placing Gateshead as narrative there, sharing a seed-cake ritual, repast of dead many voices moving from stratosphere to heart thus inspired yet with Gateshead body narrated we take our narrative to the wood through our appetite.

This spring burst engages us. The fog has been heavy, collecting poisons, not a life-sustaining circulation. This land wears the emblem of the Lowood death scourge. These snow-drops and lilies, hanging head, dew as tears, here the lily is madonna weeping for there has been a sacrifice. The crimson double-daisy flaunts the blood knowing its own majesty it shines on the field daring invasion. The red and white roses bear memory of wars, here the blood red cell of oxygen white cell of immunity they wave a circulation through the strife as even through the canker.

Yet this primrose is yellow, pale light first signal of subsiding wintry blast but failing so rapidly not to see a summer sun, vitality paling, desire resigning. Also these violets, the fragrant gratification only temporary, wasting so young, shy and tender, dying for sorrow.

This wood and this bank speak the hospital hall of camphor and burnt vinegar. Primrose plant returns us to pastille scent of the sickroom. Bright, fragrant banners of surviving the Brocklehurst wintry blast, yet only for a brief moment. The ones who teach us the preliminary survival depart from us, appear only a poignant color streak before a wasting.

We have brought out our cheese and bread, thick slices to this wood, we chat with the new worldly friend who has a turn for narrative. The typhus cradle had transformed death into food for us. We eat the portions of those who are dying. We have become as impersonal as this blooming wood. We romp well fed, or else, the lily whispers, we too will die short life ended.

We are gossiping, we have come to life on a lighter side. While we are gossiping with Mary Ann Wilson, there is someone we care most about dying in the main house and we cannot yet face it. We think we are waiting for some sort of recovery. We tell amusing stories, ask many questions, get involved superficially in others' lives, the closest friend is dying yet we cannot know it so we carry our cheese larger slice to the woods, laughing.

We take to the ordinary, we want our further lessons in air and light, must see this landscape as ordinary for we have been to the more bloody caverns and the soaring stratospheres and we seize the ordinary now with our bread, cheese, our Mary Ann. Here we prefer the sweet-briar of the common cottage garden. Our friend beside is witty and original, she knows of the world. She is not extraordinary, has not the higher taste, but she informs us of this world and we chat.

From this wooded place, address to the one who reads us, we speak to our reader directly: 'True, reader,' for after finding conscience we are read. To the reader we deliver our story that Helen Burns is ailing we would not choose the Mary Ann over the one to whom we have attached a sentiment the most 'strong, tender and respectful.'

For our faults, we are speaking to who reads us truly, this is not one of those faults, faithful to our friend would not of her tire, her absence an illness we are sure time will alleviate. When we know we are being read we have a conscience about which we remind our reader; we are faithful, yet the nascent conscience still does not let us see what is dying and the attachment indicates we have interior who she is, we have interiorization which is the explicit dialogue with reader.

This move out with the ordinary friend continues our antidote to the Brocklehurst fatal fever. He spreads when the school is in a cradle, there is not enough intercourse with a larger world and the school becomes a bed of pestilence, everywhere contagion.

Temptation to sit within a fog when his disease spreads. It is hard for us to move, the fever is in our heads and inwardly we are flailing, even delirious, but externally we cannot move. Friends are urging us out into sun and light but we cannot see them, find them, we are like glue in our bed, everything sticks. We hear vague sounds through the fog but nothing can move us out, we want to stay in it, somewhere it has been a cradle and it takes a great effort to move out.

Air, sunshine filtering through the mosaic of this leaf, building cellulose, building body, flower from roots darkly moist not moldy, there is air out here, not the fog, we reach out to a larger world in an ordinary discourse which airs out the Brocklehurst loathing.

Defended at Lowood, it was a protection so we could learn the lessons without infringement from without. But if those surrounding walls remain too sturdy then during one of his visits he will stick to our blood and spread himself there as we cramp we become captured and contaminated.

The Brocklehurst tyranny, the denigration and prohibition of a female body, has become lived unconsciously by the Lowood group. His lesson of severance at the expense of body: Brocklehurst's refusal to recognize embodiment within differentiation kills bodies. Lowood has been infected by starvation and neglected cold, the body objectified, and Brocklehurst's virulence is killing the girls who have not learned to pass him through, long division without contamination, which would be to differentiate through conscience speaking body.

When we had begun to learn of conscience, conscience as friend, typhus follows. Conscience as typhus. Typhus as our bodily symptom to tell us in conscience when we have not been dialoguing conscience yet collectively following his paternal Law without lowering it in conscience temple to unconscious body desire way out through the body.

If defended too long within the convent's spiked fortress, we become open to his invasion, spiked wall only keeps him in now working disease. In learning the discipline, an order without denigrating the female body, severance as sublimation not eliminating body, sublimation to designation wants down to body break out of wall to world of ordinary body, the passage down gets caught in disease when discipline tips too easily to harsh regimen and a temptation is for our stay to become a sort of passivity, we can shrink in it, too cold to venture forth, only skeletons in woods awaiting, we shrink in it, huddled together in our convent and it can become a sort of passivity.

Perhaps we have relied too much on those walls, perhaps we did not venture out enough, we did not rub against the world, building body. Protected we rose so high we could not sneer, we could not squint our eyes, clench those fists and with deep breaths move out the narrative into world: not stay possessed by him in a fog cradle but take the bread and cheese and move out to the proliferating greenery with our stories.

Such rubbing against the world is exercise, romping body, blood-pumping surgings: we learn to breathe correctly in the air and light which takes passing through the Lowood walls and moving friction with the worldly even as recessed green; here recessed wood has now become place of lessons of world, Mary Ann's worldly narrative, we get ready to break out to condense secondary now as densening sublimated desire when half the population of us is caught by him fevered.

Helen also becomes extremely ill when the Brocklehurst pestilence attacks but she has another relation to it, it strikes her differently, different form of disease. We hear her infection is called consumption, her body wastes, is being slowly consumed, but we are ignorant of such things and we are sure she will recover. She has taught us about his passage, she will recover. This is the place of the sunlit wood chuckling with Mary Ann, we are witty and we are making up amusing stories. But we do not go under.

It is a question of building resistance in sun and air which is not to resist him. We take our lesson from these trees, elm, ash, oak. They were beseiged by slashing gale, they stayed rooted and carried up inner resources, fluid forces under world from the earth source, inner resistance, so when whipping wind struck they let it pass over and through and they bent and twirled and moaned even raved, they have stripped down to their skeleton, becoming poignant even terrifying themselves, they manifested all that could be of hate and of terror and as that wind beseiged they did not crack nor did they resist back an onslaught, instead they stripped to certain configurations working off of external elements by the strength of their internal moving fluids and they did not crack. Their exhalation our life-force. This wood is hearty, has its pulp and its own root, it can take now this spring heat and lets it too pass through leaving it shimmering with offerings in scent and radiance.

Even this beck stayed embedded as it has been with the torrents and the whirling frosted air, letting these forces pass through, its dappled rocks aligning now jewels in its sunlit calm.

Wood and beck can take the whipping forces and transmute easily there is not here a question of morality. Oak not inferior to slashing gale storm, these whipping winds do not pronounce the tree liar or sinner or pariah. In nature the clashing forces are not scourge yet heated even fervent or ecstatic dance, without question of morality.

Humanly slashing forces take an ethics. Reed and Brocklehurst take an ethics, these masculine agents possessing. Yet we have risen to a learning of conscience and what rises is how we might carry rightly what was in locked drawer down and out.

In the presence of conscience as friend we spoke what had been rancor and hate, ethics of learning impulse delineated. After Gateshead and through Lowood, Jane knows the place of hate in her narrative which moves her through his disease. The hate at Gateshead: John Reed's eruption and she did not yet know the division operation instead direct action resistance and she was flattened.

Helen Lowood teachings to rise, mediate as infold this hate to contact of angels, words of it, message it, not direct resistance, narrative and dialogue asking conscience is this the right story. Jane moves to the larger wood when the fever settles within the walls which are spiked.

There Jane melts. Lowood had gotten so cold and split it became enflamed, delirious. Now her feet are in the tepid back, the oozing mud, wading.

We had broken out of our defense into some wooded recess and speak ordinary discourse there. The wooded place is another defense where we pause, we build body resistance, until we can return, more of Lowood desiring impartation.

She tries to bring some of this nature's lesson back to the infected school. she is carrying back the roots and digging them in the Lowood garden. It is late. She and Mary Ann had gotten lost in the wood, but now she stays out digging even as her friend goes inside because she wants these roots to take in this garden soil, does not want to wait until the morning.

Her attempt to bring nature's life-force to the diseased place is limited. It is late and she sees the surgeon leaving.

We have not tried yet to see the relation of these roots, yearning tendril, to this surgeon's black bag bearing messages from what would be corpse. We are yet young, but we are planting some of that forest pulse in the school's dirt when the surgeon leaves.

To find the message, designation of what was unspeakable is Lowood we are digging in its soil which returns us we can look further into abyss what resides Lowood, death, ask what is the message of what might be that. We begin to wonder on death.

Unfathomed gulf, vast cloud, unmeasurable depth, we stand a pinpoint, our mind's present, the rest surrounding entire abyss and we are about to totter into that chaos, it is quite unknown and we have never tried to apprehend it before.

It sits in our stomach as a dull ache, this knowledge of her dying. All around abysmal chaos. We had followed her every move, sign. We are standing fixed at some point and we begin to shudder.

Patient with our reactivity she read us the sign within the fogged veran-dah, she has sat beside. She has trimmed our inflation to size and moved along our natural contours with compassion, without cutting into us in ways violating she taught us lessons of scission, parting, of distance, of inhibition, a natural division.

We had been standing alone in the bustling classroom, we were looking out at the sleet whirling and we understood that passion and we wanted to be with another who knew it, we saw her by the fire reading in her heat. Welts she knew also from the mother's turning. She understood and she began to teach us a natural inhibition in order to speak the inherent relation of the forces beseiging.

She sat by our mortification, our death, and we cannot at first face hers. We have the strongest attachment to her and she has read our angels while holding our hand. No one has touched us through quite that same soaring spark.

We cannot at first face her death. Instead we romp. We want to see those flowers only as spring hope, we have just assumed she would recover.

Facing the surgeon's leaving and we are shuddering at this abyss we are finally peering into it. Divided speaking subject of our uneducated secret regions, to face her death is to face our own and learn that language. Shuddering we have wanted the flesh of this life we transplant root of woods. The long-arching stems are bearing numerous sweet-briar and we want to inhale that scent of spice.

But here too the pansies are golden-eyed, heartsease, we miss our love, she is in our thoughts now. Love-in-idleness she is leaving us and even with all our roots and this pansy tucked in our shirt, we cannot make her attach, no love potion in the surgeon's bag we are planting the root and from this ground a trembling pause peering through soft leather bag to its abyss.

It is not the typhus which has her; Helen did not catch the fever left by the Brocklehurst condition, she did not absorb his parasite, for she too has made it to Miss Temple's chamber, she had her own marble antidote to the Brocklehurst splittings, stylet and whip. Her disease however colludes with him because she is wasting, her adolescent body had wanted to ripen to fuller breast and now it wastes.

Here is the cough which caught Jane's attention in the first place. Consumption. Helen wastes away. She has an inspiration problem. Consuming inspiration. She has been inspiring in ways that for her body are consuming. She has been breathing in tubercule bacilli, they multiply by simple division, they leave their mass of granulation cells and the tissue is injured, here the nodular lesion, the tissue is injured by nodule and these granulation cells are degenerative.

What was tissue organic, it bound our body, it held, adhered, yet hers has the injury, wounded it becomes dry, hard, a mass which does not adhere, crumbling node this substance dry cheeselike, granulation cells of caseation, degeneration.

Her breathing is off: nodules where there once were passages for air for this oxygen to the blood, heart pulse regulated now by nodule. Body in the place of air: bacilli consolidations and caseation, the tissue injured by a consuming inspiration.

Inspiring she became of the air, her body aetherial, angel herself, translucent wing even as she stroked our hand. She animated us and we entered her philosophies, her orbits, her orbs brilliant, we breathed calmly even through impingements pounding attempt at possession. She inspired us and her stratosphere became our protection, it was gossamer, not resisting.

Rising to the heavens in her breath she breathed life into us of angels, we writhed and then we rose above dance with wording shine of her eyes are angels, messages of defect, messages of division, and of death.

She inspired until she lost enough body so body in the lungs place of air now body attempting its lowering by symptomatically saying: what was of air must be body. And this message is from her conscience as friend indicating that heart cannot get the blood sustaining only bacilli-filled, and the heart fails.

The pulse not right, the heart fails, there is difficulty in desire: difficulty in loving, there is difficulty in hating. Helen cannot rub up against what would be of love of hate. She stays isolated, above secluded in inspiration.

Her lungs rebel, incorporate the tubercule, now too much of an injured body in the lungs, caseation, cheese in lungs, feeding milk to these lesioned lungs are suffering, they have gone too far, have lifted others far to soar, they have left this earth to know the spirits of stratospheres, and these human vapors they call her back, they want her to fume.

Her spark has soared so high it has evaporated, the flame no longer in a heart circulation from a lung beating forth its oxygen. Her heart has lost its rhythm: her ardor now only of air, to the heavens and she remains untouched, sacrifice of desire and the ardor only aetherial consumes her.

Difficulty in breathing. She cannot take in the love and she cannot fume the hate. Difficulty in breathing, the blood not circulating but spitting, the pulse not right. She says no one will miss her when she is gone. No one will regret her leaving.

When Jane heard from the nurse Helen Burns was dying: 'I experienced a shock of horror, then a strong thrill of grief; then a desire—a necessity to see her; and I asked in what room she lay.' She is Jane's primary attachment even grief thrills subtended by desire and Helen cannot feel that desire even as that one crawls beside her breast to breast. Miss Temple's love not felt even as the crib has been placed beside the teacher's bed.

To inhale love, to learn to take in love, oxygen for her own tissue, love her tissues, want their health, help them heal their injury. Helen would have to love her tissue.

To fume her hate, clear out poisons, rub up against those depositing ill-will, ardor used now to expel from lungs, friction, clear passage fumed.

Helen's is an inward burning and from the beginning Jane has responded to it. Yet Helen cannot place her ardor, she has touched Jane's hand, first and final friend, only through a death cough. Helen's desire itself has remained unspoken never condensed first to language then secondary through body yet disease coagulation. Her ardor locked within was not met not lowered even in Miss Temple's chamber they resorted to the Father's lesson from high no desiring body no fuming body. Her ardor locked within as it evaporated to all heights, urging only a personal resignation.

No one will miss her and there is no place in the world for her she says she has not the talent to get on in this world not ready for Helen's ardor to lower into tissue and be taken beyond the Lowood wall.

In a Brocklehurst possession Helen's ardor is not carried out into the world and we lose her words, her design only air, never becomes art of this culture, dies in consumption, we have lost our art through Helen's resigning desire, resigning from lowering angel messages through erotic body to culture's body.

Dies to the angels yet angels urge friction with this world so they can become the embodiment of our very cell, not heeded they become symptom. Angels longing not our demise to them yet for them to be in our craving our despising, fast beating lung and pounding heart our angel our conscience. Carrying this dialogue with them is our healthy body means we carry them back to this world finding in passion a craft. In Miss Temple's chamber while under the Brocklehurst employment, Helen's gift lowered only to cough of coagulated lung, Lloyd will exonerate and can you read father's Latin of Venus beseeching Jupiter.

For when our ardent forces are not designated and then moved down and out, instead resorting to Father, kept above in his authority, we either soar and evaporate to the heavens or burn up in a delirium. This is the Brocklehurst disease, caught in splitting off ardent body in differentiation lesson.

When Brocklehurst drives us, contagious we split: we writhe as masses, all equalized in afflicted community, fused and frenzied in his fever while alongside isolated as Helen, lone little crib by the teacher's bed even as that teacher is in the room of the mass fever and the nurse sleeps. Here is this nonhuman isolation with its consuming desire, desire dying away spent in blood sputum hoarse cough singular panting only to His heaven do not grieve.

Frenzied mass while isolated desire resigns, it has been our split disease. When Brocklehurst drives us, lessons of division we get caught at splitting, he keeps us isolated, defended, not in the sun, apart from even the moss of the wood hollow, shut up as severed from our own body and we become infected in the fog of his own making. We are damp, feverish, and exhausted and we do not feel any desire.

We lose what would be message of desire, speaking subject of our desire instead we are again merely receptacle host, no movement to other sides of unique gift instead contagion and we have died without any of our pages in commemoration.

Helen would have to have strong tissue to move out from the force of the Brocklehurst disease to message her ardor, individually, and she does not want it, no one will miss her. To love and feed her own tissue, she would have to face her father's neglect and she would have to hate her father, hate Miss Scatcherd, (find her own "Gateshead" narrative), she would have to engage in some sort of friction as she would have to receive Jane's adoration, the loving care of Miss Temple.

Helen has this friction difficulty: she does not want to hate her father. To hate her father is to negotiate the loss of father, incarnate those ardent words. Ardor to its word, what is the word lowering to this ardor speaks must ultimately return to that primal hate yet she prefers to keep her ardor enclosed as only soaring aetherial in longing to return to the God Father in heaven. She says do not grieve.

At first it is true, we have not wanted to feel it. When his fever first took hold we took off to the wood to the field and sat with the lilies and the hollycocks for they were our grief as they were our hate and we burst out to inhale the breath of this wood, hearty pulp of these large trunks, layers of fern and moss our tress, tulip our open arm, rose our cheek these lips begin to color, here our body of desire, our substance in hate for how he would deliver us only in curse from ourself, and this burst takes a fuming transmuted to differentiated hue and various sorts of fragrance.

These flowers teach transmutation when we are trying to build our inner resistance and not hold onto his disease. We go to learn of their stamina. We see they take in the gaseous fumes of what carbon dioxide could be our death and they transmute these fumes to their color crackling forth lily poppy pansy rose and crocus they flower out and from what could kill us it is a gift of oxygen we breathe in the fresh air of these plants are flourishing.

> ◄§ Chlorophyll. Bacteria of the tubercule are active in the presence of oxygen yet they lack chlorophyll. Tubercule kill her body. Bacteria of the tubercule killing her body lack chlorophyll. In the presence of sunlight chlorophyll converts carbon dioxide and water into carbohydrates, has the ability to transmute what would kill us into organic compound, life of cell wall tissue cellulose. Chlorophyll takes some roots, a desire to lower to contact and suck in the earth fluids and to break through as the design of the internal forces takes shape, the buds break open. And even as this flower soon begins browning or translucent in a withering we inhale the pungent odor, see the stamina lower to its dust, we know this bloom passes through death force in its own time is not lesioned not asphyxiated not coagulated and spit. §►

She is not in the hospital portion of the school yet in Miss Temple's room. We walk at night alone now we have looked into some death abyss drawn to her presence guides us through these stairwells and the door is ajar. Will this be abyss itself we slightly brush this door peering to its opening.

We expect literal abyss at the other end of Helen's sickroom door, revert to a Gateshead contiguity expectation, yet Helen is who finds language even in dying, of death, mediating voices death's language.

When we call her name the white curtains of her crib are pushed aside. This death looks like our friend, it speaks in her voice and the voice is so calm that we wonder if she can be dying. We draw closer to her. She is cold but the smile is of old. We do not want to let her go but we want to know where she is going whether we can follow later. She sees her passing clearly how she is going to bond with the Father, return home to her Father-God, her friend.

We protest. Father. But what of us. She says do not grieve but what of us. She is choosing Him over us. She aired out our possessions, taught us perspective, severance and mediation while hand held remaining close now she chooses His air to that closeness rising from us.

She tells us to lie down beside, to cover our feet with her quilt but this is in the same breath she says it is her passing to another side she rises home to her Father and what of our full-lengthed body embracing hers? Her heart weakens as she chooses the Father yet she wants us alongside.

We do not want to let her go up. We hold, we crawl beside her our body lining hers, we place our cheek against hers more cool and pale and we hear her whispering on return to Him.

Embracing they speak language of lovers, sleep darling well kiss goodnight the one who teaches us of death is our lover.

Jane walks carefully into Helen's alcove of death; close to the fading pulse of friend begins to trace the texture and parameter of what is death. Peering inside the white curtain: where are you going? Death between women. Death at Lowood.

Death at Gateshead: non-being place of deject, the stepmother turned was our attachment to non-being, demand of that mother then desire for phantom made us happy. Here our desire mediated finding distinct words in relation until while attempting incarnation instead Latin of a Virgil read and Brocklehurst regimen of toast proportion maintained and Mr. Lloyd to be corroborated, promulation of Father law, logos a home when all of desire is diseased body in his aetherial authority.

There is a Father here at Lowood in what is death. Helen states the Father in heaven awaits her while her own father remarried, had sent her away never called her back, even when remarried never called her back, does not think of his daughter, will not regret her death, and this child lies speaking of the Father-friend awaiting open armed.

The father is absent while Father-God calls up her word and body, where we are raging at these contradictions, we found the words for our tumultuous forces when she listened alongside Brocklehurst's depotentiation, not even an admired human is he she said, condensing dryly becoming words yet she kept going up to Him even as we condensed down attempting to embody her back.

But we are tired and we rest beside her, nestle up to her. Somewhere we fume what she does not yet we hold this one dying who would not rage for father's neglect.

How father does not lower to our bodily condition according to our (revealed) desire becomes our disease. How she remains up is his malevolence in neglect is our death to a larger Father because our bodies cannot sustain it.

We let go of who dies up to Father for we have been marked in Father's descent and though she taught us to differentiate within the recess of that descent, Father's word within female desire becoming conscience speaking, she prefers rise what would rise keep that Father up is also how we have known our forces bodily become diseased.

It is true: when we hear her say she is going home to the Father, we calm. We cease protestation and her last terrible cough blood-filled subsides. We become calmer. Mighty universal Parent. When we prefer to keep Him up we die to Him our bodies cannot sustain it these bodies prefer His word disembodied to the language of our desire a glimpse we had in her temple.

All we can do is line her body with ours in her passing, show her finally its contour, that it is not of danger, even as she has chosen this Father. This young woman with a burning, Helen Burns looking up to Heavenly Father her desire to return to Him, sick-bed longing for Father who as friend is God, when her desire evaporates to Him her body burns her phlegm red and she is consumed by inspiration.

Jane has enough of her own embodied hate has found its narrative to remain well within the rampant Brocklehurst disease and Helen goes as sacrifice. Each possession requires sacrifice in its transmutation.

The Helen sacrifice to the transmutation of the Brocklehurst possession is the relinquishing of idealization of Father: a hate a friction lowering Him so this desire which has deflected to coagulated lung or frenzy becomes designated then returned to body. Transmutation of Father God Law above to a delineation of heart's desire the meaning of its distinct parts takes Helen sacrifice. Keeping the word rising to Him would not follow her own condensation lesson back down to heart wording wants out to be incarnate.

► Helen's death. I was beside the fire my book inspired when she approached, sat alongside. She waiting for me to finish the final page and then she took up my heat. Our dialogue engaged me she was an untaught little girl yet she stroked me with her desire to know to penetrate the secrets she always remained decent in it. She moved me yet I could not know it. I never knew I had to be entering her blood to teach her the interior rhythm, its eloquence, and I assumed she held me due only to my sickness. We were in the temple together exchanging histories and philosophies and nature's mysteries, fire of the temple impassioning minds I was feverish I wanted to be encircled by them both so I could learn how fever's soaring angel could become the palpable dialogue between us yet I could not know such things then.

Instead, I later lay coughing and whispered to her on

returning to Him. The consumed men who have had this
blood-cough for Him, have left this world for Him, have
written their poetries as He carried them to their other sides,
His penetration making them of the woman as yearning and
receptive and they found the poetry and made it manifest,
yet I leave empty-handed leaving nothing of any of my wisdoms the life fluids coagulated, I numbed and I became it
was a trance of sorts, and I rose adoring and somnolent up to
His arms which became stronger for receiving me. His sons
have returned their eloquence for seeking Him while we were
held up. Not carried to any other side but held up while the
sons had a turn. We leave empty until a time of returning to
her no longer schoolgirl, wisp now tissue of some desire to
meet our difference in likeness and not miss lying in a crib of
consumption white curtain covering. ह•

To let go of Helen we may forfeit our last resort to the heavenly Father
we fear it. The only way we have known the Father to soar repression all
body to Him: Jupiter, Apollo, Yahweh, Christ-Father. We have taken up
our desires and left them there.

We do not yet know the other ways, but we suspect Helen will revive,
resurgam, she will rise again, she will surge back to tell us.

The scourge at Lowood and most particularly Helen's death brings Jane
to the edge of death, not through seizure and non-relation, phantom peering phantom struck, as at Gateshead, but she walks toward it through Miss
Temple's passages and embraces Helen and speaks to it.

•ह We sleep with the woman who inspires and moves us and
we are no longer a child for her difference carries us to an
abyss. Her body is similar but it is also of other textures and
elements, how she carries the fires differently is how we pass
to the other sides through her. We are no longer yearning,
receptive and entranced, beckoning the other to form his
design upon our visage. We move toward her, we climb into
her bed, her open arms receive us and penetrated we begin
our own penetrations to the mysteries of the blood of
death. ह•

To love the death in Helen as we sleep stay on earth do not die. Jane can
love the death in Helen, which is her transmutation out of human life
impulse without surrendering human life to death literally. To love the

death in Helen is to begin a love for what is removed, beyond, symbolic, without losing and only by strengthening our relation to life, wider world.

Our calling to carry the forces from marginal realms back, find the text within the recess, Helen has taught us; and her sacrifice is the lesson to sublime is to condense reed impulse up in laconic conscience speaking now desires heart to carry out, condense down, find density, incarnation of the designation. The word that prefers instead to continue rise to Him is the Helen sacrifice for incarnating conscience mediating desire.

Invisible spirits surrounding as permeating the immediate world once we would not know them: 'My eye sought Helen, and feared to find death.' Yet Jane gets onto the crib and kisses the cold, thin Helen.

Helen dies still a messenger, unable to draw her own life substance yet responding to Jane's fervent questions leading her to the borders of the lived world as well as the human limit.

➥ It is part of the chest below the breast above what stomachs and it is hollow and abysmal unmeasurable when we begin to know that Helen is dying. At any moment we could totter into it, we are only sure of the point which holds our mind now. Her cough flagged what could be dialogue in the verandah gap we huddled.

Her resignation the body grows other bodies on itself. We are weighted on the left side groans for her. What will move us in any direction now? We are being carried in someone's arms. No one will answer our questions at first.

Everything noticed in detail. What in the world can want us here? What does this one know who unties our arms from their embrace of her death, severs us and claims we the living?

After she leaves this sky tints itself only beige we do not want to look upon it. She says, it is in our night dreams or when we darkly sit in the light of a late morning, she comes and says she will surge again, perhaps it will be a sparkling white arrow back. She will be able to afford more friction with this earth her hate with that body for we will cover her better this time in exchange of her lessons. Sacrifice to Father revealing Father's vacancy until something shifts before she returns an earlier touch coaxing her brilliance to tissue. Shiftings. Otherwise she cannot afford the friction and we can only afford to remain calm at the promise of the Father. ⁞

Bibliography

Fuller, Harry J., Zane B. Carothers, Willard W. Payne, and Margaret K. Balbach. *The Plant World*. New York: Rinehart and Winston, Inc., 1972.

Govindjee, Eugene Rabinowitch. *Photosynthesis*. New York: John Wiley and Sons, 1969.

Kerr, Jessica. *Shakespeare's Flowers*. New York: Thomas Y. Crowell, 1969.

Peterson, Roger T. and Margaret McKenny. *A Field Guide to Wildflowers*. Boston: Houghton-Mifflin, 1968.

"Photosynthesis." In *Encyclopedia Britannica*, 15th edition, vol. 25.

Sontag, Susan. *Illness as Metaphor*. New York: Vintage Books, 1978.

"Tuberculosis." In *Encyclopedia Britannica*, 15th edition, vol. 12; 11th edition, vol. 27.

"Typhus." In *Encyclopedia Britannica*, 15th edition, vol. 12; 11th edition, vol. 27.

Wilson, Edward O., et al. *Life on Earth*. Sunderland, Mass: Sinauer Associates, 1978.

Chapter 10
Pillowed Voice of Advertisement

Typhus scourge noticed; investigation of the scourge by public eye. Public eye notes school's unhygiene condition and scanty accommodation. Mr. Brocklehurst is mortified. Assigned, demoted, to treasurer and aided in his other duties by 'gentlemen of rather more enlarged and sympathizing minds.'

And the place improved. Fond of these teachers, encouraged in intellectual pursuit to a head of class and then for two years there myself as teacher. Eight years alongside the woman once mother now friend: 'to her instruction I owed the best part of my acquirements; her friendship and society had been my continual solace; she had stood me in the stead of mother, governess, and latterly, companion.' I shared with her qualities of serenity, and to others even myself I appeared disciplined and subdued.

Until the minister and marriage; and in her marriage and departure went every aspect making Lowood home. I am standing watching her chaise leave over the far hill of a wedding day expecting great despair more it is vague space, suspended in time loss spaciousness for when aware again of time gone too with her is that 'serene atmosphere I had been breathing in her vicinity.' Reason for tranquillity no longer, old emotions stir some natural element returns. And what of courage to venture to varied field amidst life's perils?

Open window, first open window at Lowood to this look out, blue peak gaze and winding white road with my prayer for liberty, then change, stimulus, yet these pleas evanescent, hollow, and they fly out this window, swept off. Servitude, the word has substance not too sweet, new servitude and it stays with me and I wonder how it is I can activate this brain to find the means of attaining my new servitude.

Sitting in bed's chilly atmosphere later, all night thinking to the next place to will it, I am ordering this brain faster and I rise from the bed, walk the room, undraw curtain and see that star or two and shivering creep into bed, head on pillow and then a voice articulation: you must advertise. And I ask this voice, suggestion from fairy, how? Smooth and prompt response indicating it is to be in the Herald, replies for J. E. at the Lowton post.

The words easily come to my pen the following morning and I write for position of governess in a private family children under 14 (as I am yet 18), qualified I say in the teaching of English, French, Drawing, and Music. Delivered at that Lowton post and then the long succeeding week until asking ' "Are there any letters for J. E.?" ' One which I take hugging to me cannot be opened now rules say back by eight. I rush and after prayers the other teachers retired I take out my letter. It says the girl is under 10, references required, signed by a Mrs. Fairfax from Thornfield.

The respectability of the sound of it as well as the woman's old-fashioned script relieves me, for I had been worrying on venturing forth on my own falling into some scrape. But here I imagine 'black gown and widow's cap; frigid, perhaps, but not uncivil: a model of elderly English respectability.' I am longing to go where life and movement more reside, this county with Thornfield lies closer to London by 70 miles than does Lowood.

Would the Superintendent break the matter to Mr. Brocklehurst and the committee for I need reference and she agrees to be this mediatrix. Returning she says Mr. Brocklehurst only requiring Mrs. Reed's approval which hastily is given, that woman saying ' "I might do as I pleased: she had long relinquished all interference in my affairs." ' Character testimonial also of capacity signed in agreement, I am given formal leave.

The lady Fairfax is satisfied, says I may come. Making preparations the trunk packed, same trunk carried from Gateshead eight years ago, now corded. I try to rest, phase of my life closing this night, I want to watch the passing, I am wandering the lobby a troubled spirit when a servant says someone below has come to see me. Assuming carrier for the trunk I go down to who is this dashing out to me from the parlour as I walk toward the kitchen, she is a well-dressed servant, matronly yet young of lively complexion. And now I am embracing this one, kissing my Bessie.

There is a little boy here. She has married the coachman and the second child is christened Jane. Immediately her appraisal: the two Reed daughters are much larger than I, Eliza is Miss Reed and in height surpasses me; Miss Georgiana in breadth. Georgiana captured a young lord whose relations against the match, about to run away together yet the sister envious finds them out, stops it, two sisters quarrelling endlessly now, cat and dog.

John plucked from his school, dissipated young man and the mother not easy in her mind by this son's conduct so expensive. No, to my inquiry she did not send Bessie here, that one heard of the letter sent and wanted a look before out of reach the child's namesake.

Her look regard and not admiration, I ask her whether she is disappointed. Never was I a beauty her frankness which appeals. Yet she says I am genteel enough, look like a lady, and she imagines I am clever, can I play the piano? This I do and I point to the painting of my hand on the wall. She asks if I also know French, can I work on muslin, these qualities decide her exceed any Reed sister; I will get on she says whether my relations notice me or not. She tells me then of an uncle's visit long ago father's brother, wine-merchant from Madeira, as much gentry as the Reeds who would not receive him properly.

We converse in reminiscence and then she leaves. I see her briefly the next morning as I await my coach, we depart at the door of Brocklehurst Arms, each our separate way hers to Gateshead mine regions yet unknown.

Crib of death. Crib death. Embrace in crib. Crib seduction. Helen's death seduces Jane into life; shattering any opposition life or death.

Who is raised out of death crib is who endured the Brocklehurst scourge, made it to beck and wood, air and speckled light. Yet in Helen's embrace mediated life to place of death, holding as travelling with the friend abyss point before turn returned to life a nurse carries. One who rises up from the Helen death is carried by a nurse and sleeping of all vulnerable posture.

When we rise from Helen's death more it is being carried and we are of another consciousness, dependent on a larger body. Helen's death is our move, we have gone to human limit in our temple lesson, interior reflection conscience dialogue mediating all impulse to limit, return now to larger body. We lean against it, we now know our tiredness, we lower to this body's need and the larger body raises us.

Helen sublimation, she mediated desire to temple, conscience, word is not paternal Law yet Helen's divided speaking reflection. Our desire sublimated to word wants down to body break out of wall to world of ordinary, building resistance, the passage down gets caught in disease until we learn the word of death. What are the words of those figures want down, figuration limit is our lesson, which is the Helen sacrifice to Father.

Who dies, Lowood sacrifice, who would not lower to angels of tissue wound, never speaking ailment, could not see how inspiration an affair of body out, instead moving to what aspired His word, out affair of body she suffered only silent crib isolation. Some Brocklehurst tyrannical purity here: no coaxing possible of that cool light ray to what may have been outstretched arm seeking solace.

Her sacrifice and the body of her vision returns resurging different form. Her vision will not exist apart from body, the place which housed even educated that vision is supported by different, larger body. The larger community notices and makes inquiry into the scourge.

In the temple chamber what had been law of ministerial father lowered passing through the passages to conscience. What was his decree lowered sweat of her hand to conscience as friend. Symbolic paternal agency, when her word is mediation, falls into conscience which taken up by larger body, community, becomes ethics.

Not morality ascribed to law's requirement and proscription, but community ethics giving law flesh. When women relation to death, two women embracing death while the mass go under, women undermining law paternal agency, in the divine death relation, relation to death in life, carry language from beyond life into life, the men of the community take notice.

Community brings Brocklehurst law to flesh and body, compassionate concern for body the new ethics, response to women death relation undermining the paternal agency. The bridge between women's singular conscience and community ethics is symptom: the frenzy of thwarted rage when desire cursed only as vile.

Our thwarted rage in frenzy symptom becomes the smoldering public. 'Inquiry was made into the origin of the scourge and by degrees various facts came out which excited public indignation in a high degree.' When his law cannot speak to our rage or desire it burns up our body until our singular conscience lowers to the community body housing the indignation becoming its ethics.

What has become mediated as conscience desires return to body. For in the Brocklehurst possession we have been too secretive behind the spiked wall, too worried of public opinion. Enclosed fog-breeding pestilence, we broke out to some larger body, we are no longer embarrassed to show it, let it be noticed: the 'brackish, fetid water,' the torn clothing never aired, the rusty cooking pot unsterilized.

Brocklehurst law, paternal "superego" wall, had cramped us in while demanding neglect the vile body. Reigned entirely in the low wood guarded by spiked wall. We have not raged against or pierced through (resisted) the paternal wall, superego morality, yet the body flared disease, the typhus smoldered and body to body some larger body takes notice, smoldering to a compassionate order, and he is diminished. Body takes the narrative of the scourge out and through compassion of larger listening body Brocklehurst becomes mortified.

The plot of the Brocklehurst disease heard beyond the Lowood grounds mortifies Brocklehurst. Against him there could be no rage and the red a disease the body can only speak the narrative of its demise to the ones of power equal to Brocklehurst himself. Compassion of larger body is what finally severs, reduces, Brocklehurst from the diseased hold on our body.

Lowood Helen's privileging of figuration (angels) over what is literal (her father's remarriage, no one will miss her) is her silencing. The way the community responds to this silencing, takes literal and contingent action, is the diminishment of Brocklehurst in the concern for body.

Helen's lesson teaching conscience speaking dialogue has all along been accompanied by the depotentiation of Brocklehurst, and her disease is his final fault, break in his strata, black pillar no longer solidly erect, has fault, he lowers and shrinks exposed his inferiority afterall.

Brocklehurst mortified. Whining he shrinks. Demoted, diminished in stature. Only treasurer, others have taken over his administrative duties. We do not abolish or relinquish him entirely—do not repeat his morality lesson of splitting off—yet we incorporate him building further body to know more than his law. We keep Brocklehurst as treasurer, using his scrutinizing eye, the sensitive and large nose to figure in the large account book.

The ones who take over the Brocklehurst administration are of more 'enlarged and sympathizing minds.' Some wealthy benevolent body has been all along in the periphery yet we could not be located in and addressed by it as we hid within the wall of only narrow minister condemnation.

When we sacrifice who could not know mediating conscience through body, we begin a care for the body, find a substantial place of health and vigor for the Lowood lesson, and such care mortifies Brocklehurst.

When concerns of the body enter the administration—'reason with strictness, comfort with economy, compassion with uprightness'—here is a disciplined regularity in conscience without prohibition and we calm to it. When Brocklehurst is transmuted to a lower position, our mind not of obsession or craving or fever, critical faculty serving body, prospering body, we flourish to a class head.

Becoming teacher: students with formal address of who we are. Claiming a profession, recovering here, something mends, we are held by these daily women, daily prayers, daily lessons have become mother discovered, something closes over which is a sort of protection, a recovering in tranquility.

We no longer give out to or await the coming man. We find profession here and receive a salary, we are not swayed and swiped at by autonomous force. What mothers becomes companion, mother lowers to our level. She moves toward us from mother through governess to companion.

Mother becomes companion after the Brocklehurst black pillar is mortified and diminished. Entire universe in these rooms in which she houses herself, we contract to it indeed our contract to enlarge learned profession as this one once of mother on our level sitting across nightly in her room adjacent chairs, we sew, discuss the pupils, shared literature.

As the paternal law has been lowered to our treasurer, regulation more to our size, so she once awesome as maternal becomes on our level, equal in dimension. Raised by a stepmother who sent us forces breaking taboo, outside convention, we have transmuted those forces until mother and father reside in convention, our size.

Sitting across eye to eye. Continual solace, after prayer every evening she is in the same chair awaiting our arrival, the intellectual conversation by the hearth, our hands on their craft.

Brocklehurst and Miss Temple of our convention, regulation more of our size, we are of a hearty enlarging body and the grip of the stepmother now entirely slack.

Satiated. We have learned of contentment without prohibition, we have assimilated even embodied the qualities of the teacher once mother. What has formed is definition: others see us as serene and disciplined.

Our transmutation of the forces emerging within fusion with that stepmother carries us to identification, which is a relation of likeness with one

211

exterior, not the same. Others see us serene and then she departs, a minister appears and she leaves.

A minister love of Miss Temple prevents our eternal bond with her, we have received definition when there has not been fusion which is also not to be split. Solidifying substance, identification, and then she leaves on her own accord, for it is not completely our natural element this nightly subdued conversation but we do not know that until she is gone and has taught us all there is of home in serenity.

We are defined solidifying substance enough to be autonomous not possessed. Curative measure to the Reed and Brocklehurst possessions, when we had been windowseat exterior as interior not knowing any difference, or boundary, we are now boundaried we know our difference, her companionship has not been a possession and we do not possess her now. She takes with her the Lowood landscape measured and serene quality.

As we watch her leave, some defining structure begins its falling away, but what is this we are left standing, suspended we gaze in another sort of atmosphere. Drifting place suspension between landscapes, not even of the daydream with no directed thought or purposeful mind, and it is some time before we are alerted to the hour or resume what would be schedule.

Old emotions stir and some natural element returns. Miss Temple leaves when our identification is solid enough to leave us standing in some suspended atmosphere when Lowood drifts away open to heterogeneous elements of our nature do not sweep us we remain who we are all we are and more rising as she drives away.

She leaves for a minister, for one who serves, acts as agent, provides. She has provided for us and now she leaves in an act of another provision. We have risen up mother's (once forbidden) body, to our hungers hidden chambers, heart to temple conscience, until we emerged in an identification with who sat nightly adjacent not fused allowing her to leave on her own path.

After Lowood we have enough sense of the precise dimensions defining our unique plot so that when the (discovered) mother leaves to marry a minister we are not thrown or swept away by arctic demons. We are left standing and we are not abandoned and have definition.

Our first mother left to marry a minister opening us up to the impingement by forces of the turning stepmother, open to death-realms, death-white realms of possessing forces besieging us until we negotiated, passed them through us remaining solid, until we even to her, our qualities are of serenity when the unconscious forces have been designated in place, differentiation within recess, divided parts still related, the Reed and Brocklehurst parts of our narrative, impulse sublimated to mediated conscience condensing what gift becomes.

When we have lowered our gift, no longer locked drawer, from temple to student body, the one identification with temple departs.

And as companions we have been in a love service, correspondents of pact, we have been practicing a fidelity to these qualities of serenity, of propriety, exercising them until they have taken our shape. The others describe us as disciplined, even subdued. Who we are reflected are the qualities which were her lesson. Final Lowood boundary lesson: evening to her we let her go over the white path.

&§ Miss Temple's departure. Waters calming as we sat together nightly we evened into it. Waves cease their roll now mirror. I would look across at her and reflect her tranquility also mine, together we would gently rock as we knit, the waters very still. I pulled in, located definition, stature, I looked upon this exercise of faculty allowing expansion in such serenity. We were gently rocking in our boat on a sea of tranquility, and I gradually pulled in. The day that all became perfectly still I realized I had evened out to her, and over her shoulder I saw him aloft on the dry land. Her service more of a ministerial nature, I was watching her chaise ride over the distant hill, gazing and afloat suspended until suddenly I felt this boat a surge of wave, old wave, natural element stirring. She went over the hill to her next place and I began to look out. I had been quite contracted into this small boat no longer stable structure as afloat and now with this sudden rocking I look out wide world of the remote blue peak. &º

At Miss Temple's departure, Jane opens the Lowood window. She says: I altered. 'I tired of the routine of eight years in one afternoon.' Lowood leaves as landscape of what was home in Miss Temple's chaise. A prominent figure departs and with her goes the landscape yet after Lowood we remain standing.

With chaise bearing teacher goes the hums and hushes of now familiar voices, the creak of aligned metal beds in the ice night, this scratch of the chairs against the slate floor when eighty girls rise as she enters from the right of the room.

&§ Prominent figures leaving. Figures depart: we have lowered to the quality we have made manifest through what they have made present for us, and we still. Some tide becomes leveled as we manifest that quality through a mutual care until finally something begins to tip from an old current.

Figures die: the qualities being exercised in their presence are not quite lowered to body. If we have loved this figure we experience the death as sacrifice. We often suffer the interruption as abandonment, feel cut off from ourselves. Their return in a different form is posited, resurgence.

Figures reject us: we have not quite manifested the quality of the other, relied too much on their carrying of it, not realized enough the pact of relationship of who we must become through it, they push us out to a different place than the one they held for us. Or we carry what neither of us want to see, what figures too dearly for both of us unconscious. ❧

We tire of eight years at Lowood in one afternoon. It had not even occurred to us to venture out before. Stirred by old emotion; emotions carry forth the prospect of other landscapes. We begin to desire liberty, excitement, for we have not turned our head in all these years to any varied rhythm, the light falling askew on the unfamiliar face, we have not turned our head yet resided in her atmosphere until we located profession gives us definition and completely still to it.

Desire to bound out the window yet we receive immediately the effects of the Lowood domain these years: we notice our plea for liberty so light it flies away of no substance. Lowood lesson, value what has substance, hollow plea now wisp now unseen, we trim some extravagance, out of the Lowood window we hold out our arms for what has weight and into them the desire is of a new servitude.

Even as the old landscape leaves us vestige of it we carry forth: servitude. Serve. Sever. The way she has taught us to sever has been of servitude. Sever from impulse dictate, trim inflation, voices of dead nourish we are serving them serving to one another the seedcake and we begin severing from grandiose animosities to inherent gift the Lowood lesson we intend to carry on what will be servitude. Will of a new servitude.

Will of a new servitude. The place summoning us from outside Lowood, to become outside Lowood, pertains to will. We are more autonomous, have learned the Lowood boundary lesson and are ready to leave Lowood when we ask on will: ' "Can I not get so much of my own will?" ' Birth from our head new this fever will springs. We lie in the Lowood bed ordering this head to will the movement out.

Will of a new servitude: the way the old place calls forth the new which will pertain to will. Lowood lesson of curbing, cool inhibition, we have not known will here, and it rises as old emotions stir, a first self-initiating direction out. We had only known as movement the Gateshead burst of bond and the Lowood servitude moved from punitive enforcement to conscience mediation yet what of will.

Dilation our temple throbs, not the temple we have known here, this is an endless question gyration: what do others do, they apply to friends, we have no friends. From where come the resources of those who look for themselves? In the passage from interior reflection to behavior, self-initiated behavior, we first try to lead with our head first, head thrusting will.

We strain to push out of ourselves and we are up and walking the floor of pressures mounting, pulling against what we have not, contrived dilation, forced friend.

Turn around the room, room turn, we think it all in our self, undrawn curtain, shivering in some starlight. When we lay our head upon the pillow we hear something, guess fairy spirit, indeed there are words of some other voice.

To be addressed by a voice, vocation. What was once voice booming without, Madame Mope, our vocation to engage with the ones sent out of her rejection. Here is the voice without toward which our movement of the windowseat, negotiation of stepmother's forces antipathetic, has educated us. It has come from some star mediation Lowood lesson we rise frenzy up and condense to word where we lay our head and we realize for the first time we are alone yet not speaking to ourselves. It is a voice without.

At Lowood we have learned when we have risen text and figuration mediating action, risen to heights sacrificing Helen there, what returned as we lowered, head to pillow, voice of conscience. To listen to it our vocation.

Miss Temple is also no longer necessary, departs, when voice of conscience is interiorized in the sense we can hear it without, apart from our will yet it sets us in motion. Voice of conscience does not advise action, for it is not up to our will, as much as indicate how to ask the "right" questions.

We have learned to listen in Lowood for the voices. They speak now what would be our will.

We had been pacing feverish push a will. Undrew that curtain, all voice of this head produced by ourselves, subject to this will. For we have a salary and profession, definition, we profess, we can figure it out.

Yet the frenzy in our brain says we cannot. None of our activity offers anything close to what we knew sitting beside her fragrance, nightly breathing into what became an emptying out to that profound spaciousness where we did not know, some unlocked drawer began its opening, voices of the dead, unfolding from where we did not know.

This activity says we do not know, we glance in frustration to those stars, we do not know, something of our dumbness begins to remember that we do not know, head on Lowood pillow and some space becomes hollowed out, lowering that head to pillowed space for what is to come, evening sky bowl.

This voice comes from outside who we know ourselves to be, from the same pillow carrying forth the dream, figures of sleep. House of the dream, our head while we slumber in its sight out of the hole of its holding a voice not of dream yet from dream's place outside who we know ourselves to be. It dialogues with us is how her word of conscience remains with us incarnate.

How conscience speaks without us is how our definition once established moves continually out of itself, emotions stir dividing and what speaks up, other suggestions not of who we are, definition tips to our inherent divisions as conscience speaks up.

This voice grants us initiating capacity how to pass out of the Lowood place into that world expanse Lowood window. This listening, head on pillow reception, does not keep us kneeling only church pew or confessional isolate, but we lay our head on the pillow and we have an open ear and some voice is telling us the moves.

Pillowed voice of advertisement. To leave through the Lowood window is not to will our brain (how do we get there, advantages or disadvantages of leaving or staying) yet to state our qualities and their desire (what is here, how is it that it is here, what does it want), advertise.

Not will desire yet state it in context of what qualities define who we are that desires, let the unconscious desire rise up starlit sublime until lowered to a speaking word clear upon the pillow.

From the moment we first entered the Lowood door, a woman with dark eyes and a pale large forehead was considering us, she stated we were young to be sent alone, hand on our shoulder she said that we looked tired and hungry. She asked of our parents, what we could do, could we read write sew, she touched our cheek with her forefinger saying she hoped we would be a good child.

From the start, we were considered at Lowood in ways allowing us to name our qualities. Delineation of our qualities and what they desire, to designate unconscious desire, the way to capture the image of the next place calling it out.

A Mrs. Fairfax calls us over the Lowood threshold. The one who responds is not alien in nature to the Lowood place, for we have been of the serene here, we would not want to risk some scrape. We imagine the black gown and white widow cap of this Mrs. Fairfax, suspect her frigidity.

The one who responds to our advertisement is called out by it and has qualities encompassing the place from where we are emerging. For we have been at a place where the mortification black slate transmuted to the white light Helen vision, and here has been at times a frigid place.

When we finally looked out the Lowood window, we saw not crevice or desert or mud terrain yet blue peak, blue where the whitened movement to our imaginative vision still contains the darkened streaks, remembering the whippings, charred still from scourge this is how we leave Lowood not with a white innocence yet blue, colored by the convent depression, noble and elevated yet working more out of a cool inhibition.

The response we get from the larger world resonates with the qualities of who we are in where we have been. Aged English respectability.

We were leaving Gateshead and Bessie asked would we kiss that aunt goodbye. To go out we are asked to go back and find the place of what swiftly is becoming past. Lowood following Gateshead was the place where we could not yet kiss the aunt goodbye yet to where we went to learn in fact that severance.

It is never a linear departure, landscape to landscape, twists and zigzags, turns back on itself. We sent the Superintendent as mediatrix to Brocklehurst. That one then returns us, as always he has done, to Mrs. Reed, his critical judgment always returning to what would be her need.

If Mrs. Reed still holds onto us through Brocklehurst he has not been diminished and leveled and we are not ready to depart Lowood. For Lowood served differentiation within what would be her recess, negotiating the forces impinging there to a mediation lifting us sublime to figuration and now we lower are we differentiated can we leave without her hold which would be to part from her rejection while still remaining related.

We would know whether we were still in Mrs. Reed's (particularly a John Reed) possession if our departure began to take a sense of urgency, some demand to burst out of Lowood gate, grasping toward a new place out of dire need, flailing scene to reinstate our dependency on her unconscious desire necessary for our movement.

Also still in Mrs. Reed's (Brocklehurst) possession if we find we have to critically condemn the place in order to leave it, or if we move only in terms of a position of power.

For Lowood has been the place of compassionate severance out of this possession, moving the stepmother's forces, transmuting them to specific voices, divided speaking angels surrounding, desiring to return incarnate what we define as quality.

If the severance has been complete, she has no interference in our affairs. We are of the recess, she is our relation, she needs to be consulted, yet with an effective Lowood severance, she does not interfere.

The trunk with which we depart is the same one which carried us here. We do not have many more articles than those with which we entered. It has not been a place to locate our qualities through our dress or material belonging. We pack, quickly filling the old trunk.

We want to watch this night of the last Lowood hours in passing. We are wakeful, pacing. We have not wanted to risk a scrape; we have been sheltered here. We entered without parent at an age too young to travel, not knowing yet what ruptured as wound or animosity. Slowly we have mended in this Lowood place of long division and its multiplication.

> ❧ We have been stitched here in the guarded place, the only
> sense of what is larger world resides in this Gateshead trunk.
> We open to its must. Brown cloth lining frayed returns us to
> a windowseat hidden as cowering, that one's tongue flaying,
> looming nursery shadow as we hear her below, eye of adver-
> sion, sisters of privilege, blood from a forehead gash, his
> promise over the majestic canopy, elastic haze of a stupor
> kept in her backroom until black column we aimed at her to
> blast her every detail dismember so that breakfast room
> sprinkled her demise. Gray field regret to a staged coach and
> no, we look into the trunk eight years filled with these
> belongings and what we know of world, we do not want to
> risk a scrape. ☙

Pacing. We are 'wandering like a troubled spirit.' As we are a troubled spirit pacing a servant tells us someone below wishes to see us.

Who brings us down for the Lowood departure (we think it is the carrier) is who embodies the past stories and knows how to narrate them.

The one waiting to see us in our last Lowood night had been one of the servants dragging us mad cat to the red-room, stood by the bed with basin in the nursery glare recovery she sang the orphan song. She pushed us in and pulled us out mother's forbidden body, that archaic desire. In the gray field first initiating I — What shall I do? — hers was the voice that replied, trace of that interior dialogue with one who differed which became the packing for Lowood.

She packed this trunk we are closing now she was saying of all we were afterall her favorite. Her presence below as we have reread the narrative of this trunk's opening requires we continue the narrative, bring its characters up to date, find out what has transpired with the Gateshead figures, for we never leave them behind and packing is to return to her who carries forth their narrative.

Bessie was always the Gateshead narrator and now we collect the past figures through her continuing narration. With her in the gray field interlocution we saw through one another's perspective, mediated the scolding exploring its meaning, with her we have perspective on heterogeneous sides, she brings them back to our history.

The narrator who returns through Bessie to continue the story perceives in ways literal (Jane is smaller in breadth and height than Georgiana and Eliza) and frank (Jane is not a beauty). The interlocution between Gateshead and Lowood the night before departure is brought forth by one from Gateshead who is not interested in figuration and brings Jane the literal information she needs, yet who eventually, viewing Jane's accomplishments in art and learning, slowly takes herself the Lowood figurative perspective granting the orphan more size than either cousin.

Georgiana has been to London where there has been a grand infatuation, young lord rebellion against relations in a run away, yet nail slash and brilliant hiss, Miss Eliza Reed takes a swipe in what becomes cat and dog they quarrel endlessly during each day cage of the Gateshead place.

Our sisterly animal nature has split into competitive faction fraction at Gateshead no benefit of the Lowood division providing heterogeneity. These sisters reside still in our design, they have grown beside us, splitting, and there has been this pull to each sister as we have been in the process of moving out.

Georgiana's London visit for liberty, for excitement, her request fell a lord, she was about to fly into it when the sister of another animal pulled her back. We were by an open window, first view beyond the Lowood grounds, blue peak stare within which a plea for liberty, excitement, for Georgiana is our breadth. Urge to a full throb excitement out, bounds breaking.

Relations pull us back in, yet at Lowood we are not coerced but we inhibit, curbing the breadth expansion of Georgiana becoming merely weightless, of no substance, vanishing. Later in the advertisement we ask for children under fourteen, for we have trimmed the one of frill extravagance and we know our limit, ourselves only eighteen.

Eliza is taller and for a while she places us in her shadow through a righteousness and insistence upon strict regulation. Hers is the exhortation to remain by Miss Temple's side night after night with our needlework, any movement only the extent of these chairs creaking as we rock steadily to some habitual sewing beside as stirrings convolute become underhand animal slash, glare an envy issuing in silence we are rocking into an old age with our needlework, Eliza has grown to pull us back ever in seclusion in a room with no window, stales, begins to turn on itself. But we have let Miss Temple go to her ministerial marriage, we have stood at the window watching the chaise mount its path other than ours.

John Reed is not doing as well as his mother would have wished. Profligate, unrestrained, plucked out of college. Slipping, he drunk and slipped into a pool of frivolity, dissolute, where he is dissolving himself (drunk) as all fragments disperse: no direction, lost vocation.

As she rode away, the atmosphere we have been breathing in her vicinity slipped away and for a while we were suspended, parts dislocating and becoming dispersed, time of no matter, we began to dissolve into what we did not yet know as another atmosphere. Dissolution as much as we grasped for solution: what do other people do to find new places, they ask friends, we have not friends. We began to slip.

We became desperate and tyrannically ordered that brain to work, no direction, throbbing yet could not order solution then feverish about to hurl for we do not know how to obtain what it is we want, we want, we want. He has been plucked out of school and he has not learned the lessons. Some star from a peripheral retina brings a focus and on the pillow a voice orients, speaking how to write out differentiated desire and quality.

For at Lowood, dissolution while in a star's holding viewpoint becomes a lowering to a voice direction from without, whereas at Gateshead without night guiding star, only profligate.

Mrs. Reed looks stout and well enough in the face but she is not easy in her mind, her son's conduct displeasing to her, he spends much of her money. She is allowing her resources to be stripped away, cannot stand for her worth, indulging the dissipated son who grabs at what is hers and she cannot stand up to him though she is stout.

She never claimed our worth, she would not have us follow that Lowood voice saying advertise what is of quality, would not have us seek tuition in this claim of where we have resource.

In order to write out such a claim in advertisement, we have to have passed through Mrs. Reed, not to give our resources over to what is greed son. His impulse mediated we have passed through this stout Reed woman and we fed her son that milk of Lowood stars, congealing stars to milk and the scattered hungers have been fed for the eight years, there is not a sustained feverish pacing here and when we touch our head to the pillow the voice tells us the right words in conscience words the advertisement of our qualities are vivid and actually quite easy to write out the following morning.

After watching Miss Temple's chaise leave, old stirrings remind us of, remind us to collect, recollect, the past place, pack it, as they announce not only is the next landscape to be about them, for they pull us out and toward it, but also that we cannot move our trunk to the next landscape without collecting our relations.

At Gateshead, Bessie led us into and then out of the red-room, she held us up to the coach taking us to Lowood and now is here for the coach departing Lowood. In and out of red-room as in and out of Lowood reminding how this Lowood also has been another aspect of forbidden mother's body, even as that landscape—stomach, heart, throat, and temple—have been ours attaining definition.

Also suggests that the next place may be a further lowering in forbidden body, returning to those places more of Gateshead yet now after the Lowood lessons. For Bessie returns at our departure and reminds us of contiguity and a literal speaking as we show her ourselves figuratively: the ways Gateshead and Lowood inform one another and reverse some is the travelling to the next place.

From interior recess heart and temple, conscience definition, Bessie's account draws us out. She looks over our surface reflecting it back. When we are first ready for external reflection, we are on our way to the place after Lowood. She notices we are still not a beauty yet we are no longer impoverished, she is reading us literally, says we are genteel. When we are writing our own advertisement, have learned Lowood lessons of our distinct qualities, we are ready to receive who reflects us externally and catches up our narrative.

She tells us we will get on whether our relations notice us or not, which is to say we are no longer dependent on relation. She notes our differentiated quality, defines us as autonomous as we are related. And we hear we have relations where we knew not. They are not poor and are of as much gentry as the Reeds, here a father's brother, wine-merchant from Madeira.

As we have delineated quality at Lowood what emerges unexpectedly is gentry. Orphan yet not impoverished, indeed genteel. We arrived an untaught little girl, coarse for we had to tug at the knots alone into the night, coarse little girl even mad cat, we struck eye for eye, we tore at the brother, nails to his scalp.

The way the Lowood rise up body's recess had mediated our differentiation to refined gentry she notices.

> ◄§ Bessie's notice. Sympathetic symbiosis. I saw a letter in the Missis' hand, heard later it was from the young Jane and I took it upon myself to ask about it. The memories had never left from me though. What first always came to me was when I was climbing the back stairs to bring her a biscuit. She sat with the dirty doll up there all alone every night, sometimes I would get on with those in the kitchen and I would forget about her but then sometimes I would remember. She never spoke to us much and I gather she scared me some, she was such a frightful child. So I put the duster in her hand and told her she was to be helper with my housework. She followed me around and she would spot

everything with those sharp eyes of hers except when she was far in her own mind and I remember I had to snap at her to get her out. The others would not speak to her, she would scare with her look, she never had no ringlets or a smile. Then one day she got to talking bolder. It was like she was holding an arm out to me but of course she would not yet I took it anyway. I got tired of my scolding and we talked it through. And I walked into the nursery to fetch her that last time at five before the light yet there she was dressed and all, she would not go in and kiss the Missis, my hand was shaking so when I raised her to that coach since that child had grown in my heart like marigold next to those tomatoes. ✌

She is who moves us in transition, lateral guardian, leading us laterally along. She has kept an eye on who we have been as we have been elsewhere. Her eye is not a Helen overview yet a lateral move through the psychic topographies.

Helen as vertical medium informing us realms of angels, gradation fiend to seraph, and we stood still on the pinpoint of only what can be present. Angels see our tortures, she whispered figurations carrying us to elevation where a perspective from which we begin ourselves as narrator.

Bessie as horizontal medium, visit night before the Lowood departure if we know enough to recognize her. She comes running out to us from the back parlour as we are passing by on the way to the kitchen to meet whom we think is carrier. Her entry is direct — ' "It's her, I am sure! — I could have told her anywhere!" ' — no circumlocution or entanglement yet direct, concrete, all in open view.

Simple wisdom accruing as she takes stock, she says we will get on whether our relations notice us or not.

She has returned the Gateshead way of knowing what is returning as old stirrings we can pack them in what is now Lowood trunk and it does not require a return to that Gateshead place actually. Having become narrator through Lowood we can exchange and part with who was narrator. We are comforted when we see her at Lowton as we await our coach the next morning, we part with her at Brockelhurst Arms.

There was a moment it came a wave of nostalgia to some longing, the dire need returning, in our question to Bessie about Mrs. Reed: ' "Did she send you here, Bessie?" ' All we have longed for in the Gateshead place returns in a rush. Does that stepmother finally desire us.

No, indeed, Bessie relies. ' "No, indeed: but I have long wanted to see you, and when I heard that there had been a letter from you, and that you were going to another part of the country, I thought I'd just set off and get a look at you before you were quite out of my reach." '

She simply sets us straight, she has come in this carrying over another threshold. Who mediates laterally cares for us, has named her offspring from what names us. Lowood differentiation has been through care. Pitchered ice, cracked and enflamed skin, whipped neck, stool mortification, blistered oozing lesion, all of what we have learned at Lowood of severance and differentiation has had a bed of what is compassion — Helen's compassion gaze distance from Brocklehurst's punishment, Helen and Miss Temple's a careful parting, compassionate larger body mortifying Brocklehurst — and in the Bessie notice we recognize the place the stepmother does not have desire of care for us which is part of our severing from her in the movement to the next place.

We part at Brocklehurst Arms, each her own way. Two separate Brocklehurst Arms for at Lowood we have seen how division returns again to multiple relation. We have learned not to remain split yet we stay related as we divide off from the Gateshead path: not a return to the Reeds yet we have paid them the narrative review as our trunk was locked and carried to its distinctive coach.

For we have felt these forces stir and have been reminded of where they are Reed as they help move us out to the terrain following Lowood. Gateshead emphasis on contiguity and immediacy now helps our action out. The next place is seventy miles nearer London: 'I longed to go where there was life and movement.'

Bessie does not arrive to pull us back yet to move us onward in memory of the Reed relations, and we leave these arms. We leave the Brocklehurst Arms fully armed, heartier, having distinguished our qualities, music, drawing, english, french. We leave when the Brocklehurst "superego" force has become arm, being armed, fortified, furnished with provision so we can well meet the next circumstance.

We leave these Brocklehurst Arms, sending Bessie back to Gateshead for she can carry it, she is matronly, she has a lively complexion, and is married to the coachman Robert Leaven.

We carry along every relation as well as the narrative of their relation, Lowood severance not a splitting, the Brocklehurst Arms are attached as they are each of their own direction. One carries Bessie back to Gateshead where she will reside in our favor with those there, raising who would resemble us. And here is also the path carrying us to some topography yet unknown.

These arms embrace as they release, we fall into the rhythm of our coach its leather stimulating nostril, amidst grating wheel we hear above the shuffling of our trunk toward the place from where in response to an advertisement we have been summoned.

❧ She was parting over the white path and I thought: here is how it is done, this moving out toward one's own nature. Parting in the favor of one's own nature, parting not a wrenching yet left with some pact of quality defined of my nature now, and I see her as I peer interior. She calms me to the voices. I am watching her depart over that path yet here she is inside on the chair armed with afghan, her needles knitting also weapon she taught me fortitude in her way that woman was ruthless. Knitting through what could be weapon. And I knew at that window she was not going to keep me for her own good. Some way we were to know our stirring parted yet not without her rocking continuous voice suggesting path now I wear her in this gift of brooch, armed.

Through who has lively complexion and cares, the relatives had found their way here and after hearing the narrative of where they pull I packed them. I want to know what stirs in the world not looking as them yet they are part of this parting to what stirs me. The last mornings before departure, in that early morning resting before rising, suspended, the fear a whale's mouth, and vast grotto moving out from where was stomach, surrounds until I become lost in it. And I wonder if I can move, do I have it in any resource to leave this Lowood place while within the hole of a fish's mouth. But then I am on my feet, broke out to some air and speckled light, trunk packed, attire for coach brooched, for it had got too still, and I wear her well. ❧

Bibliography

Corbin, Henry. *Creative Imagination in the Sufism of Ibn 'Arabi*. Trans. by Ralph Manheim. Princeton, N.J.: Princeton University Press, 1981.

Freud, Sigmund. "Some Psychical Consequences of the Anatomical Distinction Between the Sexes." *The Complete Psychological Works of Sigmund Freud*. Vol. 19. Trans. James Strachey. London: Hogarth, 1961.

H. D. *The Gift*. New York: New Directions, 1982.

Hillman, James. "Blue and the Unio Mentalis." *Sulfur* 1 (1981): 33.

Johnson, Barbara. "Metaphor, Metonymy, and Voice in Zora Neale Hurston's *Their Eyes Were Watching God*." In Mary Ann Caws, ed., *Textual Analysis: Some Readers Reading*. New York: The Modern Language Association of America, 1986.

Jung, C. G. *The Visions Seminars*. Book 2. Zurich: Spring Publications, 1976.

_____. "Psychology and Alchemy." *The Collected Works of C. G. Jung*. Vol. 12. Trans. R. F. C. Hull. Princeton, N.J.: Princeton University Press, 1953.

Kristeva, Julia. "A New Type of Intellectual: The Dissident." In Toril Moi, ed., *The Kristeva Reader*. New York: Columbia University Press, 1986.

_____. "The Novel as Polylogue." In Leon S. Roudiez, ed., *Desire in Language*. New York: Columbia University Press, 1980.

Pagels, Elaine. *The Gnostic Gospels*. New York: Random House, 1979.

Schwartz-Salant, Nathan and Stein, Murray, eds. *Abandonment*. Wilmette, Ill.: Chiron Publications, Chiron Clinical Series, 1985.

Chapter 11

Thornfield

After sixteen hours coached on an October raw day, I put my foot down to those boots of the wooden step descending but there is no word of my name and the waiter hears it without recognition. So I sit in what is private room ornamented with ceiling oil-lamp and its many portraits yet I am 'cut adrift from every connection.' Can I reach my port? Waiting in what grows a doubt and fear since there is no return to where I left, fear predominant until I ring the bell inquiring whether there is a place in the neighborhood named Thornfield. They ask is my name Eyre, there is this person waiting.

The carriage is not elegant, one horse, and this man lets the horse walk entirely the six miles, going on two hours, I have been meditating in this coach, seeing through what she sent as conveyance that Mrs. Fairfax is not a dashing sort, which is just as well for I have lived with fine people once where what I offered of my best only scorned. And if this woman is yet another Mrs. Reed, then I will advertise again. And looking out I see a different region than Lowood, 'more populous, less picturesque; more stirring, less romantic.'

She is by the fire the light of which contrasts sharply with the ride's black night, elderly lady, there the widow's cap, black silk gown, the snowy muslin apron, all as I expected yet this one seems less stately, kinder, she helps me untie my bonnet string. Clearing the way for a tray she has ordered tea noting my hands numbed by cold, surprised this way she treats me more as visitor. She hands me the tea with her own hand. We converse. My pupil is not named Fairfax for this woman has no family, the pupil is Miss Varens. And the lady begins to speak how dreary has been the fine old hall a few servants there with her, yet one must keep a distance to maintain an authority, and all last winter such severe elements and only butcher and postman at the door, melancholy breeding. Then this autumn arrived little Adela Varens with nurse, now there is a governess, the woman tells me she is happy finally to have such companions and I sincerely express my hope she finds me agreeable.

Now that I am warm, she is concerned with my rest, she leads the way: oak stairway and bannisters, the expanse and spaciousness of a gallery more like that of church than house, my small cozy bedroom considerably chosen by this woman for its human proportion, not the lonely though well furnished front chambers yet the one by hers appearing quite welcoming after the chill, the vault-like air pervading stair and gallery. The following morning sun shines on the papered wall and carpeted floor quite different from Lowood's plank and plaster; I rise with a sense that perhaps a fairer time ahead.

As I dress, I look over myself. I am not tall and handsome, red-cheeked of regular feature, no, yet I place on the black simple frock, respectable and the student would not recoil. I descend the slippery oak step. Here again imposing grandeur of the hall yet now the door half of glass is open and I walk out into the lawn, I turn around and I survey this mansion's front.

Not the seat of a nobleman, more gentleman's manor home of three stories, picturesque battlements of top, the figure of gray front stands from a background of rookery with its creatures cawing to the adjacent meadow of a sunken fence this field marked with knotty thorntrees of the mansion's appellation. The surrounding hills are not as lofty or even craggy as Lowood's, nor such 'barriers of separation from the living world; but yet quiet and lonely hills enough, and seeming to embrace Thornfield with a seclusion I had not expected to find existent so near the stirring locality of Millcote.'

How is it such a dame Fairfax lives alone in the great hall and here she is at the door greeting me warmly and in this morning talk I learn she is not great dame yet housekeeper-manager of the mansion belonging to a Mr. Rochester, she is assuming I have known all is this, the girl pupil his ward and she herself is a distant relation through marriage to his mother's side. So this kindness of Mrs. Fairfax comes from being a dependent as myself, and not the result of a condescension, relieved I am in this freer sense of my position.

Curls to her waist, the child is seven or eight years who approaches and she does not at first notice me. Adela. I am introduced as the lady who will make her some day clever. I have learned French well from Lowood's Madame Pierrot and the child is relieved I can understand her since she and the nurse are French, whereas British Mrs. Fairfax cannot understand; only now is the child just learning English. I address her in her own tongue receiving brief replies while a perusal by her hazel eyes of ten minutes at breakfast giving way to a rattling: she says Aïre, cannot say my name, tells me that on the boat over they were all sick even Mr. Rochester lying down in a fancy room called salon. She used to live with her mother who now has gone to the Holy Virgin, her mother taught her to sing and dance, the ladies and gentlemen would come to see her mama and this child would perform to entertain.

At my request here the song, she on my knee, hands folded, curls shaken back, eyes to ceiling, forsaken lady, betrayed by lover, summons servant to bejewel her to appear at ball to prove how little his desertion affected her. Song of love and jealousy strange in the voice of a small child, gesture and intonation unusual for her age, she had been coached. I do not take up her offer to dance for me instead I ask how was it she came here and I learn that after her mama died she stayed with a couple she knew not well and Mr. Rochester who used to buy her the pretty dresses and whom she knew longer came and said would she like to live in England, but he has placed her here and himself left the child says with regret.

After breakfast, I go with her to the library which has been designated as schoolroom, one book case open with ample supply, a cabinet piano, easel for painting, pair of globes. '(S)ufficiently docile, though disinclined to apply,' is the student I do not tax this first morning, at noon she to her nurse and I to

some drawing for her use as Mrs. Fairfax calls me from a room stately of
purple chair and curtain, she is opening the window in this dining room for
air and light saying they get damp when uninhabited and she points to the
adjacent room indicating it is damp as a vault. I move toward it, toward the
arch curtained as window up two steps and here to me at first a fairy place
until I see 'merely a very pretty drawing-room,' white carpets, garlands of
flowers, snowy mouldings bearing white grapes and vine-leaves, crimson
couch and ottomans, Parian marble mantle piece holding 'Bohemian glass,
ruby red; and between the windows large mirrors repeated the general blending of snow and fire.'

Chilly but one would think daily inhabited, I tell her what order she keeps
the rooms and without dust, it is she says in readiness for the visits of Mr.
Rochester though rare. To my question is he exact, fastidious, she replies not
particularly yet with a gentleman's tastes. Does she like him, is he generally
liked? The family has always been respected here, almost all the land in the
neighborhood has belonged to them. But does she like him, is he likeable for
himself? No cause to do otherwise, he is considered a just landlord by his
tenants. Yet what is his character? Unimpeachable, he is rather peculiar,
travelled a great deal of the world, a clever man yet she has not had much
conversation with him. In what way peculiar? Nothing striking yet she feels
when he speaks it is uncertain whether it is in jest or earnest, yet he is a good
master.

This woman is obviously of the class of those uninterested in 'sketching a
character, or observing and describing salient points, either in persons or
things.' My questions do not draw her out instead she wants to show me the
rest of the house, I follow her upstairs and downstairs the handsome place.
Grand large front chambers, and the third story rooms are low and dark
receptacles for furniture relics of antiquity, oak and walnut of two generations
removed from the lower floors as time past; of coffin-dust now the hands that
wove the embroidery of the cushioned stool tops; bedsteads and rows of
highbacked chairs, relics making that story 'the aspect of a home of the past:
a shrine of memory.' Hush and quaintness in the day here yet I would not
like a night in these beds of which hangings are 'pourtraying effigies of
strange flowers, and stranger birds, and strangest human beings.'

I wonder if the servants sleep here she tells me no, their smaller apartments to the back of this third floor, indeed she claims if a ghost here at
Thornfield this its haunt. To my inquiry on such ghost she claims the Rochesters more ' "a violent than a quiet race in their time" ' yet they rest quietly
now. ' " 'After life's fitful fever they sleep well,' " ' it is I saying it. Now the
housekeeper is showing me the way up to the leads, we climb a narrow staircase to the attics and here a ladder and trap door and now I am eye level to
those crows in their colony and I look over these battlements at a wide lawn
the field expanse, the wood, church at the gates, tranquil hills and this sky of
azure such contrast to what appears black vault I am descending the garret
staircase and lingering in the long passage which leads to it 'looking, with its
two rows of small black doors all shut, like a corridor in some Bluebeard's

castle.' I am going softly here while the lady is still behind shutting the trap door and I hear it: 'It was a curious laugh; distinct, formal, mirthless . . . . It passed off in a clamorous peal that seemed to wake an echo in every lonely chamber.'

She is here now and she tells me it is of a servant Grace Poole to whom she calls out but I suspect there can be no Grace here for that laugh was not of the human, tragic, preternatural laugh it was. Yet here she is appearing a square-figured woman between thirty and forty, red-haired, hard, plain face neither romantic nor ghostly. Mrs. Fairfax reprimands her for being so noisy. Grace curtseys, returns to the room. She sews and assists in the housework, Mrs. Fairfax is explaining, then this woman inquires on the lessons with Adèle and now we are in the light cheerful rooms below and here is Adèle exclaiming her hunger and we find dinner ready, waiting.

Moving from Lowood to the next landscape and no one is saying our name. We are not named or summoned in this passage from Lowood. Our foot on coach's wooden step and no one lifts an eye to us. Instead we find ourselves at some large private room, inn, not quite at the destination, 'cut adrift from every connection.'

Thornfield requires no one collects us readily yet we know our way and take it. For at the previous place, residence in the low wood we differentiated quality, head on shoulder silence, we gained our head through that silence of the convent-like school, until we lower to departure pushing off again who was nursemaid now does not have to lift us.

To Lowood there by coach travelling the entire way were guards. Also then stop to inn and fears predominant we could be taken, instead we were lifted back onto the coach carrying us directly to the Lowood door where a servant whispering our name lifted us off to a lobby where the two women entered expecting our arrival. We had guards the entire way, and we took in.

There the disciplined structure, bell, form classes, candles out, prayers, the hushes and recitations framed us within a structure until, heliotrope in our plot, we rose to defined quality.

Temple identified to her departure a differentiated definition with old emotions stirring, for we had learned our long division and moved out.

The inn of this passage also fear companioned, raised hair root, no one knows our name this time, no one tells us where we are going or collects us as part of their duty, no one is standing at the bottom of our coach. At Lowood we were on some register before we arrived.

Here still in this inn we are floating adrift as we were for a moment our first Lowood day on a verandah watching our reflections fragmented as the word Institution on a plaque formed before us, there was a cough and a girl beneath a book answered our questions before the next bell rang. There was no one within who we were then who could have formed without that Lowood discipline from without.

The inn suspension, extension of the gaze, afloat when her chaise went over the hill, spaciousness, bowl of a head's sleep to voice writing out our defining quality. We had thought that perhaps advertising was enough. We step out only to wait adrift in some private room.

We had thought advertising was enough, only to send out word of our quality and we would be picked up, but no, our private room is where we are cut adrift. On the way to Thornfield, our private inn place is not connected to world yet, and our privacy will not facilitate our way to what will be the Thornfield place.

The portraits hung here, this oil-lamp, but it is not enough to sit privately receptive our sense, that was the last place, where we learned taking in sense by sense until something interior delineated itself. However this passage is not to be a private room instruction.

Learned well in the Lowood place a patience, humility stripped to interior, some boundary to refined sense formed. Yet here in this inn if we continue with the patient withholding gaze we will sit throughout the night in private parlour.

If we do not think to ring the bell. There was no bell in the inn to Lowood only the guard's motion. The move to ring out of the solitude so heavily demarcated from world, to break out of the private parlour space, the elaborate silence in which what is interior was so carefully delineated at Lowood now wants to be rung out of: can we lift this bell?

Heavy weight of bell to ring out of the private inn leaving Lowood to where no one knows our name. We thought perhaps we could advertise and that was enough. The bell is metallic, we could sit all night staring. Daring hand reach and our question we initiate becomes Thornfield is it a place in the neighborhood?

We have to name the place which has summoned us before we can entertain any motion out. At Lowood we learned to name ourselves and our qualities. After Lowood what is required is that we know ourselves in relation to the place which has called us through, vocation. We will ourselves to get to what has called us is to be related to Thornfield.

We ask on Thornfield and its relation to where we now stand. We are ready for Thornfield only when we have articulated what from regions alone has called us out making us different from all others at the inn. We let the place name itself and we name our desire to get there: some self speaking desire to get us to the next place which is how we will initiate out.

We leave Lowood for a place. What moves us out of the sheltered Lowood school is to hold the unknown place in mind, naming it even in our worse fear. Then someone recognizes us and we find a carrier waiting there afterall in an adjacent room.

Ordinary one-horse carriage. A simple horse walks six miles in two hours. Rang bell, asked of place and here a moving shell of meditation, our willful initiation is followed by slow pace we can remain interior for a space.

What leads to Thornfield is an alteration of will and meditation. We carry the Lowood interiority forward in our movement and we do not revert to a Gateshead compulsive motion.

Not revert, nor stay with who would be another Mrs. Reed. Our resolution to advertise out of any place which might revert to her is the way we are no longer in a place of opening to the impingement by unconscious force becoming reactive compulsion, not ensnarement within forbidden mother's body yet this Lowood way we have learned to traverse within and through body to our defining qualities is what we know on the Thornfield passage will not let us remain we will advertise away from a Mrs. Reed stepmother. Slow coach ordinary resolution.

If we had not the differentiation from Mrs. Reed while still knowing her our relation we would not be on the Thornfield coach. Our resolution to advertise out of a Mrs. Reed employment is the Thornfield coach ride. Related to her but we will not work for her is being on the way to Thornfield.

And the woman is kinder than we thought we would find her, less stately and she meets us with her hands. She is untying our bonnet strings, removing our shawl, clearing the table for a tray of tea ordered for our warmth.

  ◄§ Mrs. Fairfax. This one is in her widow's cap and muslin
  apron, she is wearing what we expected yet here is a consider-
  ation which surprises us. This place reaches out to us more
  than the others, cares about our physical welfare, yet a distancing and some spacious loneliness also here, we have come
  from Lowood and we feel it: the one summoning us in leaving
  Lowood is a woman in search of companionship, she maintains a demarcated distance from the servants, she has been
  living in a chill-like vault of a mansion with no company, lacking an intercourse yet will not lose her authority to a servant
  discourse, and there has been only postman and butcher
  at the door infrequently between the frequent storm.
  Throughout what has been our Lowood winter, some woman
  has been longing for more festivity in the house, becoming
  melancholy. §►

The next place is composite of qualities of the others, the way these qualities are assorted in a different composite becomes the next place. As we have negotiated our way through the previous places we carry them differently and find aspects of them assorted in ways we had not expected: here a mansion with a woman in authority, here black and white the chill and loneliness, yet her hand removes our shawl and in care she has chosen for us this cozy bedroom closer to hers not one of the dreary front chambers elegantly furnished.

The large gallery and oak bannisters resonate still solemn spaciousness more of church. We were standing gazing on the Lowood verandah and we noticed the building looked of a church, its windows latticed. We are passing the latticed staircase window on the Thornfield passage.

Chilliness of Lowood as well as its sanctity are here also and upon awakening next morning we see that they are the corridor making room for the ornateness of the papered wall and carpeted floor of our bedroom. In this place the Lowood aspect leads to the sensate, this place is more textured, sensate, less strictly bare than Lowood though it has the chill, carries the solemnity, its woman longs for festivity.

Walking in the Thornfield place for the first time we look over our body and lineament. Not a beauty here, we note our limitation, these features 'so irregular and so marked.' At Gateshead there was no sense of differentiated body, we were scarlet curtain as ice storm as book gash; at Lowood we have put on our simple frock daily in a consistency and similarity allowing differentiation of our quality yet not of body where we heard the sermon vile body.

We have been many years in the Lowood structure and though careful even punctilious in our appearance, we have not surveyed this body. When we have advertised out from the private place of spiked wall barriers, advertised what is our difference in qualities yet are now placing them in the world we look over this body and we have arrived at Thornfield.

After we have placed our definition through her, identified our temple with her, and then let her go, divided from whom we identified, we can see ourselves for the first time from the outside, we look upon our body, body differentiation from the place as we stand, know who ourselves look like from the place as we stand where we have moved to Thornfield.

When we have made it to the Thornfield bedroom of carpet and papered wall, we wake up and look at our body. Eight years behind the Lowood wall and we had been guarded from vile body, yet slowly breaking out, to the wood in the typhus and then the opening to a larger community while we identified with who fed us at her own responsibility, some relation to our body has altered in the Lowood stay and the new relation becomes Thornfield.

We are not ready to look upon our exterior body and scrutinize it until the Helen sacrifice. We rose through impulse and possession to her over-view, sphere of angels, figures guarding and naming; and our returned body became our human limit. The survival through and departure from Lowood required a sacrifice of Helen's privilege of figuration for a more human concreteness without abandoning the figures, angels yearning human manifestation, incarnation.

The way we had become human at Lowood moved us to Thornfield where this human first takes notice exterior of herself: we want to know for the first time what we look like, and so we look upon concrete detail, human figure.

We are not ready to look upon our concrete body and scrutinize it until the Helen sacrifice, Miss Temple and Brocklehurst have been lowered, leveled, and we have distance to them, difference from them. Who taught us the mediating distance apart from Gateshead's impulse closer to con-science speaking body's desires our narrative placed in temple becoming our emotional stirring to a more sensate place becoming our Thornfield exterior reflection.

Reflection at Gateshead: who we were unconscious, her unnatural non-social phantom imp. Reflection with Lloyd: we are a human being with temporal and spatial location, reflection of where we stand in our place. Reflection at Lowood: interior image and thought becoming we have defin-ing qualities.

Prerequisite for we have gained this personal view of our concrete body from the outside only after traversing and negotiating unconscious body, temporal and place body, temple interior body. We never look upon our-selves exterior first yet earn the privilege to face ourselves exterior.

The past reflections (who we saw looking at us when we looked out to see ourselves reflected) were phantom, an apothecary, a great school girl seeing to the heart, a temple teacher. After Lowood and at Thornfield the mirror reflection is ourselves at ourselves which can only occur when we are moving to incarnate Lowood (abstract) body.

Lowood of the imaginal eye that sees to the heart, figurations surround-ing can be crafted, and interior thoughts radically conspired is our unique gift unlocked only then can there be a (defined and advertised) self to move out and reflect our concrete exterior.

Here we are interested in our feature, our material. Our lips and nose not of sweet feature, the simple and Quaker frock. We wake to this concrete body and survey it at Thornfield. For the first time we experience the bodily effects of the Lowood differentiation putting us in a new place and we are interested in this body.

To look upon our body and lineament is to survey the mansion's front.
The house delineates who we have become toward whom we are forming.

> ◄§ What curtains us, what greets us, what seats us, what
> heats us, what lights our vigilance, how we design for what
> hungers, how we take our rest, our release, where we apply
> ourselves, where we open our mouths to what feeds, the pat-
> tern of what beds us, how cluttered our corners, the silence
> of our spaciousness, the standing on wood or tile of what
> cracks, how is it plaster or board separating the voices of one
> room from another, how we place our softness, what colors
> it, how we place our mind's work, how damp our walls, these
> ways we absorb moisture, the wind's gust, the ways we expel
> our waste and how our water runs, how we weather the ele-
> ments in how wide our window, how we wall in resistance,
> what we store, what we lock, what is more daily opened.
> Speaking our intimacy and what conceals that our house. §►

Manor of gentleman not seat of nobleman: we have gained some size
even some grandeur however not grandiose yet enough imposing. Protective front, stern, battlements suggestion ammunition if invasion, yet the
battlements are picturesque. A severity yet of more design, space for what
pleases.

And it carries a history, aged place, age knots the thorn trees, the front of
the hall is hoary, this fortification we have gained at Lowood shows here;
unlike the Gateshead mansion we are not inflated as exposed to infiltration,
here a seclusion 'not expected to find existent so near the stirring locality of
Millcote.'

This manor is braced, wards off without a rigid defense system, this
stronghold has resistance yet not through splitting or an active opposition:
crows cawing from the rookery back-ground fly to the adjacent fields of the
stern front, fortifying shelter and its resistance is picturesque.

Spaciousness prevails within the interior of a certain latticed sanctity, yet
this body to which we have travelled through Lowood does not entirely bar
off from what would be world. Threshold front door half of glass inviting
some entry and this day it stands half open.

We are not intimated by nor do we idealize the stone front, not nobleman castle; its hills not as lofty as Lowood and they are not such a barrier to
exterior world.

We had risen to a lofty Lowood summit at a limit we lowered and now
with more opening to a larger community, the hills are not complete barriers yet we are fortified which shows on the front. Paradoxical hills: offering

as they do more contact with a living world, closer to London, still however facilitating seclusion.

Relief at its manageability, we have not been summoned by what is outside our reach, fortress of hoary stone and ornate oak yet it is to our size, not castle, our room is small and of ordinary furniture and Mrs. Fairfax is a housekeeper, manager equally dependent herself, not great dame, the child is a ward and we have been trained already to respond to her fluent French.

The male figure of this new place does not come through predominant mother. The one who owns the place is named Rochester and she assumes we would have known that as if by instinct. We are in the place where instinct could connect to a male figure for whom the mother-relation is employee. Here resides invisible some instinctive male force who stands above the mother-relation and owns the manor.

The child who approaches does not notice us at first. And when we are introduced, she pronounces our name as "air", we are but wisp in front of who is child in the Thornfield place. The orphan child of this mansion sings of passion beyond her years, of love of jealousy.

We were trying to coax that burning down to body in Lowood, yet it would miss, here is the one, Adela, material cause for being called out of Lowood to the Thornfield place of more intercourse with a wider world, and where we face that in the affairs of passions we are still a child.

At Lowood some desire soared until stopped in coagulation. In the affairs of passion Jane is still a child.

> ◆§ How old our passion. Lowering to a wider world descend-
> ing the Lowood stratospheres fortified we touch something
> ornate of this earth, a bannister, the door of half-glass in the
> front hall is ajar, the high backed chair seats a considerate
> lady handing to us, our walls are papered here no longer
> plank and plaster stained and we begin to smell it in the air
> again, stirrings bodily, we look over our shape the next day
> before we descend the slippery oak staircase of latticed win-
> dow to who is child redundant waisted curl child calling us
> ' "Aïre," ' sing child singing songs of love and jealously, pas-
> sion still a child. §◆

This form of a child is small featured herself and slight yet she carries some adult language and behavior. She is flighty, she is disinclined to apply her own intelligence. Another little uneducated girl we are asked to edu-cate. This child's song is that the woman was deserted by her lover and dresses up in an ornamental style, will parade to the ball and flaunt the jewels, her charm acting out to say the desertion has no effect.

The child has not learned the Lowood grieving of a stool mortification, suffering waves of cursed betrayal to a long division, heterogeneity, parting. The one who is the reason for our stay at Thornfield, the one bringing activity to what was lonely mansion, is some child who is quite alien to us, does not even notice us at first, who has not grieved desertion yet only gains attention through enactments of a surface passion.

Her mother sang and danced then left to a Holy Virgin and the child chatters and wants to entertain us. Here is some Gateshead-residue child who has not grieved mother's essential desertion. Where this desertion is not grieved yet dramatically concealed is where our passion is child. This child has not been taken to anything beyond flighty costume and parading cover: she knows the curl yet hers are redundant.

We begin to educate the Thornfield child of passion, passion as a child, with Lowood lessons, we take this child into a library transformed to schoolroom. The housekeeper calls us after our first lesson with the child and we find ourselves in a crimson drawing-room, red-room, within it a boudoir.

Child of passions uneducated and we are brought back inside what may have remained unconscious desire, withdrawing room, red place of our blood desire in the Thornfield place is subtler, cooled down by the snow-like elements: white carpets, mouldings of white grapes, the Parian mantel piece — indicating some Lowood effect.

Parting from a temple identification we found an initiation to move to another place where we could first look upon our body, and then through a passionate child needing education we move (back) down to red-room we gasp when we enter it at first thinking it a fairy room.

It may be room of fairy but we are not imp nor phantom, we have looked over our human form that very morning. We become again fascinated in a fairy place also mirrors here but this room of crimson couch and ottoman has a coolness of some borders in a whitening which is ornate, of grapes and mantel, Lowood whitened cool inhibition in the more sensate Thornfield design allowing us to reserve, note in detail, not be overwhelmed by the place. And we have entered it not alone yet with the proper Englishwoman.

Jane comes to her senses: 'I thought I caught a glimpse of a fairy place . . . Yet it was merely a very pretty drawing-room.' In Thornfield we see the fairy possibility in the room but we do not leave the room to know the fairy.

At Gateshead what was white was ice storm a split from crimson curtain the gap into which we fell in what was a violent fit. In Lowood, the white ice melted to orbs of her brilliant heightened reserve and now white becomes rich carpet and grape and vine and what is cool returns sensually to frame and support the crimson in a fitting decoration.

Our Lowood education has prepared us to advance into the red-room, not be dragged by stepmother's rule, our senses grounding our human dimension of it. Unlike the Gateshead solemnly majestic and spare chamber, this red-room is quite central at Thornfield, drawing-room adjacent by arch to dining room, not a death chamber yet available for company.

Here the boudoir is surrounded by what attracts visitors, access to worldly company, guest entertainment not isolated chamber. Here the boudoir reminiscent of fairy spirit and seizure has centrality in a daily life though the room is not much inhabited, rare visits only.

Where Jane was dragged mad cat into the Gateshead red-room, here she advances and she walks in on her own accord in the companionship of Mrs. Fairfax who has motioned her toward it saying: ' "the drawing-room yonder feels like a vault." '

We move into the dining and drawing rooms with a conversation of this housekeeper's longing for more activity, how she keeps the rooms dusted despite the empty months though the visit can be any day now. Boudoir and festive dining room have been waiting for company as we enter Thornfield.

And we see these rooms are plush. The dining room contains stately purple chairs and vases, folds of velvet curtains caught upon the arch leading to the drawing-room's crimson ottoman and snowy moulding, and yet all is very still, we are caught in some suspended moment where Gateshead's qualities meet Lowood's, these are unfamiliar yet also reminiscent rooms. A call back to appetite and desire after the Lowood stay yet only through implication.

We do not move out to wider world closer to some London hub without a return to the red-room. We have come to this place of less barrier to world and we have had a temple exchange with a child of passion which lowered us to a red-room in which our first response is to question the character of the man who owns this Thornfield place.

What this red-room mirrors is this man, his qualities, his taste, his character, for whom are these rooms of purple and crimson kept dusted ever ready? We are in a red-room and our desire is to penetrate a character, enter some unknown vault where he rests hidden until the abrupt arrival. But at Thornfield the housekeeper holds back, forcing us longer to stay on what is surface.

After Lowood we walk into a red-room with a woman who is not interested in probing, who stays on the surface, tells us how it is seen from the outside, what things look like more than what another is like. She opens the windows, draws air and light into these rooms.

We are standing in a room and this crimson reminds us. We want to penetrate who is this man owning such a room snow and fire, purple extremity, we want to know his nature, we want to know his character. Mirrored intrigue to fairy world residing: 'between the windows large mirrors repeated the general blending of snow and fire.'

Large mirrors repeating. We repeat mirroring the intrigue of a red-room of who is the man behind this place who is not here, absent landlord of the red-room we are mirroring a fascination desiring to know his design, in which way is he peculiar?

At Gateshead we were alone in the room except for fairy-sprite and we had no recourse but we went into that black vault then we looked up in order not to starve we implored who are thou father of heaven of all power, who are thou father.

The housekeeper points to the arched room saying ' "the drawing-room yonder feels like a vault," ' and in there we hear of a peculiar male figure whose visits though rare are unexpected and sudden. To Mrs. Fairfax's eyes it is Mr. Rochester, simply gentleman and landed proprietor.

At Thornfield she answers with practical discourse: the Rochesters own practically all the land of the neighborhood, are quite well respected, he is considered a just landlord, she supposes his character unimpeachable and the peculiarity whether he jests or is in earnest or that she does not understand him is not of consequence, he is a good master.

Mirrored crimson arch and we want to bend back in crimson to a spirit who owns the mansion but she guards us after we had been seized in the red-room place and sent to Lowood to learn a division without split defense, we do not open to any peculiar spirit even if fascinated now.

Guarded instead we draw on our senses to view it from the exterior, remaining on the surface first with Mrs. Fairfax who manages well. By her side we see the fairy place is actually drawing-room, we take in its natural contour and do not speak loosely of powers residing there.

We go through this new mansion her way, maintain this practical, natural attitude, and the stories begin to unfold for us, we are slowly lead into them and they are not invasive. Corners and secret nooks are revealed when we have asked of Rochester without probing the character. 'When we left the dining-room, she proposed to show me over the rest of the house; and I followed her up-stairs and down-stairs, admiring as I went: for all was well-arranged and handsome.'

Mrs. Fairfax keeps her place well arranged, she dusts these large dreary chambers even to a melancholy settling into her cloth's polish but she does not lose any ground. With Mrs. Fairfax as manager, we go out to meet each room in this place of thorn and oak and Parian marble.

Thornfield incarnate from descent out of the heights of the low wood: seizures of Gateshead sent us to a low wood where we rose in conscience unlocked gift voice says lower back to world, advertise, incarnate here is Thornfield.

We begin to climb to the top levels of this mansion with Mrs. Fairfax and they take us back to the memory of the place. Here the third story rooms are low and dark. We rise to what is 'shrine of memory,' furniture of the deceased. The top story holds the memory.

At Thornfield we rise to where deceased figures with the one who stays on the surface, grounded figuration.

Not memory residing in the cement of cavelike cellar, past unconscious, "primitive" beneath as memory dark as below where ancestral echoes but all dust of antiquity in stool's embroidery and the eerie bedhanging. Third story. We went to Lowood and learned to rise to memory. With Helen beside we placed our Gateshead past without seizure by animosity and we rose angels grading.

Unlike the Gateshead red-room, we do not leave the red-room here through beseeching Father let us rise, we walk up ourselves at Thornfield because we have made it to the temple at Lowood and we can retrace our steps up with whom has answered our advertisement, guardian of our vocation, post-Lowood education.

We rise to our memory. We go up to be taken back, learn what lies behind the place. Here angels are ancestors.

The way to the angels, rise to memory learned at Lowood, figuration is incarnated at Thornfield. Spirits not ethereal as in Lowood yet cherub head is here in the oak and walnut chests of ancestral furniture. Thornfield angel is in wood and textile of what was once daily furniture, though frightening now, these angels are embedded in ordinary earthly article.

Third story, story what was the design of hands now dust, chests reminiscent of ark of covenant marking it a sacred place, venerable chairs, here ancestors are angels are terrestrial: effigies which call up ghosts are of strange flowers, stranger birds, strangest human beings appearing on what once surrounded the sleep of the ancestors. Thornfield materializes the Lowood rise to spirit, return to what is ancestor continued red-room secret.

Mrs. Fairfax would not have us probe into the new landlord's peculiarity, not poke his secret, and our respect of her attitude allows us to know him in an alternative way: we see his quarters and pretend it is only a tour, even as we find ourselves in the bedding of the ghosts of his ancestors.

And we are not seized or taken over as we walk very close to the attic periphery earth and sky. Too directly we peered into our uncle's vault, as we did the Iceland demons, seeking the powers beyond life's gratification, death secret: in the previous mansion there were no veils and we were shocked.

After Lowood, a woman calls us back to a red-room and when we begin to probe its secrets she veils. We rise to the secrets of the ancestral memory through a veil. The chests with their carvings of cherubs' heads look 'like types of the Hebrew ark,' we are reminded that the veil of the tabernacle containing ark of covenant was also ornamented. Here to peer through veil is how we are employing a "religious" attitude: because we had been marked, we are learning to walk into the antiquity backing some red-room secrets with a religious attitude which does not shatter.

It is not that Rochester's secret tabernacle does not want to be known or spoken, instead we need to practice an approach so we are not shocked.

The eerie spirits are on a third story at Thornfield, allocated to specific rooms, not interspersed in the daily life lower stories, Mrs. Fairfax says they do not pervade the bottom floors. She tells us if there were a ghost these rooms would be its haunt yet there is not ghost and she adds that the ancestors of two generations, hands that embroidered the stool top are long the dust of a coffin, though more a violent than quiet race now stay in that coffin, resting well.

' "Yes—'after life's fitful fever they sleep well,' " ' we say what comes to mind as we stand third story looking at the relics. And perhaps somewhere in our unconscious memory we crack a secret permeating the red-room did not know until we rose to find the more concrete figures here a murdered king: "Duncan is in his grave;/After life's fitful fever he sleeps well."

‥§ "Fair is foul, and foul is fair." First he will be Thane of Cawdor then King, and he smells a murder plot. But later she says to them, "All you have done/Hath been but for a wayward son,/Spiteful and wrathful; who, as others do,/ Loves for his own ends, not for you." Hecate's desire the wayward son serve them weird in the King's Fall not himself. Banquo sees the witches vanishing are of the bubbles of the earth—"the earth hath bubbles as the water has,/And these are of them" —where the earth has air, the King is falling. Who will serve themselves to a King's Fall, the King is Father. Less than man the wife says if his hands are not red, hearing where he said not a vow to murder she claims if it were herself she would go to all lengths, plucked nipple from the babies' mouth in the midst of the smiling suck "and dashed the brains out;" herself would put that dagger in the

King's Heart: "Had he not resembled/My father as he slept, I had done't." She is neither serving Hecate, blood to that servant's face to "Out, damned spot," hands of spotted nature turning upon her on throat a death "by self and violent hands" her own demise Hecate necessitates. For those weird sisters prophecy the moving wood seen, revenge by he untimely ripped from now no mother they meet to stir their cackle "Double, double, toil and trouble;/Fire burn and caldron bubble." ࣣ

Wayward son's strife against King, would wish him dead, is some ancestral memory in the design of the upper apartments of Thornfield. Looking upon the ghostly bedhanging creatures brings out lines reminding us of a dead King resting well had been murdered by who was once favored nobleman whose mad wife was driven and possessed.

In this red-room we rise to the memory of figures are ancestors of desire to murder Father, it is in the lineage of the one who appears when we have entered the drawing room of boudoir and crimson ottoman. We rise to the ancestral memory after we evoke this man in the red-room and in Thornfield we see it with perspective.

We have come to the place of who is violent race. But we are on its top story of some overview, and here is a kind and uncomplicated woman of a Lowood sort of propriety beside us unassuming as reassuring she guides us to the ancestry of that violent life. After the Lowood education of conscience we return in the next place to stirring elemental creatures yet in rooms where we attain some distance.

While confined at Gateshead, elemental forces appeared everywhere, we were without armor, without definition, without limit. Gateshead burst volcanic heat her aspects unconscious to a flame heart chamber at Lowood, small flame revived through the Lowood scourge resistance it desires protection. We have moved to the Thornfield encasement. Encased in Thornfield armor and we rise to ancestral stories which leads to a wide view of things. We are on the leads and we are looking over the battlements.

Helen spoke of Charles 1st and his myopic problem if only he had the distant perspective, and then we rose to her perspective, small flame she located it within us we rose in distance seeing our Gateshead past in overview, placing it.

She kept rising to evaporation and we returned full body to incarnate the lessons and here are the Thornfield leads and we get some distance even as we have been exposed to the must of the past. Light here, azure sky upon lawn, field 'dotted with its ancient timber,' church, road, 'the wood, dun and sere divided by a path visibly overgrown,' hill, the hall as center we survey environs.

We have overview to see the place on which we sit, ground of the armored hall, base of this place. We survey what grounds us, sense what holds, surround of the place so rooted we can see the ancestral trace story-line, see widely back, in all directions from where we now stand.

After the Helen sacrifice, we do not continue our ascent at the Thornfield place, we begin to descend even before Mrs. Fairfax, we are in the black vault passage leading from the garret staircase, we imagine Bluebeard's corridor, and we hear a sound not like any of our Lowood past.

❧ Bluebeard. He left her all his keys. About to wed
together, he has given her all the keys to the castle, he has
said wander full reign, ample scope, keys to every chamber
but one, sole restraint, bluebeard man of "wealth and power,
mystic spells" tells her the blue room not to enter. If that door
opened dreadful punishment required. She is alone. He has
gone off to field his treasure, moated in no moving out she
roams his rooms trying every key's opening. Roaming until
the walls become blue and she hears the groan from interior
apartment. "Accent of distress," she is pulled by a "humanity
to succor the wretched soul who breathes it." Humanity
inducing her penetration to portal mystery. Door opens, the
wives are six all slaughtered. Pile's sight and the key breaks
in its lock marking her. "Damnation! Lady, this key is charm-
fraught; forged in a sulphureous cave, within whose blood-
besprinkled mouth nothing but witchcraft enters, to celebrate
her frantic revels. This speaks a damning proof against you,
and you die!"

Kinsfolk save us slaying him over and over, savior brother,
savior lover, and we return to mortal existence where we
dream of that Bluebeard his mysteries indeed "hellish incanta-
tions," yet we have given our humanity to the secret room
not moving its secrets into our humanity making us wealthy.
And we are wondering on those wives. Have they wanted us
to come to them in other ways, key of cave's mouth door's
opening their charm forged sulfur to carry to humanity, not
die or shrivel to his power as did they? ♋

We have seen our hall grounded by wood and field and we venture down the passage ahead even of Mrs. Fairfax when we hear it. It comes from behind closed doors of an unfamiliar dark corridor we become privy to what sounds preternatural.

The laugh is formal, distinct, mirthless. Cackle. It is our first forward move in the exploration of the Thornfield place, we grope into the long passage without Mrs. Fairfax though she backs us. No immediate blast into what is unknown yet step by step registering the impressions reaching us as we proceed.

On the story where we have seen ancestral relic emerges the preternatural laugh we had just thought Bluebeard corridor. The man evoked in the red-room here rises us to these figurative suggestions of desire to murder king also tortured wives in a locked room no one can enter. Witches made the key. Not a laugh denoting any of what could be pleasure.

We are on our way down after ascent gained through previous education. In Lowood a distanced overview assisted us to pass through our possessions. Here the distance returns us to what is uncanny and possessed: mirthless and formal laugh not of human joy, not a resonance of human impulse yet impersonal, not of any person individual yet distinct, left from ancestors perhaps ringing through eerie bedhanging makes our skin shiver.

At Thornfield, rising to some overview leads us back and down to a laugh rippling through generational walls allowing an impersonal sounding of what is possessed will we have the key. And we have thought it a possessed wife Bluebeard corridor.

The sound emerges from the recesses leading to beyond yet containing the furniture of two generations. We go up to go back down; when we were in the low wood we went up, now we go past to look beyond which sends us back. Still learning waves rhythm. Ascent now descends to distinct laugh which is part of the expanded vision.

Mrs. Fairfax says it is a plain servant. She is telling us that to see the preternatural as a plain servant is Grace. It is an average, middle-aged, even submissive human. We are here to learn how to know the preternatural by looking at what looks average and ordinary; the most eerie creatures in regular article and item.

How not to enter immediately as the forcefully full encounter of Gateshead blast peering directly at Iceland demon until it manifested as her rapacious tyrant at whom we lunged to a gash violent retribution on the rug where the prohibiting minister stood, the Thornfield way of Mrs. Fairfax guidance is to use what veils the story emerges never look directly, Grace as the ordinary cover.

◄§ "As calling home our exiled friends abroad/That fled the snares of watchful tyranny,/Producing forth the cruel ministers/Of this dead butcher and his fiendlike queen,/Who, as 'tis thought, by self and violent hands/Took off her life — this, and what needful else/That calls upon us, by the grace of Grace/We will perform in measure, time, and place." *Macbeth* ?

Thornfield is where we practice how to carry the figures of the ascent back down, incarnate them. We have heard the cackle resounding ghost through a Mrs. Fairfax Grace account we return to an Adela hunger and a dinner awaiting, the structure of the day resumes.

We have entered the remote Thornfield chambers of the possessions of a violent race, and we are not possessed in returning down to the ordinary structure because we have passed through in a Mrs. Fairfax approach precludes probing and invasion. Do not look too closely or ask direct questions, we turn away to take in.

This approach is our maturity gained through the Lowood education, no longer innocent in our appropriation of what lies beyond the natural, we will not call up preternatural or blast it back or poke into its secret, instead a key which will not force entry yet figuratively open by staying grounded through the one of practical attitude, learning instead veil of preternatural and letting it come to us in its measured time and ordinary form.

When we enter our curiosity of Rochester through a Mrs. Fairfax attitude, we go through relics of ancestors leaving suggestions of their forces in furniture of their ordinary days, shrine of memory figures, and in the innermost dark passage is the laugh covered by an average woman. We do not probe Rochester directly yet move through his third story to the reverberation of some preternatural source distinct and mirthless.

The Thornfield place is what houses a man who as landlord makes abrupt and unexpected visits in whose memory shrine is a murdered king resting well and a possessed woman's laugh which finds its way to the middle-aged affairs of things.

In being introduced to the third story of Rochester, through a Mrs. Fairfax guidance, we find the eerie creatures of ' " 'life's fitful fever,' " ' ancestors allowing overview returning us to a formal laugh in a Bluebeard passage covered by a squarish Grace Poole however red-haired also plain.

*Female Curiosity. Grasp of apple perhaps about to bite, Eve's touching curiosity breaking through the garden. Pandora raising cover looked inside blast of air flying every evil of the world her face blast first eyes teared shut.

Swooning in the Stygian slumber I remember his saying not to look though he would come upon me nightly. I was "a

close captive within the walls of (my) luxurious prison and
deprived of all human conversation" bringing me a great
anguish, in sweet embrace and pity he consented to a visit
from whom is sister. These sisters began whispering to me he
may be a monster, I hid the razor and after his breathing
became heavy sought the lamp there shone golden streaming
lock, even in sleep quivering the topmost feathers of his white
wing, lightning from this source more radiant than the lamp
I hold curious oil lamp shining wax to his tremulous wing
burnt, my finger then pricked blood by his arrow I am filled
with a heat heretofore unknown and I lay this passion upon
him sending me through tortuous tasks of four. Ordeals of
hell no pity lent to floating dead beseeching aid, no hands
lent to the old woman weaving, no seat or feast accepted
from Persephone, instead sitting on the hard ground lowly I
eat a crust of bread. Not to peer casket of beauty. Some
tower had spoken to me: "I bid thee, above all, beware that
thou seek not to open or look within the casket which thou
bearest, or turn at all with over-curious eyes to view the treasure of divine beauty that is concealed within."

Full face to the death demons and going under we have
been dissipated and possessed, yet this curious pull to lift up
the veil we thought our only desparate way through what
otherwise has been luxurious prison. Lover-savior to rescue
yet we remain in the Stygian sleep until we hear instruction
from a woman who manages the household, other ways to
enter recess of death forces and pretend not to see we return
with the key curious not possessed we carry the preternatural
down to the ground story here are other tasks. ক্ষ

Bibliography

Alnwick. *History of Blue Beard*. London: W. Davison, 1820.

Bachelard, Gaston. *The Poetics of Space*. Trans. by Etienne Gilson. Boston: Beacon Press, 1969.

Colman, G., The Younger. *Blue Beard or Female Curiosity. A Dramatic Romance, In Three Acts*. New York: D. Longworth, 1811.

Gregory, Eileen. *Summoning the Familiar.* Dallas: The Pegasus Foundation, 1983.

Jung, C. G. *Memories, Dreams, Reflections*. Trans. by Richard and Clara Winston. New York: Vintage Books, 1965.

Neumann, Erich. *Amor and Psyche: The Psychic Development of the Feminine*. Trans. by Ralph Manheim. Princeton, N.J.: Princeton University Press, 1973.

Rich, Adrienne. "*Jane Eyre*: The Temptations of a Motherless Woman." In *On Lies, Secrets, and Silence: Selected Prose 1966–1978*. New York: W. W. Norton and Co., 1979.

Shakespeare. *Macbeth*. New York: New American Library, 1963; quoted pp. 81, 37, 91, 44, 57, 61, 94, 131.

von Franz, M. L. *The Feminine in Fairytales*. Dallas: Spring Publications, 1972.

_____. *Shadow and Evil in Fairytales*. Dallas: Spring Publications, 1980.

Chapter 12
Gytrash

Smooth career a moderation, the woman is kind-natured her intelligence
average, we regard one another tranquilly and I am grateful for this common
pleasing regard. The child had been once indulged and can be wayward yet
there is no interference with my direction and this one neither of extreme
talent nor of vice becomes teachable,mediocre level, she chats to please me,
makes reasonable progress. Ordinary child of a simplicity affording an
attachment with which we both are content in one another's company. I
cannot flatter a 'parental egotism' to say I felt a devotion, and not an idolatry
for her yet 'conscientious solicitude.'

And I may be blamed for the restlessness rising in such comfortable
atmosphere, restlessness raising me to the top floors, leads, look to the hill
and sky line and I would long for power of vision overpassing that limit,
yearn for what lies beyond in a life of town, variety of character. Restlessness
agitation to a pain relieved only by pacing the third story corridor with my
mind's eye on its bright visions and 'inward ear to a tale that was never
ended — a tale my imagination created, and narrated continuously; quickened
with all of incident, life, fire, feeling, that I desired and had not in my actual
existence.'

'Woman are supposed to be very calm generally: but women feel just as
men feel; they need exercise for their faculties, and a field for their efforts as
much as their brothers do; they suffer from too rigid a restraint, too absolute
a stagnation, precisely as men would suffer.'

Here again Grace Poole peal, eccentric murmurs, some days I cannot
account for the sounds, occasionally I see her with basin or tray returning
with pot of porter, monosyllabic, as with the other servants I am cut short of
any effort at conversation. October, November, December pass thus; a cold,
fine January day I have been sitting still in the library all morning for Mrs.
Fairfax asked holiday for Adèle with cold. Yet I have sat too still, and I ask
to post Mrs. Fairfax's letter, to Hay, two miles I depart to walk.

Hard ground this 3:00 church bell tolls and I slow one mile from Thornfield, absolute winter still, lonely road inclining entirely to Hay and in its
middle I sit on a stile, muffed hands air freezing trickle from some brook to
ice on this causeway. Woods of Thornfield I am looking down upon sun
sinking behind as I turn eastward seeing pale moon rise above Hay these thin
murmurs of life there reaching me as 'my ear too felt the flow of currents; in
what dales and depths I could not tell,' becks weaving in the land their sough
ever remote rings in the ear.

Metallic clamping, tramp tramp, interrupting 'these fine ripplings and whisperings,' if it had been a picture it is a mass of crag of sturdy oak drawn in dark foreground effacing sun and azure hill and cloud 'where tint melts into tint.'

'The din was on the causeway,' about to leave the causeway now I pause will let this horse go by I imagine Bessie story, North-of-England spirit a ' "Gytrash" ' haunting horse, mule, or dog coming up upon the belated traveller as this one upon me. Black and white here a dog and as I expect pretercanine eyes, lion-like with long hair and following is the horse tall steed but a rider on its back breaks the spell: 'Nothing ever rode the Gytrash.' He passes I go on and then hear it sliding and a swearing. The horse fallen on the causeway ice, man is down the dog running to me only help I obey to ask the rider can I do anything? Perhaps it is swearing as he begins 'a heaving, stamping, clattering process, accompanied by a barking and baying which removed me effectually some yards distance: but I would not be driven quite away till I saw the event.'

Horse righted, dog silenced Down Pilot, limping to stile, a sprain. Fur collar riding cloak, middle height of dark with stern features, thirty-five, had he been handsome I could not have stood there services unasked offered would not have if it was a beautiful man with no qualities of any sympathy with my own, 'but the frown, the roughness of the traveller set me at my ease.' Even when he waves me away I say I will not leave him on this solitary lane until he has mounted the horse.

He had not turned his eye in my direction before though now he does and he asks from where I come. Questions on Thornfield and my post a scrutiny until I try to get the horse's bridle to lead the animal to him. Am I not afraid he asks, no until the spirited horse will not lend itself to my groping hand and of the rising forefeet I do fear a trampling and the watching traveller laughs.

Mahomet to the mountain instead and he asks me to come to him and heavy hand on my shoulder he limps to his horse. I hand him the whip to his thanks and his statement that I return as fast as possible. All three vanish ' "Like heath that in the wilderness/The wild wind whirls away." '

Incident marking. 'It marked with change one single hour of a monotonous life. . . it was yet an active thing, and I was weary of an existence all passive.' New face, masculine, in the gallery of memory I see it before me. I post the letter and in the return a pause on that stile hear again hooves to causeway but only pollard willow rising up meeting moonbeam and wind fitful in the Thornfield trees. I do not want to return to the empty hall with the tranquil Mrs. Fairfax yet desire to stir as I have just done as would any man too long in a ' "too easy chair." '

Linger at the door, pacing the front, moon's march to her zenith 'midnight-dark in its fathomless depth and measureless distance: and for those trembling stars that followed her course, they made my heart tremble, my veins glow when I viewed them.' Clock strikes return to earth entrance the hall of a light unfamiliar comes from the dining room lit small group at mantlepiece, Adèle's voice, the door shuts and I hasten to Mrs. Fairfax's room that woman not there but a dog black and white so like the Gytrash on the lane I say ' "Pilot" ' and he comes to my caress. I ring the bell to hear the master returned, Mr. Rochester with a sprain the surgeon sent, Mrs. Fairfax hurry to order tea and I go upstairs to take off my things.

After we hear the laugh for the first time loud reverberating in a bluebeard hall and it sounds outside of us, after we hear the laugh we go downstairs and settle into a ground floor mediocrity. The base of the preternatural laugh we have heard in the dark corridor is a first story mediocrity.

We ground ourselves, the conversation of the housekeeper is predictable and calming in its regular topic, the chatter of the ward is a hum of some background familiar, she is not the extraordinary child not unnatural, we settle into who is more average almost an ordinary child as these days pass, ground level.

We do not let the child's past indulgences break through, we are not asking for a stimulation in such a way, we are formal and kind as the child who could be wayward settles, pleasing chatter, no interference, we care for this child and in return receive a warm regard. There is no interruption and the rhythm of these days even. We are placing who could be wayward child in a daily structure, and she begins her learnings, slowly, of an ordinary fashion, reasonable progress.

And our heart stills to it, this Thornfield ground floor. A preternatural laugh has sounded behind the walls of some darkened corridor, we take our time. The housekeeper and pupil are who accompany our human need to rest, residence in what is nest.

We remember from Lowood the necessity of the systematic routine, daily lesson, relief in it after the Reed blasting. We do not resort to a strict Brocklehurstian defense against the preternatural soundings, for we have relativized him, other options now of containment, and upon hearing the laugh we know merely to resume what is mediocre schedule.

Residing in Miss Temple's room, rocking we stilled even current, and some force began then, perhaps it was between that Temple woman and ourselves, sounding louder as she rode off, moving us to a Thornfield mansion and we heard it in its third story corridor as laugh, stirring force, yet now we are resting still, again evening.

Here these woman are average. No dart or dip no edge staccato, yet moderation of a first story. Eventually it rises us. Current so still all we can do is rise to what stirs as force. Eventually we call the groundfloor our boredom and frustration as we find ourselves mounting to a third story imagination, endless tale of 'incident, life, fire, feeling.'

Current passing through third floor pacing we rise to its image and even as we leave them we knqw Mrs. Fairfax and Adèle are prerequisite and base for the rising: groundfloor holding regularity allowing ascent to where a more forceful current passes.

While we have been sitting in the parlour alongside a Mrs. Fairfax and child Adèle, some part has been pacing above third story where we yearn for an exercise for faculties. We are sitting with an elderly with a young girl average sitting in a parlour each to her own chore and a simple talk and from a third story pacing above we hear our plea for exercise, for what lies beyond horizon.

As we sit below in mediocrity some restless part rises to the eccentric murmur, sounds beyond any everyday account, we cannot account for the sounds as we yearn for what power of vision, force of feeling, beyond margin.

What Lowood left us. What had been Gateshead blind incorporation of unconscious force became at Lowood narrative, our tale, we rose to temple chamber echoing the many voices we were all as none, narrator. Lowood left us narrator of unconscious forces, we found there the story of what was unconscious and this brought out of a locked drawer seed-cake gift, chorals from souls of dead, becoming the images, how they nurture, our craft.

We go to Thornfield, a move closer to London hub, and we have witnessed some unconscious currents here above, felt them in a bluebeard hall, heard their echoes hair-raising. Taking our Lowood lesson, we move up, rise to what are their images, and how to word it, tale of imagination.

Thornfield is where the narrative is of what could be. At Lowood we learned narration of what was. The unconscious currents of Thornfield rise us to what could be this our narrative we are pacing at the place of overview, wider vision we desire it beyond horizon, call it longing, unconscious desires longing to manifest through what is the narrative of its images, propelling out to what could be a future.

To push out of ourselves interior, long for worldly practical experience, is to word the future narrative. To long to push out interior is where she is interior enough to be her own audience of 'a tale that was never ended.'

Old emotions stirred upon watching her chaise depart. What is the tale of their future, their place in a world to which we aspire have not touched, remaining up, first find the tale of imagination. What is unconscious desired rises to image at Thornfield—incident, life, fire, feeling—is how that tale desires to move out and 'reach the busy world.'

Thornfield our outreach of what resides interior, images ready to be worded to reach beyond horizon. Images—here is their tale—ready to be worlded, provoke. Restless. When the tale of imagination is ready to move out wording the fire is the fire it takes becoming our longing as well as restlessness. Restlessness of the possibility of the word of fire moving out makes us apologize to reader. Any man would feel it, and then we hear the strange laughter.

Narrator breaks out of text where her character could not yet, to address the reader, address to reader, apologia: woman feel as men feel, it is 'narrow-minded in their more privileged fellow-creatures to say that they ought to confine themselves to making puddings and knitting stockings. . .'

A narrow male mind would keep the woman locked in keeping the incident fire and feeling not tale desiring wide world incarnation yet reverberating laughter preternatural.

Third story Thornfield of some concealed laugh and eccentric murmur catches the madness at the male liberty concomitant with condemnation, these ways women have been held up. What begins to move the tale of imagination out is to find the word of the madness, even if it means breaking out of text.

Finding the word of the madness breaks out of our own to a wider audience, is to begin to move the tale of who we could be out, breaking text.

Yet we remain frustrated when we have only yet learned to go up. We can see the overview yet cannot break out and down. Here above where the current images itself and we pace to it yet eventually become listener to its longing for expression in wider world when we only stay above in it feels like trapped image and unaccountable sounds of laughter.

For we have basked too long in the hot attic rooms, this mansion is peeling we state our desire for an exercise for our images and this speaking is accompanied by the preternatural laugh and sounds for which we cannot account. If we do not move hidden gift imaged out in exercise incarnated then coagulation, stagnated, all dulled no faculty as currents evaporate only above to a mad murmuring.

Third floor desires imaged want experience: 'I longed for a power of vision which might overpass that limit; which might reach the busy world, towns, regions full of life I had heard of but never seen: that then I desired more of practical experience than I possessed; more of intercourse with my kind, of acquaintance with variety of character, than was here within my reach.'

After Lowood we know to let those preternatural currents rise to tale of imagination, figuration, and in the Thornfield third story its desire becoming conscious is to move figuration to wider world, concrete body, incarnate.

At Thornfield the way out is no longer up. The laugh is here to remind us though we cannot account for it. We rise to see and hear the design of our currents, to have our visions, imaginal figures in tale, figure the madness some and let the desires image themselves to eye and ear gaining momentum in some pacing.

We have gone up, ritual psychological ascent to imaged forces yet when we stay up too long image trapped above we hear a mad laugh alongside our constrained mediocrity. But we have gained some momentum and when one day has been too long, the pupil withdrawn in cold, we want to deliver the letter out.

We cannot make this move out unless we have paced above third story endless tale. Trap door, we see that remaining with tale and vision above comes up against a trap door. For we had lost the currents, no longer any feeling, no force within our daily work, in our food, in our habit, we have not been moved, frustrated we frustrate our inner voice to the skies awaiting there endless tale until she walked the corridor, listening.

Restlessness and an ascent to generation voices, stifled mediocrity now laugh and eccentric murmur, and we become ready to move from our fortress to a place of expansion. The lessons of contraction have focused us passage to entempled gift, imaged force, desires image force, we yearn to use this gift to expand to what is world yet how is it these images break forth incarnate to world and our contraction now moved into the Thornfield place becomes 'too rigid a restraint, too absolute a stagnation.'

The third story laugh accompanying endless imagination tale comes from one Grace Poole residing in a place present to the tale of fire yet trapped, only going down for more porter, she stays where enflamed visions stopped. When we have no sense how to expand imagination of fire and feeling and incident we remain trapped internal murmurs gurling, pot of porter, incarcerated up third story.

     •§ Grace Poole's laugh lies behind our hard-featured, staid appearances, under cover in a calm exterior carrying the porter. The simple servant recessed within a third story houses unnatural sounds. The laugh comes when we least expect it, in the ordinary routine, calm of things, there in the middle of carrying the tray, doing the dishes, reading by the fire, that laugh with its trailing murmurs starting outside our right ear, passing through reverberation in temple, the mind constricts now we are forced this laugh peals and we are forced to enter the fire and feeling, breaking bonds, fire and feeling, breaking bonds, we long for incident. We want to shatter any limit outstretched horizon we yearn life breaking limit, surging through sinew, snapping muscled constraint we long for expansion for it has become too moderate here as we have contracted. ξ•

For as we had been learning the lessons of constriction, we drew in and found her entempled and something began procreating, gift. We drew in, we have been carrying gift nested very still until something expanded even kicked, restlessness agitating to pain, pain of our labor, third story pacing, something begins to want to be delivered out, we are frustrated and pacing but we have never taken this step out.

We had learned at the end of the Lowood stay to advertise, called forth, arrived at the place representing larger world still secluded we have not yet taken this step out.

  ◄§ "The more concentrated the repose, the more hermetic the chrysalis, the more the being that emerges from it is a being from elsewhere, the greater is his expansion." Bachelard §►

Some part of what has been nesting in constriction wants to break out of itself. Psychic state of repose to some ending, our chrysalis has been hermetic now something we found as gift in internal passages wants to stretch even shatter, deliver. Miss Temple rode over the white path and we felt the jolt wanting exercise for faculty.

The psychic state of repose benefiting contraction has come to its natural ending and we are placed in Thornfield to experience these labor pains of expansion, restless.

We have sat still in the library all morning, we are not with pupil, something kicks within and we want to make the first steps out to deliver. It is afternoon and she decides to mail Mrs. Fairfax's letter. She has done her third floor exercises and they prepare her decision to move out of the Thornfield mansion.

We have found our way down, momentum through some eccentric sounds, we heard the laugh and some quickened murmuring, we were pacing in some heat longing for fire and perhaps we remembered the typhus scourge and we knew we were not to stay high up too long and we returned those images to ground floor even knowing it could not contain them, we sat pained labor until after many hours in a quiet library we decide to deliver it for our housekeeper has been writing a letter.

Mrs. Fairfax was part of drawing us out of the Lowood last suspension. When that familiar place suddenly had become unfamiliar we became instantly stranger and a stranger called us from Lowood to a place closer to London, and it is her letter that moves us out of the Thornfield fortress.

When we met her what surprised us was her care, the way she handed to us, handling us in care, this too an extension of Lowood lesson to sever, break away, strip off, the move out through care. A letter is a careful way to move out what is in.

Letter our images move through word to world. Missive to move interior out while remaining in. Letter moves outside while containing inside, even secret drawer content. Letter of the word of intimacy, what intimately has moved us, moves out.

Old emotions stirred upon watching her chaise depart, we are at a place where a third story calls them back, the recall becoming a paced tale of their placement in a world beyond horizon where we have become narrator and listener of differentiated interior wording what is unconscious, bring out the word of the currents, bring the letter of Thornfield tale out in a Mrs. Fairfax mode.

Since Gateshead our vocation has been to bring out the text of the unconscious, after we have learned our Lowood lesson of condensation to word, what is the world we desire unconscious desires become manifest through the Mrs. Fairfax letter.

The first morning after having arrived at Thornfield we descended to the ground floor and saw the front door half ajar, and we went out to survey. When Mrs. Fairfax saw we were out there she said to us: ' "What! out already?" ' She was telling us we were not ready that first day, she needed first to return us to a redroom remembering, to the trappings of ancestors in passages reviving gift of imagination yearning expansion until we could no longer stand pacing beside that laugh beneath staid appearances we have done third story exercises, located the vivid vision and images of fire and feeling, now lowered, fortified, for we even have stood some mad rippling of ancestral chambers through calm exterior, and we say we will post her letter.

Gift of imagination current of internal passage ready to expand out. This time it is not too soon, she knows we are ready, sensing the pain of our labor she hands us the letter.

Our road is lonely. The way we take our steps out of the Thornfield structure to what is world is through a loneliness. Intense loneliness becomes this self-initiating move from interior to exterior and we begin to move faster to warm. At Gateshead there was no interior to move exterior only a blast and seizure to remove us out. At Lowood an interior negotiating blast yet needing a summons out when ready. The sun sets and we are accustomed to this solitude as the landscape here says still: 'the stripped hawthorn and hazel bushes were as still as the white, worn stones which causewayed the middle of the path.'

Still as stone our landscape bears no apparent animation yet cool stone path. The move to world through Thornfield is where nothing moves or summons us from without, yet having traversed and withstood the interior we move the letter out on a white cool path.

Hard ground not a leaf rustle in this landscape 'whose best winter delight lay in its utter solitude and leafless repose.' We have learned to listen to landscape what is message, and as we embark to the world now our January ground says still.

We find our way out, some expansion, through the frigid constriction, we do not abandon constriction once at Thornfield in order to expand instead we know one through the other. Our way out does not require a heated assertive movement; we slow, contract as we move out. Contractions in delivery.

We make it to the one mile half-way point to the town of Hay, we are going very slowly as we take in through all senses, to deliver the letter is to become embodied, we take the message through all our senses from this surround, it is a mid-point transition and we still to a stop. Sit on stile constrict.

3:00. Mid-afternoon church bell toll half way to Hay middle of this hill inclining to the town at dusk, the setting sun transits to moon rise; we turn from our westward sunset Thornfield view to the eastward Hay chimney outline; we are at the transition point, midpoint of our transition to terrestrial world and we do not struggle against the midpoint we ease toward and then sit in it. We do not charge through nor do we pace within it, we are sitting in it January late afternoon of a hard lonely ground.

To move through the threshold to what is dimming and of moonlight is to move out. Here is not flamboyant or brilliant entry to world, city life, even as we had paced in longing for the hub, instead frozen ground, we have been sheltered and still for very long learning lessons, we move out through the same cold so much the element of what has fortified us. The causeway ices.

We stop at the midpoint where the wall between the worlds is thinnest, where threshold shifts transpire. We stop at the midpoint because something in this cold January day has told us we cannot rush our way directly to Hay. It is not up to us entirely. Here the sun sets, this sun was so lucid and dry at Lowood, we felt it in her eyes, luminary, and we rose to it until the waves calmed, we were rocking ever so gently as the cooling sun found her way to set over the hill departing and we are sitting in some transition point, still on stile, atmosphere shifts and what is this, moon rise. New guide of eastern moon, also cool yet humid becoming the fathomless dark this moon desires our crossing to another side, other side, outer side.

We have come from a place where everything calmed to a point that all began to blend, town's hub a murmur, murmurs of life from the town they are currents, currents of whispers, hub wheels circling town whispers cycling to sough of streams, tinkling blend to swirl of 'soft-wave wanderings,' pastels and we do not want, do not need to distinguish. The becks were once ferocious but now they gently weave and where their streams will take us we do not know as we fall under their ring.

Rings and we are falling under blending. We are sitting half way out on a stile when the rings encircle to our drift under. It takes this absolute suspension but we only know that afterwards. Absolute suspension for a previously unseen unknown force to crash through this scene of so many pastels its mountain melting into its sky we cannot distinguish but what is this, head alert now, rude noise, great dark oak splitting what was pastoral landscape, we snap forward to what clatters out perhaps the animal trampling.

Perhaps familiar with this creature may be one of a Bessie story of the Gytrash. For 'the din was on the causeway.' Some animal force breaks out yet only when we are the belated traveller, a step out toward some town and stilled until the atmosphere shifts to the underside of what is day, we have broken out of the domestic container, inner sanctum, moving forth delivering the letter of what was current interior, outreach while paused and what is this metallic clatter of a horse. Bessie had said horse, mule or dog spirit Gytrash spirit coming upon the belated traveller.

They have claimed such horse energies to be apart, they have said dichotomous, to the society, they have said the animal forces arise through a body's instinct ravaging antagonistic to a society as to a culture. Yet we know we hear the metallic clatter only when we have set out to that society. Something for which we were yearning in the Thornfield mansion gets released on the road during a pause shift of consciousness more to the nightside. At first we think it an eerie animal spirit coming upon us, possible collision with that of pretercanine eye.

Gytrash as dog first, huge black and white speeding low to the hazel stems, he glides low. Quietly it passes, we cannot attach to its smooth rushing whirl across our way. Large dog lion-like with long hair and the galloping horse follows. Here animal as spirit though we have heard they also have said animal dichotomous to spirit, they have called animal of the gross body while spirit of what only is ethereal, fey and without any trampling. But on the Thornfield route remembering Bessie's story some animal spirit forces delivery a way out.

A Bessie account is evoked when the delivery wants to be concrete, embodied, no longer residing with spirit ethereal. What was spirit is spirit has become animal, embodied, and of the culture even on the way out to society is of the Thornfield place. To bring the letter of what was interior out is to find the embodiment of what was spirit in a place of society which is our culture. At Thornfield what comes from beyond the horizon was unconscious, is spirit is animal, angel is terrestrial, angel as animal, as the letter is moving out.

The energy emerging our first world passage of Thornfield snorts, growls, pants; frightening even lion-like ferocious when we stop on stile it rises up and comes upon us. We have been constricted as this force on stile it rises up and comes upon us. We have been constricted as this force accumulated animal proportions of a movement alerting, frightening us, sustaining our attention.

> ◄§ H. D.: "George was like a great tawny beast, a sort of
> sub-lion pawing at her, pawing with great hand at her tousled
> garments. George had been like a great lion but if he had
> simply bared teeth, torn away garments with bared fangs, she
> would have understood, would have put narrow arms around
> great shoulders, would have yielded to him."
> Sylvia Plath: "Let me someday confront him, only con-
> front him, to make him human, and not that black panther
> which struts on the forest fringes of hearsay. Such hell. . . . I
> don't want to eat, to go to tea today. I want to rave out in
> the streets and confront that big panther, to make the day-
> light whittle him to lifesize." §►

When we stop on stile it comes upon us. If we let it pass completely, another eight years at a needlework while pacing third story to eccentric laugh repressed, we are half way out delivering and hugh animal forces come upon us.

We are ready to let it by as Gytrash, mere child fantasy, anesthesia to its ripping effect, afterall what does this force have to do with us. We are ready to let it by as Gytrash but then we see the human on the horse. When we attach to a human component of the animal energy galloping through some iced causeway, the horse falls the man down at our feet.

When we have the Thornfield letter we do not stop at seizure by a preternatural force, yet what is the human encasement of that force now incarnate stops at us.

It has taken a male human to ride through the animal forces for these generations for we have been held up, domesticated ever nested no break-ing out and he is of other, outside our parlours, from beyond the horizon riding through galloping energy as we take a step out to delivery. We had not anticipated this energy which feels somewhat familiar to be of any humankind as we had not known it would be so of animal.

We meet what first appears unbridled animal power with reticence even restraint, do not flag it down, do not prop ourselves up for its notice but as we begin to feel it pass through we stay as still as causeway ice locating what is human of it which halts it in front of us.

Ice of the causeway allows the animal forces to be humanly related, she is cool, has learned all Lowood lesson, coolly she contains these animal energies, she does not attach to them herself or go under them, the ice is what does not let the animal force move away from her direction, and she recognizes this force as she is stunned by it.

When we start out on the causeway to that wider world once seen from our battlemented fortress, some thrusting willful drive wants to go its own way and is not in touch with the natural conditions. Driven through all frostbit air and heated flank and the hooves are not wisely connected to their ground, too fast, it thinks itself beyond the natural, crash.

'(C)ommon-place human form,' no Gytrash, the rider is that moment of humanizing that would be preternatural-pretercanine, for we have been holding in, fortified even frigid for a time learning of human limited boundary, and this willful thrusting force will not get its own way. The awesome power falls down, now mere human sprain, limp.

> ⊷§ At first they are indistinguishable with the brooks lapping the winds gentle caress until louder gradually more hoof on stone rhythmic clatter and something once blending gets interrupted, rude noise, split attention to what is long-haired, low gliding now snorting and we begin to yield to what may be preternatural force coming upon us splitting our pastoral scene and something in us surrounds this dashing animal as we are immediately afraid of being overtaken by it. We remember the tales we have heard, this stallion has its legend. Then we see man as rider and we seek his human dimension, we are about to go our own way iced white stone path for we have seen the mere human and he loses charge hoof striking ice sparks to crash can we approach what limps. §⊷

That the Gytrash is merely human, no Bessie story afterall, indicates how in her narrative moving out to concrete manifestation she has had to exchange with Bessie and become her own narrator through the Lowood passage. Herself narrator mediates otherworldly force not a direct manifestation yet humanly limited, incarnate. Gytrash is human and the narrative is hers incarnate after Lowood.

In order to carry out the letter, something has to humanize of what was previously beyond the natural. The figure emerges when it is choosing us for something; figures discriminate where they land. Through a human view of him, this rider moves out of his control of the animal, some ice breaks his drive, some solitary ice path stops his strong animal-enspirited will. The Gytrash is seen through his animal, then human through his Gytrash, he loses his strong grip on things going down no longer of his will.

She has only recently begun some initiation of her path iced to world she advertised and summoned, learned the territory enough to venture out, first steps out and what erupts in a pause is a will long dormant, carried up by who has until now only been behind some other horizon.

Galloping through direct path willed long-haired energy named Pilot, he steers the way the horse is sleek and its rider has a cloak fur-collared. Will. We have been in another's directive, systematic format where we have filled out our canvas placing hungers until we filled out enough to advertise to the place where we heard the preternatural laugh while pacing in a blocked off third floor trap door we could see out but not move out, and finally first steps initiating to a world beyond and what charges through will.

At our first steps half way to town in a pause a great willed force surfaces. Energies which had been dormant behind horizon now gallop out into some suspension in what is outer world. We are stunned that this rhythmic animal flank has any relation to what we know as human at all yet we have known what is ice long enough that we halt this force, call it down in front of us perhaps we have been by a Thornfield trap door too long desiring our human counterpart, other part, part from other outer side when the ice fells it a man who we approach, can we help.

The only way we have known to relate to who can ride this animal is to minister, a nursing. We are ignored, our sweet bonnet, our gentle inquiry has no entry to his cursing, to this clamor, dog baying, bridle clanging as the hooves strike again this ice so the horse resumes some posture. Our approach has no effect, does not get noticed, yet we stay on. Our letter is forgotten as we appear paltry in front of this driving aspect, our approach has no effect, yet we stay on.

We know when we are being introduced to a figure who marks our fate. We should be on our way but we are captured too in this scene and we hesitate, we have a 'vocation to renew inquiries' here with this one. It becomes an issue of vocation to address this figure even as he waves us away. Another part of our calling.

He thinks at first it does not pertain to us, he was passing us by in a great force, we were a pallid and passive Quaker-looking girl quietly situated in the lane. Yet his dog runs over for our help: 'there was no other help at hand to summon.'

There are no other humans around, when the will long latent from the other sides of our horizon finally erupts it comes from a great solitude which finally we are bringing out to the world. The man riding animal energy charges out of a great solitude within which we are moving out.

When we carry out the solitude, not move out of the solitude but carry it out, the will emerges as riding animal.

And this force is a match for, some sound signification of energies as we had been pacing hidden, which is why our attention is halted here. What has been lingering latent in our long institutional and domesticated solitude emerges when that solitude hits world. Hugh animal energies cracking through, understood first as only magico-spiritual, yet the nested past also requires a second look to what is human and can be articulated in force.

We lost Helen to learn human limit, we have ground floor years of needlework, second look to what is human in force. And we sense a rider of middle height with large breadth of chest, dark face and his eyes and brows are of ire when there are no other humans around.

We approach him and ask of his injury, he is in his own monologue swearing as determined to proceed here heaving the horse on feet the dog silenced and he takes the place on the stile from where we have just risen. He limps saying it is a sprain, he sits where we have warmed the stone.

We break his monologue requiring interlocution. Because we have arrived at where we move out the letter we advance to dialogue with what has burst out of horizon. In beginning a dialogue we switch places, allowing varied perspective.

We switch places. Our first encounter with the new figure forecasts what we are to serve for one another. He is dark and angry and in his own direction but now he must sit. The impact of his force on our causeway path stops him to sit and we are energized, we ask again, 'questioning him against his will,' can we do anything.

Going counter will is what allows articulation of what would have remained driven force from unconscious margins. Moving counter to the will that comes out, long unconscious, as we deliver, to speak with it moves against its direction, which is to speak to it which leans toward consenting not driven will which moves us to action.

It is not heroism or a handsomeness which attracts us here, nor a gallantry or excellence of manner, but the fact that in the moon's light he appears stern, ireful, indeed not handsome. Here pact of sym-pathesis is through his frown, his roughness, the swearing and the wrathful way he casts off our quiet supplication; we would not have stayed if he had been polite or elegant, nor at a gallant suggestion that we go our way we would not have stayed for we do not desire at Thornfield to touch qualities of kindness or what is of an etiquette.

Handsome or gallant would have been antipathetic but his qualities hold for us sympathesis and we want to know what would be the forceful drive felled. His qualities reside as potential, they reside between us and it becomes our vocation to renew inquiry.

He has ridden out of a twilight's threshold, out of the prayers of a third floor pacing.

She had been asking to know power of vision overpassing horizon limit, yearned for incident fire and feeling of the margin from which he impetuously broke through the twilight in a way breaking his stride on animal energies connecting her to stern and willful forces through his ugliness also her own.

When they appear from our other sides, our ugliness, not sent through the mother though not unrelated to those the mother sent, they do not seek us out in daylight directly. Sometimes when they appear they do not want to know us. The closer they are to latent forces not of the mother's own, (we have left the mansion where the son reviled the mother's flesh; we have left the school where the son moralized in his mother's Institution her name on plaque; here the mother's relative is maid), and where the son perhaps owns his own mansion the forces try to ride by.

Mrs. Reed's male forces had direct contact with us: John Reed's search for us then assault, Mr. Reed's luminous seizure from above, Brocklehurst's column moralistic preaching at us. This male rider is not out of any Reed history, more of margin, he comes out of the twilight moving in another direction and he waves us to go on when we pause at his side.

Sometimes when they appear they do not want to know us. As with Helen and Miss Temple, we have to learn how to announce ourselves to the ones outside of Mrs. Reed. When they emerge from the dusk of what we think we lack, for which we long, when they seem to mark our fate, we have to work at getting their attention. We have looked him over, felt attracted, sym-pathesis, we hold our station when he waves us to go on.

We say we will not leave him in the solitary lane until he is fit to mount his horse. We have a stake in the bridling of the animal, that he has his animal beneath him, that his thighs monitor the muscled chest, hands check the rearing head, we have a stake that his body withstand that vibrant snort, pressing upon the sweat of the neck matted hair yet the hooves are metallic and the slash they could make on any human flesh could kill. We have a stake in his mounting the animal.

This gets his attention and for the first time he looks at us, asks our place, from where we have come.

    ◄§ Rochester. Angry eyes in the middle from pupils galloping
horses saliva's foam splashing alternate knees rising to head
pounding earth these animals charge me from your stern eyes
dark the brow as ireful as their nostrils flared and spitting for
I had been locking myself up for a long time first as curse
and then in its recovery finding voice and this hands design

yet your eyes my sign of stirrings in this open air are my
privilege rhythmic limbs of some underbrush along what
would be causeway a way out never dared before once I
thought only restless agitation my hands slipped from their
own work the stirring would come through what cracks still I
am uncertain and the air suddenly would smell differently.
Stinging cold air so fluids trickling becks now this fluid from
a nostril stung January air smelling of a frozen earth of solitary path. And I sat so still finally until that fierce horse
could break out of your eye. What, only human here limping
and a downed horse I will stay until fit mounting of that
steed for I had been locking myself up high up and you are
on the path out beyond twilight. . . . You have been drunk
throwing mud at our windows in the middle of the night
calling our name. You have run us out of the woods calling
us Bellissima, Bellissima. . . . You charge when we take a
step through what is dimly lit when we have been hidden
stilled but we were relieved to find your human form encasing that animal even as we were not sure what made us start
out on that causeway afterall. . . . One night I dreamt a tiger
mounted my leg then covered with its semen and I awoke to
tell you this dream that day we rose and walked one to each
side of your library's ladder peering between facing through
the rungs two inmates and you told me also I was born as
you year of the tiger would I come and join the others below
in your dining room. . . . Ten years earlier another dream
monstrous force trampling threatened tremendous force chas-
ing me past the statue of the reclining woman at the foot of
the stairs to mount chased past the room of the mother and
sisters they particularly the youngest were keening would not
have me go could not see that force animal and monstrous
force behind pushing me to the room at the end of the corridor, yours. ॐ

You find out our place, Thornfield governess, when we say to you that
we do not know, have never seen, Rochester, you look us over even more
scrutiny and you ask us to bring your horse to you. We tell you our post and
you ask us to get hold of the bridle of the horse, are we not afraid? You ask.

We are not ready for a Rochester exchange until we have a post.
Grounded, Thornfield with its battlements, fortified we have a post, we are
salaried, we have looked the place over and settled in, post. His relation is
to the animal and it comes from the horizon overpassing limit and we need

to be grounded in fortified post before we venture toward the horse when he asks it of us.

We have been alien to the one he asks us to approach, this animal has been alien to us as any Gytrash for twenty centuries and longer it has sounded as if from other worlds we have heard that these men have ridden this one to their wars. For they have sought to break in the wild horse for their own pleasure conquest weapon. Yet we have been placed gingerly side saddle bouncing leg touching leg never opening to flank motion never our nose to the mane this creature to us is alien we approach what may be bridle unlikely grasp now only rolled lips over yellow stinking teeth of a rearing head and we fear trampling forefeet.

Required to have nothing to do with it so we would not attempt now to negotiate this head of the horse if that man were not there. The steam from its flanks, rolling eyes as hoof stamped and then lifting, no, this an unfamil-iar 'spirited thing' we cannot take the bridle of Rochester's animal which is why he has fallen at our feet.

Some animal energy with a stern man who has been swearing is outside our region, on the margin. We see it spirited. When we approach it, it bolts. We are 'mortally afraid of its trampling fore-feet' and then the travel-ler thinks he is Mohammed.

We meet him when we are too fearful of an animal's rearing nature. We cannot approach this steed force. Our lack inflates this Rochester, for it is after we have located his human limit and he needs a compensation. ' "(A)id Mohamet to go to the mountain," ' he asks for our assistance but only through his understanding of himself as Prophet-Conqueror.

The side for the margin, this counterpart compensates for human sprain, limp, in a Prophet inflation; perhaps this one may be inspired but his announcement has more to do with the way on our shoulder now he must lean.

When he meets us on the causeway he thinks himself Great even Prophet and he falls to a sprained foot needing to lean on us to limp to his horse which he masters directly grimacing however in his spring to saddle. We meet him on our delivery interior to world when we cannot approach his horse yet he cannot get to it without us. Mutual Incapacity.

He is sprained and leans with stress. Our motion is what carries him, once it was horse but now our motion, the strides carrying him are ours, we are active in his vicinity. Touching him through his limp makes us the mover. We had asked for a new servitude to be service and serving this force stirs us to a place where the action is ours.

The letter is moving out on our own accord when we support the limp of the Prophet-Conqueror. The wound in the inflation occurs when unconscious moves out. We are not swept away in the process of posting the letter when we stay close to the limp.

He would not be limping if we had not gone through the Reed and Brocklehurst ordeals. For we have negotiated Reed thrust and Brocklehurst pillar until they were plucked, reduced, diminished. We have suffered our constriction lessons, negotiated our inflations of appetite of grandiosity of pomposity when he flashes by Secular Prophet of a single willful direction, some congealed earth ice fells him.

He had been charging forth too fast. A great charging beast erupts in our nature in our move out to world and does not note natural conditions, pushes inflated, thinks itself inspired beyond all human proportion, ambitious drive until it remembers ice. Once with limp, the spur no longer is as functional. The horse not so driven.

But we have met and somewhat negotiated the fury, it activates us and we serve his connection to his animal, something expands energized as we watch him mount trying to ignore the handicap quoting Prophet.

       ◄§ Mahomet. Muhammad. Mohammed. When Gabriel was whispering the Koran revealed into your ear you felt the weight of his wing upon your back thinking yourself poet or possessed and that the visiting spirit must be malign. Others confirmed for you the grace of the messenger supernatural you were a man visited by angels. What was it to have the human reception for angelic voice and move the doctrine out as man you were a man visited by angels remaining human decisive step your hijra from Mecca.

       Submitting you demanded submission: warfare you were on weaponed horse charging military expeditions with muslims are those-who-submit you would enforce you would command submission to your God through battle or the supervision of commando raids assassinating your more treacherous enemies. You were a man conquering Mecca, Hijaz, Khaybar, Fadak, Hunayn, Ta'if and at Badr the angels reinforced your 300 Muslims conquering the Meccan force. An entire land drops its pagan gods at your command for you are priest you are tyrant, our Islamic rituals revealed to you of washing, prayer, alms-giving, fasting, pilgrimage and/or stipulated by you as this Koran also our law of marriage, divorce, inheritance, homicide, theft, usury for you too our legislator.

       Treaties under your hand you will abandon portions of religious doctrine to ratify a treaty yet you are not foolhearty

your courage interpenetrates a patience, habitual prudence.
Apostle culmination of all Apostles would you have us say
Islam or Mohammedanism?

The ones examining you centuries later are arguing
whether religion or military conquest of most import to you
yet we know it was all the same the month you prescribe
fasting month as much military exercise as religious for you
desire your warriors accustomed to endure privation your
religion is to educate and discipline the community is central
to your doctrine where ideal lowers to the practical condition
none of that ascetic withdrawal from what they call world you
say instead "no monkery in Islam" where the embodied life of
men social activity is religion of the spirit and when the
Trumpet sounds you proclaim that heaven will split open,
mountains to dust, open graves and each guardian angel to
witness human deeds weighed in Balance some to ambrosia
Garden, blissful mansion Abode of Peace, others to the Fires
fed boiling water you proclaim Last Day will come Last
Judgment.

Your revelations come with fits we have seen you convulse
simple contorted human as we have heard through your own
vocal chord Allah beneficent despot magnificent. ❧

The one who bursts out of the margin of Thornfield associates himself
with whom transposed angelic voice to charging horse war weaponry, faith
through regiment battle carries humanly the angel's word. Angels yearning
for manifestation in the human, completing what Helen started where she
stopped in carrying them back, he breaks out.

At his request we seek and we find his whip, handing it to him.

He is off, we reel a bit. Something has struck now it is gone, vanished,
and what remains the words of a poet remembering a land once basked in
the favor of the heavens then deserted: ' "Like heath that in the wilderness/
The wild wind whirls away." '

❧ "Fallen is Thy Throne, oh Israel!/Silence is o'er thy
plains;/Thy dwellings all lie desolate,/Thy children weep in
chains./Where are the dews that fed thee/On Etham's barren
shore?/That fire from Heaven which led thee,/Now lights thy
path no more./Lord! thou didst love Jerusalem-/Once she

was all thy own;/Her love thy fairest heritage,[1]/Her power
thy glory's throne:[2]/Till evil came, and blighted/Thy long-
loved olive-tree;-[3]/And Salem's shrines were lighted/For other
Gods than Thee!/Then sunk the star of Solyma-/Then pass'd
her glory's day,/Like heath that, in the wilderness,[4]/The wild
wind whirls away./Silent and waste her bowers,/Where once
the mighty trod,/And sunk those guilty towers/While Baal
reign'd as God!. . ." Thomas Moore ❧

When the lessons become incarnate, questioning are these gods coming
through, revelation voice angelic or malign manifesting, unfamiliar and
masculine do we suspect Baal?

We are walking toward the town of Hay, we have been active, here an
incident it 'marked with change one single hour of a monotonous life.' His
face is before us masculine, stern, dark. We are walking and his face
accompanies and there are echoes, from the poet echoing here are more of
earlier verse, earlier prophet. We have been struck. Between us has been
the crash of a horse's stride, moonlight upon the baying dog, fervent plea to
assist, limp leaned upon lent, a mount, a whip. We reel a bit in the dust
galloped.

❧ " 'Let my eyes run down with tears night and day, and let
them not cease, for the virgin daughter of my people is smit-
ten with a great wound, with a very grievous blow.' " Jeremiah 14:17 ❧

He had been of the promising God as he is the abandoning God because
we are the daughter who has felt the action of incident some instinct spur-
red and as we return from posting the letter our ear opening ear to perhaps
again horse trampling at stile where is the Great Dog, no sound only
pollard willow 'rising up still and straight to meet the moonbeams.'

Our Lord. We had prayed for incident, feeling, we have desired action
and now it is past yet we hold his face before us, it is dissimilar to all others,
masculine of other, it accompanies us but we are at the Thornfield threshold now and we do not want to enter for we sense it stands for all else,
stagnation.

---

[1]Jeremiah 12:7.
[2]Jer. 14:21.
[3]Jer. 11:16.
[4]Jer. 17:6.

◄§ "Yet I planted you a choice vine, wholly of pure seed.
How then have you turned degenerate and become a wild
vine? Though you wash yourself with lye and use much soap,
the stain of your guilt is still before me, says the Lord God.
How can you say, 'I am not defiled, I have not gone after the
Ba'als?' " Jeremiah 2:21-23 ই◄

He has not emerged through the unconscious sadism or moralism of
Mrs. Reed yet blatantly he carried wrath in a stern even supercilious
manner. The forces of Reed and Brocklehurst were thrust upon us, this one
fell we approached insisting. We have gone far enough to the margins to
hear the mad laugh of a wider vision, crashing animal when the rider lost
sight of some ground, thrusting then limp.

Jane hesitates outside of Thornfield, pacing on the pavement.

◄§ "Look at your way in the valley; know what you have
done—a restive young camel interlacing her tracks, a wild ass
used to the wilderness, in her heat sniffing the wind!" Jeremiah 2:23-24 ই◄

John Reed was godless and the God which this man carries is more
savage than Brocklehurst's who though deathdealing on a Judgment Day
with Fire and Brimstone had a pristine disgust of body as animal, vile body
his ladies with the fur and plume of beast and bird.

Jane paces at the gates.

◄§ "Who can restrain her lust? None who seek her need
weary themselves; in her month they will find her. Keep your
feet from going unshod and your throat from thirst. But you
said, 'It is hopeless, for I have loved strangers, and after
them I will go.' " Jeremiah 2:24-25 ই◄

To pass through the hollow resounding gallery to our small room then
spend a long winter night of the regular topic conversed with the kind lady
of widow's cap, no, we do not want to cross that Thornfield threshold.

Difficult to hold this moment, the moon rising watches and knows, this
moon has witnessed it all, how does she hold the memory, the face was so
dark, what is the way of this moon looking so tranquil yet holding the secret
of the causeway moment when we were stepping out? Perhaps she knows
we are starstruck, veins aglow, and will they fade in the entry Thornfield
door to the simple single room? Can this moon hold all memory after we
leave her gazing beam returning here all chance stifled of erratic pulse?

We cannot condemn our stirring. We cannot condemn that we have had this exercise of a causeway moment and that we desire to continue. Any man would want it any man would want it. For we have sat too long, and as a man cramped and tired of sitting too long in a ' "too easy chair" ' we desire what stirs. We will not condemn ourselves for not wanting 'to slip again over (our) faculties the viewless fetters of an uniform and too still existence.'

> ◄§ Too easy chair and all becomes of dunce, nothing strikes, "art after art goes out, and all is night," and all still to every faculty diminished, dullness of each faculty, philosophy shrunk, metaphysic and mathematics now giddy to die, also religion expiring, "nor human spark is left, nor glimpse divine!/Lo! thy dread empire, Chaos! is restored;/Light dies before thy uncreating word:/Thy hand, great Anarch! lets the curtain fall;/And universal darkness buries all." Pope, *Dunciad*, iv, 640–656 §►

She hesitates outside. For has not "the moon-struck prophet felt the madding hour" (Pope, *Dunciad,* iv, 12) yet dullness and the obtuse night closes upon all now oblivion? And she senses this dangerous eternal gloom has transfixed the house as she paces before its gate not wanting entry.

The other side of the causeway incident, what it condemns as well as requires, dullness. Monotony and regular routine its surround, its catalyst, reagent. And within the rider's roughness is perhaps a dulling, he ignores his pain, pushes forward, insists on mounting his steed, he will ride on alone. Some dulling to pain is part of what stirs us to incident.

Jane looks up toward the rising moon as she lingers outside the Thorn-field door.

The sky is ours we know it, for he had stumbled across us and the impact entered us swelling our chest we look to the sky we are trembling from the engagement, our limbs quiver, we stop these quaking thighs and we look to that moon aspiring to zenith with its entourage stars we repeat the incident and we send it to those stars are tremulous for us we are the stars of that moon who knows we cannot rid ourselves of the man's face, man in the moon, our moon's man, ourself we are swelled to the moon is ourselves and as moon we are man in the moon Mahomet.

Something fills us, we begin expanding, rise, his chest full breadth of a chest, we expand to it yet 'little things recall us to earth.' Clock striking and we are at the door entering the Thornfield hall.

We had expected the gloom of the place to suffocate, extinguish, yet afterall the hall is not dark. Nor brightly lit, not the usual light of the hall's bronze lamp, instead a glow coming from a 'ruddy shine' of the dining room hearth. Before those doors shut to our passage we see a new room is lit up upon our reentry from the causeway. And from this room we hear voices, Adèle's and some unfamiliar tones.

The moon we want to be kept above in her course she sends us back down to some clock's ticking of an ordinary time. She recalls us to return vitality to terrestrial body not an evaporated or frenzied rise, not again Helen's sacrifice or typhus expulsion, yet home on this earth, we enter Thornfield through a side door and some radiance is there reflected off purple draperies and here some joyful sounding of voices including the child's.

We carry the animation into the old earthly residence and the previously shut-down purple dining room is lit up. We approached and engaged the causeway incident 'of incident, life, fire, feeling' and it is carried back and is already in the house when we re-enter.

Some energy source where there was none before in the inner chambers where we reside. Something deeply internal and bodily alters when we negotiate the incident on the lane when we have set out finally. She senses its presence through the ruddy atmosphere permeating the hall and the lower steps of the oak staircase.

If they are the next ones marking our fate, and if we have made the introduction properly, they will be there when we return home, we do not have to worry about losing them, they have a place in the house, perhaps they knew the place long before we did.

The dog looks like the Gytrash on the roadway, we recognize it, initiate a movement toward it calling the name, he responds to us through smelling a recognition back, he is smelling us and we are caressing this long-haired 'eerie creature' we have now approached without fear. What is Pilot responds to us now we are familiar with this pilot force in what are our old quarters.

We are able to be met on the causeway, force there a mimesis of imaged forces we have paced, we are able to be met on the causeway when the one who runs into us there is already of our house. He relates already to the third story forces, somewhere he owns the place himself.

We are called to the Thornfield psychic state, its residence, its galleries, its attic and groundfloor dimensions before we meet its figures, the ones corresponding to that aspect of the landscape housing us. It is his house and we were here all along. The psychic landscape of Jane and Rochester overlapped so they ran into one another on a causeway.

Bibliography

Bachelard, Gaston. *The Poetics of Space*. Trans. by Maria Jolas. Boston: Beacon Press, 1969; quoted p. 66.

Cook, Michael. *Muhammad*. Oxford: Oxford University Press, 1983.

Corbin, Henry. *Creative Imagination in the Sufism of Ibn 'Arabi*. Trans. by Ralph Manheim. Princeton, N.J.: Princeton University Press, 1969.

_____. *Avicenna and the Visionary Recital*. Trans. by Willard R. Trask. Dallas: Spring Publications, 1980.

Eliade, Mircea. *Shamanism*. Trans. by Willard R. Trask. Princeton, N.J.: Princeton University Press, 1964.

Gibb, H. A. R. *Mohammedanism*. Oxford: Oxford University Press, 1970.

H. D. *HERmione*. New York: New Directions Books, 1981; quoted p. 85.

Holy Bible. Revised Standard Version.

Jung, C. G. *The Visions Seminars*. Book 2. Zurich: Spring Publications, 1976.

"Mohammed." In James Hastings, ed., *Encyclopedia of Religion and Ethics*. Vol. 8. New York: Charles Scribner's Sons, 1916.

Moore, Sir Thomas. *The Works of Thomas Moore, Esq*. Leipsic: Ernst Fleischer, 1826.

Plath, Sylvia. *The Journals of Sylvia Plath*. New York: Ballantine Books, 1982; quoted p. 133–134.

Pope, Alexander. *The Poetry of Pope*. M. H. Abrams, ed. New York: Appleton-Century-Crofts, 1954; quoted pp. 101, 117.

Chapter 13

Men in Green

Agent and tenants waiting to speak to him when he rises not very early the next morning, already the child and I have moved our classroom to an apartment upstairs now the library below is a reception for callers and there are many, door knocking bell clanging steps and voices of new keys. Adèle finds it difficult to sit still wants to run to that one below is chattering now about him and his gift for her he intimated. Finally alone stare into embers castle of Heidelberg ember yet also reverie 'some heavy, unwelcome thoughts that were beginning to throng on my solitude.' Mrs. Fairfax delivering his summon to tea in a drawing room better dress says she I must put on the black silk and that I want a brooch she watches me place on Miss Temple's parting keepsake pearl ornament and we descend and pass through the arch to the 'elegant recess beyond' I keep in her shade.

Adèle and Pilot at the fire he is reclining upon a couch looking at them the fire full on his face I know my traveller that jetty eyebrow square forehead full nostrilled decisive nose of a choler, grim chin and mouth, saying let Miss Eyre be seated he stares at the fire impatient formal just as well for I could not reply to elegant discourse polite. 'Besides, the eccentricity of the proceeding was piquant: I felt interested to see how he would go on.' Statue still. Mrs. Fairfax chatters, kindly, condoling, commending and he brushes her away for tea.

Is there not a gift for Mademoiselle Eyre the child cries to his eyes become dark irate piercing did I expect gift am I fond of presents? To my general response on their pleasant quality he asks specifically what do I think? A present has many faces I would want to consider it, he is right when he proclaims I beat around the bush as Adèle is clamorous and direct I am over-modest for the child he says though not bright of no talent has done well. This I say is my gift. He stopped short takes his tea in silence until the tray is cleared and his command come to the fire.

Questions from where have I come: eight years at Lowood. ' "Eight years! you must be tenacious of life. I thought half the time in such a place would have done up any constitution! No wonder you have rather the look of another world. I marvelled where you had got that sort of face." ' He thought of fairy tales when I had come upon him on the lane and almost demanded had I bewitched his horse and asks now who are my parents? No memory of such so he surmises perhaps I was waiting for my little people in green while sitting on stile and he broke through one of my rings so I spread the causeway ice. No I reply the little men in green left ago hundred years no trace no moon summer harvest winter ever on their revels more. Mrs. Fairfax knitting dropped brow raised.

And to his further questioning on family no uncles or aunts brothers or sisters and to get here I advertised. Mrs. Fairfax chirps to my character he silences he will judge for I began by felling his horse. Life of a nun little society and when he asks my view of Brocklehurst he suspects some worship: 'convent full of religieuses would worship their director.' No, harsh, pompous, meddling, economy stripping hair, bad needles, starvèd and bored us and evening readings about sudden deaths and judgments we could not sleep afterwards. Well what did I learn there can I play and I perform that exercise he says enough I play a little but what of the sketches Adèle has shown him were they mine or did a master help. At my negative exclamation he says he pricked pride well fetch the portfolio. He scrutinizes. They have taken much time and thought where did I get the copies to which I reply out of my head he wonders the head he sees now on my shoulders and has it other furniture of the same kind within.

He surveys the pictures again alternately. To me they are only a faint representation of the vivid subjects seen by the spiritual eye, these pictures were three and in water color: (1) Cormorant upon mast half-submerged in swollen sea, bracelet in his beak and sinking below bird and mast a drowned corpse only fair arm visible from which the bracelet had been washed or torn. (2) Foreground a hill with grass and beyond and above rising to the dark-blue twilight a woman's bust with forehead starred, 'the eyes shone dark and wild; the hair streamed shadowy, like a beamless cloud torn by storm or by electric travail'; on the neck reflected pale moonlight reflected also upon the thin clouds from which rises this vision of the Evening Star. (3) Thin hands drawing up veil on head bending toward a peak iceberg resting against it, the sky polar winter, and the eye of the head is fixed hollow despair bloodless brow, folds of black drapery and above this head ring of white flame ' "The likeness of a Kingly Crown;" what it diademed was "the shape which shape had none." '

Was I happy when I did these pictures he asks, keenest pleasure I reply that I have ever known to do so, sat at them morning to night in the vacation and yet when he inquires did I feel self-satisfied on these labors, far from it, in each case the imagination far from what I could realize. Not quite, he says the shadow of my thought secured, ' "the drawings are, for a school girl, peculiar. As to the thoughts, they are elfish." ' How could I have known the eyes of Evening Star yet in a dream, making them so clear yet their brilliance the moon quells and what solemn depth what do I mean by it and who taught me to paint wind the gale of this hilltop must be Latmos where did I see Latmos put these drawings away. 9:00 what am I about keeping Adèle up so late. Movement of hand to door goodnight.

To Mrs. Fairfax I say she had said he was not strikingly peculiar, yet he is, changeful and abrupt. She says allowance, painful thoughts family troubles: lost elder brother nine years only that long in possession of the property. I wonder on such fondness for the brother yet learn then that it was more misunderstanding. Elder Rowland was not just to the younger brother, perhaps prejudiced father against the latter: the old gentleman fond of money devised a way to keep younger son with money without dividing up the property and the steps taken were not quite fair to that younger son who had just come of age. Not forgiving he broke with his family and for many years an unsettled life, shuns this old place. The answers now evasive she implies Mr. Rochester's trials are mystery to even herself so drop the subject.

'I discerned in the course of the morning that Thornfield Hall was a changed place . . . a rill from the outer world was flowing through it; it had a master: for my part, I liked it better.'

Rochester met in letter delivery to world, on the lane, and he returned into our place now his. When the Rochester energy comes riding through and we renew inquiry which is our vocation, interlocute with what emerges from unknown margins, our living space is no longer silent as a church, we have room inside for what arrives from the outside. Callers. Tenants. Affairs of business.

He thought himself Mohammed. Somewhere that which was constricted for protection now inflates, sounds off, bells, footsteps, voices of other keys. Business arrangements and tenants where only there was the whispered tutoring of a single pupil.

Secure the Hall with its master we like it better. Close to the force of who thinks himself Mohammed, we have seen and dialogued with this one and now there is noise and a peopled place in what was church solemn. Meeting Rochester, knowing we live under his roof. To meet Rochester is to know we live under his roof and are subject to unfamiliar tones, events.

Our move out to world is to let back in outer without going under. To meet Rochester is to be immediately moved in on but it is also to like that better. After the Lowood fortification exercises, we are not invaded. We rise one floor above the current groundfloor activity. Our Lowood solitude has become our desire for the bustle below as it keeps us above it.

The child with us wants to go down, bounce downstairs, we keep her up and she serves as mediatrix to Rochester; she tells us his full name, that he had inquired about us, our name, if we are not petite, pale.

Child Adèle whose excitement is frivolous when her ' "ami, Monsieur Edouard Fairfax *de* Rochester" ' has returned, is who wants to spring out to him chattering. Through the child's passion we see a master returned. We want our gift, we want to be given a surprise immediately from the master returned we want him to gift us this Adèle.

For he had ridden out of our third story desire for world to receive, embody the tale of imagination. Now his housekeeper is telling us the way he wants us to descend, carry down our stare into the fire's images, is through ceremony. We dress up. There is the black silk dress with Miss Temple's brooch at tea at 6:00.

Thornfield Hall echoed a church yet we only felt profane routine there we rose to prayer fraught we were becoming absent of spirit until we lowered to his force upon the lane mere human we thought possibly once animal-spirit now human even cursing prophet and the Hall when we return is no longer church but we descend ritual silk black through the arch the candles on mantlepiece showering this drawing room glow full-hearthed fire of child and dog foreground some sacred space speaking ritual descent.

For we have been upstairs too long, our images not incarnate, too high, become 'heavy, unwelcome thoughts,' our solitude had begun brewing unwelcome thoughts we felt it staring at the embers alone before she entered to invite us to the tea, ceremony. Unwelcome and heavy ember thoughts lend toward what is to become his ritual.

Split floors. We have enjoyed the break, how the bell rings apart from any schedule, footsteps of various timings and pressures, homogeneous routine cracked and what used to be a classroom is now reception for callers, and we split, we try to resume a private schedule in an upstairs apartment. After meeting Rochester, our private images are second floor, one story lower to ground floor than they were before.

Yet the way we have still split from the floor below is this way our stare to embers heavy unwelcome thoughts until we hear this man has a ceremony to lower them further.

Rochester brings quickened and erratic pace of a worldly life, above which we rise only throng on solitude heavy thoughts, yet our black dress, the exact tea time, Miss Temple's brooch joins the split floor sides. A quickened profane activity has broken through the old church allowing new ceremony.

At Thornfield, angels are on the ancestral furniture, the Gytrash is a limping man, and ceremony is formal human decorum; spirit incarnate, world receives not split from spirit.

Images not embodied are heavy thoughts throng solitude until we carry them down is desire for ceremony. The way these split floor sides meet, intricate, is through the ritual of a tea time. We are unfamiliar with this descent: feel the 'additional ceremony . . . somewhat stately'; we are unused to strangers and descending is strange makes us stranger.

We place on the pearl ornament gift 'parting keepsake' from Miss Temple. The way we have kept her through parting, the way we know our gift parting from her which is to keep gifted. We place on the pearl brooch and follow closely behind Mrs. Fairfax's shade through the drawing room arch.

Pearl. Nacreous concretion around foreign body. Filmy layers of carbonate of lime interstratified with animal membranes. Precious globular lustrous covering of a smooth texture surrounding foreign body. Reed and Brocklehurst foreign body we learned to place in her intimate chambers becoming precious gift and it is part of what ritual crosses us over the profane interruption of his stranger body.

In her intimate chambers not engulfed we heard chorals of dead souls becoming our word, soul on lips our craft, delineate those currents. At Thornfield pacing third story imagination tale mad murmur currents we have desired to move the letter out and this desire the causeway crash to how we now descend from high story and the request of the causeway stranger to lower the gift, carry it down.

Left alone staring into the fire earlier, images castle of Heidelberg in the embers along with heavy thoughts our earlier desire had been descend out, world embodied intercourse with world. Rochester is to whom we lower this desire we are walking by his summon into what has been chamber of desire, red-room, crimson couch drawing room, recess of what still is red, 'elegant recess beyond.'

The way out, when pacing third story desire, the way out is to proceed down and in, descend entering recess to whom summons from the red-room, entering recess, return to red-room, at Thornfield after Lowood, is the way out.

He is who sits in the red-room of Thornfield and calls us down to it now we know our entry is to be behind Fairfax cover and Temple brooch. We know our traveller. Grim choler is to what we descend, in his mouth chin jaw nose eyebrow even forehead we see the choler.

Choler brings us down when our images have become unwelcome thoughts, convoluted, too long split higher stories, we descend when the choleric figure sits in the red-room calling us down through ceremony.

Choler is what to expect when we finally carry down the stare of images.

Fully shining on his face fire as we enter. Wrath of a John Reed sort yet neither unharnassed nor concupiscent. Here also a severity of critical detachment: harsh as Brocklehurst yet not minimizing, instead he draws us out. Reed and Brocklehurst flicker through this man's 'harsh caprice,' he is someone including them as he is someone other.

To descend from the imaged forces of our private tutoring we need a ceremony of choler; we are called down by bitterness and irritation which is a critical detachment residing within what is the crimson recess.

Choler within a critical grim stare, in the 'forced stiff bow, in the impatient, yet formal tone,' choler within a critical grim stare we first face and Mrs. Fairfax chatters, consoles, compliments. Mrs. Fairfax is the immediate attempt to avoid his choler through compliment once we have descended to it.

Choler even harnassed rage when we stepped out on the causeway it came up, crashed, forerunner of this ceremony requiring descent to redroom desires less privacy yet brooch armored to face choler even rage harnessed foreign body.

He is not related. Impatient formal tone he does not want to relate to us at the moment and he will not be taken in or flattered by the Fairfax chatter. We prefer this harsh caprice to finished politeness, it is more sympathetic with qualities desiring manifestation for we have been too homogeneous, domesticated preserving needlework, only frenzied rise, pot of porter even there staid appearance, when we have been too homogeneous we have not known what manifest of latent contents our desire his choler releases.

We find his eccentricity piquant.

> ◆§ Eccentric not on center deviated axis of no central position or this point around which we are revolving is not equidistant or that conical pin no longer holds what revolves in position the bull's eye is no longer ringed he asked did we spread our rings out on that damn causeway but there is no circling for we do not pivot. Centric defining circle but what of these other circles within or around this one each of their own center therefore no center off-center multicentered or perhaps no circling at all only we hypothesize plane or are we not at all related to him at any point. Puncture, dot, prick, pointed prick a pressure most intense contact incites immediate distancing, we reflex. Something stings within and he pricks us moving off center no longer equidistant however quite distant. He has been stung or bitten and we pick it up as he moves off center pricking us. Prica. Spur to that heaving chest the horse galloped away and now we feel it yet sensation for we are not related our circles encircling different centers perhaps never will engage not the point. ੪◆

Rochester who came up when we were moving out calls us down. In order to move out we first need to go down and into a red-room, not leave it there Gateshead encrusted, but return down. There is some anger and bitterness here.

Rochester calls us down. Rochester calls us down through a piquant eccentricity and we either console (forgive/negate) the sting in the Fairfax manner or ask from it a gift as Adèle. Both ways evade the prick. Once it gifts us, if we have longed for his prick to complete, to bestow, to ravish not engage as hers through what passages we have located it, we lose gift. But when we wear pearl, this manifestation of how we have found gift in chambers before we ran into he who had to do with moving out, he does not gift cannot instead he is stung stinging out eyes irate piercing say did we expect a gift.

The one who summons us down, after our Lowood stare has congealed to unwelcome thought, does not want to give out anything. He does not want to hand our gift to us. We lower private images to a more public world through who will not impart implant gift.

In the face of Rochester we are at first over-modest and we generalize, avoid this issue of gifts when he has asked are we fond of them. ' "But what do *you* think?" ' he is who asks directly desiring we walk down and out the front door, responsible step.

We were asked to speak for ourselves once he was an apothecary tender and shrewd eyes mirroring to our desire a school where we learned among women sheltered many languages differentiating quality until old forces stirred image force desire descent into this red drawing room first story eyes are now irate asking a less sheltered more access worldly footsteps ringing can we speak.

Less sheltered though we wear the brooch. We can cringe or console or ask for our gift from him or else we can speak directly to him from what already is our present.

He had been saying not to be over-modest for Adèle of little talent has improved and when he is not expecting it we prick back. We say: ' "Sir, you have now given me my 'cadeau;' I am obliged to you: it is the meed teachers most covet; praise of their pupils' progress." ' We make his gift praise of our gift without eradicating the letter of the latter. It spurs him a turn of things stimulates him. We lower to prick to prick back. Inverted prick back the Rochester force does not have to speak as we lower our gift to larger world. Speechless, he takes his tea in silence.

Lowood taught us the figurative understanding and ours of "cadeau" stops him here. Lowood's education of language, speaking desire through image and figure, is our prick, our pin prick, our brooch, woman not with phallus yet we have a prick, received expression through Lowood, our figurative sense of gift is our gift, we need not his prick, literally. Our use of our prick makes him recessive, receptive.

Rochester does not come to gift. He arrives after we have located gift ready for delivery, as part of that labor. The dialogue would not ensue, he would not invite us closer to fire, if we were at the place of desiring from him the gift, which would maintain it an exterior affair pertaining only to a need for approbation, only to our person's need to be defined and approved exterior.

Adèle off our knee play with Pilot, this move closer to the fire is when we have shown we can brush off the Adèle cover which desires gift bestowed from him, and that invites us closer. If we descend already with gift we can take more heat.

The Rochester maneuver is to invite us closer and turn up the heat when we prick him back. We have shown ourselves worthy of the dialogue when we have matched our prick with his. In the Thornfield red-room, prick implicating distance ultimately increases intimacy through language. The way we have pricked, defense of our gift, indicates the history of our fortification and that we do not require his present and he knows we have been trained asking where.

Our Lowood training is relevant to him for he has seen our face from another world. He implies he recognizes us from another world yet is himself of this one. Mr. Lloyd saw double worlds simultaneously yet summoned us back to the natural. Rochester is for whom we serve entry to another world, world of fairy tale, of bewitchment. We are not there to draw him out, it is his drawing room, we are who invite or turn him to another world as he summons us down and through which is a move out to this world.

When we answer this question the length of the Lowood stay eight years his exclamation: ' "Eight years! you must be tenacious of life. I thought half the time in such a place would have done up any constitution!" ' Rochester is who recognizes Lowood yet he is for whom Lowood is another world. The Rochester perspective sees Lowood as another world yet suggests he knows it enough to recognize it on the face of things.

The Rochester who summons us down from another world is who recognizes the potency of that otherworld, is not dismissive of where we have spent the last eight years. The way he understands the powers of our convent life is how he calls us witch suggests perhaps we have bewitched his horse. He is the one to whom we are explicitly witch since he registers our ability to traverse thresholds which crashed his driven will power at the twilight stile.

We carry down Lowood to a red-room for whom we are witch. Rochester sees us witch as he has an investment in locating us in this world, who are our parents, he asks of our family. We deny any relative. He is the continuation, emerges out of the Lowood orphanhood, the place where what is family has been shattered.

The only way we can reenter the recess of a red-room is not to know her. We deny any relation to who in madness would push us back in as we now are traversing it to speak with him who carried in outer and we do not again ever again want to go under so we say no relation. But as we have to return to crimson recess beyond to meet who we ran into when out we have to return to her and he brings it up.

He is outside the place where we are parented, does not come through a parent, is not related to Mrs. Reed. Marvelling at our face. Even as he tries to implant us within some family system, he knows the validity, potency, of the otherworld forces to which we have risen giving us this face, admitting they felled his horse.

Another world the face speaks it. Lineament our conscience, these ways we have traversed gradation demon to angel our eye underlines laughing lines delineates and the nose its alignment signs the ways the mouth its ironic twist we have been outside, another world to what is his society.

We generate fairy tales for him, bewitchment of his horse as we carried him another world rings of our fairies the green men revelry. No parents and the break in what would be traditional structure in rush the green men.

Reciprocity at Thornfield for we had Lowood graduated to it. We carry him to rings otherworlds as he lowers us to this one which is the intercourse in the red-room the way each of us desires return. Rochester does not leave us alone another world. For we had recognized the human through preternatural spirit; grounded he speaks from the green men place as he marvels our face.

Well trained in another world for the ruptures have lent us uncanny forces. Gateshead windowseat redroom nursery gray field to Lowood trainings we were tenacious to desires force imaged gift of imagination now awaits delivery, and this one may be some sort of instrument he broke through twilight reverie but only if he sees through the way we carry another world and yes perhaps they are in green.

As it lowers what was Lowood angel now more gypsy-witch and her rings, little green men. He came out of twilight on creatures, lower spirits. We reply on the little green men as seriously as he had spoken of them. We bring him up sublime figuration as he brings us down incarnate. We bring him up as he brings us down and as with Helen the exchange is erotic.

Giving those green ones their due. When we share imaginal forces with another in exchange the exchange stimulates is closer to the fire occurring below the Fairfax level.

That woman has dropped her knitting sits wondering with raised eyebrow does not know this way we exchange until he asks how we arrived here we mention advertisement and she chirps in for our character but he does not take it returning instead to the felled bewitched horse beneath the woman's raised brow afterall.

We say England has lost its little green men for a hundred years, that is the state of things. Acknowledging that the forces of another world have lost their place in this world, we have entered a pact we are telling him that we know the green people of which he speaks us in relation indicating so we do come indeed from another world but that we have lost all worldly sense of them.

    ◄§ The men in green. Not primary in ancient world except for Democritus listing chlōron, the primaries are white, black, red. For Homer for Plato primary is "bright." Primary for Aristotle black and white whereas leek-green one of five intermediaries resulting from mixtures of white and black.

    Green named and spectrum placed Newton's eye spots it 520 wavelength (nm) in a 1660 prism view and color becomes hue saturation brightness.

    The 19th c. Young then Helmholtz eye sees green primary, red green violet, as Hering later sees pairs: red-green, yellow-blue, white-black, opposing pairs, complementary colors, white-black for rods the others of what is cone where green complements red. The ancient world had spoken of it the green of Venus pairing red of Mars of the complementary union of these two.

    A 20th c. eye, color not of hue or complement yet Land's dual camera of red and green filters sees ratio of luminance, interplay of the longer and shorter wavelengths over the entire visual field becoming our coloring not retinal cone nor prism spectrum nor Goethe's subjective yet brightness ratio where are the gods they remain on a three-dimensional color spectrum of modern physics diagramming excitations of three retinal color systems, B axis of green (pagan sees Venus) across from red A axis (Mars) and rising above here is blue/violet C axis (Jove) while below runs the dotted line some say white some black (Saturn). Green pushes on primary. In the blackest context first seen green since rod pigment in dark adapted state best catches quanta at 510 nm, green seen best at night though the color itself not registered.

    Green pushes through our dark rod state. Color of venus she opposes as complement red the mars men are red the men know their red and venus of flesh and tenderness we have said vegetation, we have called her leek from the root of luxuriance, she bends, she is pungent yet less abrasive than what is scallion or onion, suggesting broad the succulent leaves, cylindrical bulb base of leek-green we have said vegetation: *Color Symbolism*, "We should bear in mind that blossoming flowers, too, often appear green until they break down the green pigment and thus free the red, blue, and yellow pigments from their green components . . . Likewise, many fruits are green at first: only on ripening does the leaf-green colour fade and the brilliant red and yellow come into their own."

The rainbow moves up our body vertically green a heart chakra. Venus herself speaking through Ficino he is telling us to gather from her gardens laughter: "After Venus gives us this oracle for our contemplation, she sends nature, with its green things, to bloom everywhere, not just to make us alive, but younger, giving us our healthy humor back, and making us overflow with a lively spirit . . . Thus water delights us, and we take pleasure in mirrors, and enjoy everything green. In green things the light of the Sun located there has the humor of Spring and a subtle water filled with a certain hidden light. Therefore, the color green, when it is thinned, is broken down into a saffron or crocus color."

Paradise Lost. I. 781–88. "Faery Elves,/Whose midnight Revels, by a Forest side/Or Fountain some belated Peasant sees,/Or dreams he sees, while over-head the Moon/Sits Arbitress, and nearer to the Earth/Wheels her pale course; they on thir mirth and dance/Intent, with jocund Music charm his ear;/At once with joy and fear his heart rebounds."

Green. Once perhaps they wore felt layers broad and succulent feeling they bent to nature's draw the men were green, men to have a heart pushing through the darkest rod context, men to have a heart, green awakens that lotus of a heart wake up, it shakes giggling (we say something uplifts, we say something lightens us). But now for a hundred years their heart a literal red all resonance of green lost complement. Green no longer pushing through the midnight rings. They have stripped all felt. Stripped all felt that was sprite no longer giggling as venus tickles within nature's tree bark revel. War a sturdier front. The Horse is bridled, the dog named Pilot, alert, ready, straited. These men are not green. The men are red, rust. These men are rust. These men are not green. ﷼

Where we recall for him the green men, we are in the red-room to which he calls us recalls woman's recess and the men we carry to him are green, complements switch gender is where the man and woman color complement.

Before the exchange on the green men, he was not sure whether Jane bewitched his horse. After it, he announces to Mrs. Fairfax that Jane began by felling his horse, the sprain her fault. Jane's accessibility to uncanny realms potentiates her in a Rochester view. Witch crossing between the worlds, carry unconscious to conscious and back. She has halted the place he charged erect resulting in limp, bewitching gypsy-witch who knows of green men even of their absence, power to lower his thrusting animal.

He then inquires of Brocklehurst suspecting a father adoration.

Perhaps not witch yet possessed nun collected around her Minister. Not that we have our prick through access to uncanny realms yet we use a Master's force. He can only understand our residence in another world if there is a Master. Rochester is that instance of bringing image to world, and the potency that he sees the imaginal otherworlds hold for this world he attributes to a Brocklehurst ministerial. Are we merely in a novice worship.

He does not recognize our brooch. We have had Instructress allowing rise third eye vision now needing advertisement desiring out, our image not from that of a master, not copies, out of two vacations and seen by a 'spiritual eye.'

Uncanny worlds, our images lower to the drawing room, room of crimson we had desired paced above power of vision exceeding horizon is desire to lower the drawing to room of crimson room of his desire to scrutinize this manifestation of our images we present to who is Rochester. He attaches to what of our imagination.

Cormorant webbed toe bird of sea, voracious of a pouched beak storing food hoards, beaked bracelet glutton, bird of greed, bird of air accessible height spirits flight this bird knows the heights yet his feet are webbed, where there was air now ocean coils. This way previously we have known the lower world, the material primary consumption, within the Reed gluttony, the woman was drowning, unconscious.

Satan speaks. *Paradise Lost*, IV, 73: "Me miserable! Which way shall I fly/Infinite wrath, and infinite despair?/Which way I fly is Hell; myself am Hell;/And in the lowest deep a lower deep/Still threat'ning to devour me opens wide,/To which the Hell I suffer seems a Heav'n." IV, 192: "So clomb this first grand Thief into God's Fold:/So since into his Church lewd Hirelings climb./Thence up he flew, and on the Tree of Life,/The middle Tree and highest there that grew,/Sat like a Cormorant; yet not true Life/Thereby regain'd, but sat devising Death/To them who liv'd."

On the Tree of Life Satan as Cormorant overlooking the First Couple love's bliss, the woman was unconscious. Eve speaking to Adam, IV, 440: "To whom thus *Eve* repli'd. O thou for whom/And from whom I was form'd flesh of thy flesh,/And without whom am to no end, my Guide/And Head, what thou hast said is just and right." IV, 634: "To whom thus *Eve* with perfect beauty adorn'd./My Author and Disposer, what thou bidd'st/ Unargu'd I obey; so God ordains,/God is thy Law, thou mine: to know no more/Is woman's happiest knowledge and her praise."

Fusion love's bliss a hell of greed to have a Master. Master Reed. Her memory of such hell its images Rochester sees.

Woman drowning possessed by ocean's current within the scope of some greed when a demon has entered outside of Father's Law.

Until we can know her sublime. Or perhaps her exalted place, it has been revealed, we were at the house of women and we have been of subliming operation have watched the sodden corpse cremated the passionate ideas rose she was cremated and rose, aloft, inspiring, of corpse purified, we have called her the second Eve, we have called her Maria, we have known her Maria Temple of the moonlight this moon once monitoring those oceans waves wretching dismembering slamming and silencing ocean now shining full on her sublime.

Woman of the Sky Crowned with Star. Sacrality through her, we were brought closer to her hearth and the scintillation trembled us, wild eyes hair electrified Evening Star not placcid yet fervid forces, we venerated there the Venus was ardent, electric vision of the Evening Star. Forehead crowned with a star and on the neck pale reflection like moonlight. IV, 604: "Silence was pleas'd: now glow'd the Firmament/With living Sapphires: *Hesperus* that led/The starry Host, rode brightest, till the Moon/Rising in clouded Majesty, at length/Apparent Queen unveil'd her peerless light,/And o'er the dark her Silver Mantle threw."

Looking at her he sees the angel the one whispering conscience, some trace of how we were brought into her chambers and with what we emerged.

Third picture of iceberg pinnacle piercing polar sky, head against resting upon iceberg, thin hands support forehead draw veil, hollow eye fixed not a meaning alone despair's glass. Above temple amidst turban black drapery folds here pale white flame, ' "The likeness of a Kingly Crown" ' for this ' "shape which shape had none." '

II, 648-652: Before the Gates to leave the Hell two shapes. One a woman terminating in scales venomous snake, around her waist Hell Hounds yelping still barking unseen when crawling back into her womb. II, 662: "Nor uglier follow the Night-Hag, when call'd/In secret, riding through the Air she comes/Lur'd with the smell of infant blood to dance/ With *Lapland* Witches, while the laboring Moon/Eclipses at thir charms. The other shape,/If shape it might be call'd that shape had none/ Distinguishable in member, joint, or limb,/Or substance might be call'd that shadow seem'd,/For each seem'd either; black it stood as Night, Fierce as ten Furies, terrible as Hell,/And shook a dreadful Dart; what seem'd his head/The likeness of a Kingly Crown had on."

Satan while plotting conspiracy against Heaven's King became pained head from which sprung the daughter Sin, incest Father to Daughter begetting Death shapeless shape pursuing mother overtook his mother "And in embraces forcible and foul/Ingend'ring with me, of that rape begot/These yelling Monsters that with ceaseless cry/Surround me, as thou saw'st, hourly conceiv'd/And hourly born, with sorrow infinite/To me, for when they list into the womb/That bred them they return, and howl and gnaw/My Bowels, thir repast; then bursting forth/Afresh with conscious terrors vex me round,/That rest or intermission none I find" [II, 793–802].

There has been incest trying to leave hell we have faced it, remembered. The witch he causeway met had no master but these images show it, we know Death, the son of that incest himself incestually begetting what not even Hecate uglier. The witches' queen, the Night-Hag we had sensed in his attic, predicted even guided over the Father's Fall, King's lowering to caldron, Father into Daughter begetting Death.

That witch we sensed in his attic he sensed through us on a causeway, between us death and sin and incest memory, some witch without master has visions when the one who has plotted the Fall of Father is no longer only above, has offspring passed through the hell and death of the Fall of the Father into chaos unconscious (Fall from the Father) Father's Fall where our witches meet, here a hell hounds yelling woman.

What we reflect back to Rochester is that the one who left the Father's Rule, venging, is incestuous with daughter bearing Death.

Tormented by the contrast between image and craft is what we tell him. ' "(I)n each case I had imagined something which I was quite powerless to realize." '

Not quite. His response is that we have manifested interior to exterior, we are moving inside out. The drawings are peculiar, the thoughts elfish. Who we meet beneath yet in full view of the Mrs. Fairfax cover in our delivery to world is peculiar, and he finds us peculiar. We meet at the peculiar hermaphrodite, we bring him into witch, he moves witch out no longer drawing from attic.

Eyes of Evening Star attach him he gages their gaze extraordinary, out of ordinary their clear not brilliant solemn depth and this way the wind is painted and the hill-top must be Latmos. Patmos. The way to which we have been revealed.

The way to which we have been revealed irritates him. The configuration of images is placed in Rochester's drawing room we are showing him the configurations of where we have been in otherworlds, configurations of unconscious, differentiation within recess. The one to whom we show the figures differentiating recess is hermaphrodite, complements.

After he had asked of her relations, it is relative, they are no longer Gateshead literal yet through the imagination, her relations are these drawings from otherworlds to this one drawing room ground floor finally. Imagination holds the memory manifesting is her Reed relatives Lowood designed including what she must bring down from his attic their recess exchange met causeway in the crimson Thornfield drawing room.

The configuration of images is placed in Rochester's drawing room yet the way he wants guidance to image, horse fallen by those of another world, irritates him. He focuses on the second drawing, those eyes the vision of Evening Star have guided us, paced to star window gaze and voice of pillow advertisement. He has recognized hell and death but he did not know any guidance.

He went through death without her guidance and that is his peculiarity. He dismisses us irritated when he will not be guided through his Death yet his irritation is also that through which our vision lowered.

The first male figure who walks around our imaginal landscape, hermaphodite, is to whom we realize our gift, manifestation of differentiated recess. He is irritated by this look into some sacred solemn depth where there has been no Master, and the Lowood way we have been able to signify what otherwise tormenting otherworld excursion, hell. His irritation in the realization of our gift, irritation is where what we have as gift begins to realize itself.

Before he saw the pictures his assumption they were done through a Master pricked pride, he pricked Jane (back) yet the paintings themselves, the way they were revealed and not from a master and not copies, pricked him (back) to an irritation and silence, until he wanted to dismiss her. Her prick matching his, pushing his further, is in the way to which she has been revealed.

It is the dream-revealed nature of our imaginal eye which stops him, pronounces his limit. ' "And what meaning is that in their solemn depth?" ' Solemn depth limitation his own and he is irritated. He does not want us to carry him to those other realms as he demands it, he claims us gifted as commanding us to put to sleep Adèle who wants gift. The one who desires gift from another is not necessary in the room anymore, even must be carried out.

Later Mrs. Fairfax responds when we name him peculiar. We hear he has broken from Father yet still bond in bitterness. He has been the Son Not Chosen. Father and the favored elder brother, Chosen Son, took steps to obtain wealth for the younger son, which were ' "not quite fair . . . Old

Mr. Rochester and Mr. Rowland combined to bring Mr. Edward into what he considered a painful position, for the sake of making his fortune." '

He has been the Second Son excluded, pained, broken from Father yet bitter, burned, salty, pissed: ' "his spirit could not brook what he had to suffer in it." ' Rochester is not forgiving and he broke with his family to an unsettled life.

Bitter. IX, 171: "Revenge, at first though sweet,/Bitter ere long back on itself recoils;/Let it; I reck not, so it light well aim'd,/Since higher I fall short, on him who next/Provokes my envy, this new Favorite/of Heav'n, this Man of Clay, Son of despite,/Whom us the more to spite his Maker rais'd/From dust: spite then with spite is best repaid."

Paradise Lost. When Not Chosen Only Son he broke from Heavenly Father and descended. This Father lowered who was not favored son to where chaos reigned. Some couple lives in love fusion wants to wake up. This man lies outside the Father's Law of coupled bliss, woman mirroring man, and when we meet him there is no master and he mentions the green complement. Father betrayed we met on the causeway having maneuvered some chaos. Father could not protect us even lowered us into her hell hound fury chaos. To return to the red-room is to realize we have gift another world configured where he is not has not yet that his irritation is piquant and calls us down we carry down brooch's prick, we have other instruments for delivery desired images must descend through choler.

Father lowered who was not favored son meets whom the Father lowered into. Father's betrayal no Father above, on the causeway they recognize through one another's possessions witch he will call us down and in which is out if we will provide the forms, shapes, delineate the meanings which is the gift. Our gift he turns away from, he will defend from the revelation of images of dream will not rise to where he hears her laughter preternatural cackle yet perhaps through the drawings crimson drawing room laced with a green possibility he sees we have brought her down anyway we will meet her even have known her all along though we too deny the memory from the red-room in order to enter now we carry her down with the instrument to reveal her unconscious then electric then furious yet he says, tries to say, go to sleep.

Bibliography

Cornsweet, Tom N. *Visual Perception*. New York: Academic Press, Inc., 1970.

Edinger, Edward F. *Anatomy of the Psyche*. LaSalle, Ill.: Open Court Publishing Co., 1985; Chapter 5, "Sublimatio," and Chapter 6, "Mortificatio."

Ficino, Marsilio. *The Book of Life*. Trans. by Charles Boer. Dallas: Spring Publications, 1980; quoted pp. 61–2.

H. D. *The Gift*. New York: New Directions Press, 1982.

Leukel, Francis. *Physiological Psychology*. St. Louis: The C. V. Mosby Co., 1972.

Milton, John. *Paradise Lost*. New York: The Odyssey Press, 1962.

Portman, Adolf, ed. *Color Symbolism: Six Excerpts from the Eranos Yearbook 1972*. Dallas: Spring Publications, 1977; quoted p. 11.

Spignesi, Angelyn. "Verso una Comprensione Psicologica della Strega." *Giornale Storico di Psicologia Dinamica* 7 (1983): 44.

Chapter 14

Restory

I

I am sleeping in the dream of the blood sticks to my neck in a crimson covered room of locked edge. Blood is trickling then drying now only trickling down back crevices blood of her nails' extension. I am sleeping on dried leaves with a woman once of an attic running her nails down my back leaving their blood stream.

Peals accompanied as we ran her in her grey linen wrapper, accompanied by some music the peal through which I had once prayer for wider horizon, 'power of vision which might overpass that limit,' we ran through it, until we fell in the wood received us now perhaps I am not captor perhaps she understands together we have departed his manor.

In a sleep still back rivers, red fissures, I hear fragments of the brother's delirium as I was soaking his open shoulder blood sponged the same blood on her teeth. And from his fever I heard the island accounts, I pieced together the story much later after the company had left.

January causeway the way he mounted, rearing steed negating limp, tearing through my pastoral scene, mahomet, because he knew from where I had come I descended behind the pearl brooch. I had thought he could harness the animal force could ride its back but then I realized it was more prohibition for he had a madness locked up.

Feeling the blood hardening, a christianing of sorts she douses me in the red tide to say the mounting is not the way to what is outside, for he had a madness locked up and he cannot teach me of motion. Cannot release to world until the peal accompanying the desire out also descends through the redroom which is not to light it one last glimpse wings aflame like the parrot.

In a 'kind of exquisite delirium' he read my face once I was on the rug the fire scorched me the gypsy read eye, mouth, brow, and forehead, speaking

---

Single quotation marks indicate quotations from *Jane Eyre* by Charlotte Brontë. Double quotation marks indicate quotations from *Wide Sargasso Sea* by Jean Rhys.

each in what was 'rave in a kind of exquisite delirium,' when the red cloak fell off him, gem of the broad ring of the little finger I recognized he used her only as disguise, he had 'been trying to draw me out—or in.' Talking nonsense, no sense, madness. Wake or sleep. Witch's skill was devilish tricks of intimacy for his own mount. Afterwards 'Good God! What a cry!' and still kept still kept behind hidden backed so secret not even enigma kept that cry told me she was behind him and even the gypsy only disguise though it lead me to her in any case.

For I had heard her in his voice. The Fury had flown and he locked her up pacifying his guests. Later he said to the brother, 'you may think of her as dead and buried.' Then he offered me a half-blown rose asking had I been afraid, only to whomever might have emerged from the inner room, no worry says he had that key in his pocket, would never leave a lamb, his pet lamb, so near a wolf's den unguarded.

He may have a key. Way to wolf, or Fury, 'crater-crust which may crack and spue fire any day,' yet my way lead to the aunt's deathbed here the key. How all fire and violence could break out the tenth year, she said, after nine years of quiescence; she lay dying, she had written to whom had wanted to support me, uncle, that I was dead.

We go to tell her we are passionate not vindictive, and we lower to her. We lower for a kiss. 'A strange and solemn object was that corpse to me.' Sarah Reed. She died hating me still and when I lowered my cheek to her lips alive she would not touch it and later I fell through her corpse into the hate, I was sitting outside the attic door, hearing the scuffling, muffled eccentric sounds within.

He was seated at a stile writing as I was walking from Millcote back to Thornfield. He saw me as dream or shade. As we are reversing we pass through witch. He saw me walking from Millcote as dream or shade he said I came from another world, from the dead, substance or shadow. I am walking within the hate of the dead, through the corpse of Sarah Reed and now I go past him to the hate she crashed within that attic.

He tries to pull us back, he must have us for his own. We try to believe wherever he is our home, Jane will you marry me, but the horse-chestnut struck by lightning half of it split away. 'Pale-little elf,' he calls us 'fairy, and come from Elf-land, it said; and its errand was to make me happy.'

'(L)ittle sunny-faced girl with the dimpled cheek and rosy lips,' he calls us 'Fairfax Rochester's girl-bride,' he says he will be 'healed and cleansed, with a very angel as my comforter.'

Alice Fairfax wishes to put us on our guard, are we monster, no we were a sort of pet of his. Yet also with a power over him, hercules and samson with their charmers, as we were avoiding her above. He is twining soft, silken skein around his finger and its thrill to his heart conquers him.

Witchery triumph, a disguise as his. Besides, he says, shortly he will claim us—'thoughts, conversation, and company—for life.' White valley of the moon, cave, where even the child sees he will starve us; the child does not care for the fairy.

'(R)oll of the red eyes and the fearful blackened inflation of the lineaments,' the form emerges from the closet, thick and dark hair long upon her back, discolored and savage face. Purple ghost, swollen and darkened lips, veil rent in two and we fall into the fissure and we are surrounded by searing blood.

Thrusting candle to my face, her fiery eye upon me, bearing down: 'I was aware her lurid visage flamed over mine, and I lost consciousness: for the second time in my life—only the second time—I became insensible from terror.'

This redroom and its grotesque fire woman lowering to us. At first he would try to tell us it is a 'creature of an overstimulated brain,' nerves like ours not made for rough handling until he would realize the veil torn hastily: his arms then around us exclamation good god that nothing malignant did come near. Yet something did come near, not his explanation a Grace Poole exaggeration, something did come near and then I went with her, I took her out or she took me out or it us.

Orphans of some forest. No sun yet slanting through the bark tenaciously reside ants of its pore, mold. Old aged Indian Helen sat like an Indian what will this company know of bark and can I sit as still beside without my lung filling too with the blood as did hers as I romped in the woods bread and cheese with Mary Ann Wilson. Now I look at this woman beside me.

Not words yet I was lying in the red glare and the apothecary asked me to speak. I do not yet know this language yet it is coming for now I walk into that silence I learned at Lowood, silence so thick no knife could slice or pare, catches breath at first entry.

When his shadow passed over the chalk tablet that day my laugh would have been as preternatural yet stepping inside that silence its texture woven by Helen's gaze became fine linen from the high country. I shroud myself in it now I bury my chin in it inviting her coarse grey linen entry and I wait.

Gestures of her sleep suggest she desires to break out rub against tree's bark release the head knot, I cut that knot inviting her again into the folds knowing that ultimately it is her choice.

Trilling, cooing, warbling, scurrying this forest sounds itself to us, only once I knew a forest, lung decay, never learned how one's breath could remain as the forest unfolded itself in all its density the lung coagulated and was the forest part of her island I do not know and I recall that I also know nothing of the sounds of her attic.

Together we are learning to breathe in the forest, I have stayed fast steadfast even as she clawed me as captor I held fast, sitting like an Indian, and she learned my intent now her arm falls close to mine; broad, muscled, its thick splintered nails will not claw anymore as she begins to learn my smell in her sleep.

The sound hurts when it comes. Twigs at Helen's neck, this voice is low yet as it cracks I see welts. She mumbles that when he finally comes she will get his minerals, she will bury his minerals in the forest until the line of every fern shines. Forest ferns she will look in the morning where the forest ferns grow for the tree ferns are as tall and underneath them will be the orchids, octopus orchids, masses, she will swim in the ink, they were swimming once in the pools, throwing pebbles in the bathing pool for hours.

I pull in closer. I am learning of him through her sleeping mumble, and for a long while I reconsider my intent. If this is for him, I may as well return her.

Terror nightmare terror, nightmare of the forests, she was in the forest with someone who hated her, she was in the forest following a man, black hate on his face as he turned to her, her dress white and beautiful was trailing though she did not want to soil it, when the trees changed they climbed up the stairs, top, up the trees. She is in the forest and his black hatred face where will it be, the laughter.

The laughter, am I pacing still the corridor afterall? No she stirs beside me, lifting up her leg once it was well shaped. I break the china vase I was dusting in the drawing room. I am looking at this foot climb the trees, climb in the air outside her grey wrapper.

Sturdy, calloused, broad too broad, was she his servant once? This foot is dough-baked. Her cackle has words how he desired a delicate tropical flower he could pluck and place in a vase of British crystal. For him she hid this foot, would camouflage it with slipper this foot she is beating it with her fists she is kneading will we cut the bread together.

Splitting blisters her mouth to its scream. In the cavity above stomach spueing crater she is being devastated from the inside out I reach toward her now less to soothe more to withstand the extent of this final rage. It would burn his bed. It would be the fire to the thin curtains behind the red ones, red-room here finally, no, this is not to know him better yet the red-room glares around me once again, it has finally grown back to me full blown.

The mystery of why we are here together reveals itself: what was twisted root now exposed tentacle. I want to flee I think of bird plummage, who dropped me here. She is silent and she is looking at me, if I do not move I will have to stay. I see her eyes black ink pools or are they coal.

I think of my clothes in the trunk at Thornfield, corded, cards of address saying 'Mrs. Rochester, — Hotel, London,' what he will do with them.

Her leg descends, mouth closes on itself so the corners begin their scabbing once again she sleeps sounding only the gurgling at a throat's base. I pick up on her and something in my chest begins vibrating. She will turn on me once again she will bite or claw next my face if I do not pick up on her, know this current. We are here together to find its meaning; I to withstand, she to be someone finally can be withstood.

II

Riding current, barely holding to keep up with her it takes a head back, head thrown back it takes a spinning I am spinning around a knot the cavity is above the stomach now has a knot and surround a vacuum sucking spin. I cannot keep up and there is something I must do at the next stop. Head thrown back I scream for the woman she married a minister. Rochester was sent for an heirloom instead. The screams emerge regularly the lulling of cows, I am walking on the nipped grass in the country, the stone fence is missing in part, a nose broad, yet of the calf is butting in my direction, I hear the lulling I am head thrown back do they know mother this revenge of our tide defiled.

And the one who dares to come down to our tide, sent by his father who was betraying, is still nauseated and locks it up high, close to the heavens for look, he says sarcastically, look for a minister to marry.

"She'll not laugh in the sun again. She'll not dress up and smile at herself in that damnable looking-glass. So pleased, so satisfied. Vain, silly creature. Made for loving? Yes, but she'll have no lover, for I don't want her and she'll see no other."

Fuse. Fuse with his flame I would have loved my idol. What necessity he said, '(W)hat necessity is there to dwell on the Past,' when, he continued, when 'a fervent, a solemn passion is conceived in my heart; it leans to you, draws you to my centre and spring of life, wraps my existence about you — and, kindling in pure, powerful flame, fuses you and me in one.'

Fusing. My legs rent, spread as I am delivering I would want to give my life for him die in childbirth to put a child on earth for him. But he was wrapping it up. He wrapped up some madness, unmothered, scorned mother rejecting her, who with thick black hair and evening dress cut too low all she could possibly know of love was thirst becoming his thirst later he said all his life he would be thirsty and longing.

Tears scalding a cheek puffing in the delirium or hilarity a pain too pregnant for any sedative the trampling, coaches riding over me as I struggle to get to the edge of the road and leaving leaving him and 'no relative but the universal mother' who may have married a minister.

No pure flame fuses he and I in one, no legs cross now I am on the heath and then to the woods but I have taken away that madness that would marry him. The madness marrying him with favors for his slightest attention, would soothe, savor long frangipani days bathing in pools of rum and scents that are at once soporific and stimulant, she lowered with him into a trance in which they clung and moaned and she died again and again, that madness who would die for him without asking him die die you too die. And in this land it would have continued perhaps, here she would have stretched tighter corsets flushing her cheeks who would have had ringlets made for him have singed her hair with irons for a curl for him.

'Bertha Mason, — the true daughter of an infamous mother, — dragged me through all the hideous and degrading agonies which must attend a man bound to a wife at once intemperate and unchaste.'

She is folded beside me now, lumps, a tooth missing, a stench of corrosion the urine has not transmuted.

Another day without sun, the low cloud in which we awake, her hair matted in massive waves, mine stringing long oily threads of it. We hunger, roots and berries not enough the meagre squirrel supply and for the first time I understand the hunt. Here the hunger is larger than even that of Lowood for I would readily consume the burnt porridge smell of which would appetize this day.

Mud caked nails tearing ground for its root, the body swelling as it itches incessantly, too porous still. I wonder whether she feels any of it and I suspect not. The question how we can reside in this hunger or whether she will devour me first. Her chest heaves down, I have noticed the blood on her thigh, she has started, nothing matters but these leaves to her, she studies the bloodless vein of one leaf.

I stay close. What do the women who speak of the angels and then become diseased know of this scrutiny of the leaf's vein, perhaps this is their knowing now. Or the ones sitting high on the piano stool, I see them now, breasts pushed up for their Rochester, soprano perfect pitch, encircling warbling notes for Rochester. I was a watching shrinking violet on the windowseat, not diseased but not yet living, watching the others disappear either it is to life's mediocrity or to consort to sing at the extremes, always having to leave myself trailing behind a mere trembling whisper.

Here a thigh's blood stream he could not ride this river. Who can know this river's flow down the thigh of a woman locked in an attic? Is it the men with bells on their ankles, men on the rooftops making melody, carousing men who alternate a sternness, whose hardness falls into the smooth loving sometimes too slick using our thigh closeness to a mother memory, the men who can if any can afford the father's lowering without clinging to the thigh of a mother memory, yet when the blood comes what are the words of their philosophies then.

I put leaves on the woman's thigh, leaves which absorb the blood, we look at the blood veins of the leaves for a long while.

New day breeds itself as sun shafts through pitch trees, my eye begins to accustom to what can this sun want. Her back to me, the sun shaft is not yet upon her but approaching for she is to have the spotlight afterall. She is much larger than I imagined and seems in this instant to be growing, her skin expands towards this shaft surrounding it, she is large enough.

I want to touch the large back before this searchlight exposes us. As I reach tentatively she falls down at that moment on the very back. Her arms rise and she covers her eyes with large fists. Fists and clumps of hair over her eyes protecting them not from this light as much as the light withheld attic years.

I want to tell her my dreams of the forest I will take her inside yet my gaze is transfixed upon her now as the sun blinds her and I do not speak. She does not seem so diseased in this forest not even in the sun.

She begins screeching into the light. She is yelling, Pheena! Pheena! Blinding! repetitively. I tell her who I am, I tell her she bent over me with her candle, lurid visage reflected aflame to my eyes we were together surrounded by red and this wood received us, that I spoke to her before, that I left him with her. That I left him, with her. She attempts to rise, one hand covering both eyes she gropes. I too am dizzied by this vertical light. We find ourselves crawling and I am following.

Feels the dirt carefully as she proceeds. Digs beneath the moss pulls up chunks of dirt running it between her fingers and moves on, suggesting it contains not yet what she wants yet may be approximating. She moves faster, seems scared, begins smelling the dirt, tasting it. She must be ravenous also but then I wonder. She is on some other track. I stare at the tattered hem of her grey linen laughing at me, twisting mouth sneer, I feel I cannot abide though I follow. I begin to feel the dirt also, it is becoming moister. She desires watered dirt. Is this about thirst, my knees hurt, are bleeding, they feed that moss their blood in exchange we will have the water.

Erratic pace she scrambles now. Barely can I keep up. A pool, small bounces in air then she crawls in quickly, I expect submergence and greedy gulpings, yet only a sip, she is polite as any British lady, drinking clearly was not the object of this romp yet mud. Generously she covers herself with it, face first with mounds on the lids of each eye. Arms then, and the blood streaks of the thighs mud packed, then lying in the sun, the mud in piles upon her she opens her tunic, laying on her back the mud in piles upon her chest rubbing the mud across her stomach, breasts fall out. Years since this skin breathed a nature's breath or bathed now mud bath, mud caked, mud baked the way she receives the sun through the baking not of skin yet this wet earth and her breasts no longer attic stored yet freed too, loyally fall on either side of the mound of mud between them, that pyramid monument some pharoah's shrine he died.

A quickened desire to lie there on that pyramid passes through me and I recoil. We rocked side by side and sometimes facing one another, knit, discussed the lessons. Holding Helen crib death. I want to run to Eliza to tabulate account, hoard the money. Or a return to him. Let him buy the gowns he wants to make me the bride he needs; play his word games. Play for him, anything but face my desire for this mud woman of the breasts of the forest.

She leans back, watching this wife of Rochester, and she remembers him, a gaze at the bottom of the stairway. When she could no longer stand not being part yet not knowing how to move off the windowseat with her own Grace, he left the company of the drawing room as she departed it. She knelt to fix a sandal and when she rose at the stairway base there his gaze. She sees him now. He is playing billiards with the guests. Pushing a stray piece of hair across his forehead's creased sweat he bends to this shot. Blanche is beside him. The crack, balls spin yet none of the creases release as he smiles. Her perfume irritates him. "Don't put any more scent on my hair," was it shortly before their wedding night in Spanish Town she had said, "He doesn't like it." (He was so young, he was duped). The other would never wear it. His wrist suddenly falters. Twitching, he cannot bring them both up simultaneously yet they are always there at the base of wherever he goes. The colonel bends to aim. Theirs was a duel of hatreds, he thought he was ahead but death figures. She knew them, the other drew them, configured for him a reality which previously he could only suspect, of which he was suspicious. One was living in that reality, the other drew it, now they are together but he cannot in his mind hold them bring them up at once and with a good aim he shatters the pyramid of colored balls, cracking.

The fire dies down. Who sleeps is Antoinette, within the mud she repeated it: Antoinette, Antoinette, this once her name who sleeps. I am rocking by the dying fire, holding knees to chest, to keep a balance prevent a trembling for he is there, he has come between us.

She senses him walking toward her, she wants to reach out her hand. He carries a satchel. He carries her paintings inside, he has carried them back to her, returning them, he plays his last shot. He will return her paintings in exchange for taking her back. But this is a region not of any previous vision, never seen certainly by a man's eyes and she has not gone through

all of it yet. He tries sadness, he tries reprimand. His wrist twitches. He
fades. She is sitting, rocking with knees to her chest in front of the dying
fire. Antoinette stirs, remains sleeping.

She knows he had counted. He had counted upon her return through the
manifestation of the paintings, his handling of her paintings now without
irritation. Yet his closeness to her paintings is also how he is married to
Antoinette whom he locked far away far up. She will know her, arm fallen
over face, look at that face, inquire its demon. He had said, 'To tell me that
I had already a wife is empty mockery: you know now that I had but a
hideous demon.' Inquire its demon, take it to the ocean and the rivers and
let the demon swim until it sunbaked is hearty then inquire it, find its
narrative to know together its design. Who will come as midwife, who will
guide us through this pitch of which we have been petrified which has
resided beneath other selves of subverted plots to which they spiraled from
which recoiled. She ceases rocking, recedes, further recedes then shooting
forward billiard ball shooting back at Rochester pronouncing clearly: stay
where you are, it is not for you yet. Sit alone with the paintings and draw
from them. It is no longer of your will. The horse has fallen not Gytrash
afterall the man limps and this time the horse will not so immediately be
mounted. Sit on the stile with your father's betrayal not to be disguised by
our courtship. Sit on the stile weeping writing for your anguish the father's
turn on you the sun sets Thornfield falls into dusk disks of temper its rooks
caw the funeral disease she holds between her breasts we will bury until the
pyramid recognizing itself mud falls limp and the pool of blood into which
we fall can be well spoken. Neither she or I have chosen one another. It is
not yet for you. Stay out. He tries reprimand, he tries sadness. His wrist
twitches and he fades.

III

She looks at Antoinette, knows it is from regions south yet wonders how
he found her and why she returned with him, coming north to an attic for
him.

The eyes she offers me when she awakens are coals. They pull me
toward what would spit me out, skewer over coal, kettle in the gypsy's
hearth he told my fortune yet never mentioned these coals. From where did
she steal them? We do not yet know the ingredients but we have the coals
we do not know the process of distillation yet even how to articulate what
stored attic chests as we provided, protected him all the while actually
consumed by our terror of this wooded place of the madness two women
facing the mother said let sleeping curs lie and took off and threw us to the

other end of the room when we visited her madness the man came and taking her she threw us off and mothers marrying minister burning a fever leaving us residue fever pitch and mothers saying she is not fit to associate, crushing locking the red walls are their phantoms too between two women facing one another in a forest in which two coals simmer.

She reaches in her pocket and takes out two more coals saying, "At last Grace Poole, the woman who looks after me, lights a fire with paper and sticks and lumps of coal." Here are the coals of the attic's fires. As I hold them I find some in my pocket, beneath my breast. Helen's gift remaining afterall. Coals for Helen, and Maria Temple with her minister, some coal for her too we begin hearing thunder in the distance Antoinette fully awake says retort and a heating begins that the most volatile depart.

Her volatility, volare, vapor, vaporize, transient, some say fickle, changeable, what modifies, she too was once in a convent. And what primarily condensed (upward) the impulses, what uplifted, what lifted her up to the vapors not a burning intelligence of a great girl with books with angels yet cloves, cinnamon, orange blossom, scented ageless evenings of heat, wreaths of frangipani on the bed the floor strewn with her garments his endless cyclical approach and the way they would sleep together afterwards without kiss or caress.

And what cooled, what is the distillation, what cools the resulting vapor, what dropped down, de stillare, cooling and condensing secondarily (downward) to a refinement, drops, is this madness of her mother he imposed it on her in a cool hate. The mother who threw her to the other end of the room, she was in the air and then she landed. Refined.

And what condensed my volatility, the way I had at Lowood vaporized the Gateshead cruelty, coalmine crudeness, Lowood uplifted, nullified, image and symbol and voice not ours yet mediating, until the coach ride, I rang the bell and the sturdy mansion with its high laugh lowered me outside a causeway on which he fell. Lowered and condensed incarnate though I tried to keep it in the stars and moon, man in the moon, mahomet, the clock struck and I entered to a duty becoming the sponging a brother's blood of her madness.

We are distilling the coals: the way we had vaporized, benzene volatilities, and how her madness dropped us down to this refined substance becoming our figuring it and our manifesting that is thick sticky black its odor pungent heavy bituminous, resulting from this distillation it has been destructive, tar unfolding as hot as it was in her redroom and suddenly I recall the other mother, Sarah Reed, she threw me away, I was blasting and then I landed and the room was inside her body red and locked until Lowood distilled to the Fairfax veil a return with it as protection, preventive against influence of what corrodes, by-product from blast furnaces, burning under retorts, it has powerful antiseptic properties, it coats us.

We are stripped and the tar covers our skin. Our mouths distended we have dropped through projection one upon the other we have seen through the other the condensations of a mother's madness. Together we are viscous, lowered into what had secondarily condensed our previous volatilities, return again to a redroom. If we had not had our vapors, primarily been uplifted, we would not be able to begin this redroom reentry for refined delineation, what is its delineation for we have dropped into it again this time antiseptic protected.

If not for the previous volatilities what now can be speaking the redroom only would have remained crude residue, nonvolatile impurity, pitch.

Lining of this tar covering the phantom glittering eyes fascinate. The ghost, the woman with streaming hair surrounded by a gilt frame, ghost of a woman who haunts this place I released her from the attic though she lowered to me lurid and never had I received such an invitation.

Recognizing they looked into the mirror seeing through one another they fell into the redroom through the black viscous hole of a pungent odor.

It was beyond the father. The father lowered. The stepfather descended too and cheated. The last visit at the convent the stepfather gives us sweets, kisses us, critically looks us over holding us at arms length. One of his English friends will be sure to come, he has tried to arrange it. The stepfather has lowered to our kiss will sell us to this madness of our mothers afterall we are to sleep in the bed of the red curtains. Christophine's first advice is to leave him. We think of when we will live in England: "I must know more than I know already. For I know that house where I will be cold and not belonging, the bed I shall lie in has red curtains and I have slept there many times before, long ago."

Cora once said to the brother that the stepfather would not have allowed it. But the stepfather allowed it, the father allowed it, the father lowered to a vault beneath, betraying the (step)brother betraying us, allowing us to be sold to sleep in a bed of red curtains in England when our husband enters to repress rebuke retaliate for the figure of our mother's madnesses.

The fathers and sons are feuding. Betraying one another, the father is lowering and we can only take to the woods. Dear Father, he was always writing it in his head, speaking it in his sleep repetitively, he clung to his father in his sleep but the father would not reside or abide had died making a false deal, unfair, no matter his intention. And the residue, pitch, nonvolatile impurity, the pitchrage that the sons have had left over has been sold to equated with the madness of a woman close to the equator.

We came to England because we had not yet slept in the bed with red curtains nor looked in the mirror at her who released us into the woods. First we had to be locked in an attic many years because the fathers' death lowered word and law becoming our seizure, our selling into her depths, we would rather wait for his condescending cold hate look back instead of entering into this black hole facing her.

For when the father's fall leaves us without law or word locked in the room of the blood madnesses of the mothers — he was supposed to look into it too, stay there, find the new words with us but he ran all the way home, attic locked it up there. Rage at his father's selling him, not omniscient father, yet miniscule and conniving father, the rage at his father becomes instead the rage at us. It is not that he desires his mother's womb. Far from it. He runs and locks it up in the attic to distract him from his essential rage at the father for no longer protecting him through the law, for sending him below to face what the father never could, the sleep and death within the arms of a woman maddened when all borders had been ruptured and the clipped winged parrot on the railing burned.

We have focused on his rejection of us, anything to keep from her while most attached to her, we have focused on his rejections thinking it desire. Yet his rejections, the way he took us to leave us have ultimately been hers anyway (he says her madness is why he does it yet her madness is that he does it) his rejections have been hers disguised and repetitive until we coil through these repetitions first heating condense dryly vapors sublime then cooling condense incarnate we drop into we fall through the ghost in the gilded mirror to the black tar hole.

Perhaps we have attempted to distract ourselves from this second condensation by assuming the power to lower him below the equator, we hope, perhaps it is all for the father anyway, omniscient father afterall, knowing that we are the channel for him to lower further into her madness. We sense how we would invite him into our darkened den, lower him, make him strip and know her through us, we want to shoot him up with more intelligence from what resides below the waves, sea salt her blood salt makes him larger as we go to the depths, maybe we want him also to lower us, crack us open so we can get to her yet still safely within his safe regard. Instead: he would lock us up upon a return to England and we return to England to be locked up in an attic; we cannot pretend anymore it is for the father.

When the mirror cracked and the black liquid oozed we saw her ghost haunting house and we wanted to run back to the father but we did not could not any longer when we took her to the woods carrying the coals which distilling condensed to the tar, viscid, inflammable, protecting our skin. Within this tar is the memory of how we had distilled first the volatilities, vaporized contracting to figuration concisely transmuted what previously was cruder substance, she in Granbois, I in Lowood, until coolness began the second condensation incarnate it was through a woman's madness.

Condensation through her madness, what is this condensation these drops must be spoken. The ways we have been dropped again and again by her madness, if not spoken to its source, if not a condensation to word becoming new law, without a condensation resulting in language, we remain mad.

We thought he was taking us out into the world, that we would have at last conventional place, yet she emerged from our bridal gown and rent veil bent down to us peering through us eye to eye. We will not lower ourself to world, find the incarnation place for what we had learned in the higher stories until we condense through the meaning of her madness realizing no longer is he the one bringing us out.

We carry him up and in but only to the point of his father's turn, and he carries us down and out only to the point of the madwoman bending down to us after we have returned from Mrs. Reed bending to offer her our cheek. It is a woman's madness we hear hidden in his mansion, hidden in his voice, and then we begin dropping, our drops, dropping remembered through that madness.

The ways we have been dropped, at the base it was she who dropped us, what is the speaking of how to return to that fundamental hate and what lies at the bottom of that hate between two women, redroom, it wants further distillation, wanting distillation, what is at the bottom of it and how does that speak. Not to accuse her, not a breakfast room blast accusation but neither a kiss on a cheek, she knows better, her refusal to kiss us back says stay with this hate has not spoken itself must not be covered in this age with another romantic ending. We want to know what is at the bottom of this hate this madness between two women so we have taken to the woods and after we have gone past his distractions we drop into its dark hole, remembering the dropping we find the words.

If she gives up the cold metal she will take my heat. She cannot get to the heat and allow me to have mine too. When I leave frustrated, she is energized. Someone holds me horizontally. Mind dispersed all direction various colors ray. I vomit they watch I want to go below and some voices say I cannot. Parts of her fight me every step of the way, we are caught in a black hole sticky and vicious. He is outside laughing and sneering: I told you so. I scream in the hole she has folded us within. I hate her because I cannot descend with her anymore. She stops it in many underhanded ways even as she encourages further. The tar is distilled as I scream she is laughing too, while worried, she has an outside of worry but I do not trust her.

Get out. She is not holding, rather colluding. I vomit orange, bugs black and thick. Falling down the tunnel she has not wanted it yet eventually even the last resistance breaks but no candle there is no hallway like in the dream. Bumpy pitch walls I rub my hands against them as I go slowly I fall. I land on a mattress old, moldy, alone but it is preferable to where I could be. The father died here. Absolutely silent. I lay for a long while watching the bugs on the wall. I have been so afraid of this place. Let me be dead now I say to her. It is past the time of the heat because we have missed so often in it. Invaded. Bugs. Spiders. Stickings. Too many forces coming between us. Between generations, between our eyes, looking in the mirror we saw the one she rejected threw us out crushed into retort now melting tar to pitch residue I am clawing the walls. Then I realize it is no way out, my hands are bleeding. I want to force myself against the red wall but she took all the energy.

So I remain on the moldy mattress thinking these things as I feel some blood, also my nose running, phlegm, as always phlegm. The mother tantalizes or walls until I drop frustrated. Pitched to the crimson walls. Pitch, erect, pierce, transfix me here. I am slamming in a hole of tar, only pores remain breathing through what is tar antiseptic as I return again redroom. Mother held for a moment crushed or transfixed by her and then raised, uplifted so there could be the drop again into forbidden inner body. We cannot repair the father anymore, the master is divested and we cannot reconstruct. Fire out of my mouth this coal will fuel its own retort and finally I aim it at her wherever she is she is the closest yet she is not here. I am haunted and she is walking toward me and does it catch the hem of her skirt.

Recess. Swings dirt falling into the dirt from a see saw. See saw a vast plain. Clammer clatter I am on this vast plain with these clamoring children and I have no idea where she is, she deposited her demons in my room nightly so I carried them to the school. I put them on, wear them, they cackle though they are not here of any gender. The others circle, dance, red flames, stake, they have a stake in the circle of red flames around which they dance. Sleep child sleep. Even the nurses hurt us, drugged us, locked us, wanted our money to let them see the world before they die. Take me away mother from this hell which is too long part of your desire for I am only a child.

My cheek to Sarah Reed's lips. There was an unrecognized madness in that gesture yet I did not see it until I had returned and the form emerged from the closet pressing her fiery eye close to mine. I fall through your hate and it is ours the coal tar scalding skin lifts off burns through this hate we fall through to what it refines, coal tar fires an intimacy unlike any other, base of all others, mother we burn through to the borders of my unique body, my forbidden inner body.

When they have all departed, no mother, no Cora, no Christophine, no Grace and I finally fall through the cracked mirror to what does haunt in a black tar hole. Much saliva and licking now. She dropped me and with the room burning behind me I fell into a black hole and someone who says governess is there. This place has its own governing afterall, the tar takes on my dimensions and for the first time I see my shape apart from any covering, delineate its contours. Tar varying in composition according to the nature of the body from which it is distilled. Wants to explore this landscape.

Phlegm drips. Grace holds a copper cup and someone on a bed is urinating into it. Then I go into a corner to her flesh layers, at first I think it is a baby but then I see it is a grown woman. Mounds of flesh sitting in a corner. Oozing fluids from her nose and parts once private. Smells of excretions, the grease coating hair, flaxen oily and thick.

Grace. The place is fluid and heavy. Heavy fluids, this ground bends under the slightest pressure. The softness and denseness of its atmosphere threatens to absorb us. Off-whitish, beiges, hint of mauve. The flesh ripples and will be molded yet does not seek containment instead spreads. Kneading bread. The motion here is being passed from one to the other. Oozing, smells of dampness, river swamps, any bird here is low flying or webbed, of the rivers. Living under a river's wave whose crest never breaks we are suspended and though the reeds can choke we float through them. Going so far in, deepening expanse, bottomless. Oozing. Catarrh. Leucorrhea. Bog.

We turn over and begin urinating. The other landscape is harder, crust, red rimmed eye glaring. Bertha. The place is active and heated. Heat reflected off glass surface, the elements are salt and fire. Air beats around us. Acrid smells and tastes, the nails claw will claw our face perhaps this land too has knife edges, crust, crust of bread cuts us. Prickings. Scrapings. The ground is dry, cracks, fissures from the dryness, and when the wind comes it whips the skin cracks. Mounting, piercing, burning. Irritations and scintillations, enflammations. Reds oranges the deeper purple. Swept away.

These terrains at the base of our mothers madnesses when finally we have dropped to them in their own terms: Grace and Bertha. Grace and Bertha these terrains of our mother's madness now ours when all borders have been desacralized, violated and we drop to the unique borders staking these landscapes at the base to which our mothers' rigidities, obsessional arrogances, catatonias have been a defense, to which our mother's tantalizations, hysterias, manias have been a defense.

We explore a movement from Grace to Bertha from Bertha to Grace, shiftings, begin oscillating to the tensions between them. Grace landscape brings weight to body, slows to intimacies, slows our madness, receptacle protected, river or pool, slows to the place where image can be manifested. Grace indicates. Grace cooks.

The Bertha landscape moves us, inspires, surges, something in our mind snaps and we see what previously had not been seen. Quickening to unfamiliar sensation, sensitizing, exposing to what stimulates. This Bertha place thrusts, shouts, charges. Urine salt to ocean salt to blood salt let the blood flow meet the ocean foam and salt, the ocean is crashing and relinquishing itself on our fully outstretched legs. Desire in the Bertha place is to quicken, harden and heat. Desire in the Grace place is to slow and soften, sensual, to cool, poole.

And we know that a too abrupt move from Grace to Bertha (Bertha defense against Grace) results in burnings, urinary infections, irritations, skin wounds. The too abrupt move from Bertha to Grace (Grace defense against Bertha) results in blockages, paralysis, numbings. Our phlegm reddens tubucular, heart beat skips regularly, womb tumor.

We practice moving from one landscape to the other until we are no longer driven or frustrated or diseased, here becomes a movement of a pace which is not a possession, pure vastness of the place, see saw, where we learn that symbiosis is not to be antipathetic yet mutualistic, sympathetic, not parasitical living off one another attic locked yet differentiated aspects even dissimilar living together and benefiting, reciprocally. Differences residing together and flourishing. Falling in and out of the eyes of one another at every moment Bertha's scratchings and Grace's paralysis are linings, always present. We do not eradicate the two or move them to a synthetic form or exchange them with one another to demolish their original form yet we learn better their landscapes and what is required of the movement between them and what that senses like. When we have discovered these landscapes and the pacing between them, the pitch gets perfect.

Which can be this:

Dart or sword or lightning bolt in center splitting ocean and fishes flying out blue fishes silver lined heralding black hole entry. Crack of sword bolt ocean split fish release and we are still entwined in the sediment of this ocean, the way the rivers have flowed into this ocean, depositing, deposits and there is a singing in our ears coral shell singing coral shell lining of pearl of some oyster singing and you put it to my ear I hear the voices I speak them back to you and you lower into what is the moist tunnel beneath this ocean, bed of all waters, watered earth bed stilled we slow to witness as we have generations ago staked we looked across in a long arching redrimmed stare indicating we would return to it the conflation of our variant plots.

IV

Only now can we return to that manor. Not to repress him as he did her, and besides there is something to give back to him. As the tar becomes soluble, it begins to lift off the skin disease in the way we have been too permeable too passive to their advances. As the tar becomes soluble we are ready to take it back to him, that world. Galloping through it, galloping through the causeway he thinks of the governess as thief.

For did she not enter my household and leave stealing its possession? How often did I wish that demon of the attic dead but stolen and I want her back. Small-boned thief and the other a conniving criminal. And I will claim the booty and lock it up higher where no one will ever reach. "She'll not laugh in the sun again . . . *Adieu*—like those old-time songs she sang. Always *adieu* (and all the songs say it). If she too says it, or weeps, I'll take her in my arms, my lunatic. She's mad but *mine, mine* . . . Antoinetta—I can be gentle too. Hide your face. Hide yourself but in my arms. You'll soon see how gentle. My lunatic. My mad girl."

And the tar has melted on our skins, we thought we had a skin disease and that we were burning, the tar has lifted off the diseased skin and what is this coolness containing images we are just speaking to one another. We return to Rochester as we speak to one another these images, in his hearing now. Rochester will never need to know the tar as we have known it, he has yet his own distillations, but we will not stay within our diseased skin any longer. Exchange of images to their meanings takes us within his hearing. We begin to speak the conjunctive narratives, those which placed us at the same Thornfield, Bluebeard corridor afterall.

All we ask: listen to these words apart from what your father led you to expect. Beyond the father's betrayal it is not our carriage any longer. You had begun to listen, the last night before it crashed, you heard some of it configure and began to understand but said it was not what you were led to expect you said should we not leave one another; and even though you wanted to sink again into my hair that night you say now even before the drink, you were starting to listen yet father prohibited. Listen now apart.

I never told him of mother's parrot. That she fervently tried to get Mr. Mason to leave earlier. I was a sultry beauty in my white gown it slipped over my shoulder and I saw his condescending look, it was too late then for any words. We bring this symbiosis back to him, sympathetic symbiosis, we will reciprocate receiving ear and I give to her in his hearing mother's reaction to my appearance in Tia's dress she returns Mrs. Reed's whirlwind stair ascent crib crushing I give back my nightmare slowly, forest nightmare as it continued and I climbed those trees were different, she returns the uncle heights of a redroom winged, black dog trailing, the light over the grave over the ceiling descends and I give her the parrot wings alit that were first clipped by Mr. Mason making him a bad-tempered, darting, pecking bird and we begin finding the patterns, discerning the composition, she gives me back Lowood and the room of Miss Temple's seed-cake, Helen's enflamed cough. I give her back the last nightmare which will not depart of my flaming on his battlemented roof. She returns the typhus, chests of little girls aflame, reddening of phlegm and the burst of flowering even of the wood. I return my High Wood for her Lowood. She gives me her mother's short life, typhoid. I give her the five years at Coulibri of mother's desparate loneliness of a horse poisoned, my brother is not Richard, my brother her favorite is a cretin, is dead. She tells me her stepbrother also favorite has killed himself.

Christophine was telling me, her first advice, when I visited her the first time, to leave you. There was only inertia then and following. I thought of England, when I live in England. "I must know more than I know already. For I know that house where I will be cold and not belonging, the bed I shall lie in has red curtains and I have slept there many times before, long ago." How long ago? she asks. I know that bed, she says, for we have been sleeping in the same bed for many years without knowing it. In that bed we have seen the father has fallen limp and the son abuses, sells us in his name. Aunt Cora quarrelled with Richard: it was not his father's intention to hand everything the child owns to a perfect stranger, she should be protected legally.

The father's intention lowered to where his law no longer protects. Bertha attacked Richard when he said the word "legally." The fathers and the sons have betrayed each other and we have been protected only by aberrations, the manifestations too abrupt of Grace and Bertha, until the two of us took to the woods. Dear father, you were always writing it in your head, speaking it in your sleep.

"The convent was my refuge." I heard her say it also.

Either we would be burning on the glacis rail like Coco, falling screeching, clipped wings failing or dreaming it. You clipped our wings, orphan afterall, and then when we were burning we only dreamt we walked down to the hall of her ghost in the gilded mirror, woman with streaming hair surrounded by gilt frame, ghost of a woman who haunts this place they say, and we dropped the candle and ran yet could not run away from the flames licked us.

And I let them unfold, draperies of clothes falling, slithering off my press. But now they are words to her in his presence. Designating configurations designing. When we rode out of Granbois you thought you hated me I say to him. Orchids and the jasmine, the cinnamon, coconut palms, stephanotis, each another shade another scent, the lime trees and forest tree ferns like the forest of my nightmares no longer does forest have to be nightmare but you are not a man who still only hates me. Each piece of clothing unfolding off the press another image and the design I give her she reciprocates and then we hold it at arms length and analyze according to the landscapes we have negotiated.

I saw in my drawer my plait tied with red ribbons, when I first got up from the illness after the burning and Tia's rock. Her crawling into Helen's crib white curtain covering speaking of angels, her cold feet.

We bring down let drop to him what before we had previously carried back up: Lowood condensation the configurations from there we carried down and they spoke to him and he said go to sleep and how we took the drawings back up is how we knew she was locked up and that the second condensation, Thornfield wooded, how we drop down was between we two until the rediscovered configurations speak he listens.

Hours of it image interpenetrating image designates meaning. He listens. My mother with burned hair carrying Pierre out of the bedroom his eyes rolled up white. Broken slate of a Brocklehurst public denunciation, liar. Doll face doll Marionetta, Antoinetta, smiling while riding away from Granbois he calls me only Bertha saying, it was you saying, "Very soon she'll join all the others who know the secret and will not tell it. Or cannot. Or try and fail because they do not know enough. They can be recognized. White faces, dazed eyes, aimless gestures, high-pitched laughter."

You said you wanted to know the secret of the place, that place "untouched, with an alien, disturbing, secret loveliness." You wanted not what you saw but what it hides. Now I am telling you the secret, distilled, analyzed and analyzing. I was completely passive and inert, completely covered by Grace, not veiled but Grace covered Bertha to a camouflage entirely and so Bertha broke out of the attic paralysis as flame. I was completely passive to their whim from the first moment my mother rejected me and that was long before she was secluded in the madness the fat black man bending to kiss her long before she pushed me away. The parties began so we would not be white nigger. But I was always slave to her, to Aunt Cora, to Sister Marie Augustine, to Mr. Mason and to his son and to the stranger from England who took the money with me trailing after and after us both came a sobbing nameless boy who loved you so, whom you left behind in the land. I was slave to even slaves, to Amelie, and yes, to Christophine. You would drug me with your scorn and silence, your not speaking to me for hours for days and she would drug me with what she gave me of obeah and then the rum instead to a raving. Slave's slave drugged to a raving.

She says that after the teacher with the seed-cake the great girl rose the raving to images she painted them and then was sitting in the Inn at Millcote, alone for quite some time, the muff and umbrella lying on the table. She rang the bell. Ringing bell ring. Grace was the cover in that place. I took her keys when she laid her head on the table after her several drinks, scratching along the hall I entered the room to tear the veil. Bertha over Grace, the veil was rent. Ringing the bell. And then she says that the Millcote bell brought her to a third story leads and to a causeway first step out which was his fall and determination to remain mounted even as I that hag cackled: Dare to like it.

Bell brought her to a third story so I could walk down with the keys clanging and follow her to the woods where we dropped and condensed these images to narratives of beds with red curtains, locked room we have known the secret and now she will not remain in there alone mumbling to his miniature yet veiled now antiseptic protected we speak out of it in your hearing.

We preferred to be held up mad instead of returning veiled to the redroom to condense its configurations and carry them out (instead, after they were scrutinized in the drawing redroom and he said put them away we did and then we went back up, and he would say to himself we know the secret but will not cannot tell it), look across that stake, the ones before us preferred to be held up, preferred Grace and Bertha only symptomatically so the Father would not face the letter of his Fall. To oscillate within them is to receive figures not before imagined, distinctly, speak through them they come from various landscapes and they tell us the movements and they tell us the meanings.

They are in the crimson drawing room, the curtains are drawn, the tea is cool on its silver tray untarnished on the side table for he would prefer to slip to the side of things but there is no getting around the two of them now. He listens into the night. And what remains in his sight is a black and white goat with yellow-green slanting eyes, he had tied up his horse and the man Daniel, the man Daniel was venomous.

He is speaking back. An orchid with long sprays of golden-brown flowers. Touching his cheek. Is it her skirt? "They are like you," I told her. The flowers which were singed, stung by the rum. We are kneeling upon the ground and kiss the earth in front of the verandah once we saw moths fired alive in its candle far into the night, patois passions, and the rages were they hidden beneath the white dress of a barefoot servant girl with the malicious, intimate look. Glasses and plates smashed against a porthole so the sea would enter, sea salt brine returning we were returning home, dear father, I never sent it, I left the sobbing nameless boy behind, I hear it now, Dear Father.

We are speaking now as threesome what had been unspoken then. We stand on the patterns of this speaking. Patterns are threads of the rug upon which the three of us stand. Patterns of reversals, of droppings, distillations, desires. When we had finally begun speaking I said to her that her nights or days were not spoiled, that before I even drank what she poured me I longed to bury my face in her hair as before. Then the obeah and it all began again unspoken until these words standing on the rug unravelling, scrutinize each thread, hold it up for all three to see, we sharpen our eyes on the threads, run each thread between our teeth, and we speak and when the memory cuts too sharply or we lose sight of the pattern entirely, the way the two women move between themselves paces, distinguishes.

Until why was I sent down there in the first place. And they ask and I stare within their stare until it comes upon me, the long brown hair on chest and arms the arms raise and sharp descent eyes cross-eye triangulate with the pointed nose extends itself over what teeth could gnaw, arms low now and bouncing and claws. Arms coated long brown silken mass of it arms go down and chest heaves. Heavy chest, heaving chest and from it, growl. And I feel it come upon me, bear-coat, berserk. I am the bear at the base of the berserker frenzy, I have a coat that knows the frenzied fury, dear father. Rochester berserk. Becomes bear, begins to bear his own rage violent rage, bear, carry the burden of, bear away, bear off, berth, to have the space to carry it, fit distance to keep it, clear wide berth, bear away, bear off. Bearing also bring forth, birth, berth, what can carry him across the sea to the origin, place of birth, dear father. Bear the violent rage to endure it, to have the coat, the wide sea distance to endure it in order to sail it back to home, him.

To return Bertha to him, is to return him to his own animal which will not be used for mounting, yet to return the ways he can carry, withstand, endure, bear his own berserkness.

When she spoke to me the last sober evening before obeah, before Amelie, it was different from what I was led to expect. They all knew. They kept it from me. "As I walked I remembered my father's face and his thin lips, my brother's round conceited eyes. They knew. And Richard the fool, he knew too. And the girl with her blank smiling face. They all knew."

I was on the stile finally writing of these disturbances, she had gone to care for her aunt at the deathbed, and I was writing of these disturbances, continuing the letter begun often to father: "I know now that you planned this because you wanted to be rid of me. You had no love at all for me. Nor had my brother. Your plan succeeded because I was young, conceited, foolish, trusting. Above all because I was young. You were able to do this to me . . ." Though he is now dead, the letter is to be continued but that day she came upon me, substance or shadow, from another world.

I ceased the writing that day when you came upon the stile and when you later asked me of it I told you I would tell you a year and a day after our marriage. I take back this berth is mine, no Antoinette mine, but this berth is mine, Bertha returned my berserkness, the animal is how to bear how it must be endured. Endure and finally know the nameless boy of the loud heartbreaking sobs.

Take back Bertha is for me to see her eyes not blank they focus upon me they blink. They will not unite with mine yet look through mine and though they will not retaliate they go through mine and will separate, get a share of the property. Words instead of high-pitched laughter now a clear voice and flushed not whitened face. Christophine's first advice afterall but now applied to three: Thirds. They divide and sell the property. Each to a unique way: distinguishing in unison.

Perhaps Rochester to the southern regions of sharp light often dusk-like nearness of sea where he continues to write the disturbing, alien, secret letter to his father, writing out of berserkness, out of which emerges novel. He begins a garden in a way more dedicated her claws the vines his water feeds.

Perhaps Antoinette, who wants to know England finally, a Devon move. "So there is still the sound of whispering that I have heard all my life, but these are different voices." Not a stupor. Bog in the mornings does not impede yet thickens to manifest what poetry otherwise would float away.

Perhaps Jane moves to the pioneer country where leather not as coach what carries but more saddle, her paintings remain peculiar and urge others to begin and end again her autobiography as she rides on her horse she rides through where the explorers stretch that horizon of what conscious.

Companions for each not foreclosed. But for one it takes longer.

Faces to the letters. These condensations transmute distinctly. Long script scratches the parchment resounds how each sounds through each other written uniquely qualified when there is the rain no possibility of a walk today.

AFTERWORD I
Specific French Feminist Contributions

In the middle of any work requiring intense concentration and involving novel procedures, one often asks: ought I to go on? The writings of the French feminists served as the crucial Bryher-ian "go on" in such instances.[1] A brief intellectual discussion of my engagement with a few in particular is called for. Throughout, Jane Gallop's relationship with them (who she became and what she saw in dialogue with each of them) also has been informative.[2]

---

[1]This refers to H. D.'s Corfu vision, at the end of April, 1920, in the middle of which she asked her friend and patron Bryher whether she ought to go on. "Bryher says without hesitation, 'Go on.'" [H. D., *Tribute to Freud* (New York: New Directions, 1974), p. 47, see entire section pp. 43–56.]

[2]Gallop's "dialogues" with the theorists in her intelligent and cogent work *The Daughter's Seduction: Feminism and Psychoanalysis* are so interesting precisely because they are so Jungian! [See footnote 17 in the first section of the Introduction on Jung's theory of the necessity of dialoging with various intrapsychic figures for purposes of differentiation. Also James Hillman, *Revisioning Psychology* (New York: Harper and Row, 1975), *Healing Fictions* (Barrytown, N.Y.: Station Hill, 1983); Mary Watkins, *Invisible Guests*.]

Gallop's particular dialogue with Irigaray's text "The Father's Seduction: Law But Not Sex" (in *Speculum*), particularly interested me in light of my analysis in Chapter 2: the intrapsychic encounter of father and daughter in the red-room of mother's rule (mother's forbidden interior body). Even though for Gallop the daughter and father are analogous respectively to feminism and psychoanalysis, and therefore represent cultural structures, her reading (in dialogue with Irigaray's) allowed me to question whether I was reading Brontë's account of the father–daughter encounter as "seduction." What is strikingly absent from both Irigaray's and Gallop's scenarios, and which is quite present in Brontë's, is the daughter's symbiosis with a rejecting and abandoning mother (what I call antipathetic symbiosis) as the base of the father-daughter encounter. I do not see an occurrence of "seduction" yet a desparate attempt by the daughter to be rescued from the more non-being aspects of that symbiosis. The failure of this attempt, the hysterical moment, pertains not to the telos of *father's revealed desire* [as in the Gallop-Irigaray dialogue (Gallop, *The Daughter's Seduction*, pp. xv, 70-79, Irigaray, *Speculum*, pp. 37-39)] yet to the possibility for a *language* of what

◄§ *Kristeva.* With whom it has been a passionate encounter,
her texts are a woman's mind proliferating which chews even
loudly chews and converts seldom spilling. She drives ideas to
their limit of delirium and sometimes over. Constantly in
revision, she laughs over her own contradictions as they fly
over her shoulder. She has let herself be penetrated by the
Great Masters without going under; even when she tottered
from the impact what emerged is worth interest. Moving
always rapidly, bird-darting at times yet inevitably a precision in the work. Gallop senses (and I agree) a suspicion of
Mother there yet her work seems more the encounter of a
female mind with Masters, exploding them, her work has
been in domains not primarily "female," yet of the eccentric,
that anterior yet always affecting, what she would say has
been allocated to the "feminine" yet not a gender issue. The
eccentric masters and their offsides, their poetic language,
how she can be their critic, she strokes the male poet as she
pierces, this more her work. §◄

Overall, Kristeva is interested primarily in theoretical formulations of
the unconscious and its place in Western thought. The three works I read
were *Revolution in Poetic Language* (the intersection of Hegel, Marx, and
Lacan with the countertraditions of poetic language), *Desire in Language* (the
eruption of the semiotic, its effects upon the symbolic, and the cultural
results), and *Powers of Horror* (preoedipal abjection and Céline).[3] Even when
her theoretical postulations did not speak to the sort of lyrical-analytic
language I was writing, they often provoked me to ask the place of conscious signification in relation to the unconscious.

---

[2]*(continued)*
has always been mother's forbidden body (a discourse of that body and its
desires). In my view, we need to take the entire father–daughter scenario out of
paradigms of seduction (and its modus operandi of *blame*: father's guilt to daughter's guilt to mother's guilt — see Clément's essay "The Guilty One" in *Newly Born
Woman*) and recover the place of mother's womb in it. Nevertheless, the Gallop-
Irigaray dialogue has been a stimulating ingredient for such a project.
[3]Julia Kristeva, *Revolution in Poetic Language*; *Desire in Language*; *Powers of Horror:
An Essay on Abjection*, trans. Leon S. Roudiez (New York: Columbia University
Press, 1982). I recognize that Kristeva does not consider herself a feminist or
endorse feminism (Jardine, *Gynesis*, pp. 19–22) but I include her (as well as
Cixous who also has problems with the concept) as a "French feminist" because
of her inclusion in the anthology *New French Feminisms*.

I will discuss certain of her concepts or theoretical moves which interested me even where I disagreed with them. Major points of her study of the discourse of the split subject seemed pertinent to what I was attempting: that speaking subject belonging to both semiotic (*chora*) and symbolic domains, its articulation as poetic language, and the necessity of its shattering all code. Her sense is that thrusting semiotic rhythm (instinctual drive, phonic differentiation, intonation) is always limited by the "sun" (the symbolic, paternal law), and must be, if the former does not eradicate itself it must struggle with the limiting structure of language the result of which can be poetic language (e.g., Mallarmé, Artaud, Joyce). She stresses the necessity of poetic language for the destabilization (and eventual change of) any society.[4]

Her "splits" gave me something with which to struggle. I did not find the dialectic of semiotic and symbolic (which are "opposed yet inseparable") helpful (any more actually than signifier–signified or conscious–unconscious or upperworld–underworld), though I see their necessity as a place in her thought. The identification of *chora* (which, in the Platonic sense she uses, must be female) with semiotic[5] I found problematic since it too easily reverts to the polarity placing woman as nothingness: woman as involuntary, the unthought (not yet symbolic), unconscious, anonymous, without name. This split also places the domain of sequential positioning and judgment, distinction, word, boundary, at the male, which does not correspond to either the formal aspects of my study nor its conceptual findings.

Also, the scission within her rhetoric between paternal law and rhythm implies that language is something quite other than the rhythm (which lies beneath language and erupts up into it), and, by capping that rhythm, language adds something other, a limiting structure, to it. My sense is that there cannot be a semiotic completely anterior to father, that he is included within it and in fact implicated from the start, the question is how. I ask: what if the rhythm is around and is not self-destructive (threatening to eradicate itself without the solar capping device)[6] or chaotic, its natural telos not eradication, but that it requires instead a context for articulation,

---

[4]See *Desire in Language*, pp. 23–31, 132–140; and *Poetic Language*, pp. 68-85.

[5]*Desire in Language*, pp. 6–7, 133: "Plato's *Timeus* speaks of a *chora*, receptacle, unnameable, improbable, hybrid, anterior to naming, to the One, to the father, and consequently, maternally connoted to such an extent that it merits 'not even the rank of syllable.' " (her italics), p. 133; also *Poetic Language*, pp. 25–28, 32, 40, 46–47, 52, 55–56, 81–82, 88, 99–100, 149–152.

[6]See *Desire in Language*, pp. 28–34, 178–179, 276, 289.

image becoming the word it is: the aspect of poetic language which Kristeva sees as transformative even more than communicative,[7] I understand, though I aim at a poetic language which is both.

I was moved by her work on Barthes, her appreciation of the death and irony of language, writing as rupture, contestation and flight, language for the writer as problem not beauty. Her questioning of the constitution of a new heterogeneous signifying body for which literature is no longer an "object," helped me to see the place of literature as body, in fact *Jane Eyre* as my heterogeneous body newly signifying.[8]

One of the most provocative sections of her work for mine includes the statement (based on Oedipal theory) that poetic language is equivalent to incest with mother, that is, unlike discursive discourse, it does not repress instinctual drives and a continuous relation with mother, yet "the unsettled and questionable subject of poetic language (for whom the word is never uniquely sign) maintains itself at the cost of reactivating this repressed instinctual, maternal element . . . *poetic language would be* for its questionable subject-in-process the *equivalent of incest*" (her italics).[9] The questions this raises for me pertain to (1) its implications for a woman writing poetic language: is her incest with mother different at all from Mallarmé's? Is hers not Oedipal? preoedipal? and if preoedipal, how can there be a speaking at all, would not that place of incest be mute, paralyzed, engulfed without word? (2) If the only way that one can imagine the speaking of maternal desire (not the paternal discursive syntax) is in terms of instinct and incest, does not that keep maternal desire as pernicious material (having always to be capped, checked, measured with caution) which fundamentally must be repressed for language as symbolic function to be constituted, or, if the maternal element is expressed at all, the result must be an incest of a rather ominous nature ("violent silence, instinctual drive, collided void").[10] Yet do we speak of an incestual relation with his father when a man writes discursive discourse (syntactically normative sentences)? Shouldn't we? All of which precludes any sense of a speaking of maternal desire in its own *legitimate syntax—into which the paternal has descended—*which has its own systematic parameters and even internal meaning and logic (if we can conceive of such a thing beyond a subject-object antinomy).

---

[7]*Desire in Language*, pp. 102–103, 178–183; and *Poetic Language*, pp. 81–85, 101–106.
[8]*Desire in Language*, pp. 105–114.
[9]*Desire in Language*, p. 136; see also *Poetic Language*, pp. 46–51.
[10]*Desire in Language*, p. 179.

Though I found much difficulty with Kristeva's contrast between the semioticizing body heterogeneous to signification (related to incest with mother) and signification based on prohibition of incest, it did make me inquire on the relation of my lyrical-analytic language to incest. The analysis emerging from my study suggests that the incest is one involving daughter possessed within the maternal womb into which father enters (descends into), and the eventual "sublimation" of this necessarily hysterical moment (the mediation of this triangulation incest) is the baseline not only of *Jane Eyre*, but also the development of the language of the female unconscious becoming the (yet foreign) place of woman in culture.

Oedipus may or may not be the mythology most representative of male psychological development, it was never the woman's and a continual usage of Oedipal and even preoedipal structures (even by feminists) undermines any attempt to excavate or explore the mythology of female psychological domains. Perhaps it is her focus on the Oedipal (male) subject which makes Kristeva's statements on the hysteric problematic for me in various places in her work.[11]

When in Kristeva's work we arrive at the phallic mother, my wish is that

---

[11]*Powers of Horror* focuses on the primacy of the male Oedipal subject. The privileging of the Oedipal son and his triangle with mother and father in the discussion of abjection is particularly disconcerting when Kristeva speaks of prohibited incest and "confrontation of the feminine" (pp. 58f, 78–79), with no psychologizing of this privileging (i.e., questioning her own metaphorization) and, in effect, camouflaging it with discussions of generic themes. Some of her discussion on non-object and its relation to abjection as well as to primary narcissism (p. 62, 67–68) was helpful, yet this was also only discussed in terms of an Oedipal son which necessarily affects her view of its relation to maternal engulfment and paternal symbolic. The problematic statements on the hysteric are: *Desire in Language*, p. 197: the hysterical woman heterogeneous to the poet, and he experiences her only as text; p. 166: classic hystericals search for that impossible maternal fusion and are exalted in frustration; *Powers of Horror*, p. 45: Hysteria cannot produce the symbolic. Also, in my view, of the three cases she presented in "Freud and Love: Treatment and Its Discontents" (in *The Kristeva Reader*), Marie the hysteric is discussed most traditionally-pejoratively ("What was abjection for John is for Marie pure and simple inanity . . . where a narcissism without boundaries unfolds in self-satisfied fashion . . . . The way towards Oedipal identification with the father is either blocked or impeded by repression of the imaginary father . . ." pp. 265–266) and is the least heartfelt, particularly compared to schizoid Matthew with the walkman, a case filled with empathy and even poetry.

she and Lacan could have read (more of) Jung.[12] It is surprising that those who speak of the necessity of heterogeneity and shattering could maintain such a unitary sense of a phallic mother.[13] Phallic mother as if mother has one phallus, as if she is not a differentiated, heterogeneous figure herself with many psychological aspects, multiple male figures passing through her by whom the child is "possessed," with whom fused, multiple phalloi (the delineation of some primary ones is *Jane Eyre*).

The phallus is the mother because of the son's desire to be the mother's desire which must necessarily be the phallus. (Phallus — transcendent desire meeting logos — not penis. Yet the model of his extrication from her is castration.) "That the phallus could be the mother . . . perhaps allows us to remain afloat when the thetic (the symbolic) lets go."[14] I see it more that the various phalloi of the mother (and their precise form and sequence in appearance is meaningful) are beginning extrications, attempts to remove the daughter out of unconscious recesses not yet nameable to regions where

––––––––––––––––

[12]Kristeva's statements on Jung, *Desire in Language*, p. 276: "Jung's dead end with its archetypal configurations of libidinal substance taken out of the realm of sexuality and placed in bondage to the archaic mother." "Stabat Mater" (in *Kristeva Reader*), p. 179: "There thus remained for his followers an entire continent to explore, a black one indeed, where Jung was the first to rush in, getting all his esoteric fingers burnt, but not without calling attention to some sore points of the imagination with regard to motherhood, points that are still resisting analytical rationality."

Lacan's statements on Jung: *The Four Fundamental Concepts of Psycho-Analysis*, trans. Alan Sheridan (New York: Norton, 1981), p. 24, 152–153; *Écrits: A Selection*, p. 195, 233; all are on the difference between the two schools (and p. 116 in *Écrits* on Jung as spokesperson for an event with Freud, could indicate that Lacan met Jung). Yet, contrary to Lacan's sense of this difference ["that so deep a difference remains between the two schools . . . the level of their practice will soon appear to be reducible to the distance between the modes of dreaming of the Alps and the Atlantic." (*Écrits*, p. 195)] my sense is that a close examination of the two schools would find them more closely aligned. I would suggest a scrutiny of their similar uses of "imago" (which Kugler discusses in *Alchemy of Discourse*); as well as Jung's *participation mystique* with Lacan's Imaginary; Jung's anima with Lacan's petit object a; Jung's sense of heterogeneous figures in the unconscious necessitating interlocution with an ego which is then relativized by them and Lacan's sense of the unconscious as discourse of the Other and subversion of the subject.

[13]*Desire in Language*, pp. 190–195, yet Phallic Mother is discussed only in terms of the male subject. For example, "His [the poet, Dionysus] oracular discourse, split (signifier/signified) and multiplied (in its sentential and lyrical concatenations), carries the scar of not merely the *trauma* but also the *triumph* of his battle with the Phallic Mother." (p. 193, her italics).

[14]*Desire in Language*, p. 191.

she can begin to learn the linguistic and semantic dimensions of the images of those recesses, yet the mother's "phalloi" do not in themselves teach her that. "No language can sing unless it confronts the Phallic Mother."[15] And what does that confrontation involve for Kristeva: one must swallow her, eat her, dissolve her, then pierce, strip and castrate the rediscovered mother to carry her away to the symbolic.[16]

My study of *Jane Eyre* has given me another sense of it. The original fusing (step-phallic) mother is simultaneously a rejecting mother, and is to be differentiated through (and at one point that involves a bursting away from, yet this is not conceived in terms of castration), yet the differentiation takes place more through a depotentiation, the detumescence of the "phalloi" which have come from her. The negotiation and process of this detumescence is not as violent as piercing or stripping, more deflation, letting the air out of, realizing the limp within, becoming a marble indifference to the inflated erection. It is the resisting the "phalloi" of the original fusing mother, through an attempt to attack or pierce them back, that sends the daughter further into recess not language. And what moves (up and out) to symbolic language is not phallic mother or her confrontation yet a girls' school (for which that mother pays the most rudimentary tuition).

Kristeva's continual crediting of the signified (which for her must be accompanied by the transcendental ego) was helpful in the process of my questioning the signification of my lyrical-analytic language (how it generated its own analysis). I was interested in her concern for the thetic character of significance even as she saw what in poetic language departed from that (i.e., that the poetic function is not exhausted by meaning and signification).[17] In her view, in some cases poetic language produces effects that destroy even syntax itself (the discursive syntax which is the "guarantee" of thetic consciousness: of the signified object and transcendental ego); and

---

[15]Ibid.

[16]Ibid., p. 192, 195. The difficulty here is (1) not only must mother (and her fusion tendency) be an obstacle which must be castrated and severed from but (2) that Father (his Law and Symbolic) remains Savoir: saving the child from fusion with the preoedipal Mother (child as her phallus) as well as from the abjection of the child's effort to separate from that mother. See *Powers of Horror*, a study of the transposition from mother as object to Paternal Other, its mediating symbolic dimensions and the relation of that to phobia, obsession and perversions. The problem is not just that she uses the male Oedipal son as the base of her work without specifying the implications of that position, but also that the way Mother figures in such an analysis implicates negatively a female psychology.

[17]*Desire in Language*, p. 132.

yet poetic language does have a "signifying disposition [which] is not that of meaning or signification: no sign, no predication, no signified object and therefore no operating consciousness of a transcendental ego."[18] I would then ask what is the signified "object" of poetic language and its operating consciousness (though in my view poetic language resides outside of subject–object proscriptions)? What is its signifying disposition which exceeds, is heterogeneous to yet adjacent or in sight of meaning? And is that another sort of (previously "unknown") meaning?

After this study, I agree that poetic language unsettles the *position* of the signified and thereby the transcendental ego, yet this does not mean it forfeits meaning (i.e., does not mean it posits a signifying apparatus devoid of or even heterogeneous to meaning). It requires instead novel examinations of the signified (not related to referent or not even as referent yet formal relations of images carrying their own signification) which relativizes all signifying subjects (even the split subjects speaking Lacan's unconscious desire) and thereby departs from any sense of object.

In my view, Kristeva's opposing the semiotic with sentence limits of meaning (the position of a subject of enunciation as meaning) and significance (possible or actual denotation) precludes her more assiduous scrutiny of the signifying apparatus of poetic language consisting of (a specific) meaning (which in fact pertains to psychological analysis and dream interpretation).

I leave off questioning: what about an operating unconsciousness of a

---

[18]Ibid., p. 133. In the earlier work, *Revolution in Poetic Language*, however, in chapter nine, she is closer to discussing the signification of the pre-symbolic, semiotic (poetic) language (which prevents it from becoming a fetishist mechanism, i.e., the work of art and the body eroticized as an object of pleasure as substitutes for symbolic signification). Here she suggests a signification of the semiotic which, even as it dislocates signification, serves it through musicalization. She claims (p. 65) that "No text, no matter how 'musicalized' is devoid of meaning or signification; on the contrary, musicalization pluralizes meanings . . . . The text signifies the un-signifying: it assumes within a signifying practice this functioning (the semiotic), which ignores meaning and operates before meaning or despite it." In *Desire in Language*, she specifies this more precisely as a signifying apparatus which is heterogeneous to yet in sight of meaning.

I was interested in her discussion in *Poetic Language* of the transgression of the symbolic, "the thetic break," and how art does this yet without relinquishing the thetic, and how precisely this pertains to the "risk that textual practice represents for the subject" (p. 69f). Also, in this work, I benefited from her understanding of the personal "cost" of writing poetic language (p. 104), her study of desire as negation of the object in its alterity (p. 131ff), and her work on expulsion (p. 148), rejection (p. 160ff) and the renewal of divisions (p. 171ff).

transcendental ego? What of a poetic language which in and of itself had a signifying apparatus that did not forfeit meaning yet required an understanding of "signified" as regions of the unconscious necessitating other syntactical and semantical operations, autonomous to historical moments yet not unaffected by them, and not heterogeneous to signification? What would then be dismantled would be the Saussurian bar maintaining signified as beneath (and uncapitalized in Lacanian terms) without eliminating the need for a veil: veil permeated by meaning without risking sunstroke.

> ⋆§ *Irigaray.* Perhaps left-handed compliment that she is the one that should have done to her what he had done to him: excommunication. She had placed her looking glass (curved) too close to the underwear of the Fathers to reappropriate what they had stolen from "the feminine." Associating to the phrases of so many Fathers: Freud, Hegel, Kant, Descartes, Plotinus, Aristotle, Plato, then Marx, Lévi-Strauss, but through Lacan, arch-Father. Athena finally enraged at Father asking where is Mother? Her pristine stance and Gallop becomes wanton around it (Saint-Ange). Tentatively, later, began the song the voice is female and it leaves the anger on the other pages, This Sex temporarily fused of the Other Woman love songs lyric. §⋆

Those of Irigaray's publications which I read during this project were: "When Our Lips Speak Together"; "And the One Doesn't Stir Without the Other"; *Speculum of the Other Woman* (hereafter referred to as *Speculum*); *This Sex Which Is Not One* (hereafter referred to as *This Sex*).[19]
Some critics have spoken of the contrast of Irigaray's two lyrical essays with the analytical discourse of her essays deconstructing patriarchal theory. Carolyn Burke speaks of the lyrical essays (both pertaining to women-bonding) as the "other side" of the patriarchal discourse Irigaray deconstructed in the previous two volumes: *Speculum* (a critique of philosophical theories from Freud to Plato for their use of sameness-onto-itself as the baseline of identity and signification) and *This Sex* (critical analyses of Marx, Lévi-Strauss and Lacan and a reply to questions on *Speculum*).[20] Hélène Wenzel speaks of the lyrical essay "And the One Doesn't Stir With-

---

[19]Irigaray, "And the One Doesn't Stir Without the Other"; "When Our Lips Speak Together"; *Speculum*; *This Sex*.
[20]Carolyn Burke, "Introduction to Luce Irigaray's 'When Our Lips Speak Together,'" *Signs* 6 (1980), 66–68.

out the Other" as a "playful" undoing of the psychoanalytic theories Irigaray deconstructed "more seriously" in *Speculum* and *This Sex*.[21] That led me to wonder why lyric is playful and the critical examination of another's text serious. Unless, like Gallop, we use play in the sense of *jouir* here,[22] it can too easily reinforce notions of play as female in the sense of not-serious, and deconstruction as male, serious, knowledgeable. Is Irigaray "masculine" in the deconstructive essays and "feminine" in her lyrical ones?

On the other hand, as previously stated, I was perturbed that the emotional subtext of both lyric pieces is love, and that of the critical essays precise anger and distrust which continues a sort of genderized separation of the two modes. It raises the additional question: are judgment, division, and hate not possible in a lyrical essay, cannot love and even desires of fusion inform a critical mode? Nevertheless, the (separate though dedicated) development of both lyrical and critical essays (and in *This Sex* placed in the same book) supported what I saw developing in my drafts as a syntactical structure that was at once lyric and analysis. Irigaray had gotten them to one book, and, in parts of *Speculum*, even upon one page,[23] and that itself was an encouragement of what I was attempting. Also, I found the sheer energy and erudition of her work vitalizing.

In *This Sex*, Irigaray states that she does feel she tried to put a female syntax into play in *Speculum*, yet that to do so she had "to go back through the realm of the masculine imaginary."[24] Her goal (achieved in *Speculum* and discussed in *This Sex*) was to go back through the masculine imaginary to interpret the way it has reduced woman to silence and mimicry, and rediscover a place for the feminine imaginary.[25] Although she has not yet written what is actually from a feminine imaginary (or does she consider her two lyrical essays that? and, if so, must that exclude the analytical?), my sense is that she has provided for the existence of such a place.

Irigaray in fact states that she cannot "install" herself in the female syntax directly—nor does she see how any woman could.[26] This statement was provocative in a few ways. It allowed me to question my complicity with the "masters," that I used their tools in part, and how I could allow a female

---

[21]Hélène Vivienne Wenzel, "Introduction to Luce Irigaray's 'And the One Doesn't Stir Without the Other,'" *Signs* 7 (1981), 56–59.
[22]Gallop, *The Daughter's Seduction*, p. 126. *Jouir* is associated with: the maternal, body, and the semiotic, outside the symbolic.
[23]Particularly in parts of the "Speculum" section of *Speculum*, pp. 133–240.
[24]Irigaray, *This Sex*, pp. 134–135.
[25]Ibid., p. 164.
[26]Ibid., p. 135.

syntax to emerge and not be talking at or to these masters or even through their findings. Although Irigaray is more interested in the place of the unconscious in philosophical tradition, and the relation of that to woman issues, I wonder what she would say about the fact that I did not go back through the male imaginary to arrive at (through retrieving) the female unconscious or its syntax.

Her statements in *This Sex* supported my work in a number of places: the necessity of signifying feminine pleasures; all dichotomizing disrupted; woman's lack of access to language except through "masculine" systems of representation and the effect of that in severing her from herself and other women. I have already discussed ways I was assisted by her responses to questions of an unconscious that would be a woman's.[27]

The discussion concerning "feminine symbolics"[28] (what I discuss as the figuration lesson of Lowood) made me reflect on what I had discovered on such a thing. From this study, I have found that "feminine symbolics" must include the emergence of conscience from the depotentiation of paternal law (conscience mediating desire and rage through interlocution with "ego"); the articulation of ancestral memory and its unconscious desires (while keeping that veiled); the continual crafting of the images emerging from unconscious recess occasioned by the rending of fusion (paradise lost); the differentiation of psychological figures: delineation of their face, voice, and signification.

Also Irigaray's own question — *"would the operation of a 'feminine symbolics' be of such a nature that the constitution of a place for what is repressed would be implied in it?* (her italics)"[29] — pertains to my study where I found that the only way to arrive at figuration (Lowood) is that what is prior and repressed be implied (Gateshead and its movement through and effect upon Lowood in Chapter 7), and the way to delineate such figuration (Thornfield) is to go back down and through that which has been repressed (red-room). This question also prompted me to inquire whether "man" will become the unconscious of my lyrical-analysis. What is the unconscious of this study? In many ways, I consider the writing of the introduction and the afterwords a writing of the unconscious of my project (since they are in the discursive syntax which

---

[27]Ibid., p. 77, 79, respectively, as well as 134, 85, 122-25 and 138-139, 158, respectively.

[28]Ibid., pp. 122-129.

[29]Ibid., p. 124. Pertinent here are Irigaray's repetitive statements that she is interested in a non-hierarchical articulation of sexual difference, p. 146, 161-162.

must have become unconscious/repressed as what was from the start unconscious, the lyrical-analysis, was made conscious).

Irigaray explains why she still analyzes men: because she is interested in sexual difference, not reabsorption or unity or sameness or hierarchicaliza-tion.[30] Here is why I also wrote the introduction and afterwords. I am interested in (intrapsychic) sexual difference (in a woman). Irigaray dem-onstrates in many of her essays how sameness is the measure of meaning in philosophical systems of patriarchal thought. This made me consider how any homogenized discourse is phallocentric even if it consists of one female voice. All through this project I felt the importance of allowing many voices a speaking, not only within the lyrical-analysis (where there are many voices of specific figures as well as variations of the lyrical-analytical dis-course itself), but also in the inclusion of the discursive style of both the introduction and afterword. My sense here was that to include many dis-courses as well as the more traditional "male" one would reduce any phallo-cratic tendencies in the text. But then I wondered: is the goal to unsettle phallocentric discourse itself phallocentric?

As my project developed, I discovered that increased use of the first person plural was one of the major syntactical changes. Mostly I sense that this form is an aspect of a language of the unconscious; in my view, Wittig also writes from that place, and her writing supported my attempt to allow that form to continue.[31] Also, Irigaray's sense of what a female syntax might be confirmed this stylistic aspect as well as what I saw happening in general as my discursive language broke down. She says: "[W]hat a feminine syn-tax might be is not simple nor easy to state, because in that 'syntax' there would no longer be either subject or object, 'oneness' would no longer be privileged, there would no longer be proper meanings, proper names, 'proper' attributes . . . . Instead, that 'syntax' would involve nearness, proximity, but in such an extreme form that it would preclude any distinc-

---

[30]Ibid., p. 146.

[31]Wittig's use of the third person plural in *Les Guéllières* and first person singular in *The Lesbian Body* was influencial here. See her article "The Mark of Gender," [in *The Poetics of Gender*, ed. Nancy K. Miller (New York: Columbia University Press, 1986)] where she discusses her use of personal pronouns in her work. Her attempt is to make categories of gender obsolete in language. Mine is to explore different ways gender "inhabits" a text through pronouns. Also influential have been the poetic-prose works of H. D., particularly *HERmione* (New York: New Directions, 1981); *The Gift* (New York: New Directions, 1982); *Bid Me to Live* (New York: The Dial Press, 1960).

tion of identities, any establishment of ownership, thus any form of appropriation."[32]

My lyrical-analytic language has moved out of a place privileging a subject and object distinction, nor does it privilege sameness or oneness; the nearness and proximity are there (facilitated by the first person plural) but they do not preclude yet inform the discrimination of identity. In my view, there has been an unfortunate scission between ego psychologies and "unconscious" psychologies in both Freudian and Jungian schools. I work more from an understanding of the emergence of "ego" as correlative to the differentiation within the unconscious of its figures and landscapes and their meaning which does not return to discursive syntax or a semantics of oppositionalism.[33] Proximity, in my view, requires "identity," yet not an "identity" based on masculine standards or appropriation, yet one always and necessarily surrounded by the recess we call unconscious ever asking for, requiring, a delineation of its plurivocal discourse.

I already have indicated how important Irigaray's statement on woman's relation to woman in unconscious theory (the fact that it has been barely touched upon) has been for the progress of my work. Wenzel reminds us that the American feminist movement has provided much in the study of mother–daughter issues according to sociocultural roles yet, because of a general mistrust of Freud, not much has been provided in terms of intra-psychic reality.[34] Irigaray is a pioneer in speaking of the validity of that territory. When I would feel lost in the strange domain in which an alternative language was coming through, certain of her statements would be quite encouraging and would remind me that the place existed even though it had not very much been mapped and spoken ("serenely and directly").[35]

Although they lead us in different directions, immersed in very different projects, Irigaray's interest in how women's language and desire has been appropriated and repressed by patriarchal discourse related to my interest in delineating a syntax of a female unconscious, which I found necessitates a return to a lost origin in mother's body as well as an ascent and descent in our own. By the end, I found myself in a terrain of female sexuality not based on masculine parameters or theory. Any fear that might have arisen

---

[32]Irigaray, *This Sex*, p. 134.
[33]See the last chapter of *Starving Women*. Also my review essay on Marion Wood-man's *The Pregnant Virgin* in *Quadrant* 19 (1986), 90–94, as well as on Rudolph Bell's *Holy Anorexia* in *The Women's Review of Books* 3, no. 12 (1986).
[34]Wenzel, "Introduction," p. 57.
[35]Irigaray, *This Sex*, p. 135.

there and stopped the exploration was abated by my strong sense that Irigaray for one would like where I had ended up.

> ◄§ *Cixous and Clément*. Body re-inscribing that which has been repressed. Hysteric remembers sorceress. The other writes of body writing milk blood but no this body will not be essence, for who knows what will become of sexual difference. The one who says the other writes between theory and fiction herself does, moving pulsating prose-thought, and neither actually valorize body over yet this is an embodied mind thinking the way woman's body remembers. Body as theatre of the forgotten, they both look behind for what is *dramatis personae*. Their dream of transformed language becomes their urge to invent is it bisexuality. Both end there, fluid erotic, they study the woman whose passage through where the walls between the worlds are thinnest. Crossing borders exploding/ exploring perhaps beyond two-ness. Dora remembered triangles. §◄

In their major text of French feminist theory, *The Newly Born Woman*, comprised of a first essay by Catherine Clément, a second by Hélène Cixous, and a third consisting of a dialogue between them, Clément sees the hysteric residing on the cultural margins maintaining the symbolic (traditional) systems.[36] In her view, the Imaginary (and I will use their Lacanian language in discussing them), within which the hysteric and sorceress were locked (the witch "perched on the black goat," the hysteric "dolefully reclining") cannot act on the Symbolic. The hysterical effort remains only "quasi production" and is not communicable.[37]

This study suggests something else: that the hysterical moment can be transformed and transfigured. *Jane Eyre* is the narrative of the transposition of the hysterical moment (when the Imaginary cannot "rise" to the Symbolic and alter it) to a symbolic inscription just as the novel itself is the passage from Brontë's hysterical (not communicable, not a symbolic inscription)

---

[36]Cixous and Clément, *Newly Born Woman*, p. 9, 136–160.
[37]Ibid., p. 8f.

Heger letters to writing what had been repressed, which did pass over to the act of a symbolic register.[38]

In my view, Clément's dream (for her an impossible one) of the hysteric passing over to the act "and hence producing real structural transformations"[39] requires more of an understanding of how the Symbolic can and indeed does descend into the Imaginary (in which the hysteric is in fact locked within), and, in a way Clément does appreciate, the hysteric has been called liar in her attempt to narrate that.[40]

Cixous is accurate in her claim that the Imaginary persists,[41] yet, in my

---

[38]This is the August 1846 crossover. The factors in Charlotte Brontë's life relating to this crossover were many and complicated: (1) the implicit competition with her sisters: her lack of success in publishing *The Professor* (written in a male voice) whereas *Wuthering Heights* and *Agnes Grey* (both in female voices) had already been accepted; (2) the split with and renunciation of Branwell finalizing the end of the Angria period (Branwell's adultery and Charlotte's "temptation" of it—in the Heger infatuation—functionally influenced chapters fourteen onward of *Jane Eyre* as subjective fancy regarding both the appeal of and defense against adultery); (3) her father's eye operation, Brontë's biblical quote in *Jane Eyre* from Matthew on the relation of losing an eye to adultery, Rochester's loss of sight, Brontë's fear of her own loss of sight; (4) an encouraging letter from William Smith Williams, the reader of the publishing firm Smith, Elder and Co., who, in rejecting *The Professor*, intelligently discussed its merits and indicated that the firm would carefully attend a novel in three volumes by the same author (received when *Jane Eyre* was nearly complete); (5) her rage at Heger's seductive-abandonment, which became acted out as the "madness" (of and at) Mme. Heger, accompanying a desire to write for Heger, as well as write "beyond" him.
[39]Cixous and Clément, *Newly Born Woman*, pp. 9-10.
[40]Ibid., pp. 40-57.
[41]See Gallop's discussion of "Cixous's imaginary" and "Clément's symbolic," as well as the Lacanian devaluation of the imaginary and Montrelay's and Laplanche's senses of the importance of the imaginary for the symbolic, *The Daughter's Seduction*, pp. 148-150. Gallop also discusses the necessity of the Imaginary for the Symbolic, that is, to get to the Symbolic, in *Reading Lacan*, chapter two, particularly pp. 62-63. Also see the review by Phil Barrish of that discussion, "Rehearsing a Reading," *Diacritics* 16 (1986), 15-30.

A testimony of the denigration of the Imaginary is the neglect and dismissal of Jungian work, particularly by other depth psychologists. Jungians have always written (and continue with great devotion to write) not only about the domain which Lacan terms the Imaginary, yet from that very place. Jung broke from Father, and entered that space most Fathers fear to tread (yet more and more are falling into it these days): ambiguous, oppositional, replete with unconscious projective identification, elusive, polycentric. When he finally emerged to register it in the Symbolic (that is, find a Father to know it), his science became alchemy, an occult Father.

view, when the Symbolic falls into it another narrative is required and the hysterics have not been forthcoming (perhaps because of the numinosity of incest in the Imaginary so that so many prefer to live within that, repetitiously acting out the descent of the Father instead of locating the discourse of the Imaginary through the descent). *Jane Eyre* informs us on what the possibility of that other narrative might take: the negotiation of the Reed possessions, a Brocklehurst depotentiation, a Lowood context for the emergence of figuration and the Thornfield passage of that to world.

What Clément does so well is to discuss what the Jungians refer to as the "animus" problem: the woman's (particularly the woman on the margins, hysteric and sorceress) negotiation of potent male forces.[42] What she does not see is that the animus problem entails the incorporation of the Symbolic into the Imaginary: the negotiation of intrapsychic male forces (representing various aspects of appetite, desire, as well as the arbitrary and at times even abstract Law) which possess the woman, but which also imply her permeability to the unconscious, and the possibility of her creativity. If the hysteric does not learn to negotiate these as intrapsychic figures, she will stay, as Clément predicts, trapped within the Imaginary with no access out, she will not inscribe in culture, only bodily through symptom.[43]

Cixous states: "The hysteric is, to my eyes, the typical woman in all her force. It is a force that was turned back against Dora, but, if the scene changes and if woman begins to speak in other ways, it would be a force capable of demolishing those structures."[44] The structures to which she refers are those upon which the family and society are founded, which reject and despise (and in my view greatly fear) the body of women.

Clément thinks that such speech will not be forthcoming, she puts little stake in the Imaginary even as she delivers the sorceress off her stake. Though I disagree with her view of the sorceress/hysteric enclosed inevitably within the Imaginary, excluded from their own capacity for language, and therefore reinforcing the conventional social structure, what Clément

---

[42]Cixous and Clément, *Newly Born Woman*, pp. 14–39.

[43]Clément often refers to this theme, yet her most poignant statement on it is: "For the hysteric does *not* write, does *not* produce, does nothing—nothing other than make things circulate without inscribing them. 'The cough or nothing, All or nothing,' nothing is produced in between. The result: the clandestine sorceress was burned by the thousands; the deceitful and triumphant hysteric disappeared. But the master is there. He is the one who stays on permanently. He publishes writings." (*Newly Born Woman*, p. 37). My sense is that Clément does not make the connection that it is the hysteric's negotiation of the master forces which will result in breaking out of the circulation to an inscription.

[44]Ibid., p. 154.

has written on the sorceress/hysteric (and their "animus" issues) comes the closest to my view of what depth psychology of the female is about.[45]

"Women's bodies must be bound so that the constraints will make the demons come out."[46] The transition from demon to daimon (conscience) has interested me for a long while and is a major subtext of this book which examines the necessary negotiation of Reed, Brocklehurst, and Rochester forces in arriving at what is endemic to the woman, her body's metaphors, her inventions. Brontë confined at Haworth, Jane confined at Gateshead, Bertha confined at Thornfield. Devil, demon, foreign bodies as well as wizard, inquisitors, doctors. Animus figures. Mother's phalloi. To the witch/hysteric, I have added the anorexic. If the hysteric is no longer (as Clément claims, "Physically they are no more . . ."),[47] her twentieth-century counterpart is here in full disruptive force, but again, Clément's echo: disruptive to her own body or to cultural systems? Demon/daimon transition is the key.

"Each attack [spider bite] permitted a return to the lost love."[48] In the lost love place has become the foreign body, the demon which needs expulsion. The possession by John Reed in the place of his mother's rejection.

In her first essay, Clément is not as opposed to Cixous's view regarding the poignancy and effect of the hysteric as she becomes in the third essay of dialogue. Through her analysis of the women at the margins and contagion, I found Bertha Mason Rochester clearly: "All laughter is allied with the monstrous . . . . It is the moment at which the woman crosses a dangerous line, the cultural demarcation beyond which she will find herself excluded . . . . Getting away safely [for the woman knowing she was bewitched] means finding the right distance: neither too close, where one can be struck and stunned by the shock, nor too far away, where one can no longer stay alive."[49]

Perhaps even somewhat hopefully Clément leaves off her first essay with a notion of the hysteric accomplishing a "new young birth" when she emerges from the family walls within a sort of bisexuality: "I prefer to say

---

[45]See my article on the psychology of the witch: "Verso una comprensione psicologica della strega," trans. Bianca Garufi, *Giornale storico di psicologia dinamica* 7 (1983), 44–79. Also, *Starving Women*, where I indicate the relation between the anorexic and the hysteric (pp. ix–xi, 13), the anorexic and the witch (pp. 125–126).

[46]Cixous and Clément, *Newly Born Woman*, p. 11.

[47]Ibid., p. 56.

[48]Ibid., p. 20.

[49]Ibid., p. 33, 35, respectively.

that the hysteric, following where the sorceress leads, is split between man and woman, between the two figures of her bisexuality. She is between the family walls, which she does not leave, and a *jeune naissance* (a new young birth), the I-nnascence that is not yet accomplished."[50]

Both Clément and Cixous indicate the vital engagement of theory and fiction. For Cixous, the hysteric's symbolic inscription is a probability. She herself let Dora speak through a dramatic production. Her "Portrait of Dora" is the hysteric's moment of transmission into culture even as Dora's public discourse is dreamy, murmuring, breathless, laughing, mimicking, anguished, hissing, screaming, sleepy, staccatolike, exasperated, mocking, cutting and bitter.[51]

Whereas Clément spoke of animus "demons," Cixous speaks of the "whole populations issuing from the unconscious, and in each suddenly animated desert, the springing up of selves one didn't know — our women, our monsters, our jackals, our Arabs, our aliases, our frights."[52] Without "this peopling," she states that there is neither bisexuality (which for her pertains to the woman localizing within herself the presence of both sexes and "keeping alive the other that is confided to her") or creativity/invention.[53]

Cixous acknowledges that to know these "separate-people, thought-people" requires a certain amount of what once was called "possession." Very much aligned with Jungian thought here, she discusses how the same opening in a woman which keeps her accessible to the unconscious, is also the danger that she leave herself to become the other (which others, is the question I always ask). The question Cixous raises yet does not really answer is: how can she use this opening to go to the other, "a traveller in unexplored places," but not lose herself (a question quite analogous to my discussion of the anorexic's permeability to the psyche, her defense against that, and the effect on "ego differentiation"). "[N]ot to do away with the space between, but to see it, to experience what she is not, what she is, what she can be."[54] I would say that Jane's eyre, the way Jane errs and is errant, pertains precisely to this issue of opening and not losing.

In my study of woman's relation to and negotiation of forces emerging from the unconscious (and at times "possessing" her through the symbiosis

---

[50]Ibid., p. 55.
[51]Hélène Cixous, "Portrait of Dora," trans. Sarah Brud, *Diacritics* 13 (1983), 2–32.
[52]Cixous and Clément, *Newly Born Woman*, p. 84.
[53]Ibid., pp. 84–86.
[54]Ibid., p. 86.

with mother), and the relation of that to her "psychological development" and possibility of invention, I have chosen to work through a classical piece of literature. *Jane Eyre*, I believe, is the effect of a woman's self-analysis, the discrimination of her "male" figures, a delineation of their possession of her and extrication from these possessions through figuration lessons arriving at domains of creativity endemic to her nature. The people of Brontë's unconscious have become an anthology classic[55] because Brontë so precisely explored and depicted the population, the *dramatis personae* of her unconscious.

Both Clément and Cixous agree that there will not be one "feminine discourse," and I agree with them. The way Cixous has spoken to my lyrical-analytic language is in her reference to logic conveyed carnally, and the necessary involvement of one's self: "Her discourse, even when 'theoretical' or political, is never simple or linear or 'objectivized,' universalized; she involves her story in history."[56]

The permeability within each of Cixous's and Clément's essays becomes more a binary opposition in their dialogue, each taking rather fixed contrary stands regarding the hysteric (as victim reinforcing conventional structures or as actual disturber of those structures). In a sense, even as they discuss master discourse and the necessity of the Symbolic, in their dialogue they themselves are in the specular dualism of the Imaginary. In this way, they indicate, more by their position, how the Imaginary does and must persist.

Clément has said in her essay: "The result: the clandestine sorceress was burned by the thousands; the deceitful and triumphant hysteric disappeared. But the master is there. He is the one who stays on permanently. He publishes writings."[57] They then dialogue on master discourse and they discuss the hysteric behind the master, checking the master.[58] I wondered whether the unconscious of my lyrical-analysis which became the Introduction and Afterword, and my desire to make that more conscious, related to my need for a masterful position. That lead to the question: who am I

---

[55]The reference here is to Gubar and Gilbert's edition of the Norton anthology of women's literature and the inclusion of *Jane Eyre* as the only complete novel in it.

[56]Cixous and Clément, p. 92. Also: "She exposes herself. Really she makes what she thinks materialize carnally, she conveys meaning with her body. She *inscribes* what she is saying because she does not deny unconscious drives the unmanageable part they play in speech" (italics hers, p. 92).

[57]Ibid., p. 37, also see footnote 43 above.

[58]Ibid., see the third section "Exchange," pp. 136–160.

repressing as master (by masterfully bringing out the unconscious of the text which corresponds more to master discourse)? Who is the hysteric who will hold in check this mastery? Bertha. The nature of Cixous's love for Dora is astounding[59] and returns me to my love for Jane, for Helen, and also my love for Bertha. My fourteenth chapter, for which no theoretical review is possible, is Bertha's. It so permeates and depicts the silence of the entire text that it will not be summarized. Bertha is whose poetry finally speaks so lucidly that theory is redundant, yet which is a culmination as well as baseline for all the discourses of this work.

In their dialogue on the hysteric and the possibility of her dissension disturbing cultural structures, I realize, though I was not conscious of it at the time, that by writing the fourteenth chapter I have included my say in that discussion. For how Bertha was repressed is what allowed the bourgeois family at Thornfield to emerge (Mrs. Fairfax, Rochester, Adèle, Jane), yet simultaneously in the way Jane was also governess, the repressed of the master's (repressed) wife, the possibility of disturbance became greater. "[B]ut, if the scene changes . . .",[60] Cixous writes. The scene is changing.

---

[59]Ibid., for example, p. 154: "There is something else in Dora's case that is great — everything in the nature of desire. A desire that is also, often, love — for love. The source of Dora's strength is, in spite of everything, her desire." And also p. 150: "In the front line was Dora, who fascinated me, because here was an eighteen-year-old girl caught in a world where you say to yourself, she is going to break — a captive, but with such strength! I could not keep from laughing from one end to the other, because, despite her powerlessness and with (thanks to) that powerlessness, here is a kid who successfully jams all the little adulterous wheels that are turning around her and, one after the other, they break down. She manages to say what she doesn't say, so intensely that the men drop like flies." See also her "Portrait of Dora."

[60]Cixous and Clément, *Newly Born Woman*, p. 154.

AFTERWORD II
A Theory Within Female Psychology

I write this afterword with the understanding that parts of this text — certain of its more subtle workings — cannot be fully discussed yet, at least by me now. The following is what I now can summarize in a more discursive syntax. Here is yet another way of telling the story. An informing set of images in approaching and negotiating this afterword has been the Orpheus-Eurydice myth. The dangers of looking back at such a work, which took place in and through the unconscious, so close to the "navel" that is the annihilation within life and despite life, have been quite present for me. And then there comes the gaze, and the sacrifices. In another sense, however, I realize that the text itself, the lyrical-analysis, *was* Orpheus's descent, and if there had been a gaze, this work would not have manifested. Yet then I wonder how this work could exist apart from Orpheus's gaze which necessarily included the song which came before and the yearning which followed. That gaze then would make nugatory this attempt to return to the origins of the work and summarize it, since those origins would be lost. But I realize, of course, it is not Orpheus, it is not Eurydice.

All that protects us from falling completely into mother's unconscious, its phantoms and cracked vessels, from which we are not separate, is a pane. It is not that we would be "engulfed" by mother's unconscious, which is more the male initiation, yet we happily sit in it. We sit in her recessed, repressed desire to be nonsocial, unnatural. We attach to this unconscious desire which is to be rejected by her. Here is the rejection underlying the nondifferentiation with her, which is the only way to her. This is an antipathetic symbiosis.

We happily sit in the nonbeing aspects of mother's unconscious (arctic death-demons), which make her a "stepmother," and its contents engage us, perhaps even want something from us. How they want us to bring out their text to a conscious, daily world, is embodied in the outburst of stepmother's son, John Reed. He appears when the unconscious forces cannot yet be locuted or delineated in any way, and therefore seize us bodily. Such seizures take the form of repetition compulsions (where we are completely passive to them) and addictions (where we lunge back but then go under them).

These symptomatic bodily seizures appear in the more social breakfast-room: they emerge out of breaking a long fast of a complacency in the fusion with stepmother's unconscious. Huge cravings — oral, anal, genital — and releases are the John Reed seizures. No one speaks during them. The John Reed possession precludes (predates) signification and dialogue; it is an unmediated, onesided attempt to carry the unconscious to world.

The antipathetic symbiosis precludes interlocution with both stepmother as well as with the figures of the unconscious, which is the threat of our being possessed by them in entirety. This one-sided attempt to manifest unconscious is also John Reed's contiguous, immediate mode of seizure. Its necessity is that it removes us from the precarious (windowseat) edge of fusion with the nonbeing, death-demon aspects of the unconscious. We are delivered through it into the more human breakfast-room, with feeling and flowing blood.

The John Reed possession contains many cravings. The way he lunges at us as we sit with death-demons suggests that, however he seems so satiated and even indulged, he is ravenous. There are also latent cravings within our windowseat at an otherworld on the edge of a humanity: when our head bleeds we lunge, we crave the blood and flesh of humanity, we crave bodies, rushing at, tearing open, panting with bodies. What Mrs. Reed craves is Jane, and what Jane holds for her which she cannot see.

Although John Reed's call is to carry out the text (delineate the figurations of) the unconscious, his mode is one of incorporation of/by its forces. We incorporate them in the sense of including them bodily: they in fact possess us and we give them bodily shape. Yet because we are shaped by them, we are them, and so we are incorporated in the sense too of incorporeal, being yet without our (own) body.

If we lunge at John Reed, reactively engage with him in order to leave the windowseat to arrive at the more social room, it serves the opposite function of pulling us further into a symbiosis, yet this time within a more remote and solemn room, the red-room. Upon the windowseat, we were at one with stepmother's unconscious; it was not a question of body, ours or hers. Yet after the John Reed possession, we are inside the most remote, majestic and haunted chamber of her mansion, her unconscious body, the red-room.

The red-room is the place of the jewel-casket, the crimson saturation into which we are thrown at puberty, the entry and extinction of the Father, the womb. In a sense, John Reed's eruptions signal that appetite (breakfast) is off until the womb is traversed. The John Reed possession serves the purpose of moving us through the unconscious from a disembodied (even dismembered) place where there is no body — bodiless complacency with windowseat death demons — to an unconscious body.

Maids drag us into the red-room. As we have lunged back at John Reed, resisted this embodiment of unconscious force, the maids' collective morality attempts to do the same thing: resist the eruption of the unconscious as bodily craving, release, and seizure. To enter the red-room, therefore, is also to be working out a morality regarding the unconscious and its manifestation.

Mother's womb, forbidden body, where the womb engages its seed and pulverizes it, is where the imps and phantoms floating around and with us on the windowseat are now who we are in a red-room mirror. In the red-room, we are not-I, but we can be mirrored. This mirroring confirms that there is more of a body than there was on the windowseat, yet it is the unconscious body of the stepmother: the phantoms of her unconscious we bodily reflect in her hidden red chamber.

The two "temptations" which would bind us within the red-room are fascination and anorexia. A fascination for the phantom we are would keep us permanently mirror gazing within mother's unconscious: always antipathetically bound to her in an unconscious body. The next temptation would involve turning the tyrannical and deathdealing forces within that unconscious upon ourselves, to starve ourselves to death in order to become the literal skeletal manifestation of stepmother's unconscious death forces. This alternative seemingly would be a way out of the red-room, but also would keep us permanently encased in its mirror.

The way that daughters have always sought refuge from bondage in the unconscious body of mother is the final alternative Jane entertains: an appeal to a Father Spirit who would avenge. Here is a plea to Father's word (his rule holding Mrs. Reed to service) to rescue the daughter from, to split her out of (repress) the red-room of mother's unconscious. The failure of that appeal is the poignant psychological crisis of the daughter's life: the descent of the ancestor (Father Spirit) which in the modern world is experienced and studied as hysteria.

Within that crisis is the uncanny recognition of John Reed's craving: it is for the Father that he hungers and rages. Also, Mrs. Reed's antipathetic craving for Jane is based on a desire to find a way through her own rage at Mr. Reed's inability to enter and live in her enflamed, vigorous womb, and, even when he would be limp, remain seeing.

That Father's word cannot rise us out of mother's unconscious desire, yet has been descending into it, which choked us, becomes the hysterical moment. Hysteria is the moment that language lowers into the recessed desires of the unconscious and gets choked: daughter cannot yet find a way to carry out the text of the unconscious, its word which seemingly has extinguished still appears whitewinged with a black dog in a red-room.

Hysteria is a moment of the crossroads, a three-way incest: incest with mother (she has locked us in her womb) at the base of incest with father (he has entered us in her womb). There all word chokes. How the paternal word cannot rise us above yet itself descends into the maternal blood chamber, without a way to mediate its passage through what would be a language of the unconscious, is also the menstral crisis. Implicit in this crisis is the daughter contacting, even entering, the powers of the mother's unconscious womb which she knows could extinguish the Father.

The vertical descent of Father (his rule, his word, his omniscience) implies the necessity of language to contact the womb, to give form to, humanly delineate, what was unconscious womb. Therefore, this descent results in our return (which is an ascent of sorts), through the unconscious fall beneath Father, to whom is human apothecary. Mr. Lloyd, physician of the lower regions, is the fundamental necessity of having a human base in negotiating the mysteries and alchemies of the language of the unconscious.

That Mr. Lloyd is sent by Mrs. Reed indicates, as her son's assault implied, that some inherent condition of the symbiosis is that we do carry up and impart the contents of the very unconscious which binds us to her and from which she continually tries to defend through rejecting us.

The return to a conscious, daily (nursery) world is accompanied by the emotions of dread and despair as well as the sense of being "marked" in a shuddering human skin. Mr. Lloyd's appearance is our beginning skin: in his presence we have enough of a human encasement to shudder. Our shuddering skin is the humanity that has accrued through our survival of the red-room possession.

The return also is accompanied by surface excuses, a Bessie infantilizing, which denies the unconscious realms. It is in relation to this position that "self"-esteem becomes located in the unconscious. In a polarity to the Bessie position we want to stand for where we have been, we want to express it, find its narrative, and that desire is the Mr. Lloyd questioning.

Mr. Lloyd mirrors, yet his is a different mirror than that of the red-room which primarily reflected our possession by unconscious forces thereby excluding differentiated human quality. The Lloyd mirror reflects human property, the place of a located human being, and does such through interlocution and questions of unhappiness.

Where interlocution was impossible with the vertical Father, his descent is also the prerequisite for interlocution with a human paternal aspect. If we ascend from the collapse in the red-room, we emerge with the desire to find the word of where we had been and therefore the possibility of dialogue with one who knows conscious and unconscious worlds yet who has an investment in orienting us to the former. Mr. Lloyd is the relativization of the majestic Red Room — which is required if there is a return to conscious life — a humanization which allows a speaking in relation.

The speaking with Mr. Lloyd is the initiation to interlocution: words carry unconscious force, delineate it in narrative spoken in relation to human being. Finding the narrative of the red-room is to begin attaining differentiated properties accruing through dialogue. As we are beginning to relate through narrative to the figures of the unconscious (ghost ancestor, dead parents), we are in relation to Mr. Lloyd through his mirroring of our unique properties (i.e., we reply we are unhappy as adopted because of the raging stepbrother, the uncle's ghost descent). Once we speak to Mr. Lloyd we have a name, a caste, preferences, are locating ourselves in a landscape, a spatial as well as temporal dimension reaching beyond the immediate, contiguous Gateshead mode.

In our historical account, the poverty of the Eyre relations emerges: eyre/err applied to "relative," how to relate humanly is to err from the Gateshead perspective. Mr. Lloyd arrives with a certain nascent sense of our humanity which allows a development of empathy relativizing the "powers" of Gateshead, in a way that allows their figuration to be narrated, a narrative related begins to be favored over the immediacy of impulse.

Mr. Lloyd does not himself teach us how to signify the contradictory forces of the unconscious, but he is the start of our desire to find such a language which necessitates learning how to humanly relate through it. He is the catalyst to go to the place of such teaching: the girls' school is the possibility of the impartation of an infolding of openended (what was unconscious) desire compared to the cover of Gateshead need closure.

As with Mr. Reed and John Reed, Mr. Lloyd is a catalyst (signal for change, for motion) yet not transformer. Before we can get to the girls' school, we have to break the nursery bind, our unconscious desire to stay fused schismatically with Mrs. Reed. The nursery is where we are no longer within Mrs. Reed's body yet are still undifferentiated from her and the immediate effects of her unconscious: we are crushed down by her on our crib. The unmediated connection to her body while no longer *within* it is also the naiveté of the nursery attempt to keep Father's rule above (Uncle Reed in Heaven can see all you do and think, we say to her).

The way we negotiate each of the male forces emerging from the symbiosis with the stepmother affects how we subsequently are visited by and possessed by other ones. Once we have attained a level of interlocution through the Mr. Lloyd encounter, the Reed forces now possess us through language: each speaks through us in his way. The fact that we are surprised by these statements indicates that there is a possession occurring, yet it has moved to a verbal level, and we are no longer bodily seized.

The verbal possessions occur where we are not within Mrs. Reed but crib-crushed by her, suggesting an incestuous nursery bind. The mother is somewhat less archetypally ominous in the nursery (the Reed forces talk back at her through us) yet she is not humanly related to us, and the doll as transitional object, as graven image, stands for the possibility of such a passage.

The unmediated connection to Mrs. Reed in the nursery place (between archetypal Mother for whom we are the unconscious, and human mother with whom we are human in relation) is also a problematic relation to hunger and feeding. The external manifestations of the place, Eliza and Georgiana, hoard and extravagantly flaunt. They each are an excess of holding in and putting out. The hunger of the nursery is a feeding on oneself which becomes an overextended giving out to others, and this is subtended by the cruelty within the antipathetic symbiosis (which in the nursery place is a type of incest—the sexual aspect of the symbiosis, its unripe union, becomes manifest with the mother).

Although the male forces have emerged out of the vacuum-loss of "mother," which is the unconscious of mother, and though their seizures are partially our attempt to extricate from that unconscious, that is never the result. Instead they are catalysts of motion to various relations (along the passages, the eyre) within the symbiosis. We move from the complacency with the dark forces of her unconscious (windowseat) which is to be disembodied, to the imprisonment within her womb (red-room) which is to be inside her body, to the numbness of being adjacent as completely available to her (nursery), which is to be crushed beneath her body.

The black pillar, the erection of the next male agent summoned by Mrs. Reed through her unconscious connection to us, is again a call to motion, a loosening. Brocklehurst is the morality oppositionalism which provokes a rudimentary differentiation from the nursery regress. His is the critical, monocentric perspective and opinionated thought which is a beginning self-referential speaking which affects a first distancing from the stepmother.

The fact, however, that the severance from the antipathetic symbiosis necessitates the inclusion of stepmother's unconscious—that we have to bring it along—is carried by her curse. It is not a matter of splitting literally from her (her unconscious): it is "as if" the bond has burst, there is a figurative bursting required. It is more a matter of breaking the symbiotic bond keeping us identified with her unconscious, which entails a differentiation within the unconscious (which is around us both), that is, speaking the narrative of Gateshead, finding its metaphors, which is the figurative release from Mrs. Reed's hold.

The only way the nursery bond can be "as if" burst is through the anger of a critical condemnation. Anger fuels the release as finding the metaphor in the narrative effects it.

The gray field is the first place outside the symbiosis yet still on its grounds. Unlike the shadows of the nursery, this gray contains an "I," a self-referential property, the nascent trace of a self-reflective speaker. Bessie's call through this gray field is the decreased susceptibility to a moralistic scolding from without, and the manifestation of a reflective perspective, mediated speaking relation: they explore the meaning of the scolding. Interlocution with the point of view of another's perspective and mutual embrace are the departure from Gateshead.

But the issues of hunger and feeding have not been negotiated yet, and they immediately appear in the journey to as well as within the landscape of the next place. The move from Gateshead to Lowood is a move from womb regions (up) to stomach. To be on the landscape between Gateshead and Lowood is to be separating from the nursery where we are mother's hunger, yet far from autonomous: there is the pervasive fear of being kidnapped, and the inability to feed oneself. However, here also is the beginning recognition of our hunger.

Our shuddering skin was the presence of Mr. Lloyd and a temporal/spatial perspective which accompanied a move to a girls' school. The verbal outburst of the Brocklehurst possession gave us enough "objective" distance from Mrs. Reed to effect a gray field ability to see another as different as well as their perspective in metaphorical relation to our own. The entry to Lowood is the ability to locate another sensually as exterior, which is the possibility for dialogue. With the advent of such differentiation, we are not so easily bodily seized. The Lowood order is a necessary condition for a transmutation of the Gateshead seizures to figuration and craft. This order is based on consistency, uniformity and discipline.

The Lowood garden with its distinct plots, where we go at recess, presents us with the differentiation within recess which has been the inherent necessity of the Gateshead possessions. The contradictions within the Lowood recess, found in a hollow cough signal, are inscribed on its stone tablet: the Father is glorified yet women own and run the place.

When we begin to sense an exteriority now is the possibility of entering (instead of becoming) a recess, hence the possibility of reflection, an interiority. The Lowood recess, and the possibility of differentiating within it, are mediated through a reflective reading girl who is like us but different. To speak with her (who reflects ourselves but differently) within the recess is to speak with someone of ourselves yet divided, divided self-reflection.

To bring out a text of the recess is a self-divided reflection which is the move beyond the Gateshead cravings and impulse reactivity. Reflection (inner-locution) becomes possible as the Lowood girl, whose text emerges from the recess, interiorly mediates the external punishment.

The Brocklehurst possession has distanced us to a Miss Temple who is female, erotic as well as maternal and most knowledgeable. Brocklehurst is a cover for Lowood: the counterpart of mother's moralistic Brocklehurst stance is an awesome temple teacher and punished girl seeing to the heart. The Lowood lessons are a call through appetite to heart and temple.

However, this passage to heart and temple requires first that the stomach and its hungers be negotiated effectively: Miss Temple feeds the students at her own responsibility. Only then can we go into the recess, only then can we meet its differentiated plots and the reflective girl of heart's divided speaking.

The Lowood landscape is cool and dry. The move from Gateshead to Lowood is a psychological ascent: art, music, reading and language predominate, what was a craving appetite and firey outburst at Gateshead becomes elevated at Lowood to "spark of spirit" through the figure of Helen Burns.

Paradoxically, after the Gateshead extrication the Lowood ascent effects a type of solidification. The concrete body of Gateshead, which was volatile and easily influenced, is moved to the Lowood abstract body, which is firm and not swayed. The solidification of the Lowood body is based on its interiority and devotions.

The rising from Gateshead to Lowood body entails Burns's method of sublimation which is a condensation of impulse to figuration. This sublimation-condensation includes the pleasure of reading and the erotic body of text. Also involved in the Lowood sublimation and its "creed" is an overview allowing a multifaceted perspective (holding contradictions) precluding ensnarements of animosity as well as requiring a linearity: ladder ascent "burning" impulse to figuration. The modus operandi of such a sublimation process is love, love of one's enemy, the Christ love which also is the vision of an interior eye, image as body.

Lowood has a frozen landscape when we reside in its quarters while still attached (through being split off from) Gateshead. Here is a problem in division: how to divide out of the collective female body, in which we had been fused at Gateshead, yet not split off entirely (which is the Brocklehurst threat), yet remain differentiated (even heterogeneously divided) and related.

The long division is a Lowood lesson of differentiation within recess: how to be divided from yet also multiplicatively related to collective body. It is a lesson of finding the inherent heterogeneous forms within the unconscious, and this necessitates the operations of inhibition and mortification (of impulse gratification) yet not a prohibition (of desire).

Our Coming Man "paranoia" in the frozen Lowood landscape is also Mrs. Reed's fear of (unconscious) collective female body as well as our desire for Mrs. Reed (which is petrified because it has only lead to fusion).

Brocklehurst is a necessary lesson in the Lowood education of differentiation within recess since his mode of splitting and oppositionalism is the first
step in extricating from collective body in lessons of division.

The Brocklehurstian mode of splitting out of collective body is effected
through his proclamations of body as vile, his denouncement of the female
curl, and the underside of his ministerial prohibition as hypocritical proliferation and contamination. He appears in the righteous arrogance of our
own misogyny as we exhibitionistically flaunt the "feminine."

The Brocklehurstian splitting is energized through sadism and anal eroticism. The sadism inherent in the Paternal Law, which demands prohibition of female collective body and its desires, provokes our impulse to
remain fused with the antipathetic Gateshead body: through a reactive
resistance to Brocklehurst there would be a discharge (anal erotic) maintaining identification with Gateshead. Brocklehurst is the Scolding, Moralistic God we want him to be (Coming Man) who will prohibit yet also
provoke our unconscious desire to return to Mrs. Reed and the Gateshead
unmediated discharges.

An anal eroticism changes through the mediation of the Brocklehurst
possession. Anal gratification resulting from the discharge within the
Gateshead fusion changes to another sort of anal eroticism, more a pleasure, when we sit on the Lowood stool and negotiate the tremendous
impulses through the containment of Helen's gaze. The stool is another
aspect of the Lowood education of discovering an exterior (we have an
audience) which allows the dividing into an interior (proffered through
Helen's gaze) negotiating unconscious forces.

The gaze carries empathically the unspoken word of the interior negotiation of Reed and Brocklehurst. It is a message of the dissolution which
threatens upon the stool: as the forces (contradictory and heterogenous —
we are branded as evil yet Father did descend) move through us, we are
always in danger of dissolving within them (as Gateshead) instead of passing them through us. The latter involves separation (from the passage
through and out of us) as well as remaining (being) a solidified as heterogeneous body (for the passage), with an interior, with an exterior.

The moralistic oppositionalism of Brocklehurst (scrutiny and condemnation of an underside) is as necessary for an extrication from fusion with
Gateshead body as is his eventual depotentiation allowing the negotiation
and containment of heterogeneous sides of a female nature: soiled, illuminated, defected angel.

The gaze carrying the unspoken delineation of the stool experience
buoys us to solidified substance while it mortifies the Gateshead reactivity
impulse. Receiving and being held by the Helen gaze is the ability to stay
related to the inherent divisions of heterogeneous body as well as how that

requires impartation. The sublimation (division while staying in multiplicative relation to) of Gateshead body results in a Lowood body passing through and containing unconscious forces which are dividing, differentiating and approaching articulation.

Therefore, the negotiation of unconscious forces upon the stool is the attainment of a (Lowood abstract) body which is related to Mrs. Reed yet not in an antipathetic symbiosis with her: the unconscious forces once only known through symbiosis now can pass through us (Gateshead not split from yet divided through) and approach impartation.

The sublimation through the Helen gaze is the depotentiation of Brocklehurst. The condemnation by Brocklehurst was that the red-room was a lie. His law must prohibit the occurrence of the events there: that Father descended, not pulled us out of yet himself descended into the maternal crimson chamber, here is what Brocklehurst condemns. Brocklehurst's is the law which would denounce female desires (which curl, which are natural) as he is the provocation of the reactive exaggeration of female nature (through hypocrisy and impulse). Once we stool negotiate the impulse so it divides to the heterogeneous body in which we are in relation and begin to impart, the Father is descended and the figurations of the depths of a female nature are called forth, the red-room is not lie.

After the Brocklehurst depotentiation, the question emerges: what is the ordering device of the depths of a female nature, the language and law of a female unconscious, and how to impart and embody that? The move from Gateshead to Lowood is a sublimation in a primary condensation, a laconic translation of impulse to figuration, that is, the concise containment and impartation (finding the narrative) of heterogeneous once unconscious forces. This move is essentially an ascent (up and out the body) which involves the mediation of appetite (and not only the stomach but also the colon pertains here) in the figuration lessons of heart and temple. The move from heart to temple necessitates the throat, a communication of the figurations in dialogue which prepares for their densening into concrete body.

How Helen's gaze is made dense in a return to body is not in itself presented within her gaze which evaporates as the Brocklehurst possession returns to tempt us in another flailing reaction. The symptoms of a condensation going backwards (impulse as body instead of figurations densening to body) are negative inflation and whining.

The transmutation of Helen's lessons can only begin through a move to interior suffering, which is a move through grief, ascertaining its meaning, and an imparting of that in a related manner. The Mr. Lloyd dialogue was the precursor to such an occurrence which is why he was the catalyst to the girls' school. Helen's return with coffee and bread to the sinking Jane is an interiorizing of suffering which is not the Gateshead mode of exteriorizing the unconscious. The ensuing dialogue explores the meaning of the suffering in terms of relations of figurations (Mr. Brocklehurst, student body as audience, Miss Temple, kingdom of spirits, conscience). The heartfelt exchange of the meaning of the suffering is a matter of appetite. Helen carrying coffee and bread moves through the appetite, for which Miss Temple has stood, and such standing (which was part of the Brocklehurst depotentiation) is also a teaching of conscience.

Conscience comes through feeding the speaking of suffering in dialogue. The related impartation of the grief depotentiates the Law of Brocklehurst (he is not a god, Helen says) which becomes a teaching of conscience. The Helen-Jane relation is the exchange of their respective lessons: Helen teaches an upward move to conscience as surrounding spirits knowing (whether we have the story and language of the unconscious forces "right"); Jane teaches a disidentification with non-human forces in a downward move to embodied relatedness.

The interaction of the two teachings through the heart, their embrace, becomes Miss Temple's entry. She is the moment that impulse passes to a dialogue with conscience through appetite, and that conscience lowers through body in human relatedness. Here is the entry of the ordering device of conscience in whose listening we become narrator (solidified as divided speaker) of the passage of unconscious forces while disidentified with any voice or figure.

Finding conscience, an ordering device within female depths which knows its laws including the regulation of appetite, is basic to the moment Father (whose word was Law) lowered into the red-room unconscious body, and therefore it is in Miss Temple's room that the red-room is no longer lie (Mrs. Reed's curse is broken). In order to sublimate Gateshead, which is to break Mrs. Reed's bind, her curse, we have to be at a girls' school. We can only extricate from fusion with stepmother by learning how to differentiate within the depths of a female nature, which is not to split from (thereby fuse with) that nature, yet instead to enter intimacy there through dialogue while continually learning to impart the narrative of differentiated figurations of unconscious body.

The generosity of the teacher and friend (conscience as friend) is a heart matter. The heart is moved as conscience forms moving appetite through temple. The temple serving our appetite is a heart issue.

The conscience works through the heart which feeds us the food of the souls, ancient instructions. To find the conscience in the temple is to work from the heart, which is a matter of serving the appetite so it resonates with souls of the departed, their lessons. Heart feeding the soul's lesson is what from the heart speaks a dialogue that stimulates as nurtures. How to extend out the heart's lesson is to know our breasts and their unique, "right" ways of nurturing the soul, which is to receive by heart the lessons of conscience.

Conscience listening to our narrative, clearing us from imputation through the impartation, is the discovery of the language of what previously were unconscious forces, a delineation of figurations of the unconscious, which is a creative discovery, the possibility of finding our "gift." Here is the unique designation of a differentiated unconscious which becomes a study of female pedagogy: student and teacher touch qualities in one another which yearn to be manifested in each. The erotic underpinings of this dialogue become the conjunction of appetite, heart and intelligence in the temple. Temptations of idolatry appear as woman find the "right" ways of conspiring their unique intelligences.

Helen's cough is the moment the female "mentor" cannot submit to the emergence of the unconscious (desiring delineation), and reverts to a paternal authority (repressing that delineated desire) resulting in a Scatcherd power move, wrong forced friction.

How to manifest the gift we found in the temple is a lesson of a secondary condensation: the passage of figurations of the unconscious back down into the through body, which is to find their densening, their manifestation, which is our gift. This secondary condensation is an incarnation-condensation. Moving gift out through body again brings up the Brocklehurst prohibition of female body as vile, as disease. We have to pass through this disease, if we have the resistance, to carry out the gift.

To have the resistance means here not the sense of resist as come up against, yet to have a related connection to the ascended heights as well as the depths, vertical axis, and through a solidified body to hold fast as the heterogeneous forces move through: the metaphors of blossoming spring and photosynthesis are applicable here. The Helen death is the necessary sacrifice of whom would prefer that gift remain above detached from body in an essential Father idealization. Her tuberculosis asks for body in the place of air, and signals the granulation of heart failure: failure of inhalation (of desire), and fuming (of hate).

Those who go under the Brocklehurst possession at this point of the secondary condensation, are those who have not learned to mediate unconscious body through the narrative of its figurations (the typhus frenzied mass), or those (Helen isolation consumption) who mediated that to an extent where they lost all body (which is to collude with the Brocklehurst prohibition of body and be diseased).

Helen is who can see the configurations of otherworlds as well as their meaning, she has the vision yet cannot make that manifest, cannot return it to denser form. The Helen sacrifice, sacrifice of what would keep female vision disembodied in a Father idealization, is necessary for the transmutation of the Lowood lessons back down to body. Miss Scatcherd indicates what it would mean to use hate to carry the lessons (gift) out from the temple embodied, not diseased, not slattern body or neglected body.

The Helen death leaves a feeling human heart, the emotional subtext of her passing is quite poignant, and its opening is in the word of her grave — resurgam.

Helen's vision begins its return, resurgance, to world when the larger body, larger community, takes notice of the scourge. The conscience to which Helen's perspective raised Jane, when taken up by the larger community, becomes ethics. When the woman moves through her connection to death, through another woman, the Brocklehurst morality transmutes to conscience which becomes an ethics of the larger body (compassionate and fair). What mortifies Brocklehurst is the compassion of the larger community which does not enforce splitting yet dividing out, he is reduced to human dimension, mediocre employment.

When Brocklehurst is diminished and humanized, Miss Temple becomes on our level, companion. Who spoke the voice of conscience is our friend. As both Brocklehurst and Miss Temple level, the grip of Mrs. Reed slackens, our affairs are no longer her business. The differentiated unconscious where we arrived in Miss Temple's hearing is also the definition we achieve through the identification with Miss Temple; and this definition is distinguished from fusion, and is what allows the parting of Miss Temple, through care.

When Temple parts, we lower to body and first meet a strong will. A strong will attempts to break out at this point in order to get us to the next place, larger body. When this will exhausts itself is when "voice of conscience" emerges as a call without. With Miss Temple's departure, the voice of conscience is "interiorized" in the sense of being without, apart from personal will and more from the place of sleep and dreams, yet heard within. This voice is responsible for lessons on lowering our interior qualities to the larger body: incarnating them as well as carrying them to community which is vocation.

The leavetaking from Lowood requires reviewing the contents of the Gateshead trunk, the prior landscapes, catching up on their narratives, which is a Bessie visit which is the culmination of the Lowood lesson of division, differentiating the distinct aspects of recess, finding the relation of heterogeneous figures, even the most remote, catching them up.

We are ready for the Bessie surface appraisal after we have advertised our qualities, we can be looked at from without, with a strong enough definition, unique solidified substance, to be known from the perspective of another looking upon us. The interlocution of Bessie and Jane at this point requires that Bessie take on a more metaphoric understanding of Jane's gifts and Jane a more concrete and frank view of herself; and their relation and this dialogue (Gateshead body rising to Lowood perspective which is lowering back to concrete body) becomes the passage to the next landscape. The Lowood leavetaking is a summary of the Lowood lesson of long division, not splitting but parting through compassion, remaining in uniquely qualified relation.

The passage to Thornfield is not guarded or guided. It takes an act of willful initiation to move out of the private parlor place after Lowood. Thornfield is where there is to be an education of will.

Mrs. Fairfax as well as the mansion itself are a composite of qualities from Gateshead and Lowood. Here there is the possibility of the first view of our exterior, the external reflection: the importance of body as exterior appearance (ours as well as the mansions) in reflecting qualities. The move to a sensate, textual place becomes the Thornfield mirroring. Here we are descending back down in and through body from the Lowood temple. The Lowood abstract body desiring to manifest becomes the necessity of a Thornfield first reflection of exterior body.

Before we can move out the Lowood ascent (which was an ascent to figuration of what was unconscious impulse), make it manifest in world, we have to descend back into body. That movement involves the education of the mansion's child, Adèle. The education of where our passion is still a child is the return into body after Lowood which entails a return to a red-room. Thornfield, as the descent from Lowood temple back down into body, necessitates the passage through the red-room, yet this time with a Mrs. Fairfax guide of a Lowood sort of care and propriety.

When we return to a red-room after Lowood, it is a Thornfield drawing room, not unconscious body seizing us, but we enter the crimson with a conscious attitude. When we enter the Thornfield red-room, we are not as permeable and liable to possession by the imps, fairies, the phantoms of the place. With a human definition, a more solidified substance as well as the mediation of a practical Fairfax attitude, we return to the red-room desires to penetrate the character of the landlord. Instead of the result being an immediate possession by the landlord, with the Mrs. Fairfax guide we survey his possessions.

Therefore, out of the red-room we rise to the third story overview of the ancestral and unconscious passions of the place (the memory of a wayward son's desire to murder the king; tortured wives in a Bluebeard hall). In a sense, we gather the unconscious body around the red-room, and we can do that now because we know our distinct psychological qualities (we can speak our narrative without being possessed by any psychic forces) and have a differentiated exterior body that reflects them. After Lowood, we can *walk through* the unconscious body of the red-room and not be taken.

Behind it all yet most immediately in front of us is the preternatural laugh locked up.

Mrs. Fairfax offers us a veil in this purview of the ancestral unconscious. Upon our locating of the preternatural (or its locating us), she orients us to see it in terms of the average and ordinary. We are not to keep disembodied, which is to be possessed by (and thereby alienated from) the more frightening and terrestrial otherworldly forces, yet after the Lowood education, veiled, we can face them.

Once we have surveyed the possessions of the red-room's landlord, we rise to a tale of imagination through the third story forces; and some longing rises for embodying the tale in the larger world, pushing beyond horizon. Part of what the red-room desires is not to be locked up.

The move out has its prerequisites: the understanding of mediocrity as foundation; the discovery of the narrative of the imagination through the forces stirring us; and the agreement by the Fairfax practical attitude that the constriction has reached its limit, and, in fact, it is time for the primary condensation to figuration (when its laconic translation of impulse has become quite constricted) now to condense down through body to world, to carry out the letter.

A coldness and loneliness inform this movement which involves carrying out the constriction instead of departing from the constriction. The midpoint of the passage is when an animal spirit breaks through. The forces erupting after Lowood in the descent through body in wider world are spirits that are animal. Thornfield, as the embodiment of what in Lowood was the vision and narrative of otherworlds, is our encounter of the terrestrial, textured spirit, willful, driven, wanting it own way, the residue of Gateshead impulse now appearing through will. It is a driven will that breaks out through this first move down and out. For us to negotiate that driven will, through the Lowood lessons, that is, to relate to the human incarnation of the midpoint of spirit being animal, is our successful passage (consenting will).

The possibility of such a driven will being stopped, encased by human as humanly related to, is the way spirits contacted and configured through the temple education can become embodied in world. It is an erotic moment when the woman bringing the narrative (from the place of ancestral spirits) down and out collides with a male inspired animal force that no longer can go in its own direction.

Thornfield is a sensate place of locating the human encasement of what was vision and tale of otherworlds, spirit incarnate, which allows the interior a move out to society as what willfully has been of the larger world yet hidden over the horizon comes in. And this crossing is erotic.

That our move out is also a move in of what had been latent willful energies is the entry of Rochester into the mansion. That it is his mansion is also how he is a composite of Reed and Brocklehurst qualities as he is other than such composite. The entry of Rochester brings private images which had been pacing third story closer to the ground floor. He is the necessity of choler, bitterness, and irritation in the manifestation of private figuration to public body.

This manifestation involves a ceremonial descent from third to second to the first story which Rochester mostly inhabits. Yet the descent through choler is only possible with Miss Temple's brooch: the brooch is the gift representing the teaching of the articulation of ancient and lost regions, of what had been unconscious, a delineation of the unconscious, and it is what is carried down and stood behind. The brooch also is a female prick reminding us that the descent through the Rochester place is a red-room entry yet this time it is to dialogue with the man there.

After we have negotiated and placed the Reed and Brocklehurst forces through the Lowood training, and thereby transmuted the symbiosis with stepmother, the man in the red-room is not under the jurisdiction of Mrs. Reed. Therefore, the dialogue with the man in the red-room is not to be gifted by him there. Adèle who needs a gift from him is placed otherwise and then the dialogue can ensue.

The dialogue with the man in the red-room is an exchange where other-world figurations become revealed to one of a more worldly perspective, therefore it is also the manifestation of what were once unconscious forces. As Rochester is taken through the revelation to otherworlds, our figurative apprehension of unconscious forces becomes manifest in a text (dialogue) as well as a craft he can perceive.

This exchange of otherworldly figuration and manifest world is a dialogue with whom would be our complement, hermaphrodite, and thereby necessitates we ponder the complement (green) of our recess (red). This complement could return us through venusian feeling to heart, the essential midpoint and fulcrum of all our passages.

The image of the witch, the one who crosses from unconscious to conscious worlds, informs this potential hermaphroditic exchange. Themes from *Paradise Lost* also inform it: the couple is not fused; the less favored, betrayed, and rebellious son is bitter and revenges through plotting Father's fall; there is the undercurrent of father–daughter incest and offspring incest with daughter in this betrayal of the son by the father.

Rochester is a male side who can face our craft: the differentiated figurations of otherworlds which delineate the tumultuous, tortured crossing through the hell and death regions of what had been unconscious, but also that such has been guided. Rochester's defense to the female vision of guidance is also a problem in his history which he has locked up and he tells us to go to sleep. The unlocking of his secret madness, that necessary betrayal by the Father sending this son to the southern regions of the depths of intimate female nature, the place also of mother–daughter shared madness, is what we then traverse.

Angelyn Spignesi, Ph.D., is a depth-psychologist with a private practice in New Haven, Connecticut. She is the author of various essays on the unconscious as well as *Starving Women: A Psychology of Anorexia Nervosa* (Spring Publications, 1983).

www.ingramcontent.com/pod-product-compliance
Lightning Source LLC
Chambersburg PA
CBHW070837300326
41935CB00038B/781